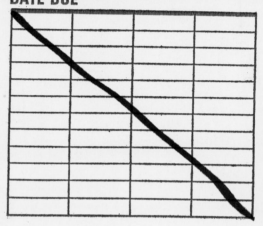

Approaches to Comparative and International Politics

Approaches

TO COMPARATIVE AND
INTERNATIONAL POLITICS

R. Barry Farrell

EDITOR

Northwestern University Press
EVANSTON 1966

Preface

IN THE HISTORY OF SCIENCE the development of boundaries within and between subjects of inquiry has both hindered and helped scientific growth. In aiding science, subject boundaries have permitted division of labor and provided classifications which have fostered focus and restrained unmanageable breadth of analysis. In hindering science, subject boundaries have fostered intellectual parochialism, concentration on one compartment of knowledge, with inadequate regard for relevant and related inquiry outside the compartment, and neglect of important problems because these have been defined out of established patterns of inquiry. Political science has not been spared such boundary difficulties, both in its contact with other related disciplines and in the subdivisions which have developed within the study of politics itself. This book deals with one of those difficulties, the boundary between two of the traditional subdivisions of our discipline, comparative politics and international relations.

It would not be accurate to say that specialists in international politics have failed to draw attention to the importance of the internal politics of the several nations. Likewise the standard textbooks in comparative politics usually contain some discussion of the foreign policies of the states whose governments are being examined. But for each specialist the other side of the boundary has not been his primary concern, and, in fact, the comparative study of the interaction of domestic and foreign politics has quite often been a no man's land—neglected not because students of politics have thought the topic unimportant but because the divisions between the two fields have tended to foster this neglect. Curriculum boundaries, research organization boundaries, and personal competence boundaries have tended to remove from primary focus many fascinating questions concerning the relationship between internal phenomena within types of states and international behavior. When members of Northwestern University's Program of Comparative Politics and its International Relations Program joined hands in the initial formulation of the Inter-Nation Simulation, the close linkages of internal and external processes were forcefully called to our attention. A group of social scientists were asked to come together and to focus their efforts on linkages between comparative and international politics about which each of them had already demonstrated deep concern. This book is the result.

Ten of the contributions are reworkings of papers originally prepared for a conference sponsored by the Comparative Politics Program of the Northwestern Political Science Department in April 1964. After the conference several of the papers were substantially rewritten, and it seemed best to delay the publication of this volume until all those who so desired had revised their papers in light of the discussion at the conference and such other factors as seemed to them important. Two additional papers—each written by a participant at the conference—have been added to the original ten. In preparing the volume for publication, the editor has included some explanatory comments and revised the order of presentation. On the other hand, every effort has been made to keep to a minimum editorial changes in the individual papers, other than changes made by the writers themselves. The Northwestern Conference on Comparative Politics and International Relations and the present book have been made possible through the generous help of a grant from the Ford Foundation to the Northwestern Department of Political Science for International and Comparative Studies.

Although the majority of contributors represented here are

professional political scientists, most have special interests and competence in other areas of research and can thus bring to their contributions here the enrichment which comes from the skills and data of other studies. The contributors also represent a variety of approaches not only to the study of comparative and international politics but also to the general study of politics. Both "behavioral" and "traditional" approaches are represented, in addition to other approaches by scholars who regard this dichotomy as uninteresting or unreal. The selection of contributors was intended deliberately to reflect the belief within the Northwestern Political Science Department that in our developing discipline no one emphasis, approach, classification, or method holds a monopoly of insight. The history of social science provides much data to suggest that it would be a rash scholar who would condemn—or sanctify—any single approach in these frontier areas of political analysis.

The organization of this book reflects the different approaches and interests of the contributors within the framework of our general subject. The discussion begins on a level of generalization which encompasses a broad range of variables and theoretical concerns in the interrelationships between national and international politics. The second and third parts each deal with one of two clusters of problems of internal politics which seem of major relevance for international politics. Thus Part Two discusses relationships between types of political society resulting from different levels of economic development and international political behavior. Part Three is concerned with the relationship between the political organization of open and closed politics and international politics. A single case, that of the Soviet Union, is presented in Part Four, with interest in its uniqueness and its generalizability in surveying in very concrete and specific terms the interaction between various internal and external factors. Part Five directs the reader to several major research concerns and challenges which the several contributors believe open the road toward future development of useful research and analysis.

In a collective undertaking such as this it is impossible adequately to acknowledge the help of all those who have contributed. The major burden of organization of the original conference was carried by George I. Blanksten, the present chairman of the Northwestern Department of Political Science. Very special words of appreciation for help, inspiration, advice, and continuous concern must go to the former chairman of the Northwestern department, Richard C. Snyder. In addition to the participation of interested members of the Northwestern social science community, the conference itself and the papers in the book benefited greatly from the presentations and good talk of guests from outside Northwestern: Vernon V. Aspaturian of Pennsylvania State University, Oliver Benson of the University of Oklahoma, Pablo González Casanova of the National Autonomous University of Mexico, Karl W. Deutsch of Yale University, David Easton of the University of Chicago, Carl J. Friedrich of Harvard University, Robert M. Holt of the University of Minnesota, Charles McClelland of the University of Southern California, and James N. Rosenau of Douglass College, Rutgers University. Personal thanks are also due Harold Guetzkow of the Northwestern Political Science Department for his counsel, trouble, and perception at various stages leading to the completion of this volume.

For many hours of extra work and for their thoughtful help in many ways the editor is indebted to three departmental secretaries, Mrs. Virginia Stewart, Mrs. Jane Taylor, and Mrs. Jeanne French. Special appreciation for assistance both with conference arrangements and with the processing of several papers must go to the graduate students and assistants in the Northwestern Comparative Politics Program, and particularly to Douglas Bwy. The difficult task of preparing the index was undertaken by C. Thomas Dienes and Mark A. Tessler.

R. BARRY FARRELL

Northwestern University
Evanston, Illinois

Contents

PART ONE

External and Internal Political Relationships

THE TWO ESSAYS in Part One explore theoretically the interaction of internal and external political influences. Professor Karl W. Deutsch is particularly concerned with external influences on the internal behavior of nations. He explores ways in which outside impacts can be reduced or increased and seeks to identify those external and internal elements which are most relevant for this process. He develops a scheme which can be used to locate sensitive spots and to make "semiquantitative statements about balances, about flows which are strong or less strong, messages which are more or less likely to be accepted or rejected." In discussing external events or deliberate external manipulations influencing internal affairs of states, Professor Deutsch offers generalizations drawing on evidence both from historical events and from descriptive and quantitative data about present-day American society.

The task of Professor James N. Rosenau is to discuss influences flowing in the opposite direction: internal influences on the external behavior of states. In addition to doing this, Professor Rosenau goes much further. He offers a pre-theory for foreign policy analysis. He suggests that in spite of remarkable strides forward there is still a paucity of theory on "the dynamics of processes which culminate in the external behavior of societies." In current writings on international relations factors themselves are presented more often than the specific variations in their influence and behavior under identified conditions; there is a profound lack of if-then propositions. "Foreign policy analysis is devoid of general theory." The tendency to treat each country and each international situation as unique and non-recurrent points to the need for developing "pre-theory which renders the raw materials comparable and ready for theorizing." In substantial and original terms Professor Rosenau then proceeds to his own pre-theory for foreign policy analysis, one which embraces the five dimensions of idiosyncratic, role, governmental, societal, and systemic variables. He then concerns himself with the rating of the "relative potencies" of these in-

3

gredients in different societies. The latter part of Professor
Rosenau's article encompasses additional variables: the issue-
area, the vertical system, and the penetrated system. In his
Table 4 Rosenau visually helps the reader to master his pre-
theory.

Though in some ways quite different in style and approach,
both Professor Deutsch and Professor Rosenau offer new theoretical possibilities sufficiently comprehensive to embrace almost
all the variables which are the specific concern of the contributors to the subsequent pages of this volume.

External Influences on the Internal Behavior of States

KARL W. DEUTSCH

Yale University

W<small>HEN</small> <small>THINKING</small> <small>ABOUT</small> the external influences on the internal behavior of nations, one should first try to define "external" and "internal," and to do so in terms of boundaries. I propose an operational definition of *boundaries* as marked discontinuities in the frequency of transactions and marked discontinuities in the frequency of responses—particularly, therefore, discontinuities in the degree of covariance.[1] If the American Communist Party (some years ago) was said to scratch when Mr. Stalin was itching, this was a way of stating that there was no effective boundary between the Soviet political system and the responses of that small subsection of the American society. On the other hand, it now turns out that when Mr. Leonid Brezhnev (and before him Mr. Khrushchev) is itching, the Chinese are not scratching, or are scratching their own place. That is to say, there is a marked, observable, demonstrable boundary now between the response characteristics of Chinese Communists and

1. For a more extended discussion of the concept of boundaries, see Karl W. Deutsch, "Autonomy and Boundaries According to Communication Theory," in Roy F. Grinker, ed., *Toward a Unified Theory of Human Behavior* (New York, Basic Books, 1956), pp. 278–97; and David Easton, *A Framework for Political Analysis* (New York, Prentice-Hall, 1965), Chap. V.

the Kremlin. Similarly the economy of New Zealand used to vary with the British economy, and this was taken to be a sign of a lack of boundaries.

Hence I would propose to define the concept of a *country* as a multiple market for goods and resources based on a market for factors of production. This would include, notably, covariance in (1) the market for labor, (2) the market for land (through the mechanism of migration), (3) the market for materials and services (including management and technology), (4) a multiple market for credit, which is capital, and (5) a multiple market for governmental services (which is sometimes called the social infrastructure). On these bases we can find out whether a country can be properly spoken of as a country or not, the emergence of national markets being a characteristic of nineteenth- and early twentieth-century economic history.[2]

Similarly, we might speak of a *general or national political community*, again as one based on multiple interdependence, the multiple taking-into-account of political actions. This contrasts with the narrow-focus political ideological system, which might comprise only a part of one nation or of several nations. The question, for instance, whether liberals in a country are part of the international liberal Masonic conspiracy was a topic hotly discussed in the 1790's, even in American electoral campaigns. In 1798 the Reverend Timothy Dwight, president of Yale College, announced in effect that "the French Revolution was simply a conspiracy engineered by the 'Illuminati' of Bavaria against government, religion, and morality; and that Jefferson was their head agent to subvert American society." [3] Against this alleged threat, he called upon his audience to support the anti-Jeffersonian, Federalist government of the day, on the grounds, among others, "that the officers of government are possessed of better information than private persons can be." [4] The Reverend Dwight did not convince the American

2. The concept of "country" is discussed in K. W. Deutsch, *Nationalism and Social Communication* (Cambridge, MIT Press, 1953, 1966), pp. 23–45.

3. Samuel Eliot Morison and Henry Steele Commager, *The Growth of the American Republic* (New York, Oxford University Press, 1942), Vol. I, p. 371.

4. Timothy Dwight, "The Duty of Americans in the Present Crisis," in Willard Thorp, Merle Curti, and Carlos Baker, eds., *American Issues*, Vol. I (Philadelphia, Lippincott, 1944), pp. 358–63. The cited passage is on p. 362.

voters. But the question of whether Roman Catholics are primarily part of an international system run from the Vatican or are members of national systems has been similarly discussed; and in Catholic countries, at times, Protestants have been viewed as possible members of foreign agencies or conspiracies. In short, the question of whether at some particular time and place there are multidimensional political communities (political systems which involve political responses on a wide range of topics) or whether particular groups are primarily extensions of narrow-focus international systems is an empirical question of fact which can be verified in terms of response characteristics and transaction flows.

From this notion of boundaries we can proceed to a definition of *autonomy*. Looking at autonomy from the outside, we may define any system as autonomous if its responses are not predictable, even from the most thorough knowledge of the environment. Looking at the same system from the inside, I should call it autonomous if it is characterized by a combination of intake and memory (that is, intake of information and recall of recorded items from memory) and if this memory itself is dissociative and combinatorial, thus providing opportunities for initiative and novelty. We may then describe sovereignty as an intensive type of autonomy.[5] Again, we may call a state sovereign, looked at from the outside, if its decisions could not be commanded or reversed dependably from the environment. This, as you notice, is not to say that decisions do not have real limits and may not have to be made in the light of environmental limitations. But it is to say that there is no decision center outside the state, from which decisions inside the state could be predicted. From the inside, then, we may call a country sovereign if it possesses a stable and coherent decision-making machinery within its boundaries.

This machinery need not be located at a single point, a single sovereign individual or committee. An "engine" may be distributed over a whole fairly large engine. There is no point in asking of an automobile engine, "Where in the engine is the engine?" And it may not be easy to see where within the national decision system is the decision system. There may not be a meaningful

5. For more detailed treatment of autonomy and sovereignty, see K. W. Deutsch, *The Nerves of Government* (New York, Free Press–Macmillan, 1963), pp. 200–29.

answer smaller than a fairly large national decision system itself. In short, there may not be an identifiable subsystem within which sovereignty can be located, but there have been, historically, times and places at which such inferences could be made. The king of France was supposed to be the subsystem in which most of the decision-making power of the French state was located in the late seventeenth century, and later on the subsystems such as the king's mistress or the father confessor of the king's mistress became dominant. The point is that the national decision system is a multi-purpose system. It works in regard to very many different topics and concerns, and it may be more highly centralized in regard to some operations than it is in regard to others.

What are some of the implications of these concepts? First, the impact of external events upon the internal affairs of a country could be said to decline with the stability and autonomy of the internal decision-making system. And second, the impact of foreign events ought to decline with the looseness of the coupling between the outside environment and the internal decision system. This is possible to state schematically. Let me picture, in a very simple way, an outside environment, E, which has generated a foreign input, F, to a national decision system. Let us assume that there is a subsystem of the national community which I will call the linkage system, designated by the letter L. This could be, if you think of economics, the world market, the market for a particular commodity such as coffee, and the coffee growers and exporters of Brazil. We will call these a linkage group from the internal economy of Brazil, and incidentally also from the political-interest arena of Brazil, to an internal environment.

The linkage group also has domestic links, which I will call d_i and l_d—that is domestic couplings to the domestic Brazilian market, to the labor market, to the tax system, the institutions maintaining some degree of political stability, the property relations, and so on. And finally, there is a large domestic system that I will simply call S. This crude model is shown in Figure I, with capital letters designating the channels of communication and small letters denoting the flows of messages or other relevant transactions.

One can then consider what some of the dynamic relationships might be. A strong impact of foreign events, through the

FIGURE I

A Simple Model of Outside Influence on a Political System

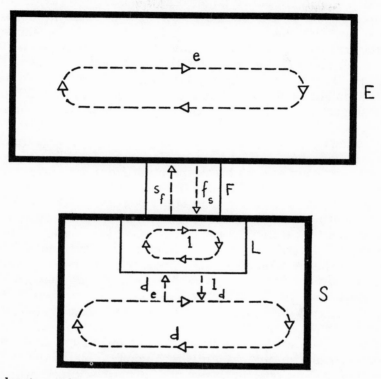

Explanatory notes:
  I. Communication
     Channels and Systems of Channels
     S = Political system under consideration, within its boundaries
     E = Environment
     F = "Foreign" input channels, from environment E to system S
     L = Linkage subsystem of S, more weakly bounded against E and more
         receptive to outside inputs F
 II. Flows of Messages or Other Transactions
     e = Flows within environment E (external flows)
     f_s = Receptor flows, from E to S, via channels L and F
     s_f = Effector flows, from S to E via channels L and F
     l = Flows wholly within the linkage group l
     d_e = Flows from system S to linkage group L (domestic to external)
     d_l = Connection between domestic system and linkage system (not indi-
         cated on figure)
     l_d = Flows from linkage group L to system S (linkage to domestic)
     d = Flows wholly within system S, including flows to and from L
         (domestic flows)

set of input channels, F, upon domestic relations requires that the environment, E, should generate relevant events. It further requires that E should be larger than F—that is to say, that the coupling from E to F should be stronger than in the opposite direction; that the coupling from F to L should be similarly stronger. If we get such a transitive series of couplings, in each of which more change migrates this way than the other, then we are likely to find a simple situation of fairly large impact.

One might then ask, What are the ways in which such outside impact can be reduced? One of the simple ways would be to break any one of the links. The most unlikely thing is that the environment, E, will disappear, and it is very unlikely that, at least in the short run, the national system, S, will disappear. It is much more easy to break the input from the environment (or reduce the input from the environment) upon the system, through an action of the domestic government. For instance, the domestic government may deliberately, by a feedback response, cut down input through nationalistic currency policies, totalitarian information controls, and so on. Or some senators may feel that Americans visiting Cuba or China will come back with all sorts of subversive tales. They may decide that whereas the Swiss and the English may have the temerity to trust their citizens to visit those strange places, the American republic may not take such a risk. It may, therefore, be the only large, free country in the world keeping its citizens on a leash when they go abroad. But in any case, this technique, to which many governments before ours have resorted at various times, will certainly reduce the impact of a foreign event. Totalitarian countries go much further, and carry out much more consistently their attempts to cut down their linkages to their international environment. Democracies do this in spasms, briefly and inconsistently, and therefore they luckily stay democracies in the long run. Nevertheless a democracy could systematically try to reduce its message intake from the outside world.

Another way could be to reduce the relevant linkage groups or institutions. You remember the crusade against "hyphenated Americans" in World War I or the Soviet crusade against "cosmopolitans" in 1948. You could put pressure on linkage groups, or you could cut the link from the linkage groups to the national community. You could isolate the linkage group in various ways.

Finally, if you did not cut the domestic ties of the linkage group, you could make the domestic system ever more stable, so that, though all the information got fed into the domestic system, the domestic system would not budge.

It is possible that the domestic system may get the same results by its sheer size. A very large country, very prosperous and with very strong holds upon its population, may be able to withstand even major impacts of foreign propaganda by tying its potential linkage groups so strongly to the domestic system that all the foreign inputs become relatively insignificant. Similar effects can be obtained by multiplying and intensifying small group ties, even in a small country. This, I think, has been the most effective method of, shall we say, psychological national defense, both in the United States and in Switzerland. The ties of integration to the main system become so strong that any inputs from abroad to potential domestic groups remain quite ineffective.

Other feedback strategies are possible. The system may work back on the linkage groups, or else they may work back, as I said, on the input to the linkage group, leaving the potential linkage group itself alone and undisturbed. Or, finally, the system may work back on the environment and effect a change in the environment itself. The first of the arrows in Figure I, attacking the linkage group alone and thus making changes only within the boundaries of the system, you could call *adjustment;* the system adjusts itself. The second you could call *isolation*. The third you could call *attempted mastery of the environment* or *attempted environment control*. All three are feedback strategies.

The effects of the environmental input can therefore be reduced by breaking the linkages, or reducing the linkages, at each of these points in the primitive model. The same effect can be achieved, without breaking or reducing the transaction flow, by reversing the strength of one or more of the relevant couplings or by reversing the proportions between the critical volumes of transactions. An economy or a political system that is strongly and vigorously developing is thus quite likely, by its sheer growth, to reverse the flow of influence without having to resort to censorship or to attacks on minority groups. Let me give a few examples of cases that I have in mind. The resources and inertia of the environment producing F, the foreign inputs, are the first major condition for an impact of change-producing changes that are transmitted from the environment to the internal communications and decisions of an acting system. The impact of prolonged war on the long-run motivation or on the war potential of an attacking power is a very obvious example. The negative inputs in the long wars of attrition against Germany, both World War I and World War II, eventually broke down its relatively strong and well-integrated political and communication systems. The size and persistence of a slump in a world market may be crucial in determining whether the reserves of a national economy and the resiliency of a national political community can be overloaded and overtaxed in the end. Similarly the resources—the attraction of an international ideological movement—could be pitted against the domestic attractions of a particular government.

A second point is the size of the current input upon the foreign events. It is not only the reserves of the environment that count, but what is actually being brought to bear upon the national political systems.

A third, and perhaps (as we see from the diagram), a crucial element, is the linkage group. A linkage group, or a potential linkage group, is a group with links to the domestic system and with some particular links to the international or foreign input. A linkage group becomes much more susceptible to the inputs from abroad if its ties to the domestic system are weakened— if it is, for instance, a segregated or a discriminated minority or if it is an economic class or social class which is disadvantaged or alienated. The theoretical danger of this was seen by Disraeli when he spoke of the English in 1839 as consisting of "two nations," the rich and the poor.[6] The development he foresaw— namely, the danger of a permanent political alienation of the English working class—was forestalled in part by policies in the shaping of which he himself had some share. In a similar way, Bismarck's comparable vision about the need for a number of welfare-state measures in order to prevent the alienation of the German working class was successful enough to lead to the political reintegration of the German Social Democrats, which

6. Benjamin Disraeli, Earl of Beaconsfield, *Sybil, or The Two Nations* (London, Longmans, Green, 1913), pp. 76–77.

was dramatically demonstrated in their support of the German war effort in 1914.[7] On the other hand, the continuing alienation of a substantial part of the wage-earning classes of France and Italy has been studied in some detail in Almond's interviews in the fields of Communism and has been documented in electoral return after electoral return to this day.[8] The other potential linkage groups are, of course, the intellectuals and the scientists who, for instance, worried the Stalin regime back in the days of its anticosmopolitan campaign in 1947–48; the labor-market groups, such as sailors and others; and export-sensitive industries or economic interest groups sensitive mainly to the international market and the international business community rather than to domestic affairs. The term *linkage groups* is used here, of course, without any evaluative connotation. And whether Mr. Castro was worried about the business community of Havana as a linkage group to, let us say, the international and particularly the American business system or whether, let us say, some conservative regime such as that of Franco in Spain is worried about its intellectuals as a possible linkage group to leftist trends, is then a question of a specific fact.

The domestic connections of the linkage groups are a very major variable. They can be greatly strengthened—this was the essence of the policies of Bismarck and Disraeli—or they can be neglected. And finally, there is the inertia of the larger domestic system.

Let us consider a few examples of this. If you again recall the atmosphere of the 1930's as described in Mary McCarthy's *The Group,* you will remember her discussions of the splits among the various intellectual circles in New York, each group picking a faction in the Spanish Civil War to sympathize with and to get excited about.[9] If I had to diagram this, I would argue that the international tensions of the incipient World War II were very strong, that the flow of news from the Spanish Civil War to people who were educated intellectuals and who read the papers every day was large and inescapable. But the

7. Cf. also Seymour Martin Lipset, *Political Man* (New York, Doubleday, 1960), pp. 127–28.
8. Cf. Gabriel Almond, *The Appeals of Communism* (Princeton, Princeton University Press, 1954).
9. Mary McCarthy, *The Group* (New York, Harcourt, Brace, and World, 1963).

ties of these intellectuals to the American community were high, and the inertia of American public opinion was very high, too.

It was impossible, then, for most intellectuals in New York to ignore the Spanish Civil War. It was quite unlikely that they would continue to feel alienated from the American community. It was also impossible for them to get the American community to mount the barricades for the Spanish Republic. Since all the pressures were there in almost irresistible force hitting at an almost immovable object, the thing that had to break was the link. The intellectual groups in New York got fragmented into innumerable splinter groups, taking out their bitterness upon each other in arguing the respective merits of Trotskyists, anarchists, Stalinists, and every other group that could command a following; even the Socialists splintered off from Norman Thomas into various subdivisions.

Another example would be the Russian intelligentsia of the nineteenth century, in which again the impact of the European environment was strong. The inflow of news from what was going on in France, England, and Germany in the 1880's and 1890's was high, but the intellectuals' ties to their domestic society were low. And the inertia of the Russian society in the 1880's was massive. One result was a partial fragmentation of the Russian intellectuals, but even greater was the breaking of the links that bound many of them to the domestic society. They became alienated Nihilists and members of various factions. Some of them tried to forge their links through the Populist movement and finally through the Russian society, which had been inert in the 1880's or at least very resistant to foreign impacts, and became highly unstable and potentially extremely responsive to change by 1917. At that time the Russian intellectuals were split. One part reestablished its links to the Russian Revolution, which by 1917 was becoming a fairly massive affair; whereas another became completely alienated from Russia and ended up as émigrés.

Another case worth studying would be the impact of Sputnik upon American public opinion in the 1950's and particularly upon one subsystem: American education. The American scientific, educational, intellectual community was, again, strongly linked to foreign affairs. It could not believe with Mr. Fulton

Lewis that a space satellite was just a bauble of no real scientific and technological significance because its linkage to international affairs was high. At the same time the cohesion and morale of the American intellectual community was considerable, and its links to the American domestic community were very, very high. The American system was not very inert; it was partially responsive in the field of education (only moderate rigidities existed there), although in the 1950's its inertia was high on basic policies. The result was a differential response in which our general image of the world changed radically and dramatically. There occurred, therefore, a very strong impact on the selected linkage group, the educational and scientific subsystems of the American community.

You could even study Edmund Burke's tactics against the French revolutionists, as described by Sir Ernest Barker in his essay on Burke and the French Revolution in his *Essays on Government*.[10] The French Revolution appealed to two sections or two subsystems of British society. On the one hand there were the rationalistic intellectuals, such as Tom Paine and Dr. Joseph Priestley, and on the other hand there were the disadvantaged chapel groups—such as Presbyterians, Baptists, and Methodists—who labored under various discriminations. If these two groups had coalesced, a considerable pressure for change would have been generated. Burke's tactic, according to Barker, was to emphasize the atheistic components of the French Revolution, so as to make impossible any kind of alignment between the English chapel sections and the French Revolution. Therefore the English extreme radicals and rationalists would be isolated and eventually driven into exile. Both Paine and Priestley did end up in the United States, and British radicalism did not get anywhere; it remained a fringe group. The chapel groups, however, were integrated to a greater extent into the English political system, and what Burke was discussing in theory was then put into political practice in the founding of the Orange Order of 1795. This for the first time united the North Irish Presbyterians, who previously had been an "out" group, with the establishment of the Anglo-Episcopalian ascend-

10. Sir Ernest Barker, "Burke on the French Revolution," in *Essays on Government*, 2nd ed. (Oxford, Clarendon Press, 1951), pp. 205–33, esp. pp. 207–14.

ancy in Ireland. The Presbyterian linkage group, particularly in Ulster, thus was greatly strengthened and tied much more closely to the British political system. Another linkage group, the Catholics in Ireland, was at the same time impressed with the horrors of the French Revolution and therefore inclined to discount and reject any messages from France appealing to Irish sympathies.

These few historical examples suggest that this extremely crude scheme can be used for two purposes. It can be used to locate sensitive spots, and it can be used to make semiquantitative statements about balances, about flows which are strong or less strong, messages which are more or less likely to be accepted or rejected. Using it in the second manner, we can make statements in terms of more or less.

How do these possibilities apply to some projections and to some proportions that might be relevant for present and future political developments? First of all, with the awakening to political activity of an increasingly larger proportion of mankind, environmental pressures and the potential pressure of foreign input messages will grow in most countries in the world. This is true because there will be more international news, and there will be more broadcasting, television, and various other ways of making some of this information potentially available. If this were the only factor, it could suggest the familiar and simple prediction that the world will become more international. However, the activities of the S and the D, the integrative links between domestic subgroups and their intranational environment, are on the whole also increasing fairly rapidly. This happens because of the monetization of the national economies, the increases in wage labor, the transition toward the welfare state, the growth of national systems of mass education and mass communication—in short, the entire process of social mobilization.[11]

In most countries the D factors are growing faster at the present moment than are the foreign inputs from their international environment. Measurable characteristics of this trend are the declining ratio of foreign trade since 1914, which is the

11. For data, see Bruce M. Russett, Hayward Alker, K. W. Deutsch, and Harold D. Lasswell, *World Handbook of Political and Social Mediators* (New Haven, Yale University Press, 1964). Cf. also K. W. Deutsch, "Social Mobilization and Political Development," *American Political Science Review,* September 1961, pp. 493–514.

opposite of the nineteenth-century data,[12] and the declining ratio of foreign mail to domestic mail, which is also characteristic of most countries (again roughly) since 1914.[13] The attention ratio in newspapers—that is, the space ratio given in newspapers to domestic as against foreign affairs—is another indicator. This is relatively weak in the elite papers—the elites stay more internationally oriented—but in the mass papers preference for domestic news is very clear, and it is even more clear in readership attention, as shown in Wilbur Schramm's studies.[14]

If there is growth both in the E and F dimensions, and at the same time also growth in the D dimension, we can predict increasing pressure on the linkage groups. They are faced with mounting overloads of communications and demands, and their increasing partial failures to cope with them may lead to rising tensions and hostilities. In many countries the position of marginal minorities is gradually becoming untenable. They are faced with the choice of much more far-reaching assimilation and integration or of increasing alienation from the national community, which may lead to their emigration or expulsion.

The mechanism I have diagramed in Figure I thus predicts some of the recent situations which we find in empirical fact: the expulsion of Greeks from Turkey and Turks from Greece in the 1920's, the split between Moslems and Hindus in India and Pakistan, the pressure on Chinese residents in the Philippines and in Thailand, the pressure on the Jews in much of the Old World and their withdrawal from Moslem countries as well as from parts of Europe; and, on the other hand, the assimilation of certain groups. Particular groups may, however, combat this double process through a vigorous cultural renaissance at the place in which they are situated. This occurs rarely, but it

12. Data are given in K. W. Deutsch and Alexander Eckstein, "National Industrialization and the Declining Share of the Inter-Economic Sector, 1890–1959," World Politics, 13:2, January 1961, pp. 267–99; and Charles P. Kindleberger, Foreign Trade and the National Economy (New Haven, Yale University Press, 1963), pp. 179–83.

13. For data, see K. W. Deutsch, "Shifts in the Balance of Communication Flows: A Problem of Measurement in International Relations," Public Opinion Quarterly, 20:1, Spring 1956, pp. 143–60.

14. Cf. Wilbur Schramm, "Communication as Part of International Relations," and memoranda with data for nine nations, April 1957, Stanford University (unpublished); and W. Schramm, ed., Mass Communications (Urbana, University of Illinois Press, 1960). Cf. also Ithiel de Sola Pool, Symbols of Internationalism (Stanford, Stanford University Press, 1951).

has happened within some sections of American Judaism, which is currently flourishing in vigorous suburban congregations. But, on the whole, the crude mechanical model I have outlined predicts pressures on linkage groups and in some cases a trend toward the partial destruction, alienation, expulsion, or else assimilation or absorption of many such groups. If this trend should materialize, then it may be that a federation or merger of a national community or larger community is likely to take place only where the linkage groups stay strong and prevail.[15] Where this is not the case, the nations will become more sharply bounded from one another.[16] Another possibility, however, is that the linkage groups will hold out and prevail because the domestic political system, the S system, is becoming either more fragile or else more responsive.

A national S system that is likely to collapse or to go to pieces will make the country remarkably sensitive to foreign impacts. This is sometimes the case in civil wars.[17] On the other hand, the highly cohesive national community, with a high capacity for adjustment and learning, may be able to absorb the impact of foreign changes, to retain its linkage groups with partial autonomy but still within the national community, and simply go on by a series of readjustments. This could be called an ultra-stable system.[18] Finally, if the linkage groups are strong and the S system is strong, the E and the F links may be broken. That is to say, we might forecast that a number of countries in the future may pass through recurrent phases during which they will try to isolate themselves. We will get waves of isolationism which will dismay the adherents of a simple one-world perspective. We will find in these stages of transitory nationalism—not only in the early stages of development but also again later—from time to time heavy pressure to cut down the for-

15. For a discussion of several historical cases, see K. W. Deutsch, S. A. Burrell, et al., *Political Community and the North Atlantic Area* (Princeton, Princeton University Press, 1957), Chaps. 2 and 3.
16. This tendency was stressed by Otto Bauer, *Die Nationalitätenfrage und die Sozialdemokratie* (Vienna, Volksbuchhandlung, 1924), p. 135.
17. Cf. Harry Eckstein, ed., *Internal War* (New York, Free Press–Macmillan, 1964); and James N. Rosenau, ed., *International Aspects of Civil Strife* (Princeton, Princeton University Press, 1964).
18. The concept of "ultra-stability" was developed by W. Ross Ashby and is defined in his *Design for a Brain*, 2nd ed. (New York, Wiley, 1960), pp. 98–99. Cf. also K. W. Deutsch, *The Nerves of Government* (New York, Free Press–Macmillan, 1963), *passim*.

eign intake sectors, whenever the balance of communication pressures point in this direction.

Thus far the problem has been viewed from one perspective —that of the government of a country trying to preserve its autonomy against foreign messages or pressures. This perspective, however, can be reversed. Supposing we were interested in manipulating a foreign country or in changing the response of a foreign country, what would be the things we could do in terms of this model?

Let us assume that the American policy is to dissuade the French from setting up an atomic force and opening the door to the diffusion of nuclear weapons to a large number of somewhat unreliable and unpredictable countries and national decision systems. We could try to increase environmental pressure upon the French political community; or we could proceed indirectly, by creating a worldwide climate of some visible progress toward measures of arms control and disarmament, by making a number of highly visible agreements with the Russians on other possibly secondary matters, but by creating an image, therefore, of a world moving toward arms control with only France out of step. (The image of a world of growing conflicts among the great powers, or of protracted wars, e.g., in Asia, would have, of course, the opposite effect.) Monsieur Pierre Mendès-France, for instance, has suggested that the image that the French would get from all the rest of the world, not only from the United States, might be decisive for the French political response.[19]

As a possible second step, we could increase F by stepping up the flow of actual and expected transactions salient to Frenchmen. The move that counts is not the total flow of transactions alone, but the changes in it. However, any changes in the rate of flow of American credit, investments, and business orders would produce only limited changes in the salience of international views in the French political landscape. To this limited extent, we could encourage cohesion among some of the linkage groups and differentiation in the S system.

France is largely beyond the reach of effective foreign manipulation, but to some extent there may be autonomous processes at work which will raise the domestic resistance to a very costly

19. Pierre Mendès-France, oral communication, Yale University, Spring 1964.

atom bomb and rocket program in France. Where there is such a balance of contending domestic forces, we can pick a considerable number of these different points; any one of them or a combination of them might produce the results intended. If, on the other hand, our research shows that none of these variables can be changed, then we can be fairly sure that verbal exhortations directed from the State Department to the French government will have very little effect.

Let me give a few quantitative conclusions. Richard Merritt and I have worked at Yale on a survey which is discussed in a chapter in Herbert Kelman's book on *International Political Behavior*.[20] I am now shifting from a discussion of the *linkage mechanisms* to a discussion of the *actual changes* in images held and attitudes expressed. In order to look at these actual changes, we assume the following: that there is a very strong correlation between the images held in the minds of particular individuals and the distribution of attitudes and responses revealed by public opinion data. If we assume that the average Frenchman thinks the United States is just indifferently good or bad, then a French public opinion poll on attitudes toward the United States will give something like a fifty-fifty distribution. If most Frenchmen have a good image of the United States, 80 per cent of the French might say they liked the United States, and so on. We are using, in other words, opinion polls as indicators of image changes. These attitudes are then in turn influenced by at least three things:

1. The impact of spectacular events, S
2. The impact of smaller but cumulative events, C
3. The actions of governments, G, together with the mass media of communication which these governments control or influence

Each of these effects, S, C, and G, could be positive, in favor of the image or proposed action we are interested in; or any or all of them could be negative, $\bar{S}$, $\bar{C}$, or $\bar{G}$, so as to reduce the attitude or oppose the proposed action in question. Some poll results of this kind, together with the S, C, and G conditions surrounding them, are presented in Table 1.

20. K. W. Deutsch and Richard L. Merritt, "Effects of Events on National and International Images," in Herbert Kelman, ed., *International Political Behavior* (New York, Holt, Rinehart, and Winston, 1965), pp. 132–87.

TABLE 1

A Summary of Predicted and Observed Changes in Images*

1	2	3	4	5
		Observed Range		Approximate Number of
Description of Case	Type of Event	Net Shift from		Cases or
		Range	Midpoint	Respondents
1. Foreign policy saliency, 1946–49	GSC	+62	±31	1,500
2. Foreign policy saliency, 1958–60	GSC	+53	±27	1,500
3. Foreign policy saliency, 1960–63	GSC	−45	±23	1,500
4. Partisan distortion of TV debates, 1960	SC	+40	±20	159–8,000 (2,200–2,672)
5. Southern voters expect integration "some day," 1956–63	GSC	+38	±19	360
6. Anxiety due to combat, 1945	S	+31	±16	2,800
7. U.S.-U.S.S.R science race, 1957–58	S	+27	±14	800–1,700
8. Impact on Western Europe of Soviet intervention in Hungary, 1956	GS$\overline{\text{C}}$	−19	±10	800–1,700
9. Impact of Sputniks on West European image of U.S.S.R., 1957–61	SC$\overline{\text{G}}$	±18	±9	800–1,700
10. German morale loss from strategic bombing, 1944–45	SC$\overline{\text{G}}$	−17	±9	3,800
11. U.S. view of Russians as "intelligent," 1948–61	SC$\overline{\text{G}}$	+16	±8	1,015–1,500
12. Cuban crisis deterrence effect, 1963	SC$\overline{\text{G}}$	+15	±8	1,500
13. Interviewer effects (Hyman), 1948	C	15	±8	
14. Germans valuing U.S. alliance, 1957–61	GC$\overline{\text{S}}$	+14	±7	800–1,700
15. German image of U.S. strength, 1957–61	S$\overline{\text{G}}$	−12	±6	800–1,975
16. German knowledge of NATO, 1954–56	C	+10	±5	1,010–1,950
17. U.S. knowledge of Okinawa and Java, 1945	S	(+7)	±4	1,500
18. U.S. opposition to invasion of Cuba, 1961–63	S$\overline{\text{CG}}$	+2	±1	1,500

* All data in column 3 are significant at the 5 per cent level. In row 18 the absence of change is significant.

What do the data in this table show? We find that about 40 per cent of public opinion hardly ever budges. That is, for instance, about 30 per cent of Americans had a good opinion of the Japanese after Pearl Harbor, and approximately 30 per cent of Americans had a bad opinion of the Japanese when they were allies in the early 1960's. The change of American opinion is mostly in the 40 per cent area. Only on some particular events do we find greater changes.[21]

The biggest change that we could find was a shift in the saliency of foreign policy. In 1946 only 11 per cent of Americans thought foreign affairs were the most important thing, but by the middle of 1948, after the Communist coup in Czechoslovakia, the Marshall Plan, and the beating of the drums by the administration and by the mass media, 73 per cent thought that foreign affairs deserved top priority. This seems to be the world record in observed shifts: 63 percentage points over two years, or, on a per annum basis, a 31 per cent shift. I know of no other case where 30 per cent of poll respondents or voters have been observed to have changed their minds within a single year; research may eventually disclose other cases, but they are likely to be rare.

In another two-year period, from Mr. Eisenhower's tranquillity in 1958 to Mr. Kennedy's concern about missile gaps and competitive Soviet and American images and standings, a 53 per cent change in the concern of American voters was accomplished. Once Mr. Kennedy was in office, and the Republicans said there was no gap because Mr. Eisenhower had done well and the Democrats said that there was no gap because they were in office, the joint efforts of both parties succeeded in reassuring 45 per cent of the American public sufficiently to let them return to tranquillity concerning international affairs. However, in October 1964 the Negro situation and the integration problems were moving to the fore, and that accounts for part of this shift. In other words, it is not only how you see foreign affairs, but what happens at home, that makes a difference to the balance.

More frequent situations, on the other hand, involved only 40 to 20 per cent shifts. For instance, the partisan effect of the Kennedy-Nixon debates may have been on the order of 40 per

21. *Ibid.*, Table 7.

cent. The deterrent effects of Cuba—that is, the number of people who said they were against invading Cuba and who also said it might involve war—were 35 per cent. There were 10 per cent all-weather invaders who said, "It will bring war, but let's go to it," and there was a group of about 15 per cent or so who said, "It won't bring war, but we are against it." Yet 35 per cent may have been influenced by deterrent considerations. Most frequent and typical is the 20-odd per cent shift. For instance, after their intervention in Hungary in November 1956, the Russians lost, in each of several Western European countries, about 20 percentage points in their popularity standing in United States Information Agency polls—polls carried out, of course, by local organizations. It should be noted that the Russians regained these 20 percentage points within two years. By 1958 they were back at their pre-Hungarian levels of unpopularity (or popularity) in Western Europe.

During World War II German morale was diminished by strategic bombings, as far as we can see, by about 17 percentage points. That is to say, in very lightly bombed cities 42 per cent of German respondents in the postwar United States strategic-bombing survey reported bad morale; in very heavily bombed cities 59 per cent reported bad morale. This may be an understatement because some of the people with the worst morale may have left the heavily bombed cities. But in any case the effect, though significant, was moderate. And if one considers the spectacular nature of the 1956 Russian intervention in Hungary or of the bombing of World War II, one can see how stable public opinion actually is against the impact of fairly spectacular events.

Events which are less spectacular do very little. The German knowledge of NATO between 1954 and 1956 grew by only 10 per cent, although Germany's joining NATO at that time should have been a reasonably impressive event. American knowledge of where Okinawa was, in 1945, was only 7 per cent better than the American knowledge of where Java was. The least change I have found in any one of these important polls has been Americans' opposition to invading Cuba. In 1961, 63 per cent opposed invading Cuba. After the Cuban crisis, this fell to 62 per cent and then climbed back to 64 per cent. That is to say, the total shift, the maximum shift was something like 2 per cent, and on an annual basis it was a 1 per cent shift.

Such data may convey some idea of the very considerable resistance of modern public opinion to quick changes. Thus they may serve to balance the emphasis on the supposed volatility of mass opinion, particularly in the United States, which has been stressed for earlier periods.[22]

Let me say three concluding things. The greatest resistance to opinion change and the greatest resistances to any foreign impact seem to me to be located in the link to the strength of the element D—that is, in the relative volume and importance of domestic communications and transactions, where there is inner strength of potential linkage groups and linkage to the strength of the ties to the large domestic community.

This is to stress, in the language of the political scientist, what Festinger would call "the importance of social support" and what I like to call the "Festinger effect": [23] namely, that cognitive dissonance between a message and a past attitude is resolved by cutting down the message and retaining the attitude, if there is strong social support for the attitude. This seems abundantly confirmed by the opinion data Richard Merritt and I have studied. The Festinger effect seems to have a magnitude on the order of about 20 per cent in changing the perceptions of the group in which it prevails.

These answers, then, should tend to balance, at least, the notion of the opposite effect, the bandwagon effect that leads people to say, "Something big is going on abroad. Let's get with it." It turns out that in politics the bandwagon effect seems to account, at best, for between 3 and 5 per cent of the votes. This is to say that the bandwagon effect may be of some use in closely contested American elections among marginal voters wavering between the two parties, if they have much social support for either attitude. But on the whole it seems to me fairly clear that wherever social support exists in enough strength, the Festinger effect outweighs the self-fulfilling prophecy, or the "William James effect," by a factor of about four or five to one.

This finding seems to me to have some important corollaries. Namely, it is not necessary for democracies to resort to pretense

22. See e.g. Gabriel Almond, *The American People and Foreign Policy*, rev. ed. (New York, Praeger, 1960, 1962), pp. xxii, 69–86.

23. Leon Festinger, H. Riecken, and S. Schachter, *When Prophecy Fails* (Minneapolis, University of Minnesota Press, 1956); and Leon Festinger, *A Theory of Cognitive Dissonance* (Stanford, Stanford University Press, 1962). Cf. also Deutsch and Merritt, *op. cit.*

quite as much as they sometimes do, in fear that if they admitted an unpleasant truth, things would become worse. In actual fact, admitting an unpleasant truth ordinarily would cost 3 to 5 per cent support, not much more. On the other hand, the more strongly linked, the more cohesive our social structures and systems are, the more we can afford to do just that. Ordinarily we can afford the morale damage which comes from facing the truth because the moral repairs of strong social support in domestic, intrasocietal links are four to five times stronger.

My last point: Very often an external event will have only limited effects on domestic affairs. The big effects on images and opinion belong to relatively rare events, and most of the things which actually happen are the frequent events at around the 10 per cent shift scale. But foreign events may have an effect on the memories of people. Even a spectacular event may shift the attitudes of adults very little, and after six weeks or two years many will revert to the views they had before. The work of Hovland, Janis, and Kelly shows some of this resurgence of old attitudes.[24]

This is not true, however, of adolescents. It is the people of fifty, plus or minus five, who respond rarely to new attitudes, as all the opinion polls show. The voter of thirty-five, plus or minus five, or the up-and-coming young man, is more resilient, and the person who is twenty years old, plus or minus five— that is fifteen to twenty-five—is relatively highly responsive to major domestic or foreign political events.

From some cases one gets the impression that basic changes in attitude, in response to spectacular events, come in waves, about every fifteen years. I would be inclined to think of a political generation as roughly half the length of a biological one. There is one generation between the student of around twenty and the young assistant professor or the up-and-coming young executive of around thirty-five; another generation between him and the department head, section chief, or senior professor of around fifty. And in these periodic political shifts you can see how innovations travel. In this sense, I am inclined to think that the impact of new events—either internally new,

24. Carl I. Hovland, Irving L. Janis, and Harold H. Kelly, *Communication and Persuasion: Psychological Studies of Opinion Change* (New Haven, Yale University Press, 1953), pp. 134–73, 241–65, esp. p. 261.

technologically new, or internationally new—is delayed, but it will tend to pack a delayed wallop, leading to changes with a fifteen- and thirty-year time lag. Hence the internationalizing impact of new events may be greater than is now apparent because of what it will turn out to be fifteen or thirty years from now. The Europeans who in 1948 met with some enthusiasm for ideas of European unification, but who sometimes then did not do so well in their political careers up to 1965, may yet get their innings by about 1978. Whether this optimistic forecast works out or not, of course, remains to be seen, but the possibility is there.

Pre-theories and Theories of Foreign Policy[1]

JAMES N. ROSENAU
Douglass College, Rutgers University

I

To PROBE the "internal influences on external behavior"[2] is to be active on one of the frontiers where the fields of international and comparative politics meet. Initial thoughts about the subject, however, are bound to be ambivalent; it would

1. This paper is part of a general inquiry into the dynamics of international politics and foreign policy in which I am engaged with the support of the Center of International Studies at Princeton University. I am grateful for the facilities the Center has placed at my disposal. The assistance and counsel of my wife Norah have also been invaluable. Neither she nor the Center, however, is responsible for the emphases and interpretations contained in this paper.

2. This is the original phrasing of the topic which I was asked to analyze for the conference that occasioned this symposium. Such influences are assumed to refer to the domestic sources of foreign policy, an assumption which is not the only one that could be made about the scope of the assigned topic. External behavior could also be defined as encompassing all the private ways in which the members of a society engage in activities beyond its boundaries. Tourists, students, soldiers, and traders are only a few of the individuals and groups whose private activities abroad can properly be viewed both as stemming from influences internal to a society and as constituting a crucial dimension of its external behavior. Notwithstanding their obvious relevance to the interrelationships of political sys-

seem to have been both exhausted and neglected as a focus of inquiry. Even as it seems clear that everything worth saying about the subject has already been said, so does it also seem obvious that the heart of the matter has yet to be explored and that American political science is on the verge of major break-throughs which will make exploration possible.[3]

The exhaustion of the subject can be easily demonstrated. While it was not long ago that the external behavior of nations was considered to be exclusively a reaction to external stimuli, ever since World War II students of foreign policy have empha-sized that the wellsprings of international action are also fed by events and tendencies within societies.[4] The literature of the field is now rich with "factors" that have been identified as internal sources of foreign policy. The role played by geographic and other nonhuman characteristics of a nation has received thorough treatment.[5] Capability analysts have uncovered a vast array of social, economic, cultural, and psychological processes which limit, enhance, or otherwise affect the external behavior of societies even as they sustain their internal life.[6] Other an-alysts have focused on political processes and delineated link-ages between the foreign policy of a nation on the one hand and the shifting opinions of its citizenry,[7] the operations of its

tems, however, such activities have been excluded from the scope of this paper on the grounds that they are not in themselves political phenomena and that as political scientists we cannot afford to dissipate our energies on matters that fall outside our spheres of competence. For my conception of the nature of political phenomena, see Calculated Control as a Unifying Concept in the Study of International Politics and Foreign Policy (Prince-ton, Center of International Studies, Research Monograph No. 15, 1963), pp. 9–15.

3. For a similar ambivalence, but one that was resolved very differently than my own, see Philip E. Mosely, "Research on Foreign Policy," in Brook-ings Dedication Lectures, Research for Public Policy (Washington, D. C., The Brookings Institution, 1961), pp. 43–72.

4. Perhaps the first to emphasize and elaborate the relevance of domestic variables was Richard C. Snyder. See his articles, "The Nature of Foreign Policy," Social Science, 27:2, April 1952, pp. 61–69, and "Toward Greater Order in the Study of International Politics," World Politics, VII:3, April 1955, esp. pp. 473–74.

5. Harold and Margaret Sprout, Man-Milieu Relationship Hypotheses in the Context of International Politics (Princeton, Center of International Studies, 1956), passim.

6. See, for example, Klaus Knorr, The War Potential of Nations (Prince-ton, Princeton University Press, 1956), Parts I and II.

7. Cf. Gabriel A. Almond, The American People and Foreign Policy (New York, Harcourt, Brace, 1950); Bernard C. Cohen, The Political Process and

press and other media of mass communications,[8] and the character of its elites—their backgrounds,[9] attitudes,[10] and solidarity [11]—on the other.[12] Nor have violent internal processes been ignored as sources of external behavior.[13] Still another group of analysts, those who follow the decision-making approach, have called attention to a wide cluster of motivational, role, and organizational variables which operate within governments as determinants of foreign policy.[14] Inquiries into the contributions of particular types of decision-makers and decision-making institutions have also become abundantly available.[15] By focusing on the perceptions and choices of officials, moreover, students of decision-making have identified a host of additional nongovernmental variables which condition the behavior of policy-makers and thus become relevant to the quality and goals of international action.[16] The past experiences and present value orientations of a society, its educational institutions, its social structure and system of stratification—these are but a few of the many societal variables which have received attention as

Foreign Policy: The Making of the Japanese Peace Settlement (Princeton, Princeton University Press, 1957); and Douglas H. Mendel, Jr., The Japanese People and Foreign Policy: A Study of Public Opinion in Post-Treaty Japan (Berkeley, University of California Press, 1961).

8. For instance, see Bernard C. Cohen, The Press and Foreign Policy (Princeton, Princeton University Press, 1963).

9. Donald R. Matthews, The Social Background of Political Decision-Makers (Garden City, Doubleday, 1954).

10. See, for example, Hans Speier and W. Phillips Davison, eds., West German Leadership and Foreign Policy (Evanston, Row, Peterson, 1957).

11. Cf. James N. Rosenau, National Leadership and Foreign Policy: A Case Study in the Mobilization of Public Support (Princeton, Princeton University Press, 1963).

12. For an impressive case study that explores and synthesizes all these variables, see Karl W. Deutsch and Lewis J. Edinger, Germany Rejoins the Powers: Mass Opinion, Interest Groups, and Elites in Contemporary German Foreign Policy (Stanford, Stanford University Press, 1959).

13. Cf. James N. Rosenau, ed., International Aspects of Civil Strife (Princeton, Princeton University Press, 1964).

14. Richard C. Snyder, H. W. Bruck, and Burton Sapin, Decision-Making as an Approach to the Study of International Politics (Princeton, Organizational Behavior Section, Foreign Policy Analysis Series, No. 3, 1954), pp. 68–117.

15. For example, see James A. Robinson, Congress and Foreign Policy-Making: A Study in Legislative Influence and Initiative (Homewood, Illinois, Dorsey Press, 1962); and Burton M. Sapin and Richard C. Snyder, The Role of the Military in American Foreign Policy (Garden City, Doubleday, 1954).

16. Cf. Edgar S. Furniss, Jr., and Richard C. Snyder, An Introduction to American Foreign Policy (New York, Rinehart, 1955), Chap. 5.

determinants of the identity, outlook, and capacities of those who occupy foreign policy decision-making roles.[17]

All this is in sharp contrast to previous tendencies either to ignore domestic variables or to deal with them through such broad and unmanageable concepts as nationalism or national character. The progress of the social sciences has rubbed off on students of foreign policy, and they are no longer content to use simple labels to explain complex behavior. Instead of explaining a policy in terms of, say, "rampant nationalism," now the inclination is to attempt to specify the components of the processes and attitudes which comprise the phenomena encompassed by such grandiose terminology. Thus have such concepts as image,[18] belief system,[19] consensus,[20] and tension levels [21] come to be part of the storehouse of equipment used by those who probe the internal sources of external behavior.

Methodologically, too, the rate of progress has been encouraging. Not only have a number of creative techniques for developing and analyzing data been perfected,[22] but, equally important, students of foreign policy are no longer ignorant of the philosophy of science, its precepts, and its tools. They are now sensitive to the distinctions between description and explanation, correlation and causation, hypotheses and models,

17. For much more thorough inventories of recent research in the foreign policy field, see Charles A. McClelland, "Articles and Books Published in 1962 in the Fields of International Relations," *Background*, 7:1, May 1963, pp. 12–57; Richard C. Snyder and James A. Robinson, *National and International Decision-Making: Towards a General Research Strategy Related to the Problem of War and Peace* (New York, Institute for International Order, 1961); and Richard C. Snyder, "Some Recent Trends in International Relations Theory and Research," in Austin Ranney, ed., *Essays on the Behavioral Study of Politics* (Urbana, University of Illinois Press, 1962), pp. 103–71.

18. Kenneth E. Boulding, "National Images and International Systems," *Journal of Conflict Resolution*, III:2, June 1959, pp. 120–31.

19. Ole R. Holsti, "The Belief System and National Images: A Case Study," *Journal of Conflict Resolution*, VI:3, September 1962, pp. 244–52.

20. Roger Hilsman, "The Foreign-Policy Consensus: An Interim Research Report," *Journal of Conflict Resolution*, III:4, December 1959, pp. 361–82.

21. K. J. Holsti, "The Use of Objective Criteria for the Measurement of International Tension Levels," *Background*, 7:2, August 1963, pp. 77–95.

22. For example, see Harold Guetzkow, et al., *Simulation in International Relations: Developments for Research and Teaching* (Englewood Cliffs, Prentice-Hall, 1963); and Robert C. North, et al., *Content Analysis: A Handbook with Applications for the Study of International Crisis* (Evanston, Northwestern University Press, 1963).

fact and value. They know that foreign policy behavior is a reaction to both external and internal stimuli and that one breaks into the chain of causation only for analytic purposes. Hence they no longer equate their inquiries with reality, recognizing instead that the operations they perform on data constitute distortions of reality that have to be undertaken for comprehension to occur. In short, the modern student of foreign policy is—or at least has the opportunity to become—a broad-gauged and sophisticated social scientist. He even has available for his undergraduate training a textbook which contains an introductory—and excellent—discussion of the nature of reliable knowledge, how it is acquired, and how different intellectual tools and perspectives can be used.[23]

II

But it is also easy to exaggerate the rate of progress. Notwithstanding the varied and impressive accomplishments outlined above, the dynamics of the processes which culminate in the external behavior of societies remain obscure. To identify factors is not to trace their influence. To uncover processes that affect external behavior is not to explain how and why they are operative under certain circumstances and not under others. To recognize that foreign policy is shaped by internal as well as external factors is not to comprehend how the two intermix or to indicate the conditions under which one predominates over the other. And in these respects progress has been very slow indeed. Rare is the article or book which goes beyond description of an internal factor and locates it in the ever changing interplay of variables—both external and internal—which combine to produce foreign policies. Even rarer is the work that contains explicit "if-then" hypotheses in which the "if" is a particular form of the internal factor and the "then" is a particular type of foreign policy. Rather, for all their philosophical and methodological sophistication, many analyses treat the internal factor under examination as the only variable in a world of constants. The different ways in which the factor can or does influence policy are described—thus making it a

23. Harold and Margaret Sprout, *Foundations of International Politics* (Princeton, Van Nostrand, 1962), Chap. 1.

variable—but the situations at home and abroad through which the influence operates are taken for granted, thus giving rise to the false impression that qualities inherent in the factor itself are the only determinants of the particular way in which it is influential at any moment in time. Even worse, the factor is often treated as a constant in a world of variables. That is, irrespective of variations at home and abroad, its influence is seen to remain unchanged. A foreign policy may be aggressive or submissive, long range or short range, economic or diplomatic, but the internal factor is nonetheless considered to be present to the same degree.

The main reason for this situation is not difficult to discern: foreign policy analysis lacks comprehensive systems of testable generalizations that treat societies as actors subject to stimuli which produce external responses. Stated more succinctly, foreign policy analysis is devoid of general theory. Perhaps it has been exhausted as far as inventorying the determinants of external behavior is concerned, but it has not even begun to take shape as a theoretical enterprise. The field has an abundance of frameworks and approaches which cut across societies and conceptualize the ends, means, capabilities, or sources of foreign policy, but no schemes which link up these components of external behavior in causal sequences.[24] No framework has energized inquiry in foreign policy as Rostow's theory of the stages of economic growth did in the economic development field,[25] as Festinger's theory of cognitive dissonance did in social psychology,[26] or as Almond's functional model did in comparative politics.[27] As one observer puts it, "The study of foreign policy . . . is one applied social science that largely lacks its counterpart in a pure science." [28] It is hardly surprising, therefore, that the influence of internal factors on external behavior has not been traced as sophisticatedly as recent progress

24. One possible exception is George Modelski, *A Theory of Foreign Policy* (New York, Praeger, 1962), but even this work is short on causal propositions and long on analysis of the points at which causation is operative.

25. W. W. Rostow, *The Stages of Economic Growth* (New York, Cambridge University Press, 1960).

26. Leon Festinger, *A Theory of Cognitive Dissonance* (Evanston, Row, Peterson, 1957).

27. Gabriel A. Almond and James S. Coleman, eds., *The Politics of the Developing Areas* (Princeton, Princeton University Press, 1960), pp. 3–64.

28. Mosely, *op. cit.*, pp. 44–45.

in the field might lead one to expect. If students of foreign policy were inclined to structure their subject in such a way as to observe the differential interplay of variables under varying conditions, then obviously a multitude of if-then hypotheses bearing on the operation of internal factors would have long since been advanced.

Occasionally, to be sure, one comes upon materials which take note of causal relationships between external behavior and internal processes. The literature on economic and political development, for example, is full of references to the ways in which the foreign policies of modernizing societies are shaped by their internal needs—by the need of elites for identity and prestige, by the need of charismatic leaders to sustain their charisma, by the need of in-groups to divert attention away from domestic problems and thereby to placate their oppositions.[29] Propositions of this sort, however, amount to partial and not general theories. Usually they are articulated in terms of a particular country and cannot be applied to other modernizing societies. Sometimes they are even developed to explain the external behavior of a particular leader or elite and then lose their relevance when a *coup d'état* or some equivalent event alters the governance of the country. More important, such propositions are partial in the sense that they are exclusively confined to internal sources of external behavior and do not posit it as also a response to events occurring abroad. No doubt the foreign policies of some modernizing elites are especially designed to divert attention from domestic problems, but they are also intended to maximize control over the international environment and must thus be adjusted to shifts on the world scene.

Much the same can be said about the emerging theoretical literature that gives a central place to foreign policy in the processes of alliance building,[30] the dynamics of supranational integration,[31] and the competition among superpowers for in-

29. Cf. Robert C. Good, "State-Building as a Determinant of Foreign Policy in the New States," in Laurence W. Martin, ed., *Neutralism and Nonalignment* (New York, Frederick A. Praeger, 1962), pp. 3–12.
30. See George Liska, *Nations in Alliance: The Limits of Interdependence* (Baltimore, Johns Hopkins Press, 1962); and William H. Riker, *The Theory of Political Coalitions* (New Haven, Yale University Press, 1962).
31. Cf. the following articles by Amitai Etzioni: "The Dialectics of Supranational Unification," *American Political Science Review*, LVI:4,

fluence in the nonaligned world.[32] While such efforts are theoretical in the sense that they posit external behaviors derived from specified stimuli, they are nonetheless partial and not general theories. They are founded on the premise that external events—individually or as structural characteristics of international systems—are the prime movers of foreign policy. Virtually none of them allow for the operation of internal causation. The external behavior called for in game-theoretical models, for example, presumes rational decision-makers who are impervious to the need to placate their domestic opponents or, indeed, to any influences other than the strategic requirements of responding to adversaries abroad.[33]

The lack of general theory is further indicated by the haphazard way in which many foreign policy analysts vary the external-internal mix from one set of explanatory propositions to the next. Sometimes policies are attributed to domestic factors and sometimes causation is ascribed to external sources, but the rationale for using one or the other explanation is never made explicit and is rarely systematic. Most foreign policy analysts, for example, are content to leave domestic causation out of their alliance theories even as their explanations of international activity in the foreign aid field contain a large mix of internal and external factors. Similarly, analysts are rarely troubled by the seeming inconsistency between their readiness to posit the behavior of individual decision-makers as cause in one instance and as effect in another. During the years between 1959 and 1964, for instance, it became commonplace to treat French foreign policy as a function of a free-wheeling and haughty De Gaulle and to view Soviet foreign policy not as a function of an unrestrained and ebullient Khrushchev, but as a consequence of stresses and strains within the U.S.S.R. and the Communist international system. Such discrepancies are not in themselves unreasonable. They may well be a reflection of

December 1962, pp. 927–35; "The Epigenesis of Political Communities at the International Level," *American Journal of Sociology*, LXVIII: 4, January 1963, pp. 407–21; and "European Unification: A Strategy of Change," *World Politics*, XVI: 1, October 1963, pp. 32–51.

32. For example, see Morton A. Kaplan, "Bipolarity in a Revolutionary Age," in Morton A. Kaplan, ed., *The Revolution in World Politics* (New York, Wiley, 1962), pp. 251–66.

33. For an elaboration of this point, see Bernard C. Cohen, "Military Policy Analysis and the Art of the Possible: A Review," *Journal of Conflict Resolution*, VI: 2, June 1962, pp. 154–59.

empirical reality. Yet, to repeat, conspicuously absent is any body of theory which would account for the discrepancies. Under what conditions does the influence of individual leaders on foreign policy outweigh that of complex societal processes? Why are domestic factors more of a hindrance in the construction and maintenance of foreign aid programs than in the formation and conduct of military alliances? No answers to such questions are at present available.

Not being able to draw on general theories, work in the foreign policy field has been largely historical and single-country oriented. An overwhelming preponderance of the inquiries into foreign policy is confined either to analyzing the external behavior of a specific country at a specific moment in time or to identifying the patterns which mark its external behavior over a period of time. Indeed, so pronounced is this orientation that most, if not all, American universities offer courses which are exclusively devoted to depicting and analyzing the patterned external behavior of various countries. Courses in American foreign policy and in Soviet foreign policy abound, and those on the external behavior of India, England, Japan, France, and other leading nations are hardly less numerous. The evolution of such a curriculum has spurred the creation of a vast textbook literature, which in turn has reinforced the tendency to approach the field from a historical, single-country perspective. A measure of the spiraling process is provided by the fact that in 1958 a text containing a separate treatment of the foreign policies of ten different nations was published and that 1963 saw the publication of a similar book covering the external behavior of twenty-four different nations.[34]

It might be argued that this single-country orientation is the first step in a slow progression toward general theory, that analyses of the external behavior of many countries constitute bases for the construction of systems of testable generalizations about the foreign policies of general classes of countries, thus leading to the eventual development of if-then models accounting for the behavior of any country. Unfortunately, however, this line of reasoning is refuted by the unsystematic and uneven

34. Roy C. Macridis, ed., *Foreign Policy in World Politics* (Englewood Cliffs, Prentice-Hall, 1958); and Joseph E. Black and Kenneth W. Thompson, eds., *Foreign Policies in a World of Change* (New York, Harper and Row, 1963).

nature of the single-country research that has been and is being done. In the first place, the premises underlying the work on each country are so varied that comparative analysis is almost, if not entirely, impossible. It is difficult to find two analyses of two different countries that consider the same variables, ask the same questions, and gather comparable data. Even the afore-mentioned compilations of ten and twenty-four foreign policies do not make comparative analysis possible. In both instances the editors presented an introductory chapter suggesting certain common characteristics of the external behavior of all nations, but in neither case did the contributors adhere to the outline. In one case, moreover, the editor himself lost interest in devel-oping his model and instead devoted the last half of his intro-duction to a discussion of "three obstacles that confound American policy-makers and that must at least be mitigated if the struggle is to be won." [35]

In addition to precluding comparison, the single-country an-alyses are themselves theoretically deficient. By placing a society's foreign policies in a historical and problem-solving con-text, analysts tend to treat each international situation in which the society participates as unique and, consequently, to view its external behavior with respect to each situation as stemming from immediate and particular antecedents. This approach does not prevent the derivation of generalizations about the goals and character of the society's behavior in many situations, but it does inhibit the construction of if-then models which link the behavior patterns to a systematic set of stimuli. Rather the stimuli, being comprised of unique historical circumstances, are conceived to vary from one situation to the next, and rarely is a construct offered to account for the variations. Consider, for example, how numerous are the analyses of Soviet foreign policy which attribute causation to a Khrushchev in one situation, to a pent-up consumer demand in another, to a conflict within the leadership structure in a third, to a reality of Russian geog-raphy in a fourth, and to an aspect of the Sino-Soviet struggle in a fifth situation. Or reflect on the differential explanations of why the United States entered a war in Korea in 1950, avoided one in Indo-China in 1954, and fomented one in Cuba in 1961. Undoubtedly each of these actions was a response to a different combination of external and internal stimuli; and no

35. Macridis, *op. cit.*, p. 22.

doubt, too, there is considerable variability in the complex of factors which determine Soviet policies. But at the same time it is also true that the variability is patterned. The stimuli which produce external behavior must be processed by the value and decision-making systems of a society, so that it ought to be possible, as with rats in a maze, to link up varying types of responses with varying types of stimuli. To repeat, however, few foreign policy researchers structure their materials in such a way as to allow for this kind of analysis. Just as it is difficult to compare the external behavior of different countries in the same international situation, so it is often next to impossible to engage in comparative analysis of the actions of the same country in different situations. One is reminded of the state that the field of political theory was in not so long ago: We have many histories of American foreign policy but very few theories of American foreign policy, and much the same can be said about research on every country presently attracting the attention of foreign policy analysts.

III

The resolution of ambivalence is never easy. A residue of unease always seems to remain, especially if the resolution is in a negative direction. Having resolved initial ambivalence with the conclusion that the endless piling up of historical case materials is leading foreign policy research down to a dead end, one is inclined to pause and wonder whether extenuating circumstances have been overlooked or, indeed, whether one's focus is so narrow as to distort perception and exaggerate defect. There must be good reasons why the lack of theory has not aroused researchers to undertake corrective measures. Could it be that the author and not the field has gone astray?

The answer, of course, is that each has special needs—the field for solutions to urgent policy problems and the author for accretions to an ever growing science of politics. The satisfaction of these needs leads down two different paths, neither better than the other.

But one wonders, too, whether the paths need be so divergent. Is a problem-solving orientation necessarily incompatible with the development of empirical materials that lend themselves to an if-then kind of analysis? Cannot historical investigation be carried out in such a way as to facilitate meaningful comparisons and generalizations that are not bound by time and place? An affirmative response to these questions is not unreasonable. Economic theory has been helped, not hindered, by work done in applied economics.[36] Sociological theory has been spurred, not stifled, by empirical inquiries into social processes.[37] Of late, political theory, as distinguished from the history of political thought, has been enriched and enlivened by research into the development of non-Western polities.[38] Surely there is nothing inherent in the nature of foreign policy phenomena which renders them more resistant to theoretical treatment than the gross data that comprise these other applied fields.

The nontheoretical state of foreign policy research is all the more perplexing when it is contrasted with developments elsewhere in American political science. In recent years the discipline has been transformed from an intuitive to a scientific enterprise, and consequently the inclination to develop models and test theories has become second nature to most political scientists. Each day—or at least each new publication—brings into the field fresh concepts, propositions, and theories about local, national, and international political systems. New models of the processes of political development abound. And so do conceptualizations of how party, legislative, bureaucratic, and judicial systems function. In each of these areas, moreover, political scientists are beginning to build on one another's work (the surest sign of a maturing discipline), and thus innovative theorizing is being accompanied by a healthy convergence on similar models of the political process.

In short, the lack of theory in foreign policy research cannot be readily justified or easily explained. Clearly it cannot be dismissed as a mere reflection of general tendencies in the discipline. Nor can it be attributed to the requirements of prob-

36. Cf. Charles J. Hitch, et al., "The Uses of Economics," in Brookings Dedication Lectures, op. cit., pp. 91–126.

37. Cf. Robert K. Merton, Social Theory and Social Structure, rev. ed. (Glencoe, Free Press, 1957), Chap. III.

38. See, for example, the studies sponsored by the Committee on Comparative Politics of the Social Science Research Council: Lucian W. Pye, ed., Communications and Political Development (Princeton, Princeton University Press, 1963); and Joseph LaPalombara, ed., Bureaucracy and Political Development (Princeton, Princeton University Press, 1963).

lem-solving and the precedents of history. Researchers in other areas of the discipline also engage in historical analysis and expend energy seeking solutions to immediate and practical problems, yet this does not inhibit their inclination to press ahead in the development of general theories. Nor, obviously, is it sufficient to speculate that in foreign policy research the "avoidance of the general in preference to the individual, unique, and empirical may be a reflection of the very recent and chiefly American origins of this field of study." [39] Other more basic obstacles must be blocking the road to general theory, else long ago foreign policy researchers would have begun to move down it alongside economists, sociologists, and other political scientists.

Two basic shortcomings, one philosophical and the other conceptual, would appear to be holding back the development of foreign policy theory.[40] Let us look first at the philosophical shortcoming. If theoretical development in a field is to flourish,

39. Mosely, *op. cit.*, p. 45. It is amusing, and perhaps even indicative of the impressionistic state of things, to note the enormous gap between this view of ourselves as nontheoretical and the view held by European analysts that "in the United States the theoretical study of foreign policy has become a thriving industry. Where Disraeli is said to have accosted aged Parliamentarians whose names escaped him with the question 'How's the gout?', American professors of international relations now reputedly ask of their younger colleagues 'How's the conceptual framework?'." F. S. Northedge, in a book review, *Political Quarterly*, 34:3, July-September 1963, p. 310.

40. A third shortcoming, so closely intertwined with the other two that its relevance is manifest throughout the ensuing discussion and requires only brief identification here, is of an organizational nature: Namely, the discipline of political science is at present organized in such a way that the external behavior of national political systems does not fall within the purview of scholars who are interested in the construction of general theories. Neither of the two groups of model builders who might be expected to theorize about foreign policy—those in comparative politics and those in international politics—is drawn by conceptual necessity to find a theoretical home for the external behavior of societies. Students of comparative politics focus primarily on national political systems and the interaction processes that occur *within* them. Once a pattern of interaction moves outside a national system, therefore, the comparative politics specialist tends to lose interest in it. Of primary concern to students of international politics, on the other hand, are the processes of interaction that occur *among* national systems. Consequently the international politics specialist tends to take internal influences on external behavior for granted and to become interested in the patterns generated by national systems only after they have crossed over into the international realm. Foreign policy phenomena, in short, are the unwanted stepchildren of political systems. They serve as outputs for one type of system and as inputs for another, but they do not constitute actions which both begin and culminate in any system that is of interest to present-day political theorists. Hence, notwithstanding their intense relevance to students of practical policy-making

empirical materials which have been similarly processed must be available. It is no more possible to construct models of human behavior out of raw data than it is to erect a building out of fallen trees and unbaked clay. The trees must be sawed and the clay must be baked, and the resulting lumber and bricks must be the same size, shape, and color if a sturdy and coherent building is to be erected. Note that the design and function of the structure are not determined by the fact that the materials comprising it have been similarly processed. The same bricks and lumber can be used to build houses or factories, large structures or small ones, modern buildings or traditional ones. So it is with the construction and use of social theories. There must be, as it were, pre-theory which renders the raw materials comparable and ready for theorizing. The materials may serve as the basis for all kinds of theories—abstract or empirical, single- or multi-country, pure or applied—but until they have been similarly processed, theorizing is not likely to occur, or, if it does, the results are not likely to be very useful.

Unlike economics, sociology, and other areas of political science, the field of foreign policy research has not subjected its materials to this preliminary processing. Instead, as noted above, each country and each international situation in which it participates is normally treated as unique and nonrecurrent, with the result that most available studies do not treat foreign policy phenomena in a comparable way. Thus it is that the same data pertaining to the external behavior of the Soviet Union are interpreted by one observer as illustrative of Khrushchev's flexibility, by another as reflective of pent-up consumer demands, and by still another as indicative of the Sino-Soviet conflict. To recur to the analogy of physical materials, it is as if one person cut up the fallen trees for firewood, another used

---

problems, foreign policy phenomena have been neglected by theoreticians and relegated to the residual category of systems theory known as "boundary problems."

The one exception to this pattern is, of course, those theoreticians for whom the boundary between national and international systems is the core of their concern, i.e., those who specialize in the processes of supranational integration. It is perhaps significant that the most promising theory in this area is presently being developed by a sociologist, Amitai Etzioni, whose training and experience does not confine him to the traditional boundaries of the discipline of political science. See, for example, his three articles cited above in note 31.

them as the subject of a painting, and still another had them sawed for use in the building of a frame house.

It must be emphasized that the preliminary processing of foreign policy materials involves considerably more than methodological tidiness. We are not referring here to techniques of gathering and handling data, albeit there is much that could be said about the need for standardization in this respect. Nor do we have in mind the desirability of orienting foreign policy research toward the use of quantified materials and operationalized concepts, albeit again good arguments could be advanced on behalf of such procedures. Rather, the preliminary processing to which foreign policy materials must be subjected is of a much more basic order. It involves the need to develop an explicit conception of where causation is located in international affairs. Should foreign policy researchers proceed on the assumption that identifiable human beings are the causative agents? Or should they treat political roles, governmental structures, societal processes, or international systems as the source of external behavior? And if they presume that causation is located in all these sources, to what extent and under what circumstances is each source more or less causal than the others? Few researchers in the field process their materials in terms of some kind of explicit answer to these questions. Most of them, in other words, are not aware of the philosophy of foreign policy analysis they employ, or, more broadly, they are unaware of their pre-theories of foreign policy.[41]

To be sure, foreign policy researchers are not so unsophisticated as to fail to recognize that causation can be attributed to a variety of actors and entities. For years now it has been commonplace to avoid single-cause deterministic explanations and to assert the legitimacy of explaining the same event in a variety of ways. Rather than serving to discipline research, however, this greater sophistication has in some ways supplied a license for undisciplined inquiry. Now it is equally commonplace

41. Briefly, by pre-theory is meant both an early step toward explanation of specific empirical events and a general orientation toward all events, a point of view or philosophy about the way the world is. Ideally pre-theories would be limited to the former meaning, but this requires that a field be in general agreement about the "proper" orientation toward its subject matter, a situation which the field of foreign policy research is far from even approximating.

to assume that one's obligations as a researcher are discharged by articulating the premise that external behavior results from a combination of many factors, both external and internal, *without* indicating how the various factors combine under different circumstances. Having rejected single-cause explanations, in other words, most foreign policy researchers seem to feel they are therefore free *not* to be consistent in their manner of ascribing causation. Deterministic theories have philosophical roots, much foreign policy research seems to say, so that in abandoning the theories it is also necessary to give up the practice of locating one's work in a pre-theoretical context. Thus, as previously indicated, rare is the observer who is troubled by the discrepancy between his attribution of causation to De Gaulle's personal qualities and not to Khrushchev's. On the contrary, many apparently believe that such discrepancies are the mark of flexibility in research and the surest sign of having avoided deterministic modes of thought.

Nothing could be further from the truth. The development and employment of a pre-theory of foreign policy does not, as noted below, necessarily lead to determinism or even to greater rigidity. It merely provides a basis for comparison in the examination of the external behavior of various countries in various situations and, to repeat, there can be no real flourishing of theory until the materials of the field are processed—i.e., rendered comparable—through the use of pre-theories of foreign policy.

Perhaps the best way to indicate exactly what a pre-theory of foreign policy involves is by outlining the main ingredients of any pre-theory and then indicating how the author has integrated these ingredients into his own particular pre-theory. Although the statement is subject to modification and elaboration, it does not seem unreasonable to assert that all pre-theories of foreign policy are either five-dimensional or translatable into five dimensions. That is, all foreign policy analysts either explain the external behavior of societies in terms of five sets of variables, or they proceed in such a way that their explanations can be recast in terms of the five sets.[42] Listed in order of

42. For approaches which assert the utility of employing two and six sets of variables, see, respectively, J. David Singer, "The Levels-of-Analysis Problem in International Relations," *World Politics,* XIV: 1, October 1961, pp. 77–92; and Robert C. North, *op. cit.,* pp. 5–7.

increasing temporal and spatial distance from the external behaviors for which they serve as sources, the five sets are what we shall call the idiosyncratic, role, governmental, societal, and systemic variables.

The first set encompasses the idiosyncrasies of the decision-makers who determine and implement the foreign policies of a nation. Idiosyncratic variables include all those aspects of a decision-maker—his values, talents, and prior experiences—that distinguish his foreign policy choices or behavior from those of every other decision-maker. John Foster Dulles' religious values, De Gaulle's vision of a glorious France, and Khrushchev's political skills are frequently mentioned examples of idiosyncratic variables. The second set of variables pertains to the external behavior of officials that is generated by the roles they occupy and that would be likely to occur irrespective of the idiosyncrasies of the role occupants. Regardless of who he is, for example, the U.S. ambassador to the United Nations is likely to defend American and Western positions in the Security Council and General Assembly. Governmental variables refer to those aspects of a government's structure that limit or enhance the foreign policy choices made by decision-makers. The impact of executive-legislative relations on American foreign policy exemplifies the operation of governmental variables. The fourth cluster of variables consists of those nongovernmental aspects of a society which influence its external behavior. The major value orientations of a society, its degree of national unity, and the extent of its industrialization are but a few of the societal variables which can contribute to the contents of a nation's external aspirations and policies. As for systemic variables, these include any nonhuman aspects of a society's external environment or any actions occurring abroad that condition or otherwise influence the choices made by its officials. Geographical "realities" and ideological challenges from potential aggressors are obvious examples of systemic variables which can shape the decisions and actions of foreign policy officials.

But these are only the ingredients of a pre-theory of foreign policy. To formulate the pre-theory itself one has to assess their *relative potencies*. That is, one has to decide which set of variables contributes most to external behavior, which ranks next in influence, and so on through all the sets. There is no need to specify exactly how large a slice of the pie is accounted for by

each set of variables. Such precise specifications are characteristics of theories and not of the general framework within which
data are organized. At this pre-theoretical level it is sufficient
merely to have an idea of the relative potencies of the main
sources of external behavior.

Note that constructing a pre-theory of foreign policy is not
a matter of choosing to employ only one set of variables. We are
not talking about levels of analysis but, in effect, about philosophies of analysis with respect to one particular level,[43] that of
national societies. We assume that at this level behavior is
shaped by individual, role, governmental, societal, and systemic
factors and that the task is thus one of choosing how to treat
each set of variables relative to the others. Many choices are
possible. One hundred and twenty pre-theories can be constructed out of the 120 possible ways in which the five sets of
variables can be ranked. Some analysts may prefer to use one
or another of the rankings to analyze the external behavior of
all societies at all times. Others may work out more complex
pre-theories in which various rankings are applied to different
societies under different circumstances.[44] Whatever the degree

43. A level of analysis is distinguished by the units in terms of which
behavior is explained, whereas a philosophy of analysis pertains to how the
units are interrelated at a given level. The same behavior, therefore, can
be analyzed both at several levels and in several ways at the same level.
Consider the act of blushing. This can be explained both physiologically
and psychologically, but S-R and Lewinian psychologists would offer different explanations of what caused the blush (as there might, for all the
author knows, be sharp differences among the physiologists). Likewise, a
presidential speech at the United Nations can be explained both physiologically and politically, but some political scientists might see the behavior
as the last act in a sequence fostered by a loose bipolar system and others
would treat it as derived from the requirements of an oncoming election
campaign. An even better example of different philosophies of analysis in
the foreign policy field is provided by the role accorded to motivational
variables by students of decision-making on the one hand and by "realists"
on the other. Both groups attempt to explain the external behavior of
societies, but the former give high priority to the motives of officials while
the latter consider the examination of motives to be "both futile and deceptive" (confirm, respectively, Snyder, Bruck, and Sapin, *op. cit.*, pp. 92–
117, and Hans J. Morgenthau, *Politics Among Nations*, 3d ed. [New York,
Knopf, 1960], p. 6).

44. Ultimately, of course, the number of pre-theories will dwindle. A
large number seems plausible at present because of the undeveloped state
of the field. So little systematic knowledge about the sources of external
behavior is currently available that fault cannot be found with any pre-
theory on the grounds that it is discrepant with observed phenomena. However, as pre-theories make theorizing possible, and as theories then facilitate

of complexity, however, the analyst employs a pre-theory of foreign policy when he attaches relative potencies to the main sources of external behavior.

Attaching causal priorities to the various sets of variables is extremely difficult. Most of us would rather treat causation as idiographic than work out a consistent pre-theory to account for the relative strength of each variable under different types of conditions. One way to overcome this tendency and compel oneself to differentiate the variables is that of engaging in the exercise of mentally manipulating the variables in actual situations. Consider, for example, the U.S.-sponsored invasion of Cuba's Bay of Pigs in April 1961. To what extent was that external behavior a function of the idiosyncratic characteristics of John F. Kennedy (to cite, for purposes of simplicity, only one of the actors who made the invasion decision)? Were his youth, his commitments to action, his affiliations with the Democratic party, his self-confidence, his close election victory—and so on through an endless list—relevant to the launching of the invasion and, if so, to what extent? Would any President have undertaken to oust the Castro regime upon assuming office in 1961? If so, how much potency should be attributed to such role-derived variables? Suppose everything else about the circumstances of April 1961 were unchanged except that Warren Harding or Richard Nixon occupied the White House; would the invasion have occurred? Or hold everything constant but the form of government. Stretch the imagination and conceive of the U.S. as having a cabinet system of government with Kennedy as prime minister; would the action toward Cuba have been any different? Did legislative pressure derived from a decentralized policy-making system generate an impulse to "do something" about Castro, and, if so, to what extent did these governmental variables contribute to the external behavior? Similarly, in order to pre-theorize about the potency of the

more systematic observation and more incisive comprehension of how international behavior is generated, consensuses will develop about the nature of empirical reality. Accordingly, those pre-theories which prove to be most "unreal" will be abandoned. Whether the number will ever dwindle down to a single pre-theory espoused by all analysts seems doubtful. Or at least many decades will have to elapse before the mysteries of international life are fathomed to the point where widespread agreement exists on the dynamics of external behavior. More likely is a long-run future in which knowledge of empirical reality becomes sufficiently extensive to reduce the field to several major schools of thought.

societal variables, assume once more a presidential form of government. Place Kennedy in office a few months after a narrow election victory, and imagine the Cuban situation as arising in 1921, 1931, or 1951; would the America of the roaring twenties, the depression, or the McCarthy era have "permitted," "encouraged," or otherwise become involved in a refugee-mounted invasion? If the United States were a closed, authoritarian society rather than an open, democratic one, to what extent would the action toward Cuba have been different? Lastly, hold the idiosyncratic, role, governmental, and societal variables constant in the imagination, and posit Cuba as 9,000 rather than 90 miles off the Florida coast; would the invasion have nevertheless been launched? If it is estimated that no effort would have been made to span such a distance, does this mean that systemic variables should always be treated as overriding, or is their potency diminished under certain conditions?

The formulation of a pre-theory of foreign policy can be further stimulated by expanding this mental exercise to include other countries and other situations. Instead of Kennedy, the presidency, and the U.S. of 1961 undertaking action toward Cuba, engage in a similar process of holding variables constant with respect to the actions taken by Khrushchev, the monolithic Russian decision-making structure, and the U.S.S.R. of 1956 toward the uprising in Hungary. Or apply the exercise to the actions directed at the Suez Canal by Eden, the cabinet system, and the England of 1956. Or take still another situation, that of the attack on Goa carried out by the charismatic Nehru and the modernizing India of 1961. In all four cases a more powerful nation initiated military action against a less powerful neighbor that had come to represent values antagonistic to the interests of the attacker. Are we therefore to conclude that the external behavior of the U.S., Russia, England, and India stemmed from the same combination of external and internal sources? Should the fact that the attacked society was geographically near the attacking society in all four instances be interpreted as indicating that systemic variables are always relatively more potent than any other type? Or is it reasonable to attribute greater causation to idiosyncratic factors in one instance and to societal factors in another? If so, what is the rationale for subjecting these seemingly similar situations to different kinds of analysis?

Reflection about questions similar to those raised in the two previous paragraphs has led this observer to a crude pre-theory of foreign policy in which the relative potencies of the five sets of variables are assessed in terms of distinctions between large and small countries, between developed and underdeveloped economies, and between open and closed political systems. As can be seen in Table 2, these three continua give rise to eight types of countries and eight different rankings of relative potency. There is no need here to elaborate at length on the reasoning underlying each ranking.[45] The point is not to demonstrate the validity of the rankings but rather to indicate what the construction of a pre-theory of foreign policy involves and why it is a necessary prerequisite to the development of theory. Indeed, given the present undeveloped state of the field, the rankings can be neither proved nor disproved. They reflect the author's way of organizing materials for close inspection and not the inspections themselves. To be theoretical in nature, the rankings would have to specify *how much* more potent each set of variables is than those below it on each scale, and the variables themselves would have to be causally linked to specific forms of external behavior.

To be sure, as in all things, it is possible to have poor and unsound pre-theories of foreign policy as well as wise and insightful ones. The author's pre-theory may well exaggerate the potency of some variables and underrate others, in which case the theories which his pre-theory generates or supports will in the long run be less productive and enlightening than those based on pre-theories which more closely approximate empirical reality. Yet, to repeat, this pre-theory is not much more than an orientation and is not at present subject to verification.

One suspects that many foreign policy analysts would reject

45. Suffice it to note that the potency of a systemic variable is considered to vary inversely with the size of a country (there being greater resources available to larger countries and thus lesser dependence on the international system than is the case with smaller countries), that the potency of an idiosyncratic factor is assumed to be greater in less developed economies (there being fewer of the restraints which bureaucracy and large-scale organization impose in more developed economies), that for the same reason a role variable is accorded greater potency in more developed economies, that a societal variable is considered to be more potent in open polities than in closed ones (there being a lesser need for officials in the latter to heed nongovernmental demands than in the former), and that for the same reason governmental variables are more potent than societal variables in closed polities than in open ones.

TABLE 2

An Abbreviated Presentation of the Author's Pre-Theory of Foreign Policy, in Which Five Sets of Variables Underlying the External Behavior of Societies Are Ranked According to Their Relative Potencies in Eight Types of Societies

Geography and physical resources	Large Country				Small Country			
State of the economy	Developed		Underdeveloped		Developed		Underdeveloped	
State of the polity	Open	Closed	Open	Closed	Open	Closed	Open	Closed
Rankings of the variables	Role Societal Govern-mental Systemic Idiosyn-cratic	Role Idiosyn-cratic Govern-mental Systemic Societal	Idiosyn-cratic Role Societal Systemic Govern-mental	Idiosyn-cratic Role Govern-mental Systemic Societal	Role Systemic Societal Govern-mental Idiosyn-cratic	Role Systemic Idiosyn-cratic Govern-mental Societal	Idiosyn-cratic Systemic Role Societal Govern-mental	Idiosyn-cratic Systemic Role Govern-mental Societal
Illustrative examples	U.S.	U.S.S.R.	India	Red China	Holland	Czecho-slovakia	Kenya	Ghana

this pre-theory, not because they conceive of different rankings or even different sets of variables but rather because the very idea of explicating a pre-theory strikes them as premature or even impossible. Those committed to the single-country, historical approach to foreign affairs would no doubt object that developing a pre-theory is a fruitless endeavor, since every situation is different from every other and no pre-theory can possibly be so coherent as to account for the infinite variation that marks international life. Other analysts, including some who are more social-scientific in their orientation, reject the possibility of pre-theorizing on the grounds that the same events can be explained in several ways and that therefore the problem of determining the relative potencies of different sets of variables can never be satisfactorily solved.[46]

The fact is, however, that one cannot avoid having a pre-theory of foreign policy whenever one takes on the task of tracing causation. Even the most historical-minded analyst makes the initial assumption that events derive from an underlying order, that every external behavior of every society stems from some source and is therefore, at least theoretically, explicable. To assume otherwise—to view the external behaviors of societies as random and impulsive, as occurring for no reason, and as therefore unknowable—is to render analysis useless and to condemn the analyst to perpetual failure. Since we cannot avoid the presumption of an underlying order, neither can we

46. A succinct illustration of this viewpoint is provided by the following: "All governments seek success in foreign policy. . . . But the determination or desperation with which they do so is due to their position in the balance of rising and declining energies and power that is a primary given, *not capable of satisfactory explanation*, of the politics of international systems. It is possible to explain particular expansionist drives as the result of a desire to escape from internal tensions; but it is also possible to impute the intensification of internal tensions and controls to the fact that a nation is committed to an expansionist policy in the first place. *The relative significance of internal and external determinants is as insoluble as is the question whether economic or political ones are more important*" (George Liska, "Continuity and Change in International Systems," *World Politics*, XVI:1, October 1963, p. 126, italics added). As indicated below, this line of reasoning assumes that there is only one "right" solution to every analytic problem, and it thus does not allow for the possibility that different observers, employing different perspectives (i.e., pre-theories), will arrive at different solutions to the same problem. In this sense the question of the relative importance of economic and political determinants is not as insoluble as Liska believes. The former determinants take on greater importance from the perspective of the economist, whereas greater significance attaches to the latter from the perspective of the political scientist.

avoid having some conception of its nature. Yet causation is not self-revealing. The underlying order does not simply manifest itself for the diligent analyst who gathers every scrap of evidence and then takes a long, hard look at what he has accumulated. Inevitably he must organize the evidence in terms of some frame of reference, crude and premature as it may seem. There may be infinite variety in international life, but analysts are not so infinitely flexible. They cannot, and they do not, ignore their prior knowledge about foreign affairs and start over, so to speak, each time they undertake to analyze an external behavior. Furthermore, even if one were to assume that each international situation is different from every other situation, it is still necessary to have some basis for recognizing and explaining the differences. Similarly, even if one assumes that the same event is subject to a variety of interpretations, depending on the perspective of the observer, it is nevertheless necessary to adopt a particular perspective if any interpretation is to be made.

While it is thus impossible to avoid possession of a pre-theory of foreign policy, it is quite easy to avoid awareness of one's pre-theory and to proceed as if one started over with each situation. Explicating one's conception of the order that underlies the external behavior of societies can be an excruciating process. As in psychoanalysis, bringing heretofore implicit and unexamined assumptions into focus may compel one to face considerations which one has long sought to ignore. Some of the assumptions may seem utterly ridiculous when exposed to explicit and careful perusal. Others may seem unworkable in the light of new knowledge. Still others may involve mutually exclusive premises, so that to recognize them would be to undermine one's previous work and to obscure one's present line of inquiry.

Nor are matters greatly simplified by emotional readiness to live with the results of explication. There still remains the intellectually taxing task of identifying the variables which one regards as major sources of external behavior and of then coming to some conclusion about their relative potencies under varying circumstances. Such a task can be very difficult indeed. Long-standing habits of thought are involved, and the analyst may have become so accustomed to them that for him the habits are part of ongoing reality and not of his way of perceiving reality. In addition, if these habits provide no experience in pre-theorizing about the processes of causation, it will not be easy to tease out variables and assess their potencies. For example, while it is relatively simple to observe that a De Gaulle is less restrained in foreign policy than a Khrushchev, many analysts—especially those who insist that every situation is unique and that therefore they do not possess a pre-theory of foreign policy—would have a hard time discerning that the observation stems from their pre-theoretical premise that idiosyncratic variables have greater potency in France than in the Soviet Union.

Great as the obstacles to explication may be, however, they are not insurmountable. Patience and continual introspection can eventually bring implicit and unexamined premises to the surface. The first efforts may result in crude formulations, but the more one explicates, the more elaborate does one's pre-theory become.

But, it may be asked, if the purpose of all this soul searching and anguish is that of facilitating the development of general theory, how will the self-conscious employment of pre-theories of foreign policy allow the field to move beyond its present position? As previously implied, the answer lies in the assumption that the widespread use of explicit pre-theories will result in the accumulation of materials that are sufficiently processed to provide a basis for comparing the external behavior of societies. If most researchers were to gather and present their data in the context of their views about the extent to which individuals, roles, governments, societies, and international systems serve as causal agents in foreign affairs, then even though these views might represent a variety of pre-theories, it should be possible to discern patterns and draw contrasts among diverse types of policies and situations. Theoretical development is not in any way dependent on the emergence of a consensus with respect to the most desirable pre-theory of foreign policy. Comparison and theorizing can ensue as long as each researcher makes clear what variables he considers central to causation and the relative potencies he ascribes to them. For even if one analyst ascribes the greatest potency to idiosyncratic variables, while another views them as having relatively little potency and still another regards them as impotent, they will have all provided data justifying their respective assumptions, and in so doing they will have given the theoretician the materials he

needs to fashion if-then propositions and to move to ever higher
levels of generalization.

IV

But all will not be solved simply by the explication of pre-
theories. This is a necessary condition of progress toward general theory, but it is not a sufficient one. Research in the foreign
policy field would appear to be hindered by conceptual as well
as philosophical shortcomings, and we will not be able to move
forward until these more specific obstacles are also surmounted.
Not only must similarly processed materials be available if general theory is to flourish, but researchers must also possess appropriate concepts for compiling them into meaningful patterns.
Although rendered similar through the explication of pre-
theories, the materials do not fall in place by themselves. Concepts are necessary to give them structure and thereby facilitate
the formulation of if-then propositions.

The need to supplement processed materials with appropriate
concepts is clarified by our earlier architectural analogy. One
cannot erect a building merely by acquiring lumber and bricks.
It is also necessary to be cognizant of engineering principles—
that certain pieces of lumber should be placed upright, that
others should be laid crosswise, and that the bricks should be
laid on top of each other rather than interspersed among the
lumber. Note again that the design and function of the building
are not dependent upon these initial uses of the processed materials. To know which pieces of lumber are uprights and which
are to be laid crosswise is not to determine how they are to be
placed in relation to each other. So long as it is not done counter
to the laws of gravity, the uprights and the cross pieces can be
juxtaposed in all kinds of ways to form all kinds of buildings for
all kinds of purposes. So it is with theories. An almost unlimited
number can be fashioned out of similarly processed data so long
as the initial organization of the data is consistent with the
subject the theories are designed to elucidate. Regardless of the
nature of a theory, however, if it is constructed out of inappropriate concepts, it is no more likely to endure than buildings
erected in defiance of sound engineering principles or the laws
of gravity.

Two interrelated conceptual problems seem to be holding back the development of general theories of external behavior. One concerns the tendency of researchers to maintain a rigid distinction between national and international political systems in the face of mounting evidence that the distinction is breaking down. The second difficulty involves an inclination to ignore the implications of equally clear-cut indications that the functioning of political systems can vary significantly from one type of issue to another. Let us anticipate much of the ensuing discussion by noting that the interrelationship of the two problems is such that a new kind of political system, the *penetrated system,* is needed to comprehend the fusion of national and international systems in certain kinds of *issue-areas.*

Myriad are the data that could be cited to illustrate the increasing obscuration of the boundaries between national political systems and their international environments. These boundaries may consist of the activities that result in "the authoritative allocation of values for a society," [47] or of the interacting roles that sustain a society "by means of the employment, or threat of employment, of more or less legitimate physical compulsion," [48] or of the processes in a society that "mobilize its resources in the interest of [positively sanctioned] goals," [49] or "of the more inclusive structures in a society that have recognized responsibility for performing, at a minimum, the function of goal-attainment by means of legitimate decisions." [50] But however such boundaries may be drawn, ever since World War II they have been constantly transgressed by nonsocietal actors. The manner of transgression, moreover, has been quite varied.

47. David Easton, *The Political System: An Inquiry into the State of Political Science* (New York, Knopf, 1953), pp. 129–48.

48. Almond and Coleman, *op. cit.,* p. 7.

49. Talcott Parsons, " 'Voting' and the Equilibrium of the American Political System," in Eugene Burdick and Arthur J. Brodbeck, eds., *American Voting Behavior* (Glencoe, Free Press, 1959), p. 81.

50. Harry Eckstein, "The Concept 'Political System': A Review and Revision," a paper prepared for delivery at the 1963 annual meeting of the American Political Science Association, New York City, September 4–7, 1963, p. 4. Eckstein notes (p. 3) seven additional definitions of a political system that can be found in the literature. Rather than digress to explain the selection of one of these—or to defend the development of still another definition—in the ensuing discussion we shall henceforth use all of the above conceptions interchangeably and assume that more or less the same phenomena are involved whenever reference is made to the authoritative allocation of values, the quest to attain legitimately determined goals, and the mobilization of support on behalf of positively sanctioned goals.

As these recent interaction sequences illustrate, even the last stronghold of sovereignty—the power to decide the personnel, practices, and policies of government—has become subject to internationalization.

When asked how he managed to continue in office despite a major shift in the control of the national government, the mayor of a city in Colombia replied, "The American Ambassador arranged it." [51]

"Ordinarily the [U.S.] aid missions have stayed aloof from local administrative differences, but there have been instances like that in Thailand where the mission served as a liaison unit among several departments of a ministry, enabling them to carry out important tasks that never would have been done otherwise.[52]

President Urho K. Kekkonen [of Finland] suggested tonight that opposition leaders who had incurred the hatred of the Soviet Union should withdraw into private life for the good of Finland.

Dr. Kekkonen made his suggestion in a radio and television report to the nation on his talks with Premier Khrushchev of the Soviet Union. The Finnish President spoke less than three hours after having returned from Novosibirsk in Siberia, where Mr. Khrushchev had agreed to postpone the joint defense negotiations demanded by Moscow October 30.

If the politicians to whom the Soviet Union objects should retire, Dr. Kekkonen said, there would not be "the slightest doubt" that Finland could continue neutral in "all situations." . . .

The suggestion that anti-Soviet politicians retire is reported to have been foreshadowed in private conversations during the last two weeks between some of the President's close associates and members of Parliament.

These conversations indicated that demands would be forthcoming for the withdrawal into private life of at least four Social Democrats. . . . Others are a couple of members of the Swedish People's party, at least one Conservative and . . . the only member of Parliament from the Small Farmer's Party.

All were prominent in the disintegrating five-party alliance that had pushed the Presidential candidacy of Olavi Honka. Mr. Honka announced his withdrawal from the race in "the national interest" while President Kekkonen was in Novosibirsk.[53]

And these are only illustrative of the obscuration of national boundaries that is observable to outsiders. Presumably similar processes are unfolding in governmental interactions that are conducted in private and not reported. Thus, to make our point

51. This incident was reported to the author by a colleague who conducted interviews in Colombia in August 1963.
52. John D. Montgomery, *The Politics of Foreign Aid* (New York, Praeger, 1962), p. 136.
53. *The New York Times*, November 27, 1961.

even more emphatically, let us add a few hypothetical—but not unreasonable—examples to the empirical ones listed above. Imagine that the barriers to observation were lowered for a moment and revealed that:

President Johnson's note of January 6, 1964, to Sukarno, in which the former protested the latter's posture toward Malaysia, was drafted by a high official of the Indonesian Foreign Office who, concerned that his country was pursuing an undesirable course in the situation, sought out the American ambassador to Indonesia and persuaded him to urge upon the President the utility of issuing such a protest.

American State Department officials, concerned about the tendency of their Indian counterparts to accept uncritically the recommendations of India's military chiefs, work closely with the Indian Foreign Office to bring about administrative reorganization which interposes more Foreign Office personnel between the prime minister and the military chiefs.

The U.S. Secretary of State and his counterparts in the Alliance for Progress engage in joint planning on ways of circumventing legislative antagonisms and achieving Congress' acceptance of a wide-ranging foreign aid program. Let us further suppose that the Latin American foreign ministers agree to take, at just the right time, a public posture of having been outmaneuvered by Secretary Rusk, in order to convey the impression of a Secretary of State who is tough with "furriners," thereby solidifying congressional support for a wide-ranging foreign aid program.

But there is no need to pile example upon example. Whether historical or hypothetical, the foregoing are common occurrences, and not isolated incidents, in the postwar era. As one observer notes with respect to underdeveloped societies, "What happens in India or Iran is no longer intelligible in terms of parochial Indian or Iranian events and forces, but must be seen as part of a world transformation in which these particular pockets of semiautonomy are working out their distinctive yet somehow parallel destinies." [54] Nor are any developed nations so self-sufficient as to be immune from internationalization. The evidence is extensive that foreign elements have become central to certain aspects of the decision-making process of the large and industrial system called the United States.[55] Even our major

54. Fred W. Riggs, "The Theory of Developing Polities," *World Politics*, XVI:1, October 1963, p. 171.
55. Cf. U.S. Congress, Senate, *Activities of Nondiplomatic Representatives of Foreign Principals in the United States* (Washington, D. C., Hearings before the Committee on Foreign Relations, 1963), Vols. 1–12, pp. 1–782.

political institution, the presidency, has been internationalized. According to the prevailing conceptualization of the office, the President is necessarily responsive to demands from five constituencies, "from Executive officialdom, from Congress, from his partisans, from citizens at large, and from abroad." [56]

In short, "the difference between 'national' and 'international' now exists only in the minds of those who use the words." [57] Unfortunately most political scientists are among those who still use the words. Notwithstanding widespread recognition that the postwar "revolution in expectations" in the nonindustrial parts of the world, the reliance of developing societies on foreign aid, the competition among industrial powers to provide aid, and the ever quickening pace of technological change have greatly intensified the interdependence of nations and beclouded the line that divides them from their environments, most analysts have not made corresponding adjustments in their conceptual frameworks and have instead clung rigidly, and often awkwardly, to the national-international distinction. To be sure, there is widespread recognition that the boundaries separating national and international systems are becoming increasingly ambiguous,[58] but it is equally true that this recognition still awaits expression in conceptual and theoretical terms. The Sprouts, for example, concede that rigorous adherence "to the distinction between intranational (or domestic) and extranational (external) factors leaves certain highly important factors out of the picture," but they are nevertheless prepared to accept these omissions on the grounds that "the distinction has value for certain purposes." [59]

56. Richard E. Neustadt, *Presidential Power: The Politics of Leadership* (New York, Wiley, 1960), p. 7.

57. Mosely, *op. cit.*, p. 50.

58. See, for example, Chadwick F. Alger, "Comparison of Intranational and International Politics," in Part Five of this volume; George F. Kennan, *American Diplomacy 1900–1950* (Chicago, University of Chicago Press, 1951), p. 99; and Otto Klineberg, "Intergroup Relations and International Relations," in Muzafer Sherif, ed., *Intergroup Relations and Leadership: Approaches and Research in Industrial, Ethnic, Cultural, and Political Areas* (New York, Wiley, 1962), pp. 174–76.

59. *Foundations of International Politics*, p. 183. Another technique for preserving the distinction, while at the same time seeming to account for the many phenomena which the distinction obfuscates, is that of moving back and forth between different levels of analysis. By stressing a readiness to analyze international events at the international level and to examine national phenomena at the national level, one can deceive oneself into

Nor do students of international and comparative politics differ in this respect. The concern of the former with international systems and of the latter with national systems remains undiluted by the postwar fusion of the two types. While those who specialize in international systems acknowledge that such systems are largely subsystem dominant (i.e., their stability, goals, and processes are primarily the result of actions undertaken by the national systems of which they are comprised), one is hard pressed to cite any models of regional or global international systems that allow for differential subsystem impacts. Instead, the builders of international models tend to proceed on the assumption that the acknowledgment of subsystem dominance is the equivalent of explicit conceptualization. Likewise, students of national systems acknowledge that international events can significantly condition, even profoundly alter, the structure and dynamics of internal political processes, but they nevertheless treat the national system as a self-contained unit and no room is made in their models for the impact and operation of external variables. At most, such variables are handled by a notation that national systems have to develop and maintain foreign policies which facilitate adaptation to the international environment. The purpose of such a notation, however, is less that of attaining comprehension of how international systems penetrate national systems and more that of isolating those factors which would otherwise confound the conceptualization of national systems. In effect, by viewing foreign

---

believing that no sequence of interaction can go unnoticed or unexplained. Wilbur Schramm, for example, recognizes that "the national system is made up of component systems and itself belongs to a partly developed world system," but he nevertheless avoids reconceptualization and preserves the national-international distinction by reasoning that "in order to deal effectively with a system of any magnitude it is sometimes necessary to shift the level of analysis from one level to another—up and down the scale—without losing trace of what units are interacting on the particular level which is being examined" ("Communication Development and the Development Process," in Pye, *op. cit.*, p. 31). This procedure, however, is not sufficient to account for the breakdown of the national-international distinction. The readiness to shift back and forth between levels only serves to maintain the premise that a clear-cut differentiation can be made between them. Such a procedure is thus not likely to result in the uncovering, much less the probing, of the growing number of phenomena that occur at the unconceptualized level which fuses the national and international ones. For a general discussion of the problem of shifting the focus of analysis from one level to another, see Odd Ramsoy, *Social Groups as System and Subsystem* (New York, Free Press of Glencoe, 1963).

policy as taking care of events abroad, students of comparative politics free themselves of the responsibility of accounting for the penetration by international systems and enable themselves to focus on the internal processes that "normally" comprise national systems.

The recent work of Gabriel Almond is illustrative of this tendency. Nowhere in his pioneering efforts to conceptualize national systems did Almond build external variables into his model, with the result that his early writings contain "a tacit assumption . . . that the polities of developing countries can be treated as relatively autonomous or closed political systems." [60] Apparently sensitive about this drawback, Almond has recently attempted to come to grips conceptually with the pervasive presence of the international system by introducing the notion of "an international accommodative capability." [61] All national systems (with the possible exception of genuinely isolated oceanic island communities) are posited as possessing such a capability, and consequently "all political systems somehow cope" with the international environment.[62] In addition, Almond stresses that the accommodative capabilities of national systems also serve as internal variables in the sense that the extent of a system's capacity for accommodating to other systems contributes to the degree to which it achieves integration, mobilizes and distributes its resources, and allows for the participation of its citizenry in public affairs. Yet despite the obvious merits of this innovation, Almond's model still contains a rigid national-international distinction. By clustering all international matters under the heading of accommodative capabilities, the model keeps national systems intact. Almond emphasizes that they may be greatly affected by the international environment and that they may even be destroyed by it [63] (presumably whenever their accommodative capabilities are insufficient), but his model does not allow for their transformation into something other than national systems. There are no "partial" national systems and no "mixed" national systems. A national system either exists or it does not, depending on whether its accommodative capa-

60. Riggs, op. cit., p. 171.
61. Gabriel A. Almond, "Political Systems and Political Change," The American Behavioral Scientist, VI:10, June 1963, p. 6.
62. Ibid., p. 7.
63. Ibid.

bilities can absorb external threats.[64] In a profound sense, in other words, Almond avoids conceptual confrontation of the impact of external variables. His scheme takes no cognizance of the fact that events abroad are not only absorbed by a national system's accommodative capabilities but might also penetrate its processes of attaining integration, its methods of mobilizing and distributing resources, and its modes of conducting public affairs.

The rigidity of the national-international distinction is further illustrated by the wide gulf that separates students of comparative and international politics. It is the author's experience that each group is essentially uninterested in the work of the other. In one sense, of course, this is as it should be. We specialize in some fields because they arouse our interests, and we avoid others because they do not. But it is regrettable that when a specialist in comparative politics and a specialist in international politics get together, they tend to talk past each other. On two occasions of lengthy professional interaction between two such specialists, they were observed to have been first perplexed, then dismayed, and finally wearied by each other's commentary.[65] The student of comparative politics is concerned about the behavior of thousands and millions of actors—voters, party officials, interest groups, elites, legislators—whereas only a few hundred serve as the focus of the student of international politics. The student of national systems is interested in what large groups of people (the citizenry) do either to each other or to the few (officialdom), whereas the student of international systems concentrates on what the few (nations) do either to each other or to the many (foreign publics). In addition, the actors who comprise national systems compete much more

64. Almond notes (*ibid.*) that national systems can also be destroyed by "internal disruptive development," but this point is not relevant to the discussion.

65. A noteworthy exception to this incompatibility is an undated collaborative paper, "National Political Systems and International Politics: Notes on the Need for Research," written by Harry Eckstein and Harold Sprout for the Center of International Studies of Princeton University. Even this effort, however, failed to avoid the dilemmas of the national-international distinction. Not only is the latter explicitly cited as the basis of the paper, but, largely as the result of adhering to it, the paper is really two papers, and the reader can readily discern which parts were written by the comparative politics specialist (Eckstein) and which by the specialist in international politics (Sprout).

extensively for each other's clientele than do those in international systems. Given these differences in the number of actors and the goals of their interaction, students of international politics accord a much more prominent place to strategy and rationality in their thinking than do students of national politics, who are preoccupied with gross behavior that is often irrational.

As a consequence of these divergent interests, researchers in the one field tend not to be motivated to keep abreast of developments in the other. The student of international politics has little familiarity with the writings of, say, Almond or Parsons or Apter, and thus he is usually bewildered when his colleague in the comparative politics field talks about political functions, goal attainment, and political culture. Contrariwise, rare is the student of comparative politics who has read the works of, say, Schelling or Snyder or Kaplan, and thus equally rare is the comparative politics specialist who can locate himself in discussions of deterrence theory, foreign policy decision-making, and the balance of power. Even worse, each group relies on secondhand and digested accounts of the major works in the other's field; as a result each acquires undue biases and misconceptions about the literature which the other regards as basic. Few political scientists can be seized with apoplexy as quickly as the comparative politics specialist who is aroused to discuss Schelling's *The Strategy of Conflict* [66] or the international politics specialist who is moved to a discourse on Almond's first chapter in *The Politics of the Developing Areas.*[67]

Deeply entrenched habits of thought also sustain the rigidity of the national-international distinction. Most analysts are trained to emphasize the differences rather than the similarities between national and international politics.[68] Rare is the graduate program that provides systematic training in the comparison of national and international systems. Hardly less rare are the programs that equip students with a capacity to compare international systems. Rather, "comparison" has a very strict meaning in political science today; one learns only to compare practices and policies at subnational or national levels. It is not

66. Cambridge, Harvard University Press, 1960.
67. Almond and Coleman, *op. cit.*
68. For an effort to elaborate the similarities, see my *Calculated Control as a Unifying Concept in the Study of International Politics, op. cit.*, pp. 16–19.

surprising, therefore, that every graduate program in the country lists comparative and international politics as two separate fields to be offered for the Ph.D. To offer a field of study in international politics is to be conversant with political activities undertaken in the absence of "a structure of authoritative decision-making," whereas to offer a field in comparative or national politics requires familiarity with the ways in which the presence of legitimacy and a legitimizing agency (government) enhance, limit, or otherwise condition the conduct of politics.[69] Indeed, students of comparative politics become so accustomed to casting their analyses in terms of the structure of authority that they even tend to lose interest in national systems when the structure breaks down and chaos and violence prevail.[70]

Of all the habits which reinforce the reluctance of political scientists to modify the national-international distinction in the light of changing empirical patterns, none is more damaging than the tendency to posit political systems as functioning "in a society" or in some other unit equivalent to a nation. This unnecessary and essentially arbitrary limitation of the scope of the processes defined as political will be found in every major conceptualization that has been advanced in recent years. As indicated above, Easton identifies the authoritative allocation of values as the core of political activity, but immediately restricts his conception by adding that the values must be authoritatively allocated "in a society." Such an addition seems more gratuitous than logical. Certainly it is not necessary to his formulation. What about the elders of a village who reapportion the land, the representatives on a city council who decide on slum clearance and provide for urban renewal, or the members of the Council of Ministers of the European Economic Community who increase the tariff on chicken imported from the United States? Surely such activities constitute the allocation of values. Surely, too, they are authoritative for persons residing in the units affected by each allocation. And surely, therefore, Easton would be inclined to investigate them, even though his focus would be a village, city, or region rather than a society.

69. This distinction between the two fields is clearly set forth in Harold and Margaret Sprout, *op. cit.*, p. 75.

70. For an illuminating discussion of this point, see Harry Eckstein, "Toward the Theoretical Study of Internal War," in Harry Eckstein, ed., *Internal War: Basic Problems and Approaches* (New York, Free Press, 1964), pp. 1–7.

Similarly, Eckstein identifies political systems in terms of structures which facilitate the attainment of goals through legitimate decisions, but he then limits his conception by specifying that the structures must be "in a society" and that they must be the society's "most inclusive" structures (i.e., the structures of a national system). Again such a limitation seems unnecessary. Again the deliberations of the village elders, the city council, and the EEC are excluded, albeit in all three cases attention focuses on action designed to determine and realize the goals of large groups of people. Much the same could be said (to take one other example) about Deutsch's conclusion that the "essence of politics" involves "the dependable coordination of human efforts and expectations for the attainment of the goals of the society." [71] His formulation would hardly be weakened and its relevance would certainly be expanded if the last two words of the definition were changed to "an interaction unit."

Obviously the tendency to house polities in societies would not serve to reinforce the national-international distinction if it were accompanied by an inclination to apply the concept of society to any social unit with shared norms and interdependent institutions. However, although lip service is often paid to such an inclination, it does not in fact prevail. Most—and possibly all—analysts have in mind national units and not villages, cities, or supranational communities when they refer to societies.[72] The

71. Karl W. Deutsch, *The Nerves of Government: Models of Political Communication and Control* (New York, Free Press of Glencoe, 1963), p. 124.

72. Despite disclaimers to the contrary, for example, Easton's exposition of what he means by a "society" is largely descriptive of a national system (*op. cit.*, p. 135). To be sure, in order to make the point that centralized governments are not prerequisites of societies, Easton cites international and nonliterate units as being societal in character (pp. 137–40). On the other hand, at no point does he specify that subnational units with centralized governments, such as villages or cities, constitute societies. Rather the impression is clearly conveyed that, except for an occasional international or nonliterate society, the world is made up only of national societies.

Similarly, in one of his efforts to delineate political systems, Gabriel Almond, borrowing from Max Weber, seeks to avoid equating societies and nations by positing "a given territory" as the home of polities ("Comparative Political Systems," *Journal of Politics*, 18:3, August 1956, p. 394). His ensuing discussion, however, is plainly cast in terms of national societies, and in a later work, the first chapter of *The Politics of the Developing Areas*, Almond's central definition not only includes societies but, indeed, defines "independent societies" as the loci of political systems (p. 7).

Political scientists, however, are not the only, or even the worst, offenders in this respect. Sociologists pay extensive lip service to the notion that any reasons for this convergence at the national level can be readily discerned. Analysts are interested in theorizing about greater and not lesser loyalties, about ultimate and not immediate authority, about the making and not the initiating of decisions; and for decades all these processes have tended to culminate at the national level. Conflicts between national societies and lesser units (such as villages or cities), for example, have traditionally been resolved in favor of the nation. So have clashes between national societies and supranational units. Legally, militarily, and politically, in other words, the actions of national officials have prevailed over those of village elders, city counselors, or supranational ministers. Faced with a choice, people have attached greater loyalty to national than to subnational or supranational units. As a result, the decision-making mechanisms of national societies have long enjoyed a legitimacy, an authoritativeness, and an inclusiveness that no other unit could match.

To restate our central point, however, major alterations in this pattern have occurred in the middle of the twentieth century. As has already been indicated, the national society is now so penetrated by the external world that it is no longer the only source of legitimacy or even of the employment of coercive techniques. The probability that most social processes will culminate at the national level has diminished, and instead the "most inclusive" structures through which groups strive to attain goals are increasingly becoming a composite of subnational, national, and supranational elements.

It must be emphasized that these changes involve considerably more than a significant increase in the influence wielded by nonmembers of national societies. We are not simply asserting the proposition that the external world impinges ever more pervasively on the life of national societies, albeit such a proposition can hardly be denied. Nor are we talking merely about the growing interdependence of national political systems. Our contention is rather that in certain respects [73] national political systems now permeate, as well as depend on, each

---

patterned interaction can be considered a social system, but the author has yet to find a sociologist who is willing to treat, say, a friendship, a corporation, and a city as major foci of analysis in an introductory sociology course. Eventually—and invariably—it is conceded or otherwise becomes clear that by social systems are meant national societies and that all other interaction patterns are subsystemic in character.

73. That is, in certain issue-areas (see below).

other and that their functioning now embraces actors who are not formally members of the system. These nonmembers not only exert influence upon national systems but actually participate in the processes through which such systems allocate values, coordinate goal-directed efforts, and legitimately employ coercion. They not only engage in bargaining with the system, but they actually bargain within the system, taking positions on behalf of one or another of its components. Most important, the participation of nonmembers of the society in value-allocative and goal-attainment processes is accepted by both its officialdom and its citizenry, so that the decisions to which nonmembers contribute are no less authoritative and legitimate than are those in which they do not participate. Such external penetration may not always be gladly accepted by the officials and citizens of a society, but what renders decisions legitimate and authoritative is that they are felt to be binding, irrespective of whether they are accepted regretfully or willingly.[74] No doubt both the Finnish president and the people were less than delighted by the aforementioned participation of Soviet officials in their electoral processes, but the decisions that resulted from such participation do not appear to have been more widely challenged in Finland than are other decisions made exclusively by members of the society.

One could, of course, reject this line of reasoning on narrow legal grounds. From the perspective of the law, the participation of nonmembers in a society's deliberations can never be regarded as more than the exercise of external influence. Strictly speaking, Soviet officials have no "right" to participate directly in Finnish affairs. They cannot vote in Finnish elections, and they are not entitled to nominate candidates for office. They are *non*members, not members, of Finnish society, and thus their actions in Finland can never be viewed as legitimate or authoritative from a strict juridical standpoint. To repeat, however, the functioning of national political systems contrasts so sharply with this narrow legal construction that the latter is hardly adequate as a basis of political conceptualization. The boundaries of political systems are defined by activities and processes, not by legalities. Our interest is in political science and not in

74. Cf. David Easton, "The Perception of Authority and Political Change," in Carl J. Friedrich, ed., *Authority* (Cambridge, Harvard University Press, 1958), pp. 179–81.

legal science, albeit the two need not be as discrepant as the situations discussed here.

The foregoing considerations not only lead to the conclusion that cogent political analysis requires a readiness to treat the functioning of national systems as increasingly dependent on external events and trends, but they also suggest the need to identify a new type of political system that will account for phenomena which not even a less rigid use of the national-international distinction renders comprehensible. Such a system might be called the *penetrated political system*,[75] and its essential characteristics might be defined in the following way: A penetrated political system is one in which *nonmembers of a national society participate directly and authoritatively, through actions taken jointly with the society's members, in either the allocation of its values or the mobilization of support on behalf of its goals.*[76] The political processes of a penetrated system are conceived to be structurally different from both those of an international political system and those of a national political system. In the former, nonmembers indirectly and nonauthoritatively influence the allocation of a society's values and the mobilization of support for its goals through autonomous rather than through joint action. In the latter, nonmembers of a society do not direct action toward it and thus do not contribute in any way to the allocation of its values or the attainment of its goals.

Obviously operationalization of these distinctions will prove difficult. When does an interaction between two actors consist of autonomous acts, and when does it amount to joint action? When are nonmembers of a society participants in its politics, and when are they just influential nonparticipants? Furthermore, how extensive must the participation by nonmembers be in order that a penetrated political system may come into existence?

In a sense, of course, operational answers to these questions

75. This designation is nonevaluative. Although the word "penetrated" is sometimes used in connection with subversive activities, nothing invidious is intended by its use here. As will be seen, a penetrated system can be authoritarian or democratic, dynamic or static, modern or primitive. Indeed, in the ensuing discussion penetrative processes are conceived to be legitimate and authoritative for the society in which they unfold.

76. For another even more elaborate systemic creation that was at least partly designed to compensate for the weaknesses of the national-international distinction, see Fred W. Riggs, "International Relations as a Prismatic System," *World Politics*, XIV:1, October 1961, pp. 144–81.

must necessarily be arbitrary. What one observer treats as direct participation another may regard as indirect influence. Further clarification of the distinguishing features of penetrated systems, however, can be accomplished by citing some concrete examples of them. Vietnam and the Congo are two obvious ones. The U.S.'s role in the former and the U.N.'s role in the latter clearly involve thoroughgoing participation in the allocation of Vietnamese and Congolese values and in efforts to mobilize popular support for the selected values. No less thoroughgoing as penetrated systems were Japan and Germany from the end of World War II to the end of their occupation by the Allies.[77] The satellite arrangements between the Soviet Union and the countries of Eastern Europe since World War II or between the Soviet Union and Cuba since 1961 also illustrate thoroughgoing penetrated systems. So does mainland China during the period between the advent of the Sino-Soviet bloc in 1949 and the latter's deterioration after the withdrawal of Soviet technicians from China in 1960. Less thoroughgoing but nonetheless significant examples of penetration are the role of American citizens, companies, and officials in Cuba prior to 1958; the participation of U.S. officials in India's defense planning subsequent to the Chinese attack of 1962; the activities of the British armed forces in postindependence Kenya; the U.S.'s abandonment of Skybolt as a weapon for the British defense system; the aforementioned behavior of American aid officials in Thailand; and indeed the operation of any foreign aid program in which the aiding society maintains some control over the purposes and distribution of the aid in the recipient society. Equally indicative of the emergence of a penetrated system is the acceptance of a growing number of nondiplomatic foreign agents in the United States.[78]

77. While no other type of penetrated system can be more all-encompassing than a postwar occupation, it does not necessarily follow that all military occupations constitute penetrated systems. France during the German occupation of 1941–44, for example, would not be classified as a penetrated system, since the French did not accept German participation in their affairs as legitimate and therefore resisted being mobilized in support of values that the Germans had allocated for them. For other dimensions of the role played by military personnel in penetrated systems, see George Stambuck, *American Military Forces Abroad: Their Impact on the Western State System* (Columbus, Ohio State University Press, 1963).

78. The number of these registered with the Department of Justice under provisions of the Foreign Agents Registration Act has risen from approxi-

As these examples indicate, penetrated systems, like international and national ones, are not static. They come into being, develop, or disappear as capabilities, attitudes, or circumstances change. Mainland China was a penetrated system during the 1950's but seems destined to be a national system during the 1960's. Contrariwise, for centuries British defenses were national in character, but now they seem destined to be sustained through penetrative processes. Cuba represents the change, rather than the emergence or disappearance, of a penetrated system; for decades its politics was penetrated by the United States, but in recent years the latter has been replaced by the Soviet Union as the penetrator.

At the same time the examples suggest that it is false to assume that penetrated systems merely represent stages in the evolution or deterioration of national systems. As indicated by the Cuban example, and even more by that of East Germany, penetrated systems can be relatively permanent forms of political organization. Recognition of the relative permanence of certain types of penetrated systems will prove especially difficult for those who cling to the national-international distinction. Such an outlook fosters the view that the integrative or disintegrative processes prevalent in a region must inevitably culminate in its consolidation into a single national system or its fragmentation into two or more national systems. Yet there is no inherent reason why the processes which lead to the solidification of national systems should not also operate in penetrated systems. Given a cold war context, what has happened in East Germany may well be prototypical rather than exceptional in the case of newly established penetrated systems.

Another characteristic of penetrated systems suggested by the examples listed above is that national societies (as defined, say, by actual or proposed membership in the United Nations) always serve as the site for penetrated systems. Unlike an international system, which encompasses interaction patterns that occur between societies, the processes of a penetrated system unfold only in the penetrated society. In no way is such a system conceived to embrace the value allocations that occur in the societies to which the nonmembers belong and which account for their participation in the politics of the penetrated society.

---

mately 160 in 1944 to nearly 500 in 1963. See U.S. Congress, Senate, *op. cit.*, p. 10.

An inquiry into China as a penetrated system in the 1950's, for example, would not require investigation of value allocations that were made in Moscow, albeit a full analysis of the Sino-Soviet bloc during that decade would involve an examination of China as a penetrated system, the Soviet Union as a national system, and the two together as an international system.

Still another characteristic of a penetrated system is indicated by the examples of the Congo and Cuba—namely, that the non-members of such a system can belong either to an international organization or to another society and that in the latter case they can either hold official positions or be merely private citizens. The existence of a penetrated system is determined by the presence of nonmembers who participate directly in a society's politics and not by their affiliations and responsibilities.

More significantly, all but the last of the examples listed earlier indicate that penetrated systems are characterized by a shortage of capabilities on the part of the penetrated society and that an effort to compensate for, or take advantage of, this shortage underlies the participation of nonmembers in its politics. The shortage may be of an economic kind (as in the case of recipients of foreign aid); it may involve military weaknesses (as in Vietnam or Finland); it may stem from a lack of social cohesion (as in the Congo); or it may consist of an overall strategic vulnerability (as in Cuba). Whatever the nature of the shortage, however, it is sufficiently recognized and accepted by the members of a penetrated society to permit legitimacy to become attached to the direct participation of the nonmembers in the allocation of its values.[79] Hence it follows that penetrated systems are likely to be as permanent as the capability shortages which foster and sustain them.

But the last listed example, that of increasing numbers of

79. This is not to imply, however, that the presence of nonmembers in a society marked by shortages necessarily renders a penetrated system author-itarian in structure or that their participation in its politics is necessarily based on superior-subordinate relationships. As illustrated by the Skybolt and foreign aid examples, penetrated systems can operate in open societies as well as in closed ones. Likewise, as the evolution of the Alliance for Progress demonstrates, many foreign aid programs are based on functional equality between the giving and the recipient societies. To be sure, some diffusion of the values of the nonmembers is bound to occur in the pene-trated society, but such values can be as variable as their bearers and thus diffusion can lead to democratic structures as readily as to authoritarian ones.

nondiplomatic foreign agents registered in the United States, cannot be dismissed merely as an exception. Capability shortages may underlie most penetrated systems, but obviously penetration of the United States did not occur for this reason. Yet because of the nature of the penetration the U.S. example is not as contradictory as it might seem at first glance. For again a capability imbalance would appear to have encouraged the growth of penetrative processes, the difference being that the United States possesses a relative abundance rather than a relative shortage of capabilities. Just as a society's shortages lead nonmembers to participate in its politics, so does the existence of plenitude serve to attract participation by nonmembers who wish to obtain either financial aid or political support.[80] Thus it is reasonable to speculate that as long as richly endowed societies maintain institutions that permit access to their resources, they are bound to become penetrated in certain respects.[81]

All the cited examples also reveal that for a penetrated system to function, there must be intensive face-to-face interaction between members and nonmembers of a society. Values cannot be authoritatively allocated, or goal-attaining activities authoritatively mobilized, from afar. Nonmembers of a society must come into contact with its officials and/or its citizenry in order to acquire sufficient information about the society's needs and wants to participate in its value-allocative processes in ways that are sufficiently acceptable to be authoritative. Moreover, even if the nonmembers could obtain appropriate information about the society without interacting with its members, their efforts to contribute to the allocation of its values would still be lacking in authority. While authority is often attached to mystical and distant entities, to be effectively sustained it requires some visible and human embodiment. The members of a society are not likely to regard the demands or suggestions of nonmembers as binding (that is, as authoritative) unless they have had some firsthand acquaintance with them.

80. For a lengthier analysis of the reasons why nonmembers are attracted to participation in the allocation of values in the United States, see U.S. Congress, Senate, op. cit., p. 10.

81. Nor is it unreasonable to contend that, for the same reasons, eventually even richly endowed closed societies are bound to experience penetrative processes. It was, after all, African students who gave Moscow its first recorded riots since the Russian Revolution of 1917.

This is not to say, of course, that intensive face-to-face inter-action between members and nonmembers of a society occurs only in a penetrated system. Nor is it to imply that nonmembers of a society can contribute to the allocation of its values only through intensive face-to-face interaction with its members. It is quite commonplace for the political processes of international systems to underlie the reallocation of values in societies and to do so either with or without face-to-face interaction. Prolonged negotiations over a treaty which reallocates the values of all the signatories to it are illustrative of the former process, and an extreme example of the latter is provided by two societies that sever all contacts and then reallocate their values in response to the subsequent threats each makes toward the other. Al-though in both cases nonmembers contribute to the allocation of a society's values, both examples would nonetheless be re-garded as reflecting international and not penetrative processes because in neither illustration do nonmembers participate directly in the allocation of a society's values. This is self-evident in the case of the two societies that sever relations, but it is no less true in the treaty example. For while the signatories to a treaty join together in face-to-face interaction in order to conclude it, each representative makes a commitment only with respect to his own society, and thus his actions at the negotiat-ing table do not involve participation in the allocative processes of other societies.[82] In other words, treaties are best viewed as the sum of autonomous acts rather than as the result of joint action.

One final point with respect to penetrated systems needs to be made. As it stands at present, our formulation suffers from a lack of differentiation. While the analysis points to the con-clusion that all national societies in the modern world are susceptible of swift transformation into penetrated systems, it treats all such systems as if they were similarly transformed and structured. Yet obviously there is a vast difference between the penetrated systems that have developed in Vietnam and the Congo and those that have evolved with respect to British or

82. One exception here would be a treaty in which one signatory agrees to allow another to participate subsequently in the allocation of its val-ues and the mobilization of support for its goals. The treaty between France and Monaco is illustrative in this respect, as are many treaties that victors and vanquished sign after a war. Such exceptions can be regarded as the one type of penetrated system that has a formal constitution.

Indian defenses. In the former cases penetration is thorough-going, whereas in the latter it is limited to the allocation of a highly restricted set of values. Nonmembers may participate directly in the determination and attainment of Indian military goals, but clearly they are not a party to the processes whereby India's linguistic problems are handled. In Vietnam, on the other hand, nonmembers have been centrally involved in efforts to mobilize support for certain religious values as well as for a military campaign. Accordingly, so as to differentiate degrees of penetration as well as the structural differences to which they give rise, it seems appropriate to distinguish between multi-issue and single-issue penetrated systems, the distinction being based on whether nonmembers participate in the allocation of a variety of values or of only a selected set of values.

V

The conclusion that national societies can be organized as penetrated political systems with respect to some types of issues —or issue-areas—and as national political systems with respect to others is consistent with mounting evidence that the functioning of any type of political system can vary significantly from one issue-area to another. Data descriptive of local, party, legislative, national, and international systems are converging around the finding that different types of issue-areas elicit different sets of motives on the part of different actors in a political system, that different system members are thus activated in different issue-areas, and that the different interaction patterns which result from these variations produce different degrees of stability and coherence for each of the issue-areas in which systemic processes are operative.

Perhaps the most impressive data along these lines are to be found in Dahl's inquiry into the politics of New Haven.[83] Using systematic survey techniques, Dahl examined the processes of governmental and nongovernmental leadership activated by situations in three issue-areas—urban redevelopment, education, and nominations. His finding is stunning: The "overlap among leaders and subleaders" in the three areas involved only

83. Robert A. Dahl, *Who Governs: Democracy and Power in an American City* (New Haven, Yale University Press, 1961).

3 per cent of his sample, and only 1.5 per cent were leaders in all three areas.[84] In effect, there are at least three New Haven political systems, and to know how values are allocated and how support is mobilized in any one area is not to be knowledgeable about the operation of these processes in the other areas.[85]

Similar findings on legislative and national systems are reported by Miller and Stokes, who employed survey data to correlate the attitudes of congressmen, the attitudes of their constituencies, and the congressmen's perceptions of their constituencies' attitudes in three major issue-areas—social welfare, foreign involvement, and civil rights.[86] Again the results compel reflection: The differences between the operation of the processes of representation in the civil rights area, on the one hand, and in the social welfare and foreign involvement areas, on the other, proved to be highly significant statistically, constituting "one of the most striking findings of this analysis." [87] Given such variability at the center of the political process, again it seems reasonable to assert that there are at least two American national systems, and to comprehend the dynamics of one is not necessarily to understand the functioning of the other.

Still another indication of the importance of issue-areas has been uncovered in studies of the processes through which political parties mobilize support. For example, using interview data, Chalmers probed decision-making within the Social Democratic Party of West Germany and was led to conclude that, in effect, the party consists of two independent organizational mechanisms.[88] He found that different party leaders and different party followers engaged in different modes of deciding upon ideological matters on the one hand and campaign issues on the other, the differences again being such that knowledge of

84. *Ibid.*, p. 175.
85. For much additional evidence that "the pattern of decision-making" varies from issue-area to issue-area in local systems, see Nelson W. Polsby, *Community Power and Political Theory* (New Haven, Yale University Press, 1963), pp. 113–14, 124–28.
86. Warren E. Miller and Donald E. Stokes, "Constituency Influence in Congress," *American Political Science Review*, LVII:1, March 1963, pp. 45–56.
87. *Ibid.*, p. 53.
88. See Douglas A. Chalmers, *The SPD: From Working Class Movement to Modern Political Party* (New Haven, Yale University Press, 1964).

the party's functioning in one area did not insure comprehension of its dynamics in the other.

Nor do international systems appear to be different in this respect. Although here the data are more impressionistic than systematic, it does seem clear that the structure and functioning of international systems can vary significantly from one issue-area to another. The current scene provides a host of examples. Consider the Communist international system; plainly it operates differently in the admit-China-to-the-U.N. area than it does in the area bounded by disarmament questions. Or take NATO; obviously it has been a vastly different system with respect to Berlin than with respect to independence movements in Africa. Likewise, to cite an equally clear-cut dyadic example, the functioning of the U.S.-U.S.S.R. international system in the Berlin issue-area bears little resemblance to the processes through which it allocates values and mobilizes support for the attainment of its goals in the disarmament or wheat-production areas.

In the foreign policy field, too, there are numerous indications that the nature of the issue constitutes a crucial variable in the processes whereby the external behavior of national societies is generated. In the United States, for example, the complex of internal influences brought to bear in the ratification of treaties would seem to be entirely different from that which underlies the allocation of economic and military assistance to other countries.[89] One has the impression that much the same could be said about other societies that maintain foreign aid programs.

Whether they are impressionistic or systematic, in short, the data on issue-areas are too impressive to ignore. Conceptual allowance must be made for them if theorizing in the foreign policy field is to flourish. Indeed, the emergence of issue-areas is as pronounced and significant as is the breakdown of the national-international distinction. Taken together, the two trends

89. Compare, for instance, the identity and number of the roles that were activated, the motives and attitudes that guided the behavior of the role occupants, and the character of the interaction that produced the external behavior in these two case studies: Bernard C. Cohen, *The Political Process and Foreign Policy: The Making of the Japanese Peace Settlement* (Princeton, Princeton University Press, 1957); and H. Field Haviland, Jr., "Foreign Aid and the Policy Process: 1957," *American Political Science Review*, LII:3, September 1958, pp. 689–725.

point to the radical conclusion that the boundaries of political systems ought to be drawn vertically in terms of issue-areas as well as horizontally in terms of geographic areas.[90] Stated in the context of the present world scene, the data compel us to cast our analyses as much in terms of, say, civil-rights political systems, economic-development political systems, and health-and-welfare political systems as we do in terms of local, national, and international systems.

However, as in the case of the national-international distinction (and in part because of it), political scientists have not been inclined to make the conceptual adjustments which the data on issue-areas would seem to warrant. Certainly the more theoretically oriented analysts, with one notable exception, have not proceeded from the assumption that issues generate structurally and functionally significant differences.[91] Even Dahl himself ignores the relevance of issue-areas in a subsequent conceptualization of politics and polities.[92] Similarly, and again with one important exception, empirical-minded researchers have not followed up the implications of the findings cited above, and one is hard pressed to find empirical analyses of particular systems that explicitly explore the relevancy, strength, and boundaries of different kinds of issue-areas.[93] Instead most researchers con-

90. Accordingly, henceforth we shall distinguish between horizontal and vertical political systems. A horizontal system is conceived to be a set of interdependent procedures through which a geographic unit (e.g., a city, state, or nation) or a functional institution (e.g., a party, legislature, or bureaucracy) allocates values and mobilizes support in a broad range of issue-areas. A vertical system, on the other hand, is conceived to encompass a set of interdependent procedures whereby a cluster of values within an issue-area is allocated by either a single horizontal system or a fusion of horizontal systems. The number of vertical systems operative at any one time is conceived to be quite variable and dependent on the purposes of analysis. Just as it is useful to posit a variety of horizontal systems at every horizontal level (e.g., 110+ sovereign states at the national level), so is it likely to prove necessary to conceive of numerous vertical systems within every issue-area (e.g., the civil rights system of the 110+ sovereign states may be viewed as 110+ vertical systems within one major area).

91. The exception is Herbert J. Spiro, "Comparative Politics: A Comprehensive Approach," *American Political Science Review*, LVI:3, September 1962, pp. 577–95.

92. Robert A. Dahl, *Modern Political Analysis* (Englewood Cliffs, Prentice-Hall, 1963).

93. Here the exception is Aaron B. Wildavsky, "The Analysis of Issue-Contexts in the Study of Decision-Making," *The Journal of Politics*, 24:4, November 1962, pp. 717–32.

tinue to treat cities, parties, legislatures, and nations as if their processes of allocating values and mobilizing support for goals were constants rather than variables.[94] To be sure, fine distinctions *between* cities or parties or legislatures or nations are recognized and closely analyzed, but the same sensitivities are not trained on the variability *within* a given horizontal system.[95]

The neglect of issue-areas in systematic inquiry is all the more perplexing because there is one respect in which intuitively, and often unknowingly, political scientists do employ the concept: although reasons are rarely given for the distinction, one is usually made between foreign and domestic policy. Throughout the discipline it is assumed that national political systems function differently in formulating and administering foreign policies than they do in domestic areas. Most universities, for example, offer both undergraduate and graduate courses in "The Formulation of American Foreign Policy," a subject presumably sufficiently unlike "The Formulation of American Domestic Policy" to warrant separate presentation. However, since the reasoning underlying the distinction is never made explicit, its implications have not been recognized, and the idea of categorizing phenomena according to issue-areas has not been applied elsewhere in the discipline. Sociologists have developed subfields in industrial sociology, the sociology of law, the sociology of education, the sociology of religion, the sociology of art, the sociology of science, the sociology of medicine, the sociology of demographic behavior, the sociology of crime, and the sociology of mental illness, as well

94. In some cases it is more accurate to say that issue-areas are treated as unconceptualized variables in the political process. In their elaborate and impressive formulation of the legislative system and process, for example, Wahlke, Eulau, Buchanan, and Ferguson note the importance of issue-areas by including them among the "circumstantial variables" (p. 20), which are in turn made central to the diagrammatic presentation of their scheme (p. 18). In the diagram, however, they accompany the box that houses the circumstantial variables with the parenthetic phrase, "not conceptualized." John C. Wahlke, Heinz Eulau, William Buchanan, and Leroy C. Ferguson, *The Legislative System: Explorations in Legislative Behavior* (New York, Wiley, 1962).

95. Researchers who focus on the behavior of blocs in international organizations might be considered an exception here. Through analysis of bloc voting in the United Nations, they have turned increasingly to the question of how different issues affect the cohesiveness and functioning of blocs. See, for example, Thomas Hovet, Jr., *Africa in the United Nations* (Evanston, Northwestern University Press, 1963).

as in the sociology of the family, urban sociology, rural sociology, political sociology, and the sociology of particular societies.[96] Yet political scientists do not offer courses in, say, the politics of employment, the politics of transportation, the politics of conservation, the politics of foreign aid, the politics of civil liberties, the politics of agriculture, the politics of defense strategy, the politics of health, the politics of commerce, the politics of education, and so on.[97]

The conceptual and empirical neglect of issue-areas would appear to stem from several sources. One is the sheer force of habit. Most analysts have become accustomed to perceiving and structuring political phenomena in terms of horizontal systems. Hence, confronted with findings like Dahl's, most researchers would be inclined to treat them merely as interesting characteristics of local communities rather than as pervasive phenomena that necessitate reconsideration of one's approach to the discipline.

The habit of horizontal analysis is reinforced by the tendency of some, and perhaps even many, researchers to view horizontal political systems as dominated by a "power elite" who perform the function of allocating all the system's values. A legislature has its "inner club," a party its "bosses," an executive his "kitchen cabinet," a community its "influentials," and an international organization its "powerful"—all of whom are believed to interact in the same way whenever they make decisions for, or mobilize support in, their respective systems. Such an approach is obviously incompatible with a recognition of issue-areas as a

96. Cf. Robert K. Merton, Leonard Broom, and Leonard S. Cottrell, Jr., eds., *Sociology Today: Problems and Prospects* (New York, Basic Books, 1959).

97. Exceptions, of course, can be cited. Some institutions, for example, are now offering courses in the politics of disarmament and the politics of civil liberties. As a general trend, however, political science is still organized in terms of units (local, national, and international) or institutions (party, legislative, administrative, and judicial) that process all types of issues, rather than in terms of issue-areas that activate all types of units and institutions. Even the exceptions do not usually extend beyond a particular unit. Courses in the politics of disarmament tend to focus on the Nuclear Club of the 1960's, and those dealing with the politics of civil liberties are concerned primarily with the United States. The scope of the former is rarely extended to the problems of weapons management in other contexts, and the scope of the latter rarely encompasses civil rights problems in South Africa, Great Britain, or the Soviet Union.

meaningful concept. Notwithstanding the findings uncovered by Dahl and others, however, power-elite theories still abound, and the strength of the habit of horizontal analysis remains undiminished.

Neglect of issue-areas would also seem to stem from a view that the issues which preoccupy horizontal systems are unique rather than recurrent and that therefore any model which posits them as variables encourages the writing of case histories rather than the testing of hypotheses and the construction of theories. Issues are temporary and situational, the reasoning seems to be, and to see horizontal systems functioning in terms of them is thus to reduce actors and action to a level of specificity that inhibits the discernment of patterns and regularities. Unlike the power theorists, in other words, some analysts appear to accept the validity of the issue-area data even as they discount them on the grounds that such data reflect historical rather than political processes. The difficulty with this line of reasoning is that it is based on an excessively narrow conception of the nature of an issue-area. Both vertical systems and the issue-areas in which they function are best conceived in terms of broad types of values and the recurring need to allocate them. Hence, although issues may be temporary and situational, issue-areas are persistent and general. Each area must be conceptualized at a high enough level of abstraction to encompass a variety of vertical systems, and each of the latter must in turn be conceived as based on a continual processing of the values that its structure is designed to allocate. This is why Dahl, for example, constructed his three issue-areas out of data for fifty-seven, eight, and ten occasions when questions pertaining, respectively, to urban development, education, and political nominations were at issue during periods of nine, seven, and twenty years. Similarly if the "Berlin situation" were conceptualized as a vertical political system, the crises of 1948–49, 1958, 1961, and 1963 would all serve as data from which the boundaries, processes, and stability of the area would be inferred.

The boundaries of issue-areas and of the vertical systems within them would seem to be the focus of another more sophisticated line of reasoning that neglects both the concept and the evidence of its importance. The reasoning is that a system con-

sists of "a boundary-maintaining set of interdependent par-
ticles" [98] and that while issue-areas and vertical systems certainly
contain interdependent parts, their boundaries are not self-
maintaining. Why? Because the processes of allocating values
and mobilizing support within an issue-area are too vulnerable
to continuous and significant external interference to justify
treating their interdependent parts as political systems. And
why should the boundaries of issue-areas be so vulnerable? Because bargaining among issue-areas is a major characteristic
of geographic and other types of horizontal systems. Indeed,
the stability of such systems is considered to be crucially dependent on their ability to resolve conflicts in one area by
compromising in other areas. Hence, the argument concludes,
the essential characteristic of boundary-maintenance—that the
components of a system be so related as to divide the system
from its environment—will at best be obscure and at worst nonexistent in vertical systems.

There can hardly be any dissent from much of this reasoning.
It is certainly true that the outcome of interaction patterns
within an issue-area can be greatly influenced by external variables. The strong pull which national security considerations
can exert in the area of civil liberties provides an obvious example. And surely it is also incontestable that bargaining among
issue-areas can frequently occur in horizontal systems. Indeed,
this is virtually a defining characteristic of legislatures, especially those in which logrolling processes are predominant.

The recognition of these points, however, does not diminish
the potential relevance of the issue-area data. For the fact is
that no political system has unmistakable and impermeable
boundaries. Legislatures are penetrated by executives and parties; executives penetrate legislatures and parties; and parties
in turn are penetrated by executives and legislatures. Local
communities are penetrated by regional ones, and regional units
are penetrated by national systems; and, as we have seen, it is
increasingly difficult to distinguish national systems from their

98. Schramm, *op. cit.*, p. 30. The author adds that "the key words are
boundary and interdependent. By interdependence we mean a relationship
of parts in which anything happening to one component of a system
affects, no matter how slightly, the balance and relationship of the whole
system. By boundary-maintaining we mean a state in which the components are so related that it is possible to tell where the system ends and its
environment begins."

international environments. In short, the boundaries of horizontal systems are also far from invulnerable, perhaps no less so than those of vertical systems.[99] Certainly bargaining among horizontal systems can be just as consequential for the participating units as that which occurs among vertical systems. Executive-legislative relations and inter-nation relations provide obvious examples. Consider the former: Plainly the extent of the impact which executives and legislatures can have on each other is no less than the pull which issues can have on each other within even the most logrolling type of legislature.

In fact, one can think of some horizontal systems that are *less* boundary maintaining than some vertical systems. To take an extreme example, compare the horizontal system known as Vietnam and the vertical one known as disarmament, as they appear to be functioning in 1964. The boundaries of the former are so obscure that classifying it as a penetrated system is the only way in which its processes of allocating values and mobilizing support become comprehensible. On the other hand, it is not nearly so difficult to discern the line dividing the disarmament area from its environment. Governments take positions, seek support from other governments, send representatives to Geneva, and then attempt to allocate values with a minimum of penetration from other issue-areas. To be sure, in the end values are rarely allocated and deadlock usually results, but this outcome is due less to the intrusion of other issues than it is to the rigidity of the positions which actors bring to disarmament negotiations. A good illustration of the relative ease with which the boundaries of the disarmament area can be discerned is provided by the last paragraph of these excerpts from a recent news story:

Geneva, Feb. 12—Semyon K. Tsarapkin, leader of the Soviet delegation to the disarmament talks, accused Swiss authorities today of

99. Conversely, the structure of vertical systems can remain just as impervious to the effects of bargaining with other units as can the structure of horizontal systems. That is, the bargaining that occurs across issue-areas need not have any greater impact on the identity, motivations, and interaction patterns of the actors who conflict over the allocation of a particular set of values than, say, treaty negotiations would have on the identity, motives, and decision-making processes of the actors in the national systems that are signatories to the treaty. The resolution of the conflict in the vertical system, i.e., the way in which the values are allocated, may be affected by the intrusion of other issues, but the distinctive behavior which forms the boundaries of the system may well continue unaltered.

having shown a "clear lack of desire" to help find Yuri I. Nossenko, an "expert" who had defected from the delegation.

Mr. Tsarapkin also accused the Swiss of permitting "provocative activity on their territory by foreign intelligence agents." He called on them to utilize "their sovereign rights" and to take "all necessary measures" to assure Mr. Nossenko's return "to his place of work, to his family and children." . . .

Washington announced Monday that Mr. Nossenko was a staff officer in the Soviet security agency and had requested political asylum in the United States.

At a suddenly called news conference, Mr. Tsarapkin said that "if Mr. Nossenko was in United States hands, it could mean only that the Swiss had not provided delegates to international conferences with elementary security." . . .

Observers noted that Mr. Tsarapkin had not directed any accusations at the United States. His only reference to Washington was to acknowledge its announcement that Mr. Nossenko had applied for asylum. . . .

Conference sources interpreted the avoidance of an attack on Washington as evidence that Moscow did not want to damage the arms talks or disrupt the current relaxed atmosphere in relations between the two capitals. . . .[100]

In other words, the argument that vertical systems are vulnerable because of the stability requirements of horizontal systems may not be as valid as it appears at first glance. Precisely opposite considerations may prevail in some instances. To maintain stability, horizontal systems may have to insulate certain issue-areas and prevent bargaining across their boundaries. Such a process of insulation may occur under two considerations: First, it may be precipitated whenever the actors of a horizontal system have common goals in one area but their lack of agreement on other matters results in the recognition that progress toward the attainment of the common goals can only be achieved through insulating the issue-area. The disarmament area within the U.S.-U.S.S.R. system would seem to be illustrative in this regard. Second, the process of insulation may be initiated whenever the actors of a horizontal system lack agreement in one area but their concurrence in other areas leads them to agree to contain the conflict in order to prevent it from destabilizing the other areas or the entire system. For many years the handling of civil rights issues in the United States corresponded to this pattern.

100. *The New York Times*, February 13, 1964, p. 1.

In short, further elaboration, rather than continued neglect, of the issue-area concept would seem to be in order. None of the arguments against the construction of vertical political systems out of identifiable issue-areas fully offset the compelling evidence that horizontal systems function differently in different areas. Let us turn, therefore, to the task of specifying more precisely the nature of issue-areas and the location of vertical systems within them.

Stated formally, an issue-area is conceived to consist of (*1*) *a cluster of values, the allocation or potential allocation of which* (*2*) *leads the affected or potentially affected actors to differ so greatly over* (*a*) *the way in which the values should be allocated or* (*b*) *the horizontal levels at which the allocations should be authorized that* (*3*) *they engage in distinctive behavior designed to mobilize support for the attainment of their particular values.* If a cluster of values does not lead to differences among those affected by it, then the issue-area is not considered to exist for that group of actors, and their relationships with respect to the values are not considered to form a vertical system. If a cluster of values does divide the actors affected by it but if their differences are not so great as to induce support-building behavior, then the issue-area, and its vertical systems, is considered to be dormant until such time as one of the actors activates it by pressing for a reallocation of the value cluster. If a cluster of values induces support building on the part of the affected actors but if their behavior is not distinctive from that induced by another cluster of values, then the issue-area is considered to encompass both clusters, and both are also regarded as being processed by the same vertical system.

It will be noted that the boundaries of vertical systems are delineated not by the common membership of the actors who sustain them (as horizontal systems are), but rather by the distinctiveness of the values and the behavior they encompass. The actors determine the state of a vertical system—whether it is active, dormant, or nonexistent—but the boundaries of the system are independent of the identity of the actors who are active within it. In fact, the horizontal affiliations of its actors may be quite varied. Some might be members of local systems. Others might belong to national systems. Still others might be participants in penetrated or international systems. The cluster of values associated with economic development provides an example of an issue-area that encompasses actors at every horizontal level.

This is not to imply, of course, that either the actors, the values, or the behavior that form the parameters of a vertical system are simple to identify. A number of operational problems will have to be resolved before empirical research on vertical phenomena yield worthwhile results. In particular, answers to three questions must be developed: How are the values over which men differ to be clustered together into issue-areas? At what level of abstraction should they be clustered? What characteristics render the behavior evoked by one cluster of values distinctive from that stimulated by other clusters?

The general line of response to the first two questions seems reasonably clear. A typology of issue-areas ought to be something more than a mere cataloguing of the matters over which men are divided at any moment in time. For vertical systems to be of analytic utility, they must persist beyond the life of particular actors. As has already been implied, not much would be accomplished if "issue-area" meant nothing more than the conventional usage, in which an "issue" is equated with any and every concrete historical conflict that ensues between identifiable individuals or groups. In brief, a typology of issue-areas must be cast in sufficiently abstract terms to encompass past and future clusters of values as well as present ones. Obviously, too, the level of abstraction must be high enough to allow for clusters of values that evoke behavior within all types of horizontal systems, from local communities to the global community. At the same time the typology cannot be so generalized as to erase the distinctiveness of the behavior which characterizes the vertical systems in each of its areas.

For the present, of course, any typology must be largely arbitrary. Until systematic and extensive data on the distinctive nature of certain issue-areas are accumulated, the lines dividing them cannot be drawn with much certainty. In order to suggest further dimensions of the concept, however, let us adopt a simple typology which seems to meet the above criteria. Let us conceive of all behavior designed to bring about the authoritative allocation of values as occurring in any one of four issue-areas: the *territorial, status, human resources,* and *nonhuman resources* areas, each of which encompasses the distinctive motives, actions, and interactions evoked by the clusters of values that are linked to, respectively, the allocation of territorial jurisdiction, the allocation of status within horizontal political systems or within nonpolitical systems, the development and allocation of human resources, and the development and allocation of nonhuman resources. Examples of vertical systems located in the territorial area are the persistent conflict over Berlin, the continuing Arizona-California controversy over rights to the Colorado River, and the recurring efforts to effect a merger of the Township and Borough of Princeton, New Jersey. Status-area systems are exemplified by the long-standing problem of whether Red China should be admitted to the United Nations, the unending racial conflict in South Africa, and the perennial question of higher pay for policemen faced by every American town. Enduring efforts to provide medical care for the aged, unceasing problems of population control, and periodic disputes over the training of teachers are illustrative of vertical systems that fall in the human resources area. Certain foreign aid programs, most housing and highway programs, and many agricultural policies illustrate the kinds of vertical systems that are classified in the nonhuman resources area.

In other words, each of the four issue-areas is conceived to embrace a number of vertical political systems, and the boundaries of each vertical system are in turn conceived to be determined by the scope of the interaction that occurs within it. Thus, as implied above, some vertical systems may function exclusively at local horizontal levels; others may be national in scope; still others may be confined to interaction at the international level. Given the interdependence of life in the nuclear age, however, empirical inquiry would probably find that an overwhelming preponderance of the world's vertical systems ranges upward and downward across several horizontal levels. The pervasiveness of penetrated systems is indicative in this respect. So is the large degree to which so-called local government in the United States is in reality a local-state or local-state-federal system in most issue-areas. Table 3, by using brief identifying labels for currently existing vertical systems in all four issue-areas, is designed to provide an even more concrete set of examples of the extent to which vertical systems extend across horizontal levels. Each system is entered in the table at the approximate horizontal level at which it came into existence,

TABLE 3

Examples of Vertical Systems in Each of the Four Issue-Areas
*Arrows suggest the degree to which the scope of each
system was extended across horizontal levels
subsequent to its activation*

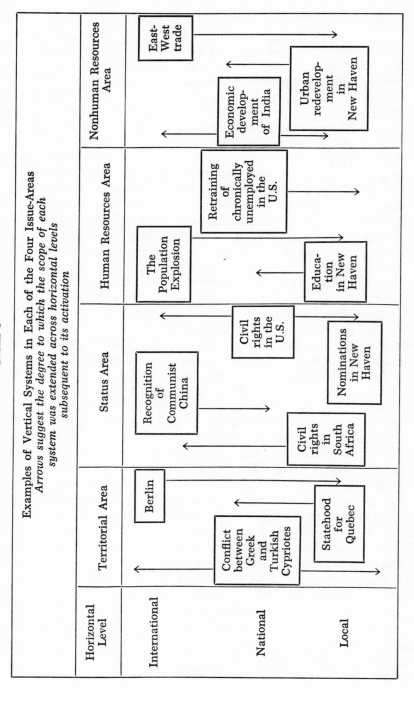

Horizontal Level	Territorial Area	Status Area	Human Resources Area	Nonhuman Resources Area
International	Berlin	Recognition of Communist China	The Population Explosion	East-West trade
National	Conflict between Greek and Turkish Cypriotes	Civil rights in the U.S. Civil rights in South Africa	Retraining of chronically unemployed in the U.S.	Economic development of India
Local	Statehood for Quebec	Nominations in New Haven	Education in New Haven	Urban redevelopment in New Haven

but crudely scaled arrows have been attached in order to suggest the subsequent extension of its scope. The scarcity of systems without arrows is intentional and designed to represent the small degree to which life in the nuclear age can be confined to a single horizontal level.

But how, it may well be asked, does this particular typology meet the criterion that the value clusters in each area must evoke distinctive motives, actions, and interactions on the part of the affected actors? Granted that the values themselves differ, why should it be presumed that these differences are sufficient to produce differentiation in the functioning of the systems that allocate the values in each issue-area? As previously indicated, the answers to these questions must of necessity be somewhat vague. Since the issue-area concept has not been the focus of systematic inquiry, data which would allow for comparisons of the functioning of vertical systems are not available, and any typology has perforce to be constructed out of crude impressions about the reasons for the findings uncovered by Dahl and others. In the case of the foregoing typology the four issue-areas were derived from an impression that the motives, actions, and interactions of political actors are crucially related to the degree of tangibility of both the values which have to be allocated and the means which have to be employed to effect allocation.[101] With respect to motives and actions, it was reasoned that the affected actors would be more strongly motivated and more persistently active the *greater* the tangibility of the *means* (since the rewards and costs to the actor of allocating a particular cluster of values are likely to be clearer the more easily comprehensible are the means necessary to realize the values); and that the more actors affected and active, the *lesser* the tangibility of the *ends* (since tangibility involves specificity, and thus the aspirations of a greater number of actors are likely to be encompassed by issues in which intangible goals are at stake). With respect to interaction, the presumption was made that the *greater* the tangibility of both

101. For traces of the idea that ends-means tangibility may be a central variable in the generation of issue-area differences, see Samuel P. Huntington, *The Common Defense: Strategic Programs in National Politics* (New York, Columbia University Press, 1961), pp. 242–48; and Raymond A. Bauer, Ithiel de Sola Pool, and Lewis Anthony Dexter, *American Business and Public Policy: The Politics of Foreign Trade* (New York, Atherton Press, 1963), pp. 124–26.

the *ends* and *means* involved in an allocative process, the more the tendency to bargain among the affected actors would increase. In short, among the distinctive characteristics of an issue-area are the number of affected actors, the intensity of their motivations to act, the frequency with which they act, and the extent of their readiness to bargain with each other.

That four main issue-areas derive from the foregoing is readily apparent. The processes of allocating tangible values through the use of tangible means will differ significantly from those in which intangible ends and means are involved; both of these will in turn be distinguished from the processes whereby tangible values are allocated through the utilization of intangible means; and still a fourth pattern of distinctive motives, actions, and interactions will occur whenever tangible means are employed to achieve intangible ends. In short, we have fashioned a 2 x 2 matrix, each cell of which corresponds more or less closely to one of the four kinds of values that are presumed to sustain political behavior:

		M E A N S	
	I n t a n g i b l e	Intangible	Tangible
E N D S		Status area	Human resources area
	T a n g i b l e	Territorial area	Nonhuman resources area

Although crude and impressionistic, this derivation of the distinctiveness of the issue-areas does seem to hold up when one engages in the exercise of locating empirical findings in the matrix. Let us take Dahl's data as an example, and assume for purposes of illustration that the tangible-intangible scale of ends is operationalized in terms of whether the values involved can be photographed with a camera and that the tangibility of means is measured by the extent to which money must be expended in order to acquire the values. The values represented by education cannot be photographed, albeit money is necessary to build the schools and pay the teachers—prerequisites to the realization of educational values. Hence vertical systems designed to process educational issues fall in the human resources area of the matrix. Similarly, nominations in New Haven are not photographable, and, unlike the building and maintenance of a school system, money is not needed to have them allocated in a desired fashion. Thus they would be classified in the status area. Likewise, urban redevelopment in New Haven—or the need for it—is readily photographable, and great quantities of money must be committed to its realization, thereby locating it in the nonhuman resources area. Since Dahl offers no data for the territorial area, let us conclude this exercise with the example of Berlin as a vertical political system. In this case recent history —especially since the erection of the wall in August 1961— testifies poignantly to the photographability of the values involved. Yet diplomatic persuasion, rather than money and the military capabilities it buys, must obviously serve as the means through which a Berlin settlement will ultimately be accomplished.[102]

The impression that the fit between this formulation and empirical phenomena is sufficient to warrant further development of the typology is reinforced by one other consideration. The assumption that the tangibility of ends and means determines the number of affected actors and the extent of their readiness to bargain with each other permits specific conclusions about distinctive characteristics of at least two of the issue-areas. On the one hand, the status area, being composed of both intangible ends and means, is likely to evoke more uncompromising political behavior on the part of more actors than any of the other three; on the other hand, the nonhuman resources area, being

102. It must be emphasized that these examples are provided only for the purpose of illustrating how an issue-area typology might be developed. The classification of data in terms of the tangibility of ends and means is clearly far more complex than this exercise implies. In each instance a case might be made for classifying these particular data in one or more of the other areas.

composed of both tangible ends and means, is likely to evoke more bargaining on the part of fewer actors than any of the other areas. That these two conclusions correspond to the differences between concrete vertical systems in each area can be readily demonstrated. Compare, for instance, the processes whereby values pertaining to civil rights are allocated with those that mark the allocation of values in the field of transportation (e.g., the development of rivers, harbors, and roads). Clearly more persons are aroused by the former cluster than by the latter, and plainly, too, uncompromising positions are as characteristic of civil rights issues as horse-trading is of rivers and harbors allocations.

Indeed, it is noteworthy that these characteristics of the status area would seem to be so powerful as to create still another distinctive characteristic of that area: The boundaries of vertical systems in the status area would appear to be more capable of expansion than are systems in any other area. Because they arouse a greater number of actors and a more uncompromising set of orientations, status issues can quickly move upward, downward, and sideward, once they are activated. The demand for civil rights in Angola, the attempt of James Meredith to enter the University of Mississippi, and the recognition of Communist China are illustrative of the vertical dynamism of status issues. Their horizontal dynamism—their capacity for intruding upon other issue-areas—is exemplified by the current civil rights debate in the United States. It was equally apparent in November 1963, when the arrest of Professor Frederick C. Barghoorn proved to be far more unsettling to the U.S.-U.S.S.R. system (as it was then being sustained in wheat and disarmament negotiations) than a concurrent flare-up of the Berlin crisis.

VI

The implications of the foregoing conceptual adjustments for the construction of foreign policy theory are clear.[103] If the above formulation has any validity, the external behavior of

103. Of course, if the issue-area concept is at all valid, its implications are not confined to foreign policy research. As indicated above, for example, it would seem to provide a useful way of assessing the political stability of horizontal systems. From an issue-area perspective, a stable—though not necessarily desirable—polity is one in which the boundaries of its vertical

horizontal systems at the national level is likely to vary so greatly
in scope, intensity, and flexibility in each of the four issue-
areas that any theory of foreign policy will have to include
if-then propositions which reflect these variations. Similarly
theoretical account will have to be taken of the external behavior of penetrated systems. Their relations with the rest of
the world will obviously be partly a function of differences in
the degree and nature of the penetration they experience. Moreover, since the extent and manner of penetration are likely to
vary from one issue-area to the next, any theory will have to
encompass these additional differences.

Indeed the penetrated and vertical systems concepts would
seem to be sufficiently important to warrant revision at the pre-
theoretical level. It seems reasonable to presume, for instance,
that the relative potency of systemic variables would be greater
in penetrated systems than in those which are strictly of a
national kind. Thus the pre-theory summarized in Table 2 could
fruitfully be doubled in scope by subdividing each of the eight
columns into "penetrated" and "nonpenetrated" categories and
introducing eight new rankings which elevate the systemic variables, say, one notch in each of the eight penetrated systems.
Likewise, if the distinctive characteristics of the status and
nonhuman resources areas have been correctly estimated, it is
easy to envision still another expansion of the pre-theory—a
twofold expansion in which societal variables are elevated one
position in the rankings for status areas (because more members of the system are likely to be aroused to make more
uncompromising demands) and lowered one rank in those for
nonhuman resources areas (because fewer system members are
likely to make less stringent demands). Table 4 presents these
possible expansions of the pre-theory which the penetrated and
vertical systems concepts facilitate.

While these concepts greatly complicate the task of theory
building, they do not dictate or limit the kind of theory that can
be constructed. As emphasized throughout, all we have done in
this paper is to identify and amplify the materials out of which

---

systems are insulated from each other, whereas an unstable polity would
consist of processes whereby one or more issues dominate political activity
within the entire system. For other possible avenues of research opened
up by the issue-area concept, see my "The Functioning of International
Systems," *Background*, 7:3, November 1963, pp. 116–17.

TABLE

A Further Elaboration of the Author's Pre-Theory of Foreign Policy,
Societies Are Ranked According to Their Relative Potencies in

Large Country																							
Developed Economy												Underdeveloped Economy											
Open Polity						Closed Polity						Open Polity						Closed Polity					
Penetrated			Non-penetrated			Penetrated			Non-penetrated			Penetrated			Non-penetrated			Penetrated			Non-penetrated		
status area	nonhuman resource area	other areas	status area	nonhuman resource area	other areas	status area	nonhuman resource area	other areas	status area	nonhuman resource area	other areas	status area	nonhuman resource area	other areas	status area	nonhuman resource area	other areas	status area	nonhuman resource area	other areas	status area	nonhuman resource area	other areas
so	r	r	so	r	r	r	r	r	r	r	r	i	i	i	i	i	i	i	i	i	i	i	i
r	sy	so	r	g	so	i	i	i	i	i	i	r	r	r	so	r	r	r	r	r	r	r	r
sy	so	sy	g	so	g	g	g	g	so	g	g	so	sy	sy	r	sy	so	sy	sy	sy	g	g	g
g	g	g	sy	sy	sy	so	sy	sy	g	sy	so	sy	g	so	sy	so	sy	so	g	g	so	sy	sy
i	i	i	i	i	i	sy	so	so	sy	so	sy	g	so	g	g	g	g	g	so	so	sy	so	so

i=idiosyncratic variables   r=role variables   g=governmental variables

4

in Which Five Sets of Variables Underlying the External Behavior of
Sixteen Types of Societies and Three Types of Issue-Areas

Small Country																							
Developed Economy												Underdeveloped Economy											
Open Polity						Closed Polity						Open Polity						Closed Polity					
Penetrated			Non-penetrated			Penetrated			Non-penetrated			Penetrated			Non-penetrated			Penetrated			Non-penetrated		
status area	nonhuman resource area	other areas	status area	nonhuman resource area	other areas	status area	nonhuman resource area	other areas	status area	nonhuman resource area	other areas	status area	nonhuman resource area	other areas	status area	nonhuman resource area	other areas	status area	nonhuman resource area	other areas	status area	nonhuman resource area	other areas
sy	sy	sy	r	r	r	sy	sy	sy	r	r	r	sy	sy	sy	i	i	i	sy	sy	sy	i	i	i
so	r	r	so	sy	sy	r	r	r	sy	sy	sy	i	i	i	sy	sy	sy	i	i	i	sy	sy	sy
r	g	so	sy	g	so	i	i	i	i	i	i	so	r	r	so	r	r	r	r	r	r	r	r
g	so	g	g	so	g	so	g	g	so	g	g	r	g	so	r	g	so	so	g	g	so	g	g
i	i	i	i	i	i	g	so	so	g	so	so	g	so	g	g	so	g	g	so	so	g	so	so

so=societal variables   sy=systemic variables

any theory of foreign policy must be fashioned. A wide range of theories can be built out of these materials, and nothing inherent in the latter determines the design, elegance, and utility of the former. These qualities must be supplied by the analyst, which is what makes the task of theory building awesome and challenging.

PART TWO

The Developed–Underdeveloped
Dichotomy

THE THREE ESSAYS in this section are addressed to the question of whether or not interrelationships can be found between the level of development of a political system, on the one hand, and, on the other, its foreign policy. Problems of terminology and definition at once become apparent. Social scientists have been struggling for some years with issues of development and social change, and have wrestled with such terms as "non-Western," "underdeveloped," "developing," and "emerging" as applied to many of the countries of the world. While several of these terms remain awkward and consensus has not yet been achieved on either their definitions or the propriety of their use in contemporary social science, students have at least become accustomed to the recent growth of a literature concerned with what are increasingly called the underdeveloped, or developing, areas.

A perhaps ironic concomitant of the expanding acceptance of these terms as labels for, in general, non-European countries is the remarkable absence of a terminology to identify the states near the other end of the developmental process. These terminological difficulties are, however, minor when compared with the definitional and conceptual problems involved in developmental theory and its relationship to economic and political change in today's world.

Despite these formidable problems, the authors of the following essays have embarked upon an inquiry about the nature of the interplay between the developmental process and foreign policy. Carl J. Friedrich of Harvard University, George I. Blanksten of Northwestern University, and Pablo González Casanova of the National Autonomous University of Mexico have addressed themselves to varying aspects of this interplay. Concerned with "Western" or "developed" systems, Professor Friedrich seeks out the relationship between the intranational politics of these states and their foreign policies. In the course of his discussion he pays special attention to the problem of national minorities, a problem relevant for both developed and developing nations.

95

Professor Blanksten, concentrating his focus on the developing nations, addresses himself to such questions as the nature of development, its implications for the structure of domestic politics, and the relevance of these matters to issues of foreign policy. Speaking from a still different cultural vantage point, Professor Casanova deals with the foreign policies of underdeveloped areas, raising, among other problems, the question of the relationship between ideology and analysis.

Few will deny the boldness and ambitiousness of the undertaking attempted here. Lacunae no doubt remain. But if the authors have advanced our insight into the quality of the dichotomy distinguishing developed from underdeveloped systems and identified some of the interrelationships between the intranational politics and the foreign policies of each, the collective purpose will have been served.

Intranational Politics and Foreign Policy in Developed (Western) Systems

CARL J. FRIEDRICH
Harvard University

FOREIGN AND DOMESTIC POLICY in developed Western systems constitutes today a seamless web.[1] The former sharp division which expressed itself in such principles as the primacy of foreign over domestic policy is no longer tenable and has not been for some time. These principles, never fully operative, were not merely descriptive but contained expedient normative propositions; now they have become utopian.[2] The division remains,

1. I am not going to take up the Soviet Union, the Fascist dictatorships, and related totalitarian regimes, though some of them no doubt constitute developed systems. The problems they present are too different, and our knowledge of the impact of internal party politics on foreign relations is too fragmentary. Cf. Zbigniew K. Brzezinski, *The Soviet Bloc*, rev. ed. (New York, Frederick A. Praeger, 1961), esp. Chaps. 6–8, for some essentials. Characteristically, however, Merle Fainsod in his magistral *How Russia Is Ruled*, rev. ed. (Cambridge, Mass., Harvard University Press, 1964), while noting that "domestic and foreign policy are intimately interrelated" (p. 597), discusses foreign policy in a brief three pages (342–45) under the heading of "goals of the Soviet leadership." Cf. also Friedrich and Brzezinski, *Totalitarian Dictatorship and Autocracy*, rev. ed. (Cambridge, Harvard University Press, 1965), Chap. 27 and pp. 357 ff.

2. Cf. my *Foreign Policy in the Making* (New York, W. W. Norton and Co., 1938), Chap. 3, and a later article "Das Ende der Kabinettspolitik," in

of course, but it resembles that between agricultural and fiscal policy, calling for a distinct organization and a separate set of specialists, but certainly not calling for a separate kind of political theory. It is the more curious that just such a theory has been demanded in recent years by very able writers in the field of international relations.[3] Such demands seem to spring from a certain lack of theoretical framework in the study and teaching of international relations and foreign policy. Nor can there be any question that the field of foreign relations raises distinctive issues which call for treatment within the context of a general theory of politics.[4] But these distinctive issues, or at least some of them, bear close resemblance to patterns and processes characteristic of other kinds of political relations, e.g., negotiation, employment of violence, compacts. Some of these have been explored in the interesting papers on behavior.[5] As a matter of fact, the intermeshing of domestic and foreign policy is so intricate that it has even become difficult to define foreign policy satisfactorily. For what is genuinely foreign in a world shaped by a great variety of international organizations? Even if we draw reasonably neat lines between such organizations as the Council of Europe, on the one hand, and the European Community of the Six, operative as ECSC, EEC, and Euratom, on the other, they are apt to become blurred once the details are taken into account.[6] Hence such terms as "international federalism"

Aussenpolitik, I (1950), pp. 20 ff., and the critical reply by Hans Rothfels, *ibid.*, pp. 274 ff.

3. Stanley Hoffmann, ed., *Contemporary Theory in International Relations* (Englewood Cliffs, N.J., Prentice-Hall, 1960), esp. the editor's own comments, and Raymond Aron, "The Quest for a Philosophy of Foreign Affairs," as well as the latter's *Paix et guerre entre les nations*, rev. ed. (Paris, Colmann-Lévy, 1962), esp. pp. 16 ff. These *prises de position* are focused in terms of the "autonomy" of an academic "discipline" of international relations, but such a discipline must necessarily be part of political science when theoretically considered.

4. I have dealt with some of these in *Man and His Government* (New York, McGraw-Hill, 1963), esp. in Chaps. 27, 30–32, and 35.

5. See the papers by K. Deutsch and J. Rosenau in this volume and the literature cited there, and Deutsch, *The Nerves of Government* (London, Free Press of Glencoe, 1963), esp. Chap. IV and pp. 205 ff.

6. Stanley Hoffman made a valiant effort in this direction in the paper entitled "Discord in Community" which he contributed to *The Atlantic Community—Progress and Prospects*, ed., Francis O. Wilcox and H. Field Haviland, Jr. (New York, Praeger, 1963). Cf. for contrast the paper by Haviland.

have come into vogue,[7] and the protests against "community" are not likely to halt the internalization of international politics.

In considering the impact of intranational (domestic) politics on international affairs, we are confronted with a host of widespread prejudices and stereotypes. At the outset, some of these deserve mention in order to set the stage for the analysis. For one, the people are seen as desiring peace and are therefore presumed to render a country's foreign policy more pacific—if granted greater influence, either directly or through their representatives. Experience suggests that while the premise is correct, the deduction is in error; for the general public, uninformed about the complexities of foreign relations, often insists upon the very policies which make for conflict. In this connection, some of the specific dynamics of democratic politics, such as the predominant impact of the well-organized group, are frequently neglected. The notion, often advanced by well-meaning persons and by no means only academic ones, that it is possible to cope with these difficulties by education has little support in actual experience.

The history of the development of democratic politics shows that democracies were not organized to deal with foreign affairs. The classic theorists of democracy, John Locke and Jean-Jacques Rousseau, paid slight attention to the issues. "What matters principally to every citizen," Rousseau wrote, "is the observance of the laws internally, the maintenance of private property, and the security of the individual. As long as all goes well with regard to these three points, let the government negotiate and make treaties with foreign powers. It is not from this quarter that the dangers will come which are most to be feared." [8] The rise of totalitarian dictatorship in the twentieth century, intimately linked to crises growing out of the miscon-

7. Cf. the collective volume, ed. E. Plischke, entitled *Systems of Integrating the International Community* (Princeton, N.J., Van Nostrand, 1964), and my own paper therein, "International Federalism in Theory and Practice." The latter was elaborated for the IPSA Round Table on Federalism, Oxford, 1963 (published in *Politische Vierteljahrsschrift*, 1964.) Cf. also fn. 38.

8. Rousseau, *Contrat Social*. Cf. also Locke, *Second Essay on Civil Government*, Section 147: "What is done in reference to foreigners . . . must be left in great part to the prudence of those who have this power committed to them," the reason being that this power is "much less capable to be directed by antecedent, standing, positive laws."

duct of foreign affairs, provides an eloquent rebuttal to such illusionism. But the notion persists in generally held views upon which such approaches as isolationism, neutralism, and other forms of escapism are based.[9] How to structure the process of foreign-affairs decision-making in a nation which is democratically organized so as to insure an effective conduct of its foreign policy is an unsolved problem. Numerous eloquent appeals have been made, especially in the United States, but the Republic stumbles along, muddling through crisis after crisis as best it can.

Another common assumption is compounded of the two notions that a country should have an integrated foreign policy and that this foreign policy should be animated by active, if not aggressive, concern with some kind of central purpose, usually described as "national interest." Actually, an integrated foreign policy is a rare and marginal case even in the history of autocratic regimes (Charles V, Richelieu, Bismarck, and other "masters") and is typically based upon some central aggressive and/or imperialist design; its closest parallels in our time are the world-revolutionary thrusts of totalitarian foreign policy. The United States has not had such an integrated foreign policy. The foreign affairs of the United States and other democracies (as well as many other states) have been a pragmatic patchwork of a plurality of policies,[10] dealing with particular issues as they arise and inspired by some general defensive notions related to specific areas and defined in terms of concrete advantage and disadvantage, symbolized by a tariff reduced or a military involvement avoided. In his path-finding study on the national interest,[11] Charles Beard years ago showed how this patchwork is woven by officials, special interests, and occasional outbursts of popular concern. Let us therefore agree that we

9. *Foreign Policy in the Making, op. cit.,* Chap. 2, gives some illustrations of this notion. Recently, G. J. Mangone has published interesting findings, *Foreign Policy and Onandaga County* (1964).

10. The volume edited by Joseph E. Black and Kenneth W. Thompson, *Foreign Policies in a World of Change* (New York, Harper & Row, 1963), while organized in terms of the foreign policy of various countries, actually serves to prove what is said in the text.

11. Charles A. Beard, *The Idea of the National Interest—An Analytical Study in American Foreign Policy* (New York, Macmillan Co., 1934), esp. Chap. XII. For an approach based upon the assumption that the "national interest" is more or less self-evident, see Hans J. Morgenthau, *In Defense of the National Interest—A Critical Examination of American Foreign Policy* (New York, Alfred A. Knopf, 1951).

are not talking about foreign policy but about foreign policies, and accept as a working hypothesis that such a pragmatic and reactive approach to foreign affairs may work as well in the long run as any grand designs.

Let me turn, then, to the so-called principle of the primacy of foreign affairs—that is to say, the principle that foreign policy considerations take precedence when they clash with those of internal politics, or that they ought to do so. For as usual in politics, the existential and the normative are intermingled (and confused). It is readily apparent that to the extent that foreign and domestic issues can be distinguished, there is no such principle at work, as far as the actual conduct of foreign affairs is concerned. In all democratic countries the dynamism of popular participation in foreign affairs produces in the mind of all politicians a continuous balancing of foreign and domestic concerns, with now one, now the other in the ascendancy. That is the reason why a democracy's foreign policy is rarely more than a hodgepodge of separate policies, propagated and in turn opposed by various groups and organizations. Though it may be urged by informed observers [12] that those in charge of foreign policy should not allow internal issues to determine the course of foreign policy, how are these makers of foreign policies to escape the constellations in party and parliament that bring about such determination? Admittedly the British parliamentary system is better able to withstand the pressures of Parliament and the general public, but only at the expense of being more vulnerable to those within the governing party; the American situation is just the reverse. It stands to reason that a system which expressly proclaims that all power stems from the people will be subject to the people's preoccupations; it is found to be so in all democratic states—but not only in the democratic ones. Totalitarian governments, while somewhat freer from a general public opinion and its gyrations, are demonstrably subject to the push and pull of party divisions.[13] Hence in both democratic and

12. Joseph-Barthélémy, *La Conduite de la politique extérieure dans les démocraties* (Paris, Publications de la Conciliation Internationale, 1930). The same view has often been voiced since, notably in the book by Morgenthau cited in the previous note. See also the books in note 16.
13. Merle Fainsod, *How Russia Is Ruled*, rev. ed. (Cambridge, Mass., Harvard University Press, 1964); Z. Brzezinski, *The Soviet Bloc*, rev. ed. (New York, Praeger, 1961), Chaps. 1–7. For the belief system which provides the framework for the shifts, that is to say, the guiding continuity, see Nathan Leites, *A Study of Bolshevism—An Analysis of Soviet Writings to*

totalitarian regimes the people may force a bad policy, they may prevent a good policy from being adopted, they may allow special interests to deflect national policy, and they may even provide the government with ready excuses for a policy which is unpalatable to other powers.[14] Communist theory explicitly acknowledges the interdependence of domestic and foreign policy and rejects the principle of the primacy of foreign policy in favor of a primacy of domestic policy. This principle is, however, in flagrant contradiction to the world revolutionary goals of the Communist ideology, and a detailed examination of Soviet foreign policy in no way supports the contention that domestic policy has precedence over foreign policy.[15]

Overall appraisal of recent experience forces one to the conclusion that the formation of foreign policy is part of the continuous process of policy formation, responding in kaleidoscopic fashion to the interaction of a great number of interests and viewpoints. Foreign policy will dominate the decisions only to the extent to which the interests active in a particular foreign area successfully press for adequate concern and/or the general public happens to respond. One view or another may dominate for a time, and considerable uncertainty may surround particular policies.

This last observation leads me to comment briefly upon another "principle" of cabinet-style foreign policy, that of the so-called continuity of foreign policy. It too has been stated both as norm and as fact with some measure of empirical evidence to support it. The idea that foreign policy is or ought to be continuous has clearly some factual basis; yet like many expediency norms, continuity depends upon circumstances, and a sharp alteration in the situation ought obviously to elicit a rapid alteration and adaptation in policy. The principle that foreign policy is and ought to be continuous applies, therefore, only *rebus sic stantibus,* other things being equal, and only on the basis of the further understanding that "continuity" means steady and gradual transformation of policy to adapt it to evolv-

---

Find a Set of Rules Governing Communist Political Strategy (Glencoe, Ill., The Free Press, 1953). Despite the changes depicted by Brzezinski, these rules still largely apply.

14. Beard, *op. cit.,* Chap. IX. For the role of the party in integrating foreign-interest diversities, cf. W. Y. Elliott, ed., *United States Foreign Policy* (New York, Columbia University Press, 1952), pp. 133 ff.

15. Cf. the paper by Vernon V. Aspaturian in this volume.

ing conditions. The principle is intended to exclude the discontinuity of sudden reversals, gyrations, and oscillations. How such a principle is to be made operative in a regime based upon a system of parties, geared to sharply antagonistic conceptions of policy, is the problem. It has become the more perplexing as foreign and domestic policy have become increasingly intertwined. One answer has been bipartisan foreign policy, but while that conception works for short periods of national emergency, it is so contrary to the very spirit of party politics that it cannot be the answer for long. The American situation is deceptive in this respect, because of the fact that the real operative party division in international affairs cuts across traditional party lines, the true division being between internationalists and nationalists (formerly isolationists).[16]

Neither in England nor in the Federal Republic of Germany has a bipartisan foreign policy conception found favor with the opposition party. And rightly so, because too many vital issues are bound up with international affairs to make such an approach workable if there is to be a real opposition. To the extent, then, that party outlook and ideology impinge upon foreign policy, it will necessarily be discontinuous. This means in terms of our overall problem, of course, that intranational politics molds the handling of international affairs. A very striking instance of the resulting discontinuity occurred in connection with British Prime Minister Macmillan's efforts to bring Britain into the European Common Market. Space forbids a review of the case in its complex totality, but we may note that the party cleavage became very pronounced, some Labour politicians going so far as to indicate that they would not honor a treaty bringing Britain into the Common Market but would take her out again. It is not possible to know to what extent these vigorous hints at radical discontinuity influenced President de Gaulle's judgment in declaring himself against British entry. They are likely to have been a factor, since they suggested a

16. See H. Bradford Westerfield, *Foreign Policy and Party Politics—Pearl Harbor to Korea* (New Haven, Yale University Press, 1958), for richly documented case studies; James A. Robinson, *Congress and Foreign Policy-Making* (Homewood, Ill., Dorsey Press, 1962), speaks of the "secondary role" of Congress in international relations. He attributes this decline to (1) the need for large amounts of technical information, (2) short decision time, and (3) financial cost. While true, it in fact reinforces what is said in the text.

fairly widespread disinclination among the British public to join the Community of the Six.[17] Democratic politics is party politics, and hence the progress of democratization has brought about an emphasis upon alternative lines of foreign policy. There are, of course, certain basic guide lines to a national policy which are said to escape the immediate impact of party conflict, but it is doubtful that any such basic issues are really immune. The British case just cited touches the very core of British foreign policy. What could be more central to German foreign policy than reunification? Yet the three German parties differ considerably on how to approach it. The solidarity of the Americas as expressed in the Monroe Doctrine was believed to be sacrosanct, but did it really remain beyond party and intraparty controversy, even before the Cuban revolution put the entire doctrine in jeopardy? It has from time to time been suggested that one might deal with the problem by distinguishing the goal, such as reunification, from the means or way to achieve it. While such a distinction may at times be useful, it is often seen on closer inspection that the agreement on the goal is merely verbal and that behind the common formula there are hidden very important differences in substance. Thus reunification may mean a good many things to different people in Germany, and the same is true of Britain's joining the Common Market and of the Monroe Doctrine.[18]

The possibilities which merely verbal agreement offers for achieving an appearance of unity and continuity, where it does not in fact exist, have led to the development of formulas as a method of democratic foreign policy. Such formulas are often

17. *Foreign Policy in the Making*, Chap. 4. The case of Britain's entry into the Common Market was most interestingly analyzed by Roland Young and James A. Robinson, "Parliamentary Decision-Making in Great Britain— The Case of the Common Market," paper delivered at APSA meeting, 1962. For a vivid, if biased, account see Drew Middleton, *The Supreme Choice— Britain and Europe* (London, Lecher & Warburg, 1963).

18. For Britain, see U. W. Kitzinger, *The Politics and Economics of European Integration—Britain, Europe, and the United States* (New York, Praeger, 1963), Chaps. V–VII, and Royal Institute of International Affairs, *Britain in Western Europe* (London, New York, 1956); for the United States, see Dexter Perkins, *A History of the Monroe Doctrine*, rev. ed. (Boston, Little, Brown, 1955); on Germany, see James H. Wolfe, *Indivisible Germany—Illusion or Reality?* (The Hague, M. Nijhoff, 1963), and Wilhelm G. Grewe, *Deutsche Aussenpolitik der Nachkriegszeit* (Stuttgart, Deutsche Verlags-Anstalt, 1960), esp. pp. 169 ff.

expressed under the heading of "doctrines." Monroe, Truman, Eisenhower, as well as Hallstein and others have been credited with such doctrines concerning highly controversial fields of foreign policy. Those doctrines introduce a certain degree of continuity into democratic foreign policies, although they tend at the same time to "rigidify" specific areas and thereby to contribute to the lack of unity of such policies. They possess, however, the very distinct advantage that they can be made the focal point of official efforts to commit the general public and a majority of the representative bodies (parliament) to a particular line. They may be compared to brand names, which allow a comparable concentration of advertising efforts. In other words, such formulas allow a party to "sell" its approach in a particular field of foreign policy. At the same time they provide a convenient facade behind which policy can be evolved and adapted to changing circumstances. While the American people and Congress remained committed to the Monroe Doctrine, American policy toward Latin America underwent a steady evolution from protectorate to partnership.[19] It would seem that such formulas give foreign policy an ideological slant, and like ideologies they are subject to elaborate manipulation.[20]

Party-conditioned discontinuity (including the intraparty conflicts over the party line) is said to be transcended by those factors determining foreign policy which operate regardless of human preferences and decisions. Among these factors (if we exclude the elusive and highly stereotyped "national character") geography has been urged recurrently as a permanent determinant of foreign policy. Not only the discredited exponents of *Geopolitik* but many others have taken the view that "the geographical position of a nation is the principal factor conditioning its foreign policy."[21] But mountains, lakes, and rivers determine policy only after its objectives have been set by peoples or rulers; or, to put this proposition more accurately, they do not determine, but condition, foreign policy. Geography does not play

19. Cf. Dexter Perkins, *op. cit.*, pp. 314–70.
20. *Man and His Government*, Chap. 4; *Totalitarian Dictatorship and Autocracy* (1956), Chap. 9 (with Z. Brzezinski).
21. Jules Cambon, in his discussion of French foreign policy, contained in a collective volume issued by the Council on Foreign Relations entitled *The Foreign Policy of the Powers* (New York, Harper and Brothers, 1935). This view is no longer prominent in the volume cited above, note 10.

the role of fate; it merely does or does not present obstacles, when a government pursues a policy of expansion, or of protection if the policy is one of defense. A body of water illustrates the point; it can become a sea lane for attack as well as an obstacle assisting in the defense. Similar comments may be made about such matters as mineral resources, climate, and the rest of geographical givens. They inject a persistent conditioning factor into national foreign policy, but they do not determine it or provide it with genuine continuity.

A comparable, though slightly more flexible, situation is presented by the existence of national cultural minorities within the boundaries of a national state, especially if such minorities are regionally distributed in fixed and historically well-established habitats. The situation ought not to be confused with that in the United States, where such groups are widely scattered and most of them have recently arrived, being composed of immigrants with a determined will to become American citizens. Even here pressure groups of such minorities have been a continuing problem of American foreign policy makers, who have, however, been traditionally inclined to pay as little attention to their pressure as the democratic process will allow.[22] In Europe, by contrast, these minorities were, after World War I, given explicit protection by the peace treaties and under the League of Nations. This protection proved rather feeble, but the impact of these situations on foreign policy was nonetheless considerable. The existence of such cultural minorities is a serious challenge to the homogeneity and equality of all citizens which democratic theory presupposes.[23] In Europe such minorities have tended to reinforce the idea of an over-arching, supranational European community, especially since quite a few of them are survivals from an older European order containing supranational communities of language, religion, and so forth. In the period between the two world wars such minorities, often with distinct political aspirations, constituted almost 10 per cent (32 million) of the European population. The vast migrations following World War II have considerably reduced this figure, and the totalitarian structure in Eastern Europe has further

22. Cf. Bradford Westerfield, *op. cit.*, pp. 77–78, 227–39.
23. Heinz O. Ziegler, *Die Moderne Nation: Ein Beitrag zur politischen Soziologie* (Tübingen, Mohr, 1931); Hans Kohn, *The Idea of Nationalism— A Study in its Origins and Background* (New York, Macmillan Company, 1944).

reduced the problem.[24] Even so, the problem remains a serious one.

At the present time ideological issues arising from the world-wide Communist movement are often claimed to be the true factor of continuity. As long as the world-revolutionary ideology and the thrust toward world conquest continue, the foreign policy of all those states which are in the posture of defending themselves against this thrust is rendered continuous to that extent. But this continuity obviously depends upon the continuance of the threat. Such constellations have existed in earlier times and undoubtedly account in part for the principle itself. At the same time they reveal it as somewhat tautological; no separate principle of continuity is required for explaining the persistence of ideological orientations or for the response to them on the part of those who are threatened by such ideological expansionism. The apparent continuity is deceptive. In fact, periods of great revolutionary upheaval have usually been accompanied by a pronounced lack of continuity in foreign policy. The impact of revolutionary ideas is itself the primary factor making for lack of continuity. Attempts to delineate and interpret Soviet foreign policy in terms of tsarist foreign policy have ended in failure, even though some common traits and parallel problems can be shown to prevail. To the extent that all regimes, even the most autocratic ones, depend upon a limited measure of popular approval and general consensus, continuities springing from persistent factors in a nation's location and tradition are likely to be operative. But there is no need to look upon such continuities as norms of expedience; they may even constitute distinct disvalues and cause permanent handicaps, such as Poland's wide-open frontiers. On the other hand, the discontinuities caused by party conflict in developed political orders are a positive advantage, especially because of the continuous vigorous criticism which such conflict engenders.

In this connection a relatively free and competitive press such as is found in developed democratic societies deserves brief mention. Not only does such a press provide a continuous flow of information gathered by self-reliant correspondents and reporters, although this information is undubitably of vital im-

24. For the situation about 1930, cf. Wilhelm Winkler, *Statistisches Handbuch der Europäischen Nationalitäten* (1931), pp. 153 ff.

portance in the shaping of foreign policies. Such a press also continually scrutinizes a country's foreign policy and provides suggestions and at times directives to the policy-makers.[25] It is difficult to know precisely what the degree of impact may be and whether it currently goes beyond mild irritation. There can be no question that writers like Walter Lippmann, Raymond Aron, and James Reston, to mention only three eminent examples, have at times occasioned more or less "agonizing reappraisals" of particular policy lines and specific decisions. By molding public opinion and arousing parliamentary and congressional attention, such writers may affect the conduct of foreign policy in subtle and devious ways. It is uncertain, but nonetheless probable, that the British press, notably *The Times* and its editor, Geoffrey Dawson, had a good deal to do with British appeasement policy.[26] Since these writers and the press are part and parcel of the national political scene, their minds provide some of the most interesting transmission channels for intranational political issues and for their projection upon the international level of policy conflict. This sort of projection has had some of its most deleterious effects during wartime, when journalistic interest in particular stereotypes fitting the emotional state of war, especially prejudicial views on the national character of the enemy, may serve to fix lines of policy which prevent the making of peace.[27]

The role of the press, the absence of continuity, and the subordination of foreign to domestic issues have, along with other related studies and observations, suggested what I have called the three-level theory of democratic foreign policy.[28] It

25. Cf. the bibliography given by Ralph O. Nafziger, *International News and the Press* (New York, H. W. Wilson Co., 1940), *passim*, and such special studies as Eber M. Carroll, *French Public Opinion and Foreign Affairs, 1870–1914* (New York, London, The Century Co., 1931), which concentrate on the press.

26. Martin Gilbert and Richard Gott, *The Appeasers—The Decline of Democracy from Hitler's Rise to Chamberlain's Downfall* (London, Weidenfeld and Nicholson, 1963), pp. 66 ff. See also B. Granzow, *A Mirror of Nazism—British Opinion and the Emergence of Hitler—1922–1933* (London, Gollancz, 1964).

27. Harold Nicolson, *Peacemaking—1919* (Boston and New York City, Houghton Mifflin Co., 1933); also his *Sir Arthur Nicolson, Bart., First Lord Carnock; A Study in the Old Diplomacy* (London, Constable & Co., Ltd., 1930); John L. Snell, *Wartime Origins of the East-West Dilemma over Germany* (New Orleans, Hauser Press, 1959).

28. Carl J. Friedrich, "Die öffentliche Meinung Amerikas in der Krise," *Aussenpolitik*, VII, 1956, pp. 502 ff. Gabriel Almond, *The American People*

seems that part of the complexity and discontinuous opaqueness of contemporary foreign policy is due to the fact that in increasingly democratized political regimes foreign policy decisions occur on three distinct levels: (1) the technical and bureaucratic level of professional diplomacy, (2) the one-sided level of particular interest groups, and (3) the emotional level of broad popular participation. Marked deviations occur as policy decisions move from the first level to the second and from the second to the third. The first level, continuously involved in the day-to-day decisions of state department and foreign office, is distinguished by its careful attention to detail, by its reference to specific advantage or disadvantage defined in relation to the particular adversary at hand, by its operative relation with comparable technicians working for the other powers—whether partners, friends, neutrals, or enemies—and by its acceptance of a general code of conduct, called the rules of diplomacy (still a potent factor, even though considerably changed by the world-revolutionary situation).[29]

The second level is reached when an issue of foreign relations vitally affects a particular interest group, or several such groups, so that it is induced to mobilize its resources for influencing both the experts and the popular representatives, as well as the general public, especially the press. Under this pressure the technician may retreat into inaction, he may fight back, or he may adopt the interested position in whole or in part.[30]

The third level heaves into view at those infrequent intervals when the general public becomes aroused. Such occasions may

and *Foreign Policy* (New York, Harcourt, Brace and Company, 1950), distinguishes four levels which he calls the general public, the attentive public, the policy and opinion elites, and the legal and political policy leadership, pp. 138–39. He does not relate these to the policy process in quite the way I have, but rather elaborates the classification of elites, pp. 140 ff.

29. Harold C. Nicolson, *Diplomacy*, 2nd ed. (London, New York, Oxford Press, 1958). For a more personal approach, cf. Charles W. Thayer, *Diplomat* (New York, Harper, 1959).

30. Perhaps the most interesting of the older studies is the well-documented story of oil politics by Alfred Vagts, *Mexico, Europa und Amerika unter besonderer Berücksichtigung der Petroleumpolitik* (Berlin-Grunewald, W. Rothchild, 1928); my *American Policy Toward Palestine* (Washington, Public Affairs Press, 1944) shows another pressure group at work; cf. also Frank Manuel's more recent *The Realities of American-Palestine Relations* (Washington, Public Affairs Press, 1949). The oil politics in the Middle East are discussed by George Kirk, *The Middle East, 1945–1950* (London, New York, Oxford University Press, 1954), who also discusses Palestine within the general context of Mideastern international relations.

arise in connection with a threat to peace, a flagrant aggression, or some other overt act touching profound national sensibilities. When on these occasions the general public—the people's voice of old—is heard, both technicians and special interests are apt to respond by adapting themselves to the mass reaction. It is here that some of the most dramatic turns and even reversals of foreign policy have occurred. It takes extraordinary mastery, such as was displayed by John F. Kennedy at the time of the Cuba crisis, to avoid rash and irrevocable errors. This sort of third-level decision may occur after a previous technical or interested decision has been reached, as in the case of British policy after Suez, or it may be the decisive stimulant in the first place, as was true at the time of the outbreak of hostilities in Korea and again at the time of the stand-pat rejection of Soviet demands regarding Berlin in 1958.[31]

Since the three levels interact in various ways, the distinctions between them ought not to be exaggerated, but an inspection of, say, American policy in the Middle East proves the value of drawing attention to the dependence of international relations upon these factors. They suggest why the extent of the dependence of the foreign policies of developed constitutional systems upon intranational politics allows of no facile generalizations. It very much depends upon whether the issue involves a response on the first, second, or third level.

The foregoing sketch does no more than indicate some of the basic issues. Many others deserve treatment, such as the role

---

31. W. Phillips Davison, *The Berlin Blockade: A Study in Cold War Politics* (Princeton, N.J., Princeton University Press, 1958), esp. pp. 149 ff., while sound on the leaders, fails to take into account the popular support which made Truman's and Clay's position viable. The curious lack of corresponding action in the summer of 1961 when the Berlin sector boundary was sealed off has never been satisfactorily explained; cf. Hans Speier, *Divided Berlin—The Anatomy of Soviet Political Blackmail* (New York, Praeger, 1961); there is little doubt that the public would have supported action corresponding to the airlift, if the U.S. government had taken it. Davison has also given a general analysis of the German position in his two chapters contributed to the volume he edited with Speier, entitled *West German Leadership and Foreign Policy* (Evanston, Ill., Row, Peterson, 1957); this study also contains interesting analyses of other aspects of the German democracy's problems in foreign relations, with pressure groups producing various policies in specific contexts. For France, see Jean-Baptiste Duroselle's interesting chapter in Stanley Hoffmann, et al., *In Search of France* (Cambridge, Mass., Harvard University Press, 1963), pp. 305 ff., and the same author's *De Wilson à Roosevelt, Politique Extérieure des Etats Unis, 1913–1945* (Paris, A. Colin, 1960).

of minorities in affecting foreign policy in the regimes we have considered, the special problems presented by such interest groups as churches and trade unions, and the difficulties arising from the built-in propensity of democratic regimes to minimize the role of foreign affairs through such devices as isolation, neutrality, and the transfer of responsibility to supranational groupings, whether regional or worldwide.

Even more significant is the range of issues presented by the framework of political theory and its propositions that was mentioned at the outset. Power, rule, and influence, authority, legitimacy, and the problem of justice, equality, and freedom, as well as the problems of decision-making, negotiating, arbitrating, and fiscal control are part of the problem of intranational politics and the formulation and execution of foreign policies by developed (open) systems.[32] The extensive literature on these and other related issues of foreign policy-making has added much to our knowledge in all these fields. And yet very sizable research tasks loom ahead. Apart from the relatively limited, though important, areas in which quantitative studies are becoming possible, in none of the developed systems of government today is the dynamics of foreign policy determination adequately known and understood. It is clear that foreign affairs are not being conducted as they once were in the bygone days of cabinet policy fashioned and directed by small cliques of insiders, whether aristocratic or bureaucratic. Yet there are at present so much experimentation and innovation, so many failures as well as successes in a variety of terms of reference that research has been able to cope with only a limited part of the whole. The rapidly increasing areas of international federalism pose a whole set of new questions, as the interdependence of domestic and foreign policies is further complicated by their conduct on two or more territorial levels.[33] Boundaries are becoming problematic as it appears increasingly uncertain what is *intra* and what not.

A functional approach to policy processes will therefore (1)

32. See *Man and His Government* (New York, McGraw-Hill, 1963), *passim;* and Raymond Aron, *Paix et guerre entre les nations* (Paris, Colman, Levi, 1962). An interesting general theory was put forward by the late Eugen Fischer-Baling, *Theorie der Auswärtigen Politik* (Köln, Westdeutscher Verlag, 1960).

33. Besides the work cited in note 6, see *Systems of Integrating the International Community,* ed. Plischke (Princeton, N.J., Van Nostrand, 1964).

treat foreign policy as part of the policies of developed political systems, seen as an interdependent collection of approaches to concrete problems having both a domestic and a foreign dimension, and (2) understand foreign affairs not only as the external aspect of self-contained systems but also as the internal aspect of supranational (regional and worldwide) systems of policy formation and control.[34] Such a treatment will enrich the understanding of intranational politics, by building an awareness of the continuous interaction between domestic and foreign issues —an interaction which is increasing steadily as the political community grows beyond the boundaries of national states. An issue of particular complexity already alluded to earlier deserves further detailed exploration: namely, the problem of national minorities. It may serve to deepen the general discussion of intranational politics and foreign policy in developed Western systems, but it has its applications to the problems of emergent nations as well. For national cultural minorities can operate as a force deeply disturbing to national foreign policies, as they did in Europe in the period between the two world wars.

The lack of homogeneity caused by national cultural minorities creates peculiar difficulties between democratic and non-democratic states, which did not receive serious attention in theory and practice before the First World War.[35] These difficulties were obscured by the fact that such cultural minorities had themselves been in the vanguard of democratization. The Poles and Danes in Germany, no less than the several Slavic nationalities in the Hapsburg empire, sought an outlet for their cultural aspirations by clamoring for parliamentary democracy.

34. The clashes and conflicts between politics and morals, often stressed in connection with foreign policy, e.g., K. W. Thompson, *Christian Ethics and the Dilemmas of Foreign Policy* (Durham, N. C., Duke University Press, 1959), are peculiar neither to Christianity nor to foreign policy. Cf. my *Constitutional Reason of State* (Providence, R.I., Brown University Press, 1957), for the basic issues in Western developed systems of constitutional government.

35. This statement needs to be qualified, as far as the Hapsburg empire is concerned. Here a number of scholars and publicists, notably Joseph Redlich and Karl Renner, were making an effort to stem the tide of centrifugal nationality sentiment, especially as it aggravated the relations of Austria-Hungary and Russia, which led to the outbreak of the First World War. Note especially Joseph Redlich, *Das Österreichische Staats und Reichsproblem*, 2 vols. (Leipzig, P. Reinhold, 1920, 1926); and Karl Renner, *Der Kampf der österreichischen Nationen um den Staat* (Leipzig und Wien, F. Deuticke, 1907).

Little did they realize, though Rousseau could have taught them, that a democratic majority can be a harsher oppressor than a formal autocracy. They soon learned the lesson, as it is at present being learned by minorities in many emergent nations where national integration threatens them with extinction.

When the state is being identified with the nation, any group refusing to identify with the twin sacred beings is in danger of being looked upon as a traitor to the national cause. One answer is the forcible removal of such minorities, such as was organized even in the 1920's, when more than 600,000 Greeks were "relocated" after their presence in Asia Minor had come to be considered intolerable by the Turkish minority. But before the advent of the totalitarians and the Second World War, this population transfer remained an isolated instance as new democratic states in Central and Eastern Europe struggled to develop policies which would encompass the aspirations of cultural minorities within the national frame. As against the classical concept of the *nation* (*Staatsnation*) developed during the French Revolution and epitomized in the work of Rousseau, Fichte, and Hegel, the idea of nationality in Herder's sense of a people was promoted actively, building on notions that had been worked out in prewar Austria. The hope sprang up that it might be possible to contrive some kind of national cultural corporatism such as Karl Renner and his friends had advocated as a solution to the Austro-Hungarian empire's problems.[36] Unfortunately the advent of Hitler to power in Germany ruined what chances had existed for such a development. Presumably it would have been viable only within the broader context of a federally united Europe, as envisaged by Briand and Stresemann.[37] Meanwhile the relations between these newly formed democratic states were frequently strained to the breaking point by the existence of these national cultural minorities. The ex-

36. Cf. Renner, *op. cit.*, and *Nation und Staat*, 1918. For the theoretical framework, cf. my *Man and His Government*, Chaps. 30, 32. Yet this can hardly be considered practical politics where the cultural minority forms compact settlements, amounting to millions and antedating the formation of the state; the brutal consequence has been the post-Second World War policy of resettling large minorities of Germans; but could this policy be adopted toward anyone except a defeated enemy?

37. Rich materials are contained in *Gustav Stresemann—Vermächtnis* (Berlin, Ullstein, 1932), ed. H. Bernhard, et al., esp. Vols. II and III. In the very abbreviated English edition, some bits can be gathered from Pt. III, Chap. IV.

perience contains significant lessons for anyone concerned with the problems of intranational politics and foreign policy.

To reduce the analysis to its most typical form, one might concentrate upon those situations in which the government is engaged in carrying on a policy which the minority considers contrary to its vital interests; for this was almost universally the case at the time, though the degrees of alienation and suppression varied greatly. In short, the analysis is focused upon more or less oppressed minorities. The effect of such a minority is different, depending upon whether the minority belongs to a people which constitutes the majority in one or more other states. For the government of the adjoining state may then be inclined to act as a guardian of the rights of the oppressed minority, or indeed be impelled to do so by its own public opinion. Thus when in February 1928 the government of Estonia took away the Cathedral of Reval, which belonged to a Lutheran congregation of the German minority, the German diplomatic representative felt obliged to absent himself from the Estonian national festivities. Thereupon the Estonian government demanded his recall; yet it is obvious that the man had no choice but to express his disapproval, since the German minority would have made his continued service equally impossible. Hundreds of similar situations have occurred since that time, and the Estonian case has been cited partly for its nostalgic aspect, Estonia having long since been deprived of her national independence by the Soviet Union. She was particularly paradigmatic for minority problems during the interwar period, because she had organized a system of corporate federalism; each nationality was incorporated as an electoral body without reference to territory on the basis of personal choice.[38] Although the workings of this system are not well known, it may have considerable importance for the future.

There is another aspect of this Estonian case worth remarking, and that is the involvement of Germany. For whenever a minority belongs to a nationality in another state, particularly a major state, its needs and wants will often be reinforced by that

38. Evald UUstalu, *The History of the Estonian People* (London, Brown Publishing Co., 1952), unfortunately gives only the briefest reference. This interesting experiment was, to my knowledge, never studied with any care as to its actual workings, though references to the legal provisions are available. Cf. also my comments in "Recent Trends in the Theory and Practice of Federalism," *Jahrbuch des Offentlichen Rechts*, 1965.

state's foreign policy. To be sure, minorities have at times been able to secure the protection of another state without being bound to it by such ties of nationality. Particularly Great Britain and the United States have over the years assisted minorities, especially when such protection afforded them an opportunity to advance some aspect of their own national interest. But the nationality tie produces a different kind of emotional dynamism which may even become very bothersome to the protecting state, if it is democratically organized and provides for popular participation and pressure. Parliamentary influence may be used both by the minority itself and by its sympathizers abroad to influence the course of foreign policy.[39]

In the interwar years relations between Germany and Poland were constantly disturbed by friction developing out of the presence of national minorities in both countries, which eventually provided the pretext for Hitler's attack upon Poland. These tensions had set a pattern of mutual hostility which aggravated each negotiation. Thus during the debates over the ratification of a commercial treaty between the two countries in the German parliament, the treatment of the German minorities was repeatedly referred to.[40] This kind of situation may in turn suggest to a government the advantage of maltreating a minority in order to extract concessions from the state where a majority is vexed by such maltreatment in exchange for the cessation of such oppression—a tendency which shows that the existence of a majority elsewhere may not prove an unmixed blessing for a minority.[41] Such "related" minorities are therefore the primary cause for a complex disturbance of foreign policy under democratic conditions. The international procedures set up under the Covenant of the League of Nations were intended to modify this situation somewhat. Indeed this procedure was an invitation to interfere in minority situations, since it provided that any member of the Council of the League of Nations had not only the right but the duty to bring violations of the rights of minorities to the attention of the Council as a whole.[42] In fact, a

39. A careful study of the foreign policy aspects of the Tyrolese question is badly needed; so is one of the situation in Cyprus.
40. Reichstag, Stenographische Berichte, 438:1387.
41. This aspect was repeatedly referred to in the Proceedings of Europäischer Nationalitätenkongress, of which there were eight before 1933.
42. Felix Morley, The Society of Nations (Washington, Brooklyn Institute, 1932), pp. 261 ff., 418, 431; C. Howard-Ellis, The Origin, Structure

minority belonging to a majority represented on the Council, like the German one, was more likely to find its complaints presented to the Council. Thus the German Council member presented to the sixty-seventh session of the Council in 1929 a statement in which he called attention to what the German government considered a violation of the rights of German minorities in Poland, in connection with the application of the agrarian reforms in two Polish provinces.[43]

In addition to this kind of international negotiation through friendly governments, groups of related minorities undertook at that time to organize international pressure along distinctly national lines, by creating a framework of the nation outside of the state to which the majority belonged but with this majority as a center. This sort of approach was started by the Poles, who in the 1920's organized the Council of Poles Living Abroad, which held congresses in Warsaw and thereby sought to coordinate the scattered groups of Poles in all countries and to bring about cooperation among them. The Czechs and Slovaks followed suit in 1923. The publicly declared primary object of these organizations was to maintain the cultural unity of the peoples concerned. But such an innocuously cultural purpose is easily perverted, when such an organization turns into a political tool of international power politics. During the third congress, held in 1931, the Polish Council, after sharply criticizing the U.S. senator who was then chairman of the Foreign Relations Committee for rejecting the Polish access to the sea, resolved among other things that "the Council strongly protests against the interference with internal Polish affairs." Thereupon the secretary-general of the International Congress of Nationalities immediately objected to such an attempt to mobilize Polish citizens of other states on behalf of a policy which had nothing to do with maintaining the cultural integrity of Polish groups abroad, even though it was admittedly of very great importance for the Polish state. He added that the peaceful cooperation of nationalities beyond state boundaries can be assured only if their activity is limited to matters of cultural concern. True enough, but the de-

---

and Working of the League of Nations (London, G. Allen and Unwin, 1928), p. 111. Both authors illustrate the very limited scope of League authority.

43. League of Nations, *Official Journal*, "Documents relating to the Protection of Minorities," Special Supplement, No. 73, Geneva, 1929.

velopment followed the negative alternative, and such cooperation became virtually impossible after Hitler and the German
National Socialist regime proceeded to exploit the German organizations abroad for their political objectives of expansion and
conquest.[44]

The problem of the disturbing influence of related minorities
is compounded when the unrelated minorities come to the support of a related one, as has often been the case. Then the minorities form a bloc in parliament which may endanger the very
operation of government, especially when, as in Czechoslovakia
in the interwar period, the minorities constituted nearly a third
of the population. It is doubtful whether under such conditions
a national foreign policy can be maintained, except possibly in
situations where the minimal agreement is buttressed by a federal system which reduces the tensions among the several
nationalities. It may also be made more tolerable by a supranational system which includes the several rival states and
thereby attenuates the difficulties. This sort of resolution of the
foreign policy problems created by the existence of national
minorities under democratic conditions was attempted by the
aforementioned system of minority protection under the League
of Nations. But even here national rivalries inject themselves.
Generally Germany—in the few years when the Weimar Republic was a respected member of the League—became the most
outspoken defender of minority rights. Yet such leadership did
not go unchallenged; the Poles particularly were inclined to
question it. Comments like the following highlighted the situation: "It is high time to call the attention of the civilized world
to the situation of the Polish minority in Germany and to make
it clear how hypocritical and cynical the role of the Germans as
guardians of the rights of minorities is." [45] The Germans replied
in kind by claiming that the Poles were "working up" the case of
the Poles in Germany in order to veil the oppression of Germans
in Poland. These conflicts are briefly recalled here because they
illustrate how nationality conflicts and the issue of minority

44. Ralph F. Bischoff, *Nazi Conquest through German Culture* (Cam-
bridge, Mass., Harvard University Press, 1942). For the general setting, cf.
Carl J. Friedrich and Zbigniew Brzezinski, *Totalitarian Dictatorship and
Autocracy*, rev. ed. (Cambridge, Mass., Harvard University Press, 1965),
Chap. 27.

45. Cf. *Kurjer Poznanski*, Jan. 27, 1932. See also Stresemann's speech
in the Council, June 13, 1929.

rights poisoned foreign policy and international relations prior to the advent of Hitler. The seeds of Hitler's aggressions lay hidden in the activities of rival minorities. Democratic foreign policy, which is difficult enough under conditions of cultural homogeneity, becomes almost unmanageable where the diversities of national cultural minorities impinge upon it.

This conclusion is especially clear in situations where national minorities live close to the boundaries of the state which is populated by their own national "relatives," for in such situations the minority is looked upon with suspicion and distrust as a menace to the host state. The Germans in Sudetenland (Czechoslovakia) were a much greater threat than the Germans living in Siebenburgen (Hungary and Rumania) or the Wolga Republic. Such border minorities are a constant source of friction unless the two adjoining states enter into a close alliance or supranational combination. Thus in recent years the German-speaking part of the population of Alsace has ceased to seem a threat to the French Republic, and it has become easier for France to concede to this minority the degree of cultural autonomy it believes it is entitled to. A similar trend can be observed in the South Tyrol, although the problem is far from having been satisfactorily settled. Were Austria a part of a united Europe, it might become possible. A revival of nationalism and "independence" may, on the other hand, lead to new complications and the revival of irredentist sentiment.

In conclusion, it deserves to be repeated that foreign policy in mature democratic societies is closely interwoven with domestic policy without either always having precedence or always being subordinated to it. It all depends upon the extent to which the particular issue of foreign policy touches the sentiments of the public at large. In matters which profoundly arouse the people, all considerations of domestic and party politics are apt to be swept aside; in more limited matters considerations of party politics may seriously affect the outcome. Where nationalities intertwine, the passions are especially apt to be engaged, and hence democratic foreign policy becomes especially unreasonable and difficult to manipulate in the interest of peace and international cooperation. In any case, the international relations of mature and sufficiently large-scale constitutional democracies are apt to be congeries of distinctive policies suitable for particular areas rather than to constitute any "grand design." And the task of the chief policy-maker, whether president, prime minister, or secretary of state, is likely to be the most difficult and politically the most unrewarding.

International Politics and Foreign Policy in Developing Systems

GEORGE I. BLANKSTEN
Northwestern University

Let me attempt to define the term "underdeveloped"; to me it seems to have an objective and an analytical meaning. I see it primarily as an economic concept, although it has noneconomic, especially political and social, implications. Professor Bert F. Hoselitz of the University of Chicago, who has done much pioneering work in the field of underdeveloped areas, has said he may not be able to define an underdeveloped area, but he certainly can recognize one when he is there.[1]

I would like, in a sense, to develop two models. Let us say Country A has an advanced economy and Country B we can call underdeveloped. If we remember that I think of "underdeveloped" primarily as an economic concept, we can identify certain inputs of Country A's economy—things like raw materials, natural resources, available labor supply, etc.—the ingredients, so to speak, that go into this economic process. Country A subjects this input to a certain technology which I look upon as a way of mixing these ingredients together. I am tempted to call the result the "output," but economists now are more taken with

1. Cf. Bert F. Hoselitz and Wilbert E. Moore, eds., *Industrialization and Society* (Paris, UNESCO, 1963), *passim.*, especially pp. 11–31.

terms like "per capita gross national product." In general, it represents the standard of living. This is our model for the developed or the advanced economy. We know the input in terms of the national resources, raw materials, labor supply, and so on, subjected to a technology which gives us the standard of living of the advanced or developed economy.

Let us compare this with the economy of Country B, which I call underdeveloped. The difference, it seems to me, is not in the input. We can say that the input into Country B's economy is the *same* as the input into Country A's. This is not really an unrealistic proposition; the economic characteristic of underdeveloped areas is not a shortage of things we have called input. Many countries in Latin America are thought of as "El Dorado"—places of untold wealth—and so I think it is not too unrealistic to say the problem is not one of input. There are impressive amounts of available input in these countries. The difference is in the state of the productive arts, in the way the input is handled. For this largely technological reason there is a different standard of living, or a different per capita gross national product. The basic point is that in this illustration, where we assume the inputs to be the same, the standards of living could be the same too, if only the technology were. But because of the technological problem in underdeveloped areas, it is not possible to obtain, from the available input, as near a realization of their potential as in developed areas.

We can then ask, "Aren't all countries underdeveloped?" They are, in the sense that in every country some further technological improvement or advancement is probably possible. I don't see these as absolute terms; I think this is essentially a relative proposition. The United States is in many ways underdeveloped, but compared with many other countries in the world it has a relatively developed economy.

Logically, technology and techniques are means rather than ends. There was a time, especially in the 1930's and 1940's, when anthropologists put great emphasis on cultural relativism. Each culture defined its own values; all cultures were equal; all values were equal; and no country had any kind of right, within the context of cultural relativism, to tell other countries that their values or their cultures were inferior. The point that acquires interest with respect to underdeveloped areas is this: We still subscribe to a certain amount of cultural relativism. In various societies and cultures throughout the world there are different standards of goodness, beauty, truth, and other values. But there does seem to be cross-cultural agreement about certain values, especially two.

In the first place, there is consensus about standards of living. It is generally agreed that it is better to live on a high standard of living than a low standard of living, that it is better to be rich than to be poor. This is one area of cross-cultural agreement on values. Another has to do with sickness and health. It is generally agreed that it is better to be in good health than to be ill. We still recognize variation among cultures about other values, but there does seem to be agreement on these two.[2]

As more efficient technologies and more developed economies bring a fairly differentiated division of labor in a country, so we find a kind of a political division of labor. This differentiation of functions is a political concomitant of the economic division of labor.[3] To illustrate this in the Latin-American area, we can cite militarism. Armies are prominent in the politics of many of the Latin-American countries. That seems to be a relatively simple illustration of the differentiation of functions. In underdeveloped Latin-American countries armies are not specialized or differentiated. In addition to performing specialized military functions, they do a variety of things: They run the government, they administer elections, they even cultivate the national music in some countries. There have been many jokes about Latin-American armies. The Mexican Army has borne the brunt of them, especially the barbs ridiculing the ratio of high-ranking commissioned officers to enlisted men. I have often thought these jokes unfairly aimed at the Mexican Army when other armies really are much better targets. In Costa Rica, for example, for a time over half of the Army was in the band. This made a kind of sense because one of the main things the Army did was perform at band concerts. The function of political socialization might also be mentioned. If we follow the career of a typical recruit or conscript drawn into the Army, we find that our hero is

2. Walter Goldschmidt, *Man's Way* (New York, Holt, Rinehart, and Winston, 1959), *passim*. See also George I. Blanksten, "The Aspiration for Economic Development," *The Annals of the American Academy of Political and Social Science,* Vol. 334, March 1961, pp. 10–19.

3. This scheme of analysis pursues the general system set forth in Gabriel A. Almond and James S. Coleman, eds., *The Politics of the Developing Areas* (Princeton, Princeton University Press, 1960).

illiterate and has very few ideas that we would call political ideas. Somebody simply jumps out of the woodwork and says to him, "Congratulations! You're in the Army." But look at him two or three years later, after he has done his military tour of duty and, let us assume, has been released with a reasonably honorable discharge. We find that our hero is now, because of his army experience, literate, that he now has ideas that we would call political—I am not saying that we would necessarily agree with them; that is another kind of question—that he has notions about the relationship between citizen and government. He has been socialized, and by the Army. The role of the church in politics in many Latin-American countries is much the same. This is one of the political implications of the underdeveloped economy.

There is also in many of these societies a lack of integration that expresses itself along a number of dimensions. I think three are probably especially important. There is the vertical dimension: society is pretty sharply divided into rigorously separated classes, and class systems are very rigid. Then there is the horizontal dimension: political regionalism is often very severe, as in Brazil and Mexico. The third dimension, the fundamental difference between rural and urban life, is a major political characteristic of most underdeveloped societies. In sum, there are political implications in this kind of model, but the model is primarily economic in character.

We should be suspicious of causal theories in social science. It is enough to say, if we can demonstrate it, that certain things co-vary, that known technological changes occur with identified political changes. Such an approach provides a researchable and definable form, and economic development defined as technological change tends to co-vary with the kinds of political change mentioned here.

Another important question is: How much are economic change and political change different phenomena, and how much are they just different ways of looking at essentially the same data? For research purposes many problems of economic development in the underdeveloped areas are easier to deal with on the latter basis. If the economist looks at the same set of data with a different focus than a political scientist does, the group theory of politics becomes especially relevant. It may well provide an analytical bridge between what the economists do when they talk about division of labor and economic interest groups and what the political scientists do when they deal with the differentiation of functions and political interest groups. It thus becomes significant to ask how much of what economists have already done is really useful as political concepts. An economist concerned with economic interest groups is interested in labor unions; the political scientist concerned with political interest groups and pressure groups is interested in labor unions. Are these sufficiently similar so that we political scientists can build on what the economists have already done for us in these areas? I suspect the answer is yes.[4]

What of the foreign policy of the underdeveloped country? What do we say about Country B's role in the Cold War that is related to the underdeveloped economy? All Gaul was once divided into three parts. Now we hear that the world is divided into three—the so-called West, the so-called Communist world, and the underdeveloped areas. Are the underdeveloped countries separate and neutral in foreign policy?

Another significant problem is the interrelationship between intellectual systems or ideological systems on the one hand and their slogans on the other. To put the question another way, do people in these countries understand the ideology their leaders talk about? Some ideologies are fairly sophisticated as philosophies and intellectual systems. There are countries where these ideologies are, in a sense, the truth from headquarters—official doctrine. But there is, I think, an important question of the extent to which the people at large, especially in the underdeveloped countries with large percentages of illiterates, understand the ideology. There is a tendency for people to derive certain slogans, or phrases, or words, or, at the most, groups of words, from an ideology. In a sense these slogans get to be just that—slogans or taboos or symbols—and the meaning of those things in the ideology or in the philosophy becomes lost. I believe this is what has happened especially with Karl Marx as a thinker, as an intellectual, as a writer. Throughout the world and in many of the underdeveloped areas there are people who have drawn slogans out of Marx with meanings that he certainly would not have accepted. I first came into dramatic con-

4. Blanksten, "Political Groups in Latin America," *The American Political Science Review*, LIII: 1, March 1959, pp. 106–27.

tact with this problem when I worked in Argentina, where Marxist terminology is used by many of the political parties. The Socialists are accepted as the intellectuals of the Marxist movement, and they are the people who ask strict constructionist questions. The use of a word like "imperialism" to mean what Marx meant by it is important to Socialists. They ask questions like, "Did Marx mean to say imperialism was the *highest* or the *last* stage of capitalism?" In some of the languages into which *Das Kapital* has been translated the same word may mean either "last" or "highest," and the difference is an important one to a Socialist.

In Argentina there were not only debates among the Socialists but also between Socialists and Communists as to what the Bible really meant. Another group, the *Peronistas*, weren't really Marxists, but they stole much of the vocabulary and jargon of Marxism. They used words like "imperialist" and "capitalist," and they were very effective at developing them into street slogans. At *Peronista* rallies it was interesting to notice how people were trained. Whenever they heard certain words they were expected to cheer. If they heard "proletariat" or "the workers" or "the exploited," they cheered. What those words meant in Marxism was a separate question. During the formative period of the *Peronista* movement the Socialists complained that the *Peronistas* were stealing Marxist vocabulary. A great Argentine Socialist leader, Americo Ghioldi, set out on a campaign—I think he was probably unsuccessful—to persuade his followers to use Marxist jargon judiciously. He urged them not to say "imperialist" unless they meant what Marx meant by it. He took a similar position on terms like "exploited," "exploiter," and so on. At a certain political stage in Argentina the Socialists carried on a concerted campaign to try to preserve the integrity of the jargon, the vocabulary.[5] I don't think it was a successful campaign because the stealing of the vocabulary, the slogans, and the symbols of Marxism still flourishes. We might say that a writer has really arrived when people steal his jargon. Probably a mark of great prestige in the intellectual establishment is to have one's ideas rejected but to have his own peculiar jargon used in the

5. For further discussion of this intellectual plight of the Argentine Socialists, see Blanksten, *Perón's Argentina* (Chicago, University of Chicago Press, 1953), pp. 378–86.

attack against him. Karl Marx shares membership in this fraternity with such other thinkers as Sigmund Freud and W. W. Rostow.

There is, then, significant verbalism in the underdeveloped areas—a use of Marxist jargon without his ideas. The words are used as slogans, symbols of what people are for and what they are against. In foreign policy questions this fact may be important in identifying friends and enemies of the underdeveloped countries. Almost everybody I ever met in any underdeveloped country was against imperialism and imperialists. In effect they said, "Never mind what these words mean; we are against it." At the time of the Indian invasion of Goa, there was an emergency session of the United Nations Security Council. Delegates opposed to this action referred to India as an invader, an aggressor, and an imperialist. The Indian delegation stood for all of these names except "imperialist." That one almost induced apopolexy.

Certain of these slogans, the words without the ideas—like "imperialists," "capitalists," "colonialists"—play a verbalistic role in largely illiterate societies where one cannot really discuss ideologies anyway. In a society with a 20 per cent literacy rate, I could see these slogans on the walls: "Down with the Capitalists!" "Imperialists, Go Home!" To try to talk with people in that society about the system of ideas that produced those words is to joke in a foreign language.

Let me move on to the effect of foreign aid on the international role of underdeveloped areas. To what extent is it an oversimplification to say that the purpose of foreign aid is to buy friends? Is foreign aid a bribe influencing the foreign policies of the governments of underdeveloped countries? Some years ago the late Jawaharlal Nehru, then prime minister of India, made a statement touching on India's relations with China. In the United States some members of Congress believed that Nehru's statement was not sufficiently anti-Chinese, since he was receiving foreign aid from us. Many said that we should therefore cut off foreign aid to India. In more recent years there have been similar incidents. Indonesia's Sukarno told us to "go to hell," even though he was receiving foreign aid from the United States. A more recent political cartoon showed Gamal Abdul Nasser receiving a CARE package and saying, "Thank you. Go to hell." And West Germany threatened to terminate its aid to the United Arab Republic if it gave a twenty-one-gun salute to Walter Ulbricht, the visiting East German leader. Are the underdeveloped areas really bought or bribed with policies of this kind?

To answer that question, it is necessary to distinguish among types of foreign aid. A wide variety of different public programs go by the same name, foreign aid. We have three types of policies under this umbrella—a policy of military assistance, a policy of economic assistance, and a policy of technical assistance. Sometimes the same U.S. governmental agency administers all three, but they are fundamentally different from one another.

Military aid is the current form of the old lend-lease idea of making military materials or supplies available to the governments of any countries whose defense the American President deems necessary to the defense of the United States. Economic aid has a history dating from the Marshall Plan and is a form of emergency assistance. A country devastated by war, flood, an earthquake, or crop failures and in an emergency situation is eligible for economic aid. Technical assistance is different from the other two in that it deals with the technological problem. Its purpose is to stimulate technological change or innovation in an underdeveloped country.

One difference among these types of foreign aid is that the first two are political in their objectives and short run in their conception, while technical assistance is not. If we give military assistance to a country we do it for a political reason, and we expect a fairly obvious foreign policy result in the immediate future. We give economic aid or defense support to a country, frequently in conjunction with military aid, for the same kind of immediate, short-run political purpose. Thus, military aid and defense support might be viewed as bribes that can be withdrawn from people who say, "Go to hell," but this is not true of technical assistance. Essentially long run and economic in its objective, technical assistance is directed toward the basic characteristics of the underdeveloped country's economy.[6]

All three of these programs are operating concurrently, each for a different purpose. Problems arise in the combinations of

6. For a useful theoretical discussion of the differences among types of foreign aid programs, see National Planning Association, *Technical Coöperation in Latin America* (Washington, D. C., National Planning Association, 1956).

the different types of foreign aid made available to the governments of various countries. In some, military aid and defense support are combined, and properly so. In others—and I think this is largely true of Latin America—there is not much military assistance or defense support, but the main United States program is technical assistance.

A question for the United States is whether the foreign aid packages available to participating countries are made up of relevant programs and proper combinations of programs. We may then ask what the effect of our foreign aid is on the countries involved. When a Sukarno or a Nasser says, "Thank you. Go to hell," it may be that the military aid and the defense support are not functioning properly, but that does not tell us anything about the value of our technical assistance. If I were insulted by what a Nasser or a Sukarno said, I might consider stopping military aid or defense support in his country, but that decision would be irrelevant in the matter of technical assistance.

If this basic theory of the nature of the underdeveloped economy is correct, in the long run the most important kind of foreign aid for underdeveloped areas is technical assistance. I think it would be ridiculous to terminate technical assistance to governments on the ground that they were not appropriately grateful.

A final point has to do with whether a species of evolutionism might not be involved in the concept of economic development. W. W. Rostow argues, for example, that there are identifiable stages of economic development—the traditional stage, a precondition to takeoff, the takeoff itself, then the mature economy, then the stage of high mass consumption. The differences among the stages involve, in the first place, the speed of change. In the traditional stage the rate of change is very slow; it is faster in the precondition stage and fastest of all in the takeoff. In the mature economy the rate of change slows down, but the level stays high.[7] This formulation has its problems. There is, for

7. Among W. W. Rostow's leading writings on the stages of economic growth are "The Take-off into Self-Sustained Growth," *The Economic Journal*, March 1956, pp. 25 ff.; *The Process of Economic Growth*, rev. ed. (New York, Norton, 1960); "Trends in the Allocation of Resources in Secular Growth," in Léon H. Dupriez, ed., *Economic Progress* (Louvain, 1955); "The Stages of Economic Growth," *The Economic History Review*, Series 2, XII:1, August, 1959; and *The Stages of Economic Growth* (New York, Oxford University Press, 1960).

example, the question of what we use the word "stage" to mean. If we define it as a condition that contains within it the seed of the next one, then we are in theoretical trouble. If, on the other hand, we use the term "stage" only as a handy or a convenient device for classification, the difficulties are fewer. Regardless of whatever else we may say about Rostow, I believe that economic development takes different forms and that rates of change differ in underdeveloped areas. It may well be that these areas are, among other things, the theaters of the most rapid change in the world today.

Does this suggest anything about foreign policy? Would a country in "takeoff," because it is changing rapidly, have a different kind of foreign policy than a country which is moving at a different rate of change? I suspect the answer is yes. Consider Mexico, for example. Because of its current state of economic development, Mexico really needs peace. If Mexico got involved in a serious war, it would be disastrous to the kinds of change going on in that country today. I would say the same thing about the stage of development of India today. India would be harmed internally by a major war.[8] Indonesia, however, is different. We might even argue that Indonesia needs a war or an international crisis for reasons related to the internal change process. Lucien Pye's analysis makes what to me is a fairly convincing case for saying that Indonesia at this stage in its development needs serious international crises (1) to hold the country together and (2) to try to get it into a more constructive phase in the change process.[9]

All this sounds intriguing, and I wish I could believe it more than I do. I also wish it could be more complete. I can pick out places like Mexico, India, and Indonesia, but obviously big, important pieces are missing. Cohesion of the society, including the economy, is a necessary thing in economic development. Indonesia needs that cohesion, and the only framework it has so far for the development of a national community and an identifiable culture is the one the Indonesians reject because it is associated with the Dutch. They desperately need one that they

8. On the Indian and Mexican cases, see Richard L. Park, "India's Foreign Policy," and Blanksten, "Foreign Policy of Mexico," both in Roy C. Macridis, ed., *Foreign Policy in World Politics,* 2nd ed. (Englewood Cliffs, Prentice-Hall, 1962), pp. 291–334.

9. Cf. Lucian W. Pye, "The Politics of Southeast Asia," in Almond and Coleman, *op. cit.,* pp. 65–152.

will not reject. Mexico, on the other hand, within the last generation has been through a major revolution and is now at the stage of remarkable industrialization and economic development, which is just reaching the point of institutionalization and bureaucratization. The whole country is like plate glass. We must not hit Mexico with an international crisis if we are to avoid shattering things that are important there. I think that in foreign policy Mexico will go to unreasonable extremes to avoid breaking the plate glass, but I wish I could be more complete on this. Obviously much is missing.

Internal and External Politics of Underdeveloped Countries

PABLO GONZÁLEZ CASANOVA
University of México

Two Aspects of Research

BEFORE STARTING the principal theme of this work, we should like to point out the fact that the politics of underdeveloped countries has two theoretical aspects: (1) as a problem of developed societies and (2) as a problem of underdeveloped societies. Although these two aspects are obvious, what is less obvious are their consequences throughout the total process of research, from the planting of hypotheses or assumptions up to the determination and formation of conclusions.

The difference between the aspects springs from various factors, among which we must point out the following: (1) the theory of what constitutes a problem in political science or political sociology; (2) predominant or acceptable rules for research and analysis of the problem; (3) techniques of interpretation; (4) ideology and rationalization; and (5) the basic intent of the research insofar as political science or political sociology is applicable.

These factors create a large dichotomy between the politics of underdeveloped countries as a problem of the developed world and as a problem of the underdeveloped world. Certainly there exist—and perhaps in ever increasing numbers—

researchers and intellectuals from underdeveloped societies who have studied in developed societies and who, by a
process of imitation or reflection, have taken on the outlook of
developed societies, their traditions and scientific disciplines,
their techniques and ideology, and have identified with them in
the course of their research. But these intellectuals do not easily
make the bridge between the two frames of reference, for various reasons. Some identify fully with the tradition of political
science in the developed countries, with the precepts, techniques, etc. They convert themselves into performers of a type
of research using models and theories borrowed from the
developed societies, arriving at data, confirming or rejecting
hypotheses, etc., and thereby canceling the possibility of enrichment of the academic life of the developed societies with the
viewpoint of the underdeveloped societies. Others, upon return-
ing to their countries of origin, acquire the viewpoints of these
countries and "forget" the traditions of the developed society.
They apply precepts and techniques with a freedom and irregu-
larity not permissible in the academic world from which they
have come.

In the background of this lack of scientific exchange is the
real difference in social and cultural systems as they apply to
these two types of researchers and the form in which their research disqualifies itself when conducted with the perspective
of an irrelevant society.

In the underdeveloped societies this process of disqualifying
the political science of researchers from advanced countries
(and their emulators) takes place promptly for two reasons:
First, to do valid research it is necessary to get at the real data of
the undeveloped country and not to imitate or import ideas from
the developed country with a "cosmopolitan" or "colonialist" attitude. Second, it is necessary to apply the political science of the
advanced country with due regard for the ideology and reasoning
of the underdeveloped country's own interests.

To these conclusions must be added the socio-cultural circumstances which move the intellectual from the underdeveloped
countries to his college, whether Oxford or Harvard; the lack of
concrete frames of reference, which facilitates his administrative and political career but hampers the progress of his research
and his academic life according to the pattern of the developed
countries; the lack of economic and human resources, which

prevents him from continuing his research with recognized principles and techniques; his youth or a lack of scientific attitude in the environment, plus the need of confining himself to political limits; his scientific vocabulary, reflecting a lack of technical terms and of the more sophisticated tools of analysis; the needs and functions of new nations, which eliminate or leave to one side the traditional problems of political science in order to solve a series of problems having no traditional place in the political science of the developed countries.

All this change in political science and ideology in the underdeveloped world results in a process which the scholars in developed countries do not identify as a science—that is, as a source of problems or techniques of analysis—but more as an ideology or object of study. And to this is added various well-founded arguments. Actually the ideologist or researcher who has experienced the metamorphosis of the underdeveloped society does not strictly adhere to the principles of analysis and research. He takes great liberties with interpretative techniques, relating these to the disqualifying ideologies and rationalizations of his own political situation. These arguments are likewise relatively definitive, and evoke a clear image of the problems of appropriate rationalization and the problems of the intellectual leaders of the underdeveloped world as researchers.

Under such circumstances certain psychological problems are engendered at international scientific conferences and in scientific exchange between the intellectual elites of developed and underdeveloped countries—problems of courtesy, of excessive sensitivity, of the difficulty in carrying on objective dialogue with regard to "tabu" problems, and the like. Yet it is not this fact alone that we wish to emphasize here, but rather the importance it assumes in political science research, in analyzing the work, speeches, and writings of the ideologists and leaders of the underdeveloped world, in order to understand what experiences they reflect and what has influenced them in reaching their concrete political conclusions. The chief problem in collecting and recording the conclusions of the intellectuals and leaders of the underdeveloped countries is to consider them as mere theories of investigation and to apply to them the techniques of investigation, of the rigorous analysis and interpretation commonly accepted by the academic world in advanced countries.

The adopting of "conclusions," "watchwords," and "principles" by leaders in underdeveloped countries and the formulation of hypotheses of research with a method such as McClelland proposes for a study of philosophers, historians, and economists of the developed world [1] should have two important results: (1) usefulness, experience, the "trial" of development as it may relate to the premises or conclusions of the leaders who have changed these societies and (2) the enrichment of political science in the developed countries as far as hypotheses concerning the development of underdeveloped countries are concerned.

With this objective we may now select some political ideas of the leaders of the underdeveloped world that show most clearly the relationship between internal and external politics. We shall state them in the form of assumptions, in order to point out the method of research on this problem in its ultimate stages.

SOME POLITICAL PRINCIPLES OF UNDERDEVELOPED COUNTRIES THAT CONTAIN A THEORY ABOUT INTERNAL AND EXTERNAL POLITICS

There exists in our time a group of principles, relatively generalized among intellectuals and leaders of new nations, which establish a form of practical theory with regard to development and are tied to internal and external politics. These principles have several characteristics: (1) They are the result of a struggle against magic and metaphysical misconceptions, against the emotional elements of mere enthusiasm and mere goodwill which give free rein to fantasy and imagination without allowing opportunity for positive action.[2] (2) There exist side by side, and frequently blended with the rationalizations, the ideologies of traditional and modern society. These can be distinguished by common sense—intellectual and even practical— and by the form in which they recur in administrative and economic programs. (3) They recognize the history of underdeveloped countries, experiences which repeat themselves there, and they involve generalizations about development and

1. See David McClelland, *The Achieving Society* (New York, Van Nostrand, 1961), pp. 22 ff.
2. See Gamal Abdul Nasser, *Egypt's Liberation: The Philosophy of the Revolution* (Washington, D. C., Public Affairs Press, 1956).

differences in development. From this point of view they constitute rejection of the undifferentiated generalizations concerning
development which characterized philosophical and scientific research in the nineteenth century. (4) They correspond to intellectual preoccupations of a strategic type necessary in studying
the requisites of action, plans, programs—with an attitude
similar to that of the military or guerrilla leader. (5) They
are formulated in very unaffected language, easily transmissible
to the masses as conclusions or procedures for effective political
action. (6) This type of communication varies its rational and
dogmatic characteristics, depending upon the leaders and the
culture of the public.

Determination of principles or premises—a development
which finds itself in vogue in the new nations—is the ideological
and political instrument of its leaders. The degree of popularity
and the limits of its acceptance in these countries have not been
studied sufficiently. For this reason it is possible that we are
going to declare the continuation of some principles that are
less common than others, that spread less generally. Similarly,
it is certain that our enumeration means nothing without the
most important principles or premises:

*Independence.—No country is able to develop without inde-
pendence, which permits it to enter into relationships with other
countries on an equal plane.* Any struggle or violence against
independence, sovereignty, and the free will of the people is an
attack against the development of the country. "If the problem
of man," says Sékou Touré, "were reformulated, for colonial
peoples the only true problem that can be advanced is the
problem of obtaining independence." [3] "The first objective is
political independence," says Nkrumah, and there is a "bridge
of gold" between total independence and economic, political,
and cultural development.[4] And Sukarno states, "To set back or
to violate on whatever pretext the independence of a people is
to violate its total development." [5]

This struggle for political independence does not imply a struggle for isolation or autarchy. Quite the contrary. It implies the

3. Sékou Touré, *L'Action politique du parti démocratique de Guinée*
(Paris, Présence Africaine, 1959), p. 26.
4. Kwame Nkrumah, *I Speak of Freedom* (New York, Praeger, 1961),
pp. vii–viii.
5. Sukarno, in a release by the Department of Information, Republic of
Indonesia, Djakarta, November 10, 1960.

elimination of colonialism, and it means the cooperation of free nations—in particular those with a common heritage and similar background (Latin America, Africa, Asia). It implies the establishment of political and economic bonds between the weak, poor, and underindustrialized in order to strengthen their independence. From Caracas to Bandung and to the most recent congresses in Cairo the necessity of union, of cooperation and alliance between former colonies with a common legacy or similar background—this has been the moving principle of independence for these countries. Isolation has been, and is, a symptom of weakness and colonialism. Union is symptomatic of, and a motivator of, independence.[6]

Total independence.—Mere political independence is not enough, but it is unquestionably necessary, as is military, economic, and cultural independence. With such independence a country breaks at the same time the colonialist political, military, economic, and cultural monopoly, also that of production and export markets. The importation of goods and capital is diversified, as well as international relations, cultural ties, and sources of information. "All revolution of the twentieth century occurs simultaneously in all spheres of life and human existence," writes Sukarno. "In the political area and also the economic area, and in the social and military field—all at the same time. It does not happen as in former centuries when revolutions were frequently only political, or only economic, or only social, or only military. Revolution in our time is a simultaneous revolution: social, cultural, of every type."

To make a revolution or a struggle for independence affect development, it is necessary deliberately to affect at the same time political, economic, and cultural independence. "That which in other countries has taken three hundred years or more must, in dependent territory, be brought to a head in a single generation in order to survive." [7]

Total independence and social justice.—If independence ought at the same time to be political, economic, and cultural, independence at its very roots must maintain individual in-

6. Cf. *Asia-Africa Speaks from Bandoong* (Republic of Indonesia, Ministry of Foreign Affairs), pp. 161–69; for the Cairo conference, see Jacques Arnault, *Procès du colonialisme* (Paris, Editions Sociales, 1958), pp. 297–301.
7. Kwame Nkrumah, *op. cit.*, pp. VII–VIII.

dependence and promote development accompanied by social, economic, political, and cultural revolution. "All the peoples of the earth have gone through two revolutions: first, a political revolution in which they exchanged tyranny or an army of occupation for the rights of self-government. And, at the same time, a social revolution, implying class struggle, terminating only when justice is assured for all the citizens of the united nation." [8]

Thus the struggle for independence has to be at the same time a struggle for social justice. Without social justice, concurrent with or immediately following independence, independence is neither obtained nor maintained. Separate government of the people is easily destroyed by colonialism or by colonial and semicolonial oligarchies. In order to strengthen independence, the state must redistribute wealth, land, profits, culture, power. In order to maintain and strengthen independence it is necessary to abolish social plurality, characteristic of colonial societies, and abolish social and geographic isolation, with its unequal treatment of indigenous populations and its national disintegration. Where such objectives are not held in view, independence is weakened or lost.

Consciousness of this need for social justice and national integration as essential factors of development is very generalized. It frequently expresses itself as a phenomenon not only of international but internal character, i.e., decolonialization. "When we speak of decolonialization," says Sékou Touré, "we think implicitly of destroying those habits, conceptions, modes of behavior of colonialism. We think of replacing them with national formulae, concepts of our people adopted to the conditions, means, aspirations of the people of Guinea. . . . Decolonialization ought to put an end to exploitation, spoils, injustice—and ought to assure the reform of these particular disgraces, of these various practices of division and opposition, into the practice of unity and cooperation." [9] Thus the measure of gain of social justice, equality, and integration is a measure of independence. The measure of gain in eliminating colonialist and neocolonialist exploitation is the measure of independence. On the other hand, the measure in which social injustice, inequality, plural society, and segregation are maintained is also the

8. Nasser, *op. cit.*
9. Sékou Touré, *op. cit.*, pp. 64–65.

measure of the existence of labor exploitation, the measure of forces resisting independence.

Social justice and development.—Now, then, if independence is a requisite for development and social justice, a requisite for the continuation and growth of independence, social justice, then, is a requisite of development. Without independence there is no development. Without social justice there is no continuation of independence. Without social justice there is no development. At worst, there is an increase in colonialism or paracolonialism.

The principle, stated solely in economic terms, is this: Underdeveloped countries that depend fundamentally upon an external market for their development cannot industrialize themselves and are highly vulnerable. Without internal markets there is no development, and in order to have internal markets it is necessary to instigate (1) a redistribution of wealth and (2) a redistribution of profits. (Perhaps one of the most notable examples of the affirmation of this principle exists in Mexico— from Cárdenas up to the present day. It is characteristic, ideologically, not only of the leaders but also of the Mexican school of economics, influenced by revolutionary and Keynesian ideas.)

The market is historically the main factor in development. Capitalization and investment depend upon the market. For one thing, expansion of trade generally follows an expansion in investment, capitalization, and industrialization. In the beginning, development of trade preceded capitalization and investment. So while ancient empires were able to initiate development apart from the external market and while great monopolistic enterprises in our time have artificially created an external market where there was none, founded either on wartime or peacetime penetration, the new countries are not able to depend upon the outside market for their development. They are not able to pretend to dominate the colonial market or whatever may be the base of their capitalization, their investments, their industrialization. New nations can only rely upon the growth of their internal market and the protection of their products and imports to the outside market.

The internal market is thus primarily for development; it is an essential part of development. And as underdeveloped countries are fundamentally agricultural (and the reason for bad distribution of investment, for limitation of monetary economy is the large estates and plantations which impede the existence of a national market) the first requisite of politics of development is agrarian reform, which distributes the land to the people, frees the worker from the traditional society, and increases the monetary economy. Without agrarian reform it is not possible to have development in the present underdeveloped nations.

Yet agrarian reform is not enough. Redistribution of investment by strata, branches, and sectors is necessary in order to maintain and increase internal trade and to enable the ultimate consumers to maintain incentive for investment in capitalizing industrialization. To this end, above all a policy of higher wages is required—as well as every type of fiscal and anti-inflationary measure—in order to promote the most equal redistribution of investment and finally to increase trade.

Thus whatever limitation there is in agrarian reform, in the policy of wages, in the levying of progressive and direct taxes, in the earning power of money that exists is a limitation of development.

Capitalization, expropriation, and industrialization.—A clear model of the policy of development requires taking a series of steps to facilitate national capitalization. Even though it is false to say that poor countries, in order to develop themselves, need capital and technical aid from abroad, and also false to convert foreign capital and foreign technical aid into the cornerstone of development, what is absolutely certain is that the poor countries need capital for development. Lacking colonies which would permit the acceleration of capitalization and needing to increase their internal trade, the only means of accumulating capital left to them are (1) to expropriate foreign goods and industries, particularly communications, transportation, basic industries (a practice defended and practiced by various leaders from Cárdenas to Ben Bella) and (2) to protect the price of raw materials and the balance of exchange—this last policy even more generally practiced by leaders of the underdeveloped countries—as well as to recognize alliances and establishments of commercial agreements with countries producing similar products, such as sugar, coffee, silver, etc.

On the other hand, in order to develop its economy it is necessary for the country to industrialize. A commonly accepted theory, and one defined by Colin Clark, is that economic development implies the augmentation of per capita production in primary, secondary, and tertiary activities (intensive capitalization) and transference of manpower from minor to major activities of production (extensive capitalization). In a capitalist system of free enterprise this requires an increase in incentive for native investment, the establishment of a system protecting national industry and a system of currency control, a control of external commerce,[10] and a control of foreign investments. Thus in order to have development, a policy of national capitalization is necessary, and capitalization requires a policy with regard to expropriation and nationalization of industries and foreign properties. Also necessary is a policy of industrialization and with it a revised policy pertaining to the control of exchange and the decontrol of foreign investments and foreign commerce.

The state and its development.—Nevertheless these requirements are still not sufficient. To encourage investment and to stimulate national capitalization necessitates the intervention of the state. Opposing large economic units and the wealth of the large monopolies of our times, the government of the underdeveloped and weak nation must have the necessary strength to defend itself in the economic struggle, liberating itself in its own country. Native and private unity is always weaker than monopolies and easily dominated or destroyed. Not only for this reason is the intervention of the state of the new country or the underdeveloped country necessary in economic life, but also, in these countries where natives are accustomed to regarding trade as something alien and mysterious, the only thing that can promote investment is the state. Its investments generate a demand which in turn generates other investments. "It is not a question, as one supposes, of choosing between the alternatives, *laissez faire* or interventionism; but between development or economic stagnation." [11] The state must step in and organize development and must assume the role of producer. This principle has signified a "boom" ever since 1918 and has had antecedents throughout all the history of capitalism and development. Since World War II it has been the common heritage of all economists partial

10. Caio Prado Junior, *Esboço dos fundamentos da teoria econômica* (São Paulo, Editora Brasiliense, 1957), pp. 219–21.

11. Aldo Ferrer, *et al., El estado y el desarrollo económico* (Buenos Aires, Editiones Raigal, 1956), p. 151.

to "interventionism" and the ideology of the underdeveloped world. It does not derive from a "specific ideology," nor is it reducible to "in the main, similarities found in Russian motives and forms." [12] "It is not inspired by any conception of general order," [13] and today thinkers of the most diverse ideologies support it. "The governments of underdeveloped countries that endeavor to move their economy from a dead stop must carry out most coordinated planning and make real the labor of stimulation and guidance in social and economic areas, much more than is required in highly-developed countries," states one frankly conservative author.[14]

Connected with state intervention is the programing of project-making and the planning of economic development. In fact, in our times it is a commonplace that development must be planned, that it requires a rational, coordinated technical use of resources. India, Indonesia, Guinea, Cuba (even before becoming socialist) had elaborate plans for national development.

To have effective national development, it is necessary that a country apply, and have recourse to, all techniques of economic and social planning. Never has this premise been so popular as in our time and in our countries, to the degree that no technician or leader can avoid admitting that planning is necessary and undertake, at the very least, partial tasks of planning. The idea that planning is contrary to liberty and human respect does not flourish in underdeveloped countries. "It is obvious that any honest plan," says Nehru, "is capable of effecting a free national government, sufficiently strong and sufficiently popular only by meeting the possibility of introducing fundamental changes in the social and economic structure." [15]

Development and democracy.—The politics of development requires an independent government, and the only way of obtaining this independent government is through close ties between government and people. Under these conditions democracy exists in its genuine sense, since participation of the people

12. Alfred Bonne, *State and Economics in the Middle East and Society in Transition,* 2nd ed. (London, Routledge and Kegan Paul, 1955), pp. 75–76.
13. Prado Junior, *op. cit.,* p. 218.
14. Eugene Staley, *The Future of Underdeveloped Countries* (New York, Harper, 1954), p. 235.
15. Jawaharlal Nehru, *The Discovery of India* (London, Meridian Books, 1956), p. 401.

in the economy, the culture, and the power, as well as national unity, is necessary to the state's being an effective instrument of development.

Yet the definition of democracy can be limited to forms which have obtained historically in modern Europe or in the United States, with bi-party or multi-party systems, with groups that periodically alternate in power and stand for diametrically opposed political platforms, with a government that maintains a Montesquieuan division of power with a Madisonian system of checks and balances. The experiences of the underdeveloped countries which have applied this model of democracy are known well enough; in reality a simulated democracy is arrived at with the concentration of power in an authoritarian head of state or in the landowning oligarchy or in the military caste. The system operates with democratic forms in an authoritarian reality, disuniting the mass of people. The division of government and the division of the parties are formidable instruments of oppression of great colonialist or neocolonialist powers which play with these divisions or manipulate them so as to affect the interests and the power of the governments in these lesser examples of political independence.

By definition democracy must mean a type of government really working for development and truly democratic. To keep the essence of democracy in at least one or two of its aspects— government of the people, by the people, and for the people— and to assure participation of the people in the government and the development of the country is a clear goal not to be confused with the diminution of democracy in its classical European and North American forms. As Sékou Touré says, "There are democratic and non-democratic states and they are distinguished, one from the other, by the importance of the role the masses play; by the importance of participation of the people in the affairs of State." [16]

The government that works best for development is that in which democracy depends upon maximum participation of the people in the government, with the help of, and the surrender to the public of, the resources and instruments that enable them to govern: economic, military, political, cultural. In this sense a government is democratic in the way in which it hands

16. Sékou Touré, *op. cit.*, p. 49.

over to the people the instruments of economy and war, the political know-how and the political organizations of farmers, workers, and administrators. It is democratic when its representatives are designated by popular vote, with respect to units of production and service, and when it is oriented to the masses with respect to technicians and technical advisers—thus educating and explaining reasonably to the masses the motives of political and technical decisions. A government which hands over to the people the military apparatus, the basic organizations, and the technical and political reasoning is a government founded on the necessity of public service—one in which politics is respectful of the organized popular forces, strongly based internally and strongly facing external pressures.[17]

With reason David E. Apter says, in speaking of nationalist leaders of the underdeveloped countries, "These leaders face a tremendous dilemma. They must reconcile the need for extensive popular participation in political life, yet it is indispensable that they maintain themselves and also exhibit highly integrated and effective leadership, . . . and they must fulfill such needs as education, social well-being, and the increase of revenue." [18] Apter concludes that the ideal policy is that of an open fraternal party of the masses deriving legitimacy from a broad base and acquiring social mobility through participation of its members. This type of party has socialistic characteristics in its ideology and practices. Its emphasis on democracy succeeds in promoting development and promotes, as well, both equality of opportunity and the major participation of all.[19] Lipset also says with reason that "given the pressure of rapid industrialization, and for immediate solution of the chronic problems of poverty and hunger through the means of political instruments, it is unlikely that many of the new governments of Asia and Africa will characterize themselves by a system of open parties representing different class positions and values." [20] "Democratic centralism,"

17. Fidel Castro, *Discurso del 1° mayo* (La Habaña, 1960).
18. The author uses the word "oligarchy," a phenomenon occurring with frequency in this situation, but not with necessity.
19. See David E. Apter, "Nationalism, Government, and Economic Growth," in *Economic Development and Cultural Change* (Chicago, University of Chicago Press, 1959), pp. 117–36.
20. Seymour Martin Lipset, "Some Social Requisites of Democracy: Economic Development and Political Legitimacy," *American Political Science Review*, LIII:2, March 1959, pp. 69–105, quotation from pp. 101–102.

"guided democracy," and "directed democracy" can augment the participation of the people in the government and are the most effective instruments for national development, for national integration, and for self-determination of the state.

National unity and development.—Apart from the type of democracy pointed out above, the instruments most suitable for development are national unity, the national conscience, and the elimination of division in the national population according to location, tribe, community, party, or region. The state, as a functional instrument of development, accomplishes national unity by political and economic ideology, implants national symbols, as opposed to foreign, tribal, and factional symbols, and increases internal trade—thus alleviating differences of class, region, and race through a redistribution of wealth and income. The policy best suited to development is the policy invoked by national unity and by a "nationalist anti-imperialist front" which underdeveloped peoples formulate upon the basis of historical experience and their political needs, which are only incidentally tied to Communist slogans and tactics. This policy, which represents the essence of nationalism in underdeveloped countries and is surely the least understood in the developed world, most directly binds the problems of internal politics to external politics.

"Undoubtedly," says Sukarno, talking about the delay in accepting this policy, "they do not understand, because, without doubt, they are not experts in revolution, that the basis for any national revolution opposing imperialism-colonialism is the concentration of national forces and not the breaking of national forces." [21]

Following this principle, the most suitable policy for recently liberated or weak nations is their internal union and their federal union when cultural, economic, and political differences do not admit greater integration and in international alliances and treaties when they belong to different geographic zones and different continents. Whatever limitation there is to national unity, national conscience, national integration, and the alliance of nations and new states is a limitation to development.

The principles and premises enumerated above are, as we

21. Statement by Sukarno, Djakarta, August, 1959.

have said, the commonplace of a political science of nations and a policy for development. Products of extensive historical experience and reflection about the necessary means for development, one finds them in scattered or partial form in the speeches and writings of the leaders of underdeveloped countries and in the political conscience of the most active of the poor nations. Some of them appear formulated as accounts or conditions of the politics of development, and there is a permanent possibility of expressing them in one way or the other.

But the simple acceptance or pronouncement of these principles is not enough to accomplish development, and the generalizations they point up do not always have a necessarily constant character. Instruments of development—independence, social justice, etc.—although they cannot be fulfilled at every moment or in a permanent manner, do convert themselves into goals and require a strategy that analyzes concrete conditions, circumstances, and sequences. This strategy is the theme of a political consideration no less important, although perhaps even more removed from the academic consciousness of the developed world. Based upon a kind of trial and error in the underdeveloped countries, upon their failures and successes, upon their history, it effects ties, in the political truth of our time, with the Socialist and Communist movements, although it does not derive necessarily from the establishment of this type of government. But its single tie to the Marxist ideology does make still more difficult its consideration as far as the theory of development is concerned. Only occasionally does the non-Communist academic world take account of this circumstance.[22]

Some of the principles are as follows:

Revolution and development.—The development of a nation and the instruments necessary for this (independence, agrarian reform, social justice, decolonialization, democracy, national unity) generally have taken place through capitalistic or socialistic revolution. In order to have economic growth in certain sectors of a territory or a nation, as a function of colonialist or neo-colonialist forces—in order to have development—social revolution is necessary.

Revolution and "revolutionaries."—But to recognize this principle is not enough; it is necessary to apply it, and only

22. Cf. C. Wright Mills, *The Marxists* (New York, Dell, 1962).

revolutionary force can apply it—the middle classes, the workers, the farmers. The leaders of great power or landowning classes cannot apply it, although ideologically they recognize the need for agrarian reform, for social justice, for democratization. They cannot because these social revolutions are directly against their interests and precisely because they are the enemy of agrarian reform, of the redistribution of income, of democratization. Although they discuss theories or laws ostensibly favorable to reform, even up to and including revolution, at the moment of effective political action they are the bitterest of enemies and use every force at their disposal to eliminate the theories and laws with ideologies and rationalizations based upon classical liberalism.

The difficulty of a "bourgeois" revolution or "democratic" revolution of the classic type.—On the other hand, in our time it is constantly more difficult to create a national, capitalistic, and democratic revolution of the classic type. Imperialism, with all its weapons of force—boycotts, embargoes, mercenaries—nips in the bud this type of revolution by using constitutional law, parties, freedom of the press, the conditions of internal and external trade, and other devices to destroy revolutionary movements at their start, giving the nationalist and democratic groups the alternative of defeat or the establishment of a government of national unity and directed democracy (or, in extreme cases, a Socialist or Communist government).

Revolution and socialism.—Finally, in ever increasing numbers the leaders and the intellectuals of new nations maintain that the best system of development is socialism, since it permits in a suitable manner the achievement of national integral independence, decolonialization, social justice, national capitalization, state intervention and planning, the new democracy, and national unity as well as the highest standards of development. Although the definition of what constitutes socialism differs greatly from leader to leader, the idea that socialism is the most suitable instrument for development exists throughout the underdeveloped world among both Communist and anti-Communist leaders.

In 1951 an expert at the United Nations wrote: "In our opinion, today there are a good number of underdeveloped countries in which the concentration of economic and political power in the hands of a small class, whose main interest is in the preservation of its own wealth and privilege, eliminates the possibility of considerable economic progress until a social revolution brings about change in the distribution of income and power." [23] Slowly, in the course of these last years, principles which were formerly exclusive to the underdeveloped world are being adopted into the political ideology and the academic thinking of the developed world. The need for agrarian reform, the need for a planned economy, and the usefulness of a single party are several examples of ideas and generalizations formulated in a distant world and adopted by the administration of the great powers and by their intellectuals. Nevertheless, until today it was exceptional to consider them as hypotheses of development, defining and analyzing them with the most advanced methods of the social sciences either for a study of the internal and external politics of these countries or for the specific study of interaction between internal and external politics of the underdeveloped world. It seems plausible to predict that political science and political sociology will advance significantly if they make a systematic analysis of this type.

All the principles enunciated above register a series of relationships existing between internal and external politics, visible in the underdeveloped world. In continuation we will make a résumé of these relationships:

Independence—internal development.

Equality of the states—internal development.

Interalliances of underdeveloped countries—internal development.

Integral independence (political, military, economic, and cultural)—internal development.

Independence—social justice.

Decolonialization with regard to the outside—internal decolonialization.

Lack of external trade, with favorable currency relationships (colonial or semicolonial)—internal trade as a mover of development—agrarian reform, including foreign ownership.

Industrialization as a form of development—protection of industry against foreign interests.

23. United Nations Technical Assistance Administration, *Standards and Techniques of Public Administration, with Special Reference to Technical Assistance to Underdeveloped Countries* (New York, United Nations, 1951), II, B, 7.

National capitalization—expropriation of energy resources in foreign hands—control of foreign investments.

International monopolistic rivalry—need for the intervention of the state in the economy of the underdeveloped country.

Multipartitism, the division of powers and federalism— weakness of internal and external government.

Disunity of government and people—weakness toward foreign countries.

Classical "foreign" democracy not suitable for development— democracy of a new type, directed and controlled, with one sole or predominant party—the definition of democracy in the function of the people's participation in government, culture, and economy.

The politics of national unity—opposed to foreign penetration, opposed to the division of the population by locality, tribe, class line, community, region.

Social revolution against national and foreign-effected interests—national development.

Social revolution—socialism—zones of influence—cold war.

All these principles or generalizations receive ideological confirmation or rejection in the developed world. The main question is to know whether it is a matter of viable hypothesis or mere rationalization. To this end there are various problems to take into account:

1. The rationalizations of the developed world concerning the politics of the underdeveloped world tend to exaggerate as evils the importance of internal factors (racial, cultural, political).

2. On the contrary, the rationalizations of the underdeveloped world tend toward overestimation of external factors (colonialism, imperialism).

3. The true interaction of the internal and external factors and of internal and international politics alone can clarify a system of hypothesis to which we can apply the most rigorous techniques of today. If we fulfill this task in analyzing the suppositions and generalizations of the underdeveloped world we need:

First, to define the most significant principles or generalizations and their frequency among chiefs of state, leaders, and intellectuals; in political organizations (movements, parties, syndicates); among masses, classes, groups (the theoretical participants); among employers, employees, workers, urban and rural populations). Techniques of content analysis and direct inquiries are necessary to this end.

Second, to reduce the most significant principles to true hypotheses, through a study of their formation, definition, language, logical sequence, and empirical base; level of generalization and degree of differentiation; and degree of rationality and dogmatism.

Third, to elaborate the operating definitions of each hypothesis and choose the most suitable indicators from among those which are certainly found frequently and from those which Deutsch has pointed out.

Fourth, to use forms of analysis similar to those used by McClelland and to add others from diverse researches, analyses of coincidence, etc., that promise an empirical research with political hypotheses objectively formulated.

Fifth, to remember, as did Lipset and Bendix years ago, that "the methodology of research can only measure the present behavior of the people and the changes produced in recent periods" and "only bring limited perspective"; and to decide whether it is necessary to complete these perspectives with old and new methods of historical analysis.

We believe that if political science enriches its field of investigation with regard to the underdeveloped world not only with data and ideologies of this world but with its hypotheses, and if it applies to them the rigid techniques of investigation, it can advance with the greatest rapidity in its theoretical and applied aspects.

PART THREE

The Open–Closed Polity
Dichotomy

IT IS PERHAPS UNFORTUNATE that in recent years the open-closed polity dichotomy has received less attention as a subject for the development of general empirical theory than has the developed-underdeveloped dichotomy. There has been much attention to individual countries, and historians and political specialists have suggested important links between the internal politics of a given country and its foreign policy. Although, as Professor Rosenau's pre-theory suggests, the open-closed polity question may be an important one for foreign policy analysis, there is a dearth of new general theory. On the other hand, this has been a topic which has profoundly interested political theorists in the past, from Plato to Locke to Marx.

Professor Norton Long's discussion is intended to remind the reader of some of the major questions regarding the open and closed political societies which have interested earlier thinkers—and at the same time to relate some of their thought to modern problems. Although his concern is not alone with foreign relations, he points to some of the implications of closure from Plato to Marx on the affairs of politics and society. If contemporary closed societies must have a comprehensive ideology which is incompatible with others, the question remains whether that ideology must always guide action. Professor Long observes that "in the history of the world many fighting, totalitarian, and logically hopelessly incompatible faiths have learned to live together." And he asks the question "whether with time the dependence of the Communists on the myth of incompatibility and ultimate victory can be dispensed with."

The second paper, by the editor, attempts to relate foreign policy to the organization of government according to whether the polity is more open or more closed. It suggests some tentative generalizations about characteristic aspects of closed and open societies which in the areas of foreign policy may affect the perceptions of decision-makers, the decisional context, and the interrelations between structure and process and decisional outcomes. The effort has the limitations of travel in uncharted ways. Conclusions lack the firmness one might wish for and must suffer from the absence of previously developed rigorous general theory in several areas.

Both authors are troubled by the normative problem posed by the terms "open" and "closed." There is a tendency to place a value of "good" on the open society, which may unconsciously bias one's estimate of its qualities while depreciating its opposite. In this respect the open-closed dichotomy poses problems similar to the developed-underdeveloped dichotomy. For both we probably need new terminology. And for both we must offer a further caution: that though the dichotomized opposites may have some meaning for classification and analysis, the real cases are somewhere in between—more or less open, more or less closed, more or less developed, more or less underdeveloped. The current theories of economic development have introduced concepts of levels of development; the analysis of open and closed societies usefully moves toward similar refinements.

Open and Closed Systems

NORTON E. LONG
Brandeis University

ATHENS AND SPARTA have come to assume almost Weberian ideal typicality as exemplars of open and closed political systems. The funeral oration of Pericles, as reported by Thucydides and the writings of Plato—especially the *Republic*, the *Statesman*, and the *Laws*—have given them magnetic imaginative power in the political tradition of the West. So much so that Karl Popper,[1] in his defense of the open society against its totalitarian enemies, feels it necessary to attack Plato and all his political works, including his past and present influence in the history of political ideas. The defense of Plato has been hard put to transform Plato into a friend and ally of modern, liberal, constitutional democracy rather than of the closed society. The case for Aristotle, while not on philosophical grounds completely reassuring, is, in the realm of political ideas and influence, far more supportive of constitutionalism and liberty. A consideration of the critical dimensions of open and closed political systems may well begin with Plato, since his writings provide the most thorough philosophic exposition of a closed system and

1. Karl Popper, *The Open Society and Its Enemies* (Princeton, Princeton University Press, 1950).

155

since his influence, at least in the realm of ideas, has been in-calculable.

Popper may not be right in classifying Plato as a totalitarian. The Greek city-state is so lacking in comparability to the modern nation-state that comparisons between the two are at best of un-certain value. The criteria that Friedrich and Brzezinski adopt as standards by which to identify totalitarian dictatorships would certainly exclude Plato from their classification.[2] In fact, of course, they find totalitarian dictatorship a strictly modern political phenomenon, impossible without modern technology. In this they may well be right. At all events Plato's concern with the political life was total and the appropriate concern of government, in his view, utterly comprehensive. In the identifi-cation of public, private, economic, and religious life as all proper subjects for political direction, Plato was certainly a totalitarian.

At the center of Plato's political system, giving to the whole a kind of deductive logical coherence, is a political ideology of a near-unchanging perfection. Final truth is open to the vision of the philosophic ruler and in a measure attainable by the ap-propriate manipulation and indoctrination of the subjects. Change is the great enemy of nearly achieved human perfec-tion, and it must be guarded against by all means possible. Stability is the highest good, and it must be achieved by every imaginable device. Given the near realization of perfection, no other position is acceptable. The same, of course, applies to paradise. Hamilton's acid comments on angelic behavior are in point. Since men are not angels they must be made as angels to accept paradise and learn to live in it and enjoy it in a whole-souled contentment. The problem of realizing paradise on earth and conditioning men to accept it voluntarily has plagued politi-cal theorists from Plato on. As Talmon shows, it was a major difficulty of those messianic prophets of totalitarian democracy, the Jacobins.[3]

Hannah Arendt put her finger on the one opening most difficult for the closed system to guard against, the infiltration of

2. C. J. Friedrich and Z. K. Brzezinski, *Totalitarian Dictatorship and Autocracy,* rev. ed. (Cambridge, Harvard University Press, 1965), Chap. 2.
3. J. L. Talmon, *The Origins of Totalitarian Democracy* (New York, Praeger, 1960).

mutant strangers into the system by the accidents of birth.[4] Indeed Plato appears to have believed that the decline of his earthly paradise would follow a failure in the breeding arrangements that might upset his educational conditioning. "The greatest principle of all," Plato writes, "is that nobody, whether male or female, should ever be without a leader. Nor should the mind of anybody be habituated to letting him do anything at all on his own initiative, neither out of zeal, nor even playfully. But in war and the midst of peace—to his leader he shall direct his eye, and follow him faithfully. And even in the smallest matters he should stand under leadership. For example, he should get up, or move, or wash, or take his meals . . . only if he has been told to do so. . . . In a word, he should teach his soul, by long habit, never to dream of acting independently, and to become utterly incapable of it. In this way the life of all will be spent in total community. There is no law, nor will there ever be one, which is superior to this, or better and more effective in ensuring salvation and victory in war. And in times of peace, and from the earliest childhood on, should it be fostered—this habit of ruling others and of being ruled by others. And every trace of anarchy should be utterly eradicated from the life of all men, and even of the wild beasts which are subject to men."[5] Plato's deep concern with the individual as a source of change, which means decay from a state of perfection, is shared by later protagonists of the closed system. According to Sabine, "In 1958 Khrushchev told the party, in words that Lenin might have used, 'Spontaneity, comrades, is the deadliest enemy of all.'"[6]

Plato's concern with change is directed toward conserving as perfectly as possible the initial imprint of the divine forms on the human material. Thus the best possible society is to be achieved at a stroke through massive education and the exclusion of all unwanted and uncontrollable influences that might corrupt the system. Closure is desired both because the best possible state has been achieved and the sole task is its maintenance and because it must be protected from sources of contamination and

4. Hannah Arendt, *The Origins of Totalitarianism* (Cleveland, Meridian, 1950).

5. Quoted in Karl Popper, *op. cit.*, p. 9.

6. Quoted in George H. Sabine, *A History of Political Theory*, 3rd ed. (New York, Holt, Rinehart and Winston, 1961), p. 881.

decay by internal malfunctioning and noxious external contact. Much of Plato's totalitarianism may be due less to the necessary elaboration of the idea of the good than to the fear that no area could be allowed to escape control because of its possible contaminating effect on areas deemed vital. Friedrich and Brzezinski suggest that totalitarian elaboration occurs as a result of opposition within the regime rather than as the result of a preconceived dogma of total coverage. In fact, for those with a messianic creed it may be difficult to conceive of any area as indifferent and to be tolerated as the private area. The Muslim conqueror is reputed to have asked if the books in the Alexandria Library agreed with the Koran. If they did, they were superfluous; if they did not, they were noxious and so in any event should be destroyed. The Jacobins, in their passion for an egalitarian uniformity, seemed to regard the desire for privacy as a kind of excuse either to plot against the general will or to neglect the all-embracing civic role. De Tocqueville found a similar majoritarian tyranny developing in the conformist demands of mass democracy. This may be contrasted with the explicit defense of privacy and the right to differ expressed by Pericles.

The various exponents of the closed system, whether Plato, the Soviet Marxists, the Fascists, or the messianic totalitarian democrats, all claim a vision into final human perfection and a special capacity for understanding and bringing the vision to realization. This claim is the core of their varying principles of legitimacy by which they justify to themselves and others their right to power. Since, in effect, all these visions represent a heaven on earth and a final point in history, they provide an ethic of all-embracing and ultimate ends. As they are not based on any controllable, piecemeal empiricism, their appropriate methodology is logical elaboration, with Ptolemaic epicycles to account for any indigestible bits of inescapable fact. The entangling of the principle of legitimacy in a web of such broad scope renders it vulnerable at all points to controverting evidence that may undermine it. Instead of the beneficiaries of the principle of legitimacy speaking rarely ex cathedra and allowing much to remain outside faith and morals, the claim to special knowledge is invoked so widely that reality must be reconstructed to fit the theory. As Talmon has pointed out, this was precisely the dilemma of the messianic democrats. It is the same for the adepts of *diamat,* who have yet to learn completely the self-denying wisdom of our Supreme Court and decide only when they have to and on narrow grounds.

The position of the Catholic Church, faced with Galileo and the altered view of the world that was emerging, differed considerably from that of the other totalitarians. The Church was faced not with the discrediting of a view it had itself created, but rather with the erosion of a vulgarized popular conception that it had adopted. To be sure, its claim to a universal infallibility opened the Church to the conflict with modern science that its pretensions made inevitable. Unlike other totalitarians, it is possible for the Church to abandon or reinterpret the view of the physical world with which it had become entangled. In a sense, the problem of the Church resembles that of tribal society, where a world view has come to be elaborated and life wholly regulated by an embracing set of conventions viewed as natural. This tribal set of customs is highly sensitive to internal mutation and external contamination. It is not a conscious artifact like that of Plato or the self-conscious proponents of closed systems, but is an evolutionary product of the tribe's adjustment to its environment. As a going technology it is defended both consciously and unconsciously, and for very sound biological reasons.

Popper charges Plato with seeking to reinstate an arrested tribalism by reconfounding nature and convention and thus seeking to escape the burden and strain of civilization. However that may be, the nature of a preliterate and prescientific society may well require an embracing and unquestioning ritualism to retain and transmit the level of technology and adaptation achieved by the tribe. A fortunate adjustment becomes frozen in the routines in which it was accomplished. In a preliterate state any but the most careful preservation of the routines would occasion the rapid loss of the advance through progressive deviation from correct patterns. Since the real essentials of the fortunate advance are unknown, the whole elaboration with which it is connected must be preserved. This rigidity obviates the "strain of civilization," since it provides comprehensive answers and lines of conduct. Dewey's "quest for certainty" is unnecessary because certainty is routinized in the unquestioned round of use and wont.

The totalitarianism and the closed system of the tribe are

related to the preliterate means by which a social system preserves the going state of its technology from dissipation and loss. This is quite different from the case of an artificially and deliberately created totalitarian closed system where these qualities are a matter of conscious design rather than an unconscious response to social and environmental necessities. They point to critical differences between traditional closed systems, whose response to external and internal change is still largely that of tribal fear of altering an order of nature that is felt as both divine and beneficent, and the contrived totalitarian closed system, whose arrangements are deliberately adopted to bring about some future desired state.

The reaction of the Tokugawa Shogunate in Japan to external influence is instructive. In an early and sanguine stage it was receptive to foreign ideas and missionaries in the hope of digesting what it found of value and turning this to its internal and external advantage. After the Shinabara rebellion the attitude was reversed. Sanguine feeling gave place to fear and lack of self-confidence, which occasioned the massacre of Christians, the virtual closing of the islands to foreign influence, and the intensification of police controls.[7] Fear of inability to digest external influence is a major reason for seeking to close a system externally. Similar reasons are also relevant to attempts to close the system from internal sources of change.

As so often, Plato has clearly expressed the argument for closure. He says, "Intercommunication between states necessarily results in a mixing of characters . . . and in importing novel customs; and this must cause the greatest harm to people who enjoy . . . the right laws." Another passage of the *Laws* indicates that though foreign contacts are perhaps inescapable, they must be guarded against. The following has a modern ring: "First, no man under forty years shall obtain permission for going abroad to whatever place it may be. Secondly, nobody shall obtain permission in a private capacity; in a public capacity, permission may be granted only to heralds, ambassadors, and to certain missions of inspection. . . . And these men, after their return, will teach the young, that the political institutions of other countries are inferior to their own." [8]

7. Cf. George M. Beckman, *The Modernization of China and Japan* (New York, Harper and Row, 1962), p. 101.
8. Plato, *Laws,* 950 d.

The models of evolution suggest two broad strategies of meeting the challenges of the environment. One might be considered defensive, the other adaptive. A fortunate development that exploits potentialities in the environment may be frozen in a defensive armature and the features of the development fully and even awesomely elaborated. The price of this elaboration may destroy all plasticity, on which further adaptation depends. Survival then depends on the defensive capacity, since innovative potential has been precluded. Man as a physical creature has had the advantage of the plasticity of an imperfectly elaborated organism, and in his extension of evolution to the symbolic cultural realm he has had the choice between defensive, fully elaborated, or adaptive postures. His own survival seems to have been closely related to his adaptive and plastic qualities.

However, pursuing the analogies of evolution for what they may be worth, a major requisite of an organism is the capacity to preserve its character or structure. Plasticity beyond a point would mean dissolution. Change must be made compatible with the preservation of structure. This is what Aristotle addressed himself to when he discussed the question of when is a constitution the same. The members of the state, like the cells of the human body, could change, and yet the constitution would be the same. The preservation of the constitution is the preservation of identity through change. Two kinds of preservation are important. One is the preservation of what Aristotle called the constitution.[9] The other is the preservation of the state as an independent collectivity apart from the preservation of the constitution. Differing constitutions call for differing methods for effectuating their preservation. Thus the methods of the closed system are appropriate to certain types of constitution and the methods of the open system to others. Any type of constitution will find certain things indigestible and will require methods to defend itself against subversion of its character from within as well as forceful or other sources of change from without.

The literature of small group studies shows that at the beginning of the group's life great and disproportionate amounts of energy have to be spent on maintaining the group as a going concern. Certainly the establishment of the principle of legiti-

9. Aristotle, *Politics,* Books III and IV.

macy in a new regime is a major objective, to which nearly all others must of necessity be subordinated. Survival involves not only external but also internal struggle. But beyond the inevitable trauma of birth, a period which the idealized version of the American experience has ill equipped us to understand, there is the question of the political culture available to newly arrived actors on the political stage. The political technology, like other cultural artifacts, may be homemade from trial and error experience or borrowed from what is ready-made and available. Even our own open society had to learn its way. As Professor Levy has shown, Jefferson himself had a darker side in the area of civil liberties. Those who were not the beneficiaries of Whig nationalism and an opulent economy are far more likely to opt for integral nationalism and messianic totalitarian democracy as the mythical base of their principles of legitimacy than for any base more compatible with an open political system.

Political success stories are apt to be imitated. The United States was rapidly superseded as a model in Japan by imperial Germany. To the hard-pressed new regimes in the under-developed countries the closed system of the Soviets offers not only its relevance to the solution of their economic problems but equally, and perhaps even more persuasively, a technique for the rapid consolidation and stabilization of the regime. The almost uniformly unhappy experience of new parliamentary regimes since World War I makes the choice between the two major competing systems anything but even. The case of India, with a comprehensive national party and a political system that is still leaning toward the open, is undecided. In fact, for both India and Pakistan the critical question may not be whether they will be open or closed political systems but whether they can maintain their integrity as unified systems at all.

The open political system that is characterized by a plurality of power centers, a relatively free flow of information, considerable social and political mobility, and government by compromise and negotiation is the outcome of a lengthy and favorable history. It is much more difficult to transplant ready-made from the few countries in which it is successfully operating to other societies. It has been carried with them by the bearers of such a political culture, but precisely because it depends on a pluralistic and complex balance of attitudes and institutions it is far more difficult to imitate successfully than simpler governmental and societal systems. Countries seeking to collapse the creation of a unified government that England achieved under the Conqueror, a unified legal system, a national bureaucracy, representative institutions, the commercial revolution, the agricultural revolution, the Industrial Revolution, and the welfare state into one simultaneous and well-nigh instantaneous program of action will scarcely find their program compatible with the pluralistic compromise and delay of the open system. Many of these institutions have to grow, and while hothouse methods are feasible for some, for others time is an inescapable need.

It seems that the polar opposition between open and closed political systems will be difficult to maintain. The open system has remained open to a large degree because of a sense of confidence in its ability to digest whatever comes its way and to transform this into a part of itself rather than itself be transformed. England believed in free trade only when it could outcompete the world. Our own momentary and belated partial conversion to freer trade seems unlikely to outlive the demonstration that foreign steel and autos can compete in our domestic market. Immigration gave the Statue of Liberty a confident meaning that has been lost since World War I.

The Jeffersonian slogan of free trade in ideas is held with increasingly shaky conviction. The open system can only stay open to the degree that its institutions are powerful enough to achieve by social processes the stability that is elsewhere achieved by coercive governmental action. The nongovernmental tyranny of the majority noted by De Tocqueville successfully insures the degree of conformity necessary for systemic stability. As sanguine confidence in the capacity of the social melting pot to achieve reasonable political homogeneity disappears, alarm arises over political and cultural deviancy that earlier would have been treated with genial contempt. The protagonists of the open society discover that they may have to be intolerant of intolerance and that they may feel it necessary to make it unlawful "to conspire to teach to advocate."

Yet even an alarmed open society may not seek to make its principles of legitimacy exhaustively explicit and to elaborate their logical consequences to all areas of society. The increasingly intimate connection of foreign and domestic policy powerfully presses in this direction. Washington congressmen see in an exhibition of modern art sponsored by the State Department a subversive attack on sound American values. To be sure, their aesthetic criticism was, perhaps unknown to them, shared by Hitler and Stalin, who each from his own standpoint regarded this kind of art as subversive. Apart from personal ethical predilections, a major value of the open society is the extent of its plasticity and hence its capacity for creative adaptation, which results from the large area that is exempt from authoritative determination from above. Fear can cause that area to be vastly contracted. Inevitably this occurs in wartime. In the world of the Cold War the degree to which an open system can or will tolerate uncontrolled areas of freedom depends on its sanguine or nonsanguine attitude toward the course of events. As yet despite passport controls that have kept some Americans at home and some others from visiting Cuba, China, and Albania, we have nothing like a Berlin Wall. In fact, if the real measure of success or failure could be decided by the popularity contest of who would opt to go to the open system of the United States and who would opt to go to the closed systems of the Communists, there is little doubt of at least a favorable numerical result. That the old test, looked down on by the Statue of Liberty as it went on at Ellis Island, is no longer available is among the most powerful reasons for growing uncertainty as to the world's choice—or, perhaps more important, whether for most of the world such a choice exists.

If change affects the open system so as to cause some reconsideration of the degree to which it can afford to be open, it likewise has its effects on the closed systems. The iron curtain was never completely successful and couldn't be. As the stability of the Soviet regime has stood the test of time, war, and other disasters and as it has accumulated an impressive record of success in certain areas, its confidence in its capacity to withstand subversion has increased. The internal necessities of its own development have compelled the creation of an educated and scientifically competent population. The eighteenth-century optimism that such a population automatically spells at least a major thrust toward an open society is probably utopian. Highly authoritarian regimes have come to power and remained in power for long periods of time, ruling over relatively docile literate publics. The Hitler regime was too soon upset by war to reveal whether the internal feudalism that Trevor Roper describes would have made possible its disintegration from within.

As Friedrich and Brzezinski point out, the facile advocates of revolution have given little careful consideration to the means available for its effectuation. On physical grounds alone it would seem that modern military and police means are adequate to maintain power. Castro's success does not disprove this.

While physical violence may not be at the disposal of would-be revolutionaries there are ways by which revolution occurs other than through conspiracies and force. Boredom and apathy, as Sabine suggests, may have been the greatest foes of the theological authoritarians of the past. The most deadly weapon, in his judgment, was indifference. Interest in nonideologically orthodox studies in philosophy and even sociology has become evident in the Soviet Union. Its appearance in Poland is an old story. Elsewhere among the satellites, trains of deviously independent thought are in evidence, thinly masked in orthodox wrappings reminiscent of the techniques of the Middle Ages. Of course these stirrings of independent thought can be checked. While the extent of the forces let loose by de-Stalinization must have shocked its authors, the success of its repression should caution those who pinned great hopes upon it.

More promising than de-Stalinization and the growth of independent thought is the seeming emergence of two Romes within the Communist world. It seems impossible to achieve a closed system within Communism from the currents at work through world Communism. The now existing possibility of playing off the giants against each other must be reckoned with.

National interests among Communist countries without authoritative policing can produce a variety of doctrinal deviations. Doubtless Moscow and Peking will not work out a *cuius regio, eius religio* agreement of toleration, but dilution of orthodoxy under the circumstances will be difficult to prevent. Differences in preexisting political cultures may well give different countries their own brand of Marxism. Western social democracy in Germany and Sweden has already shown this possibility.

If Moscow should establish an institute of Christology, manned by renegade divines and dialectical students of comparative religions, to deduce logically what President Johnson, Prime Minister Wilson, and General de Gaulle will do because they are, after all, Christians, even though they may be bad Christians, it would be little more fanciful than some of the efforts in Marxology.

In the history of the world, many fighting, totalitarian, and logically hopelessly incompatible faiths have learned to live together. The problem of logically excogitating what people in fact must do from their doctrine is well illustrated by the writings of Blanshard on American Catholicism. What they logically must do they don't in fact necessarily do. Hume's observation that what is true in logic is not necessarily true in fact is a warning against facile deductions from doctrine. Even the past is only a more or less probable guide to the future.

In the meantime it is true, as the late Professor Sabine has said, that "the excessively dangerous consequence of believing that a society must be put together according to a single organizing principle is that the relation between societies is then thought of as a contest between incompatible systems." [10] He goes on to say that the belief that this is so creates an international situation in its own image. The question is whether with time the dependence of the Communists on the myth of incompatibility and ultimate victory can be dispensed with. Certainly it seems central both to the present regime's claim to the legitimate exercise of power and to the justification of the continuance of dictatorship. It seems also necessary for the sense of goal orientation that messianic totalitarian democracy requires. But again, that it seems necessary does not make it so. Only firsthand empirical investigation could satisfactorily answer that question, and that only for the present. The most vital question concerning the future of the closed society is that of the cultural and psychological forces playing upon its leading elements. For them the system is less and less closed. Like the Spartans, once outside Sparta they are exposed to the corruption Plato feared.

10. Sabine, *op. cit.*, p. 927.

Foreign Politics of Open and Closed Political Societies

R. BARRY FARRELL
Northwestern University

H ERE AN ATTEMPT will be made to suggest some hypotheses about the relationship between internal political arrangements and international politics in selected political societies with contrasting internal political organizations. The particular political arrangements of concern will be those associated with the "open" or "closed" qualities of national political organization. What difference does it make to a state's foreign policy if its polity is open or closed? How does the factor of an open or closed political society affect state foreign policy?

It seems preferable not to linger on the question of defining open and closed political societies. Nor is it appropriate here to join with Karl Popper and many others in assigning values of good or evil depending on whether a political society is in the category of "open" or "closed." [1] Professor Long has already discussed some of these questions. The most that will be attempted here will be to suggest some characteristics of the two types

1. K. R. Popper, *The Open Society and Its Enemies*, 2 Vols. (London, Routledge and Kegan Paul, 1945). See, for example, the introductory chapter, pp. 1–4.

which may help in the problem of definition. The term "open political system" will be used as synonymous with constitutional democracy. Among its characteristics are competitive regular electoral contests, legalized two- or multi-party organizations aimed at offering alternative governmental leadership, a high degree of toleration for autonomous groups in politics, and an acceptance of constitutional restraints on governmental power.[2] Closed systems for this discussion will be thought of as coming closer to the totalitarian model. The syndrome of six characteristics identified by Professors Friedrich and Brzezinski can be accepted here as identifying the totalitarian form of the closed society. Those six characteristics, in summary, are: an official ideology, a single mass party consisting of a relatively small percentage of the total population, a system of terroristic police control, near-complete party control of all means of effective mass communication, similar control of all means of armed combat, and a central control and direction of the entire economy typically including most associations and group activities.[3]

A further general comment on open and closed political systems: It is probable that no political system has fully fallen within the model form of constitutional democracy or totalitarian dictatorship. Many political systems fall somewhere between the types described. Professor Friedrich, in his useful volume *Man and His Government*, provides the very apt caution that "a dichotomic classification, while impressive on account of its simplicity, is suspect from a realistic viewpoint, because nature tends to be pluralistic, rather than monistic or dual-

2. Concerning the use of the term "system" in this chapter it has seemed sufficient to accept conventional usage rather than the more specific meaning discussed by David Easton, "An Approach to the Analysis of Political Systems," *World Politics*, Vol. IX, 1957, pp. 383–400, and, by the same author, *The Political System* (New York, Knopf, 1953). It is unfortunate for the present chapter that foreign policy is not a primary concern of Arthur S. Banks and R. B. Textor, *A Cross Polity Survey* (Cambridge, MIT Press, 1963). This valuable pioneering volume in "raw characteristics" 26, 28, 29, 30 provides classifications which can differentiate 115 "independent polities" with more subtlety than the rough classifications "open" and "closed," although it will be noted that in defining "open" the present study comes close to the Banks-Textor classifications. The volume has proved very useful in developing hypotheses concerning the decisional context in foreign policy formation.

3. Carl J. Friedrich and Zbigniew K. Brzezinski, *Totalitarian Dictatorship and Autocracy*, 2nd ed., rev. by Carl J. Friedrich (Cambridge, Harvard University Press, 1965), p. 22, also pp. 31–275.

istic." [4] It nevertheless may be useful here, for purposes of analysis, to examine some political systems which come closer to the two extremes, even though it may be correctly argued that in one respect or another they do not completely qualify.

For most of this discussion, data concerning open political societies come from the experience of the United States congressional system and the British and Canadian examples of the cabinet-parliamentary system. Data for closed systems, with one exception, come exclusively from the Soviet Union and the Communist countries of Eastern Europe. The exception is Nazi Germany. Though recognizing that there were fundamental differences in ideology, duration, and political style, it has been useful to draw from time to time on Nazi experience for further information on modern closed political systems coming close to the totalitarian form. It must be further recognized that since 1956 several of the Communist countries in Europe have become far less closed and as a consequence the Friedrich and Brzezinski totalitarian syndrome is less applicable to them.

It has been pointed out by many scholars that the line between foreign and domestic affairs is a very blurred one if it exists at all.[5] Certainly there are very few foreign policies which do not have domestic effects, and conversely domestic affairs may profoundly influence foreign policies. Nevertheless, it is difficult to escape the worry illustrated by John Locke's separation of the "federative" power from the "executive" power. That difficult-to-delineate aggregation of subjects having "reference to foreigners" does seem to manifest evidential characteristics of

4. Carl J. Friedrich, *Man and His Government* (New York, McGraw-Hill, 1963), p. 183.

5. See for examples, W. Y. Elliott, ed., *United States Foreign Policy: Its Organization and Control* (New York, Columbia University Press, 1952); Richard C. Snyder, "The Nature of Foreign Policy," *Social Science*, Vol. 27, April 1952, pp. 61–69; Richard C. Snyder and James A. Robinson, *National and International Decision-Making* (New York, Institute for International Order, no date); or James N. Rosenau, *National Leadership and Foreign Policy: A Case Study in the Mobilization of Public Support* (Princeton, Princeton University Press, 1963); C. J. Friedrich, *Foreign Policy in the Making* (New York, Norton, 1938); C. F. Alger, "Comparison of Intranational and International Politics," and James N. Rosenau, "Pre-Theories and Theories of Foreign Policy," both in the present volume. The simulation of the relationship between internal and external state decision-makers in international relations is discussed in Harold Guetzkow, et al., *Simulation in International Relations: Developments for Research and Teaching* (Englewood Cliffs, Prentice-Hall, 1963).

interest to political science. These characteristics appeared sufficiently distinct before World War II so that Professor Friedrich, as an apologist for constitutional democracy, nevertheless felt it necessary to assert that "popular governments simply are not organized to cope with the problems which arise in their dealings with foreign powers. . . . Constitutional democracy is not as yet geared to the task of conducting foreign affairs." [6] The challenges of total war and cold war have dramatized the indictment and forced efforts to meet it.

The direction in which the constitutional democracies have had to move in coping with the problems of foreign policy formation was in some respects forecast by Locke, writing at the end of the seventeenth century, in his *Second Treatise on Civil Government*. The "federative," or foreign policy, power (which included military policy) by its nature called for fewer institutional and legal limitations and more discretion in the hands of its executors. Said Locke: "What is to be done in reference to foreigners, depending much upon their actions, and the variation of designs and interests, must be left in great part to the prudence of those who have this power committed to them, to be managed by the best of their skill for the advantage of the commonwealth." [7] High stakes, the need to preserve confidences, the demands for special expertness, unusual requirements of timing, and numerous and often unpredictable diverse external events may require some special arrangements for democracies in their treatment of foreign policy. At least in the expansion of the size and professionalism of their foreign policy bureaucracies and in the area of governmental secrecy, the constitutional democracies in the formation of foreign policy have come closer to the practice of the closed political systems. The subject of the relationship between public opinion and the necessities of foreign policy expertise have been carefully explored by Gabriel Almond, James Rosenau, and others.[8] But we must still be haunted by Carl Friedrich's question of 1938: Are constitutional democracies as yet geared for the task of conducting foreign affairs?

6. Carl J. Friedrich, *Foreign Policy in the Making*, op. cit., pp. 47, 60.

7. John Locke, *An Essay Concerning the True Origins, Extent and End of Civil Government* (London, 1690), Chap. XI, par. 147 (reprinted New York, Hafner Publishing House, 1947, pp. 195–96).

8. James N. Rosenau, *op. cit.*, Gabriel A. Almond, *The American People and Foreign Policy* (New York, Harcourt Brace, 1950).

The literature on the formation of foreign policy and the policy outcomes of the process is rather more adequate for the United States than for the United Kingdom, Canada, or the Communist systems. Some of those who have treated the British and Canadian parliamentary foreign policy systems are Ashton-Gwatkin, Bishop, Cadieux, Cohen, Deener, Eayrs, Farrell, Glazebrook, Keenleyside, London, Morrison, Skilling, Strang, and Windrich.[9] The principal single work on the Wilhelmstrasse was published in 1954 by Paul Seabury, although several other scholars have examined Nazi foreign relations.[10] We are still remarkably in the dark on many of the details of foreign policy formation for the Communist countries. There are available several excellent volumes on general Soviet government which include data on foreign relations and from whose general treatment of the system inferences can be drawn.[11] But specialized

9. Frank T. Ashton-Gwatkin, *The British Foreign Service* (Syracuse, Syracuse University Press, 1950); Donald G. Bishop, *The Administration of British Foreign Affairs* (Syracuse, Syracuse University Press, 1961); Marcel Cadieux, *Le Diplomate Canadien* (Montréal, Bibliothèque Économique et Sociale, Editions Fides, 1962), also by the same author, *Premières armes* (Montreal, Le Cercle du Livre de France, 1951); Maxwell Cohen, et al., "The Department of External Affairs," in Royal Commission on Government Organization, Vol. 4, *Special Areas of Administration* (Ottawa, Queen's Printer, 1963); David R. Deener, "The Treaty Power in Canada," in H. L. Keenleyside, et al., *The Growth of Canadian Policies in External Affairs* (Durham, Duke University Press, 1960); James Eayrs, *The Art of the Possible* (Toronto, University of Toronto Press, 1961); R. Barry Farrell, *Formation of Canadian Political Foreign Policy*, to be published by Northwestern University Press, Evanston; G. P. deT. Glazebrook, *A History of Canadian External Relations* (Toronto, Oxford University Press, 1950); Hugh L. Keenleyside, *The Growth of Canadian Policies in External Affairs, op. cit.;* Kurt London, *The Making of Foreign Policy* (New York, Lippincott, 1965); Rt. Hon. Lord Morrison of Lambeth, *Government and Parliament*, 2nd ed. (London, Oxford University Press, 1959); H. Gordon Skilling, *Canadian Representation Abroad* (Toronto, Ryerson Press, 1945); Lord William Strang, *The Foreign Office* (London, Allen and Unwin, 1955); Elaine Windrich, *British Labour's Foreign Policy* (Stanford, Stanford University Press, 1952).

10. Paul Seabury, *The Wilhelmstrasse* (Berkeley, University of California Press, 1954).

11. See especially, Merle Fainsod, *How Russia Is Ruled*, rev. ed. (Cambridge, Harvard University Press, 1963). On the countries of Eastern Europe, see Z. K. Brzezinski, *The Soviet Bloc, Unity and Conflict*, rev. ed. (New York, Praeger, 1961). Both volumes contain extensive bibliographies. Several journals are most important sources of data. Among them are *East Europe*, New York; *Current Digest of Soviet Press*, New York; *Problems of Communism*, Washington; *Slavic Review*, Seattle; *The Russian Review*, Hanover, New Hampshire; *Journal of Central European Affairs*, Boulder, Colorado; *Soviet Studies*, Glasgow.

treatment of foreign policy formation—apart from analysis of policy outcomes—is very limited. For the Soviet Union, probably the best single descriptive account available at present is the chapter by Vernon Aspaturian in *Foreign Policy in World Politics,* edited by Roy C. Macridis.[12] A discussion of some interesting theoretical and other questions posed by this chapter is to be found in Professor Aspaturian's contribution in Part Four of the present volume.

Our discussion suggests that a comparison of foreign policy formation in open and closed societies ought to proceed on the assumption that there will be similarities as well as differences and that the differences fit into the designations "more" and "less" rather than "either" and "or." We should also proceed with the caution that variables other than whether a society is open or closed may be as significant or more significant in affecting policy results. For example, the analysis of Professor Gustavo Lagos in developing and applying categories for international stratification suggests that economic and other variables may be at least as important as a national political system in shaping national foreign policy.[13]

In attempting to compare the foreign policy differences between open and closed societies it seems useful to use in modified form a grouping suggested by Snyder, Bruck, and Sapin in the introduction to the republication of their paper on decision-making.[14] Three of the four analytical groupings they suggest are the following: (1) perceptions of decision-makers and the definition of the situation, (2) the decisional context as a set of intervening variables, and (3) the interrelations of structure and process and decisional outcomes. These categories will be used here—perhaps changed and stretched further than was intended—to group some hypotheses and observations about for-

12. Vernon V. Aspaturian, "Soviet Foreign Policy," in Roy C. Macridis, ed., *Foreign Policy in World Politics* (New York, Prentice-Hall, 1958), pp. 132–210. In a later edition of this book published in 1962, this chapter is on pp. 133–99. See also A. Dallin, ed., *Soviet Conduct in World Affairs* (New York, Columbia University Press, 1960); John S. Reshetar, *Problems of Analyzing and Predicting Soviet Behavior* (Garden City, Doubleday, 1955); Philip E. Mosely, *The Kremlin and World Politics* (New York, Vintage Books, 1960).

13. Gustavo Lagos, *International Stratification and Underdeveloped Countries* (Chapel Hill, University of North Carolina Press, 1963).

14. Richard C. Snyder, H. W. Bruck, and Burton Sapin, *Foreign Policy Decision-Making* (New York, Free Press–Macmillan, 1962), pp. 5–9, 14–185.

eign policy and its formation in the particular open and closed societies which have been identified.

PERCEPTIONS OF DECISION-MAKERS

Among the factors which must affect the way in which those who shape foreign policy are influenced in defining what is important and how they should look at the world are (1) ideology, (2) education and personal expertise, and (3) external, opportunistic, or policy priorities.

Ideology in all probability plays a more important role in influencing the foreign policies of closed societies than it does in open societies. Of course, it is untrue that philosophical values are not influential in the foreign policies of the United States or the parliamentary countries. There is a strong propensity to impute good or evil to American policy.[15] In the Far East, for example, the whole discussion of the recognition of Communist China has had a heavy bearing on moral commitments to Chiang Kai-shek. American allies are "the free world" regardless of data which would suggest that several American allies fall more within the category of closed political systems. Wars have been fought to "make the world safe for democracy." In the early days of the United Nations the traditional normative stance of the United States against imperialism was often reasserted.

In spite of these and many instances of philosophical motivations of foreign policy in open societies, the hypothesis is suggested that there is far greater emphasis on ideological factors in closed societies as influences on foreign policies. One of the characteristics of closed societies, including all the examples we are discussing, is a single ideology which prescribes in detail over a far wider range of human experience than is true of the belief systems to be found in constitutional democracies. In Nazi Germany, in the Soviet Union, and in all the other Communist countries, the role of ideology covers the widest range of human conduct, and its precepts are often quite specific. Democratic

15. See Hans J. Morgenthau, *In Defense of the National Interest* (New York, Alfred A. Knopf, 1951). According to Carl J. Friedrich, *Man and His Government, op. cit.*, "Recurrently, states in either camp are found to be prevented from taking apparently rational actions and adopting corresponding policies because of taboos imposed by their respective beliefs and convictions" (p. 123).

pluralism is rejected for a single truth. Students are schooled year after year in the precepts of ideology; diplomats are trained on textbooks which purport to present a world "system" grounded on ideological doctrines.[16] Advancement in career is at least partly related to protestations of belief. The ideologies of closed societies have specific foreign policy aspirations, although it may be noted that more space is given in Communist ideological writings to domestic rather than to foreign affairs.

We may recall some examples of Nazi ideological precepts of direct relevance for foreign affairs: The German Nazis were to bring other Aryans within the Reich and regard the Aryan race as superior to other races. The German Nazis were to accept the inequality of men and races and thus attribute a moral correctness to the commands of the Nazi Führer and his immediate coterie. Non-Aryan states were to be regarded as inferior in Nazi diplomacy. The Nazis were to regard the Jews and the Slavs as subhuman. The Nazis were to attribute to the German state a special mystical role which made it superior to other states.

The precepts of historical Soviet ideology have included: The Communist system is superior and destined to triumph over other systems. The nonsocialist state is controlled by a class which exploits and dominates it, and the analysis of that class and its institutions provides special insight into state policies. There is a basic antagonism between capitalist and socialist states. In former imperalist holdings and in underdeveloped

16. For the fusion of ideology and Communist scholarly analysis re foreign relations in the Soviet Union see, for example, V. P. Potemkin, ed., *Istoriya Diplomatii,* 3 Vols. (Moscow, 1945); D. B. Levin, "K Voprosu o Ponyatii Diplomatii," *Sovetskoe Gosudarstvo i Pravo,* No. 9, September 1948, pp. 14–28; A. Y. Vyshinsky and S. A. Lozovsky, eds., *Diplomatichesky Slovar,* 2 Vols. (Moscow, State Publishing House, 1948, 1950). Compare A. A. Gromyko, S. A. Golunsky, V. N. Khvostov, *ibid.,* 2nd ed., 3 Vols. (Moscow, 1960, 1961, 1964). On the current Soviet Communist interpretation of postwar international relations see A. G. Mileykovsky, ed., *Mezhdunarodnye Otnosheniya Posle Vtoroy Mirovoy Voyny, 1945–1949,* Vol. 1 (Moscow, State Publishing House of Political Literature, 1962); and A. A. Lavrishchev, D. G. Tomashevsky, *ibid., 1950–1955,* Vol. 2 (Moscow, Publishing House of Political Literature, 1963). The third volume on the post-1955 period was delayed for revision to cover the new interpretation following the dismissal of N. S. Khrushchev. A short Soviet interpretation of the postwar period is provided by V. G. Trukhanovsky, *Istoriya Mezhdunarodnykh Otnoshenyi Vneshney Politiki S.S.S.R.,* Tom. III, 1945–1963 (Moscow, International Relations, 1964). For an approach to international relations from the perspective of ideology see O. V. Kuusinen, chief ed., *Osnovi Marxizma-Leninizma* (Moscow, State Publishing House of Political Literature, 1962), particularly pp. 214–535 and 655–76.

areas are to be found the weakest links in the capitalist chain, and it is the responsibility of the Communist to exploit the contradictions of imperialism in economic and political development to the disadvantage of the capitalist and the advantage of the Communist. Likewise, the Communist believes there is a correct doctrine about revolution, coexistence, and war. Regarding the latter, "wars of national liberation" are still approved. A Communist is expected to believe that business leadership groups in capitalist societies wish to unleash a new imperialistic war if the opportunity is presented. The Communist believes that in the acceptance and execution of the wishes of the party leadership there is a special moral virtue. The party has a special obligation to prepare long- and short-range plans in foreign and domestic affairs, with which all should conform because these enable the society to move correctly in the direction of dialectical historical progress.

These few examples will suffice to illustrate some ideological beliefs which may be relevant in influencing the foreign policies of the two major systems of the modern era which have come closest to being totalitarian. It is impossible to generalize with assurance about the extent to which precepts of this kind influence each individual foreign policy decision-maker in his perception of the world about which he must think. Professor Hans Morgenthau has argued that ideology is a more or less conscious disguise "for the true nature of the policy." "While politics," he asserts, "is necessarily pursuit of power, ideologies render involvement in that contest for power psychologically and morally acceptable to the actors and their audience." [17] In sharp contrast to this view of the significance of ideology, Professor Nathan Leites, in his book *The Operational Code of the Politburo*, implies that Stalin's politburo behaved predictably and that prediction could be significantly derived from a study of chosen ideological texts from the holy books of Marx, Lenin, and Stalin.[18] Both positions have the disadvantages of excess. The importance of ideology appears to be variable and to depend on the private attitudes and ideological knowledge of the individual, the nature of the occasion, the perceived relevance of ideological

17. Hans J. Morgenthau, *Politics Among Nations,* 3d ed. (New York, Knopf, 1961), pp. 87–88.
18. Nathan Leites, *The Operational Code of the Politburo* (New York, McGraw-Hill, 1951). See also by the same author, *A Study of Bolshevism* (Glencoe, Free Press, 1953).

doctrine, and undoubtedly several other factors. We have seen in the correspondence between Stalin and Tito, and more recently in the dialogue between the Chinese and Soviet Communists, that the precepts and language of ideology appear to be of great importance in internal discussion between Communists.[19]

For the individual decision-maker in foreign affairs at the top of the hierarchy in a totalitarian society, it is probable that ideology may influence his own thinking and that it serves as a "prism"—as Professor Aspaturian has called it—biasing the selection of data and analysis he has received from subordinates. The fact that the pressures of the system try to make ideology monolithic in totalitarian societies, rather than heavily pluralistic as in constitutional democracies, limits the possibility of the kind of questioning of eternal verities which may be possible in an open society inside and outside the government. The closed system decision-maker is thus to some extent a prisoner of dogma—dogma which has precepts about foreign policy or of relevance to foreign policy; dogma which is only to a very limited degree susceptible to questioning about its utility and factual relationship to changing world conditions.

Sometimes ideology is linked with aggressiveness in foreign policy. Both Nazism and Communism have had a highly aggressive revisionist quality, and it has often been argued from these cases that closed societies tend to be more anxious for rapid and radical change, more aggressive in foreign and military policy than are open societies. It is nevertheless possible to argue that at present there appears to be a slowing down of aggressive tempo in the Soviet Union. It is admittedly true that much past experience with the Nazis and the Communists would seem to impute a high propensity to foreign policy revisionism and aggression for their types of closed society. On the other hand, there have been highly revisionist periods in the diplomatic history

19. *The Correspondence Between the Central Committee of the Communist Party of Yugoslavia and the Central Committee of the All-Union Communist Party (Bolsheviks)* (Belgrade, Jugoslovenska Knjiga, 1948). One of the most interesting documents of the Sino-Soviet dispute illustrating the association of ideology and policy is the editorial which appeared in *Hung Chi*, Peking, February 4, 1964, accusing the Soviet of "splitism" and calling for the Communists of the world to unite on the basis of Marxism-Leninism. Reprinted in *The New York Times*, February 7, 1964, p. 6.

of constitutional democracies. It is therefore not clear that all the evidence is in to support the hypothesis that the closed society must necessarily be more aggressive than the open. This is a subject about which useful research could be undertaken.

EDUCATION AND PERSONAL EXPERTISE

It is at least a tenable assumption that the perspective of a decision-maker may be affected by both the level and the subject matter of his education. Without pushing too hard on the advantages of mind gained from university training, it can probably be presumed that the recipients of such training may have a wider range of knowledge and skills in the application of scientific methods to problem solving than do those who have completed only a high school and pre-high school education. Higher educational training generally aims at improving the sophistication of intellectual perspectives and techniques and at creating an awareness of alternatives, limitations of data, and complexities. We shall examine here the presence or absence of university-level education and the nature of that education as well as other forms of training.

The backgrounds of two groups of people may be examined here. The first group are the professional officials concerned with the development of foreign policy—members of the foreign service and those brought in association with the foreign service on the official level at the foreign ministry or in embassies and legations abroad. The second group are the political heads of a country concerned with foreign affairs, and here we emphasize particularly the national leader, the foreign minister, and the defense minister. Though others are also involved, our interest will be concentrated on these two groups. The official governmental foreign affairs specialists will be discussed first.

Today educators and foreign service officers on both sides of the iron curtain share a large measure of agreement on the desirability of higher education for future professional diplomats, but disagree on the type of higher education which is most appropriate for those who would make their careers in international relations. Several years ago Mr. George Kennan advocated the establishment in the United States of a sort of West Point for future foreign service officers—a college-level institution which would provide training in subjects directly related to international relations.[20] At present the American foreign service examination system accepts students with more diverse training than would probably be provided by Mr. Kennan's academy. Nevertheless the present examination expects the candidate to be well informed in public and international affairs and to show some skill in political and economic analysis. Recruitment to the Canadian foreign service demands less command of the specific data of national and international politics and economics and more skill in the analysis of problems in this area. It also looks toward breadth of knowledge in various fields and is so designed that one does not have to be a college major in history or social science in order to pass the examination. Both countries require foreign language competence on admission, or shortly after admission, to the foreign service. Both countries provide tests of English language writing skills, general knowledge, and intelligence.

The British system of examination seems less concerned with specific fields of knowledge pertaining to international relations. There is considerable stress on literary ability, although one paper does deal with public affairs. The British also try to assess the suitability of a candidate psychologically by talking with him and examining his behavior. For forty-eight hours he associates with other aspiring candidates at a country house in the presence of a team of examiners, consisting of civil servants and a psychologist. All three countries attempt to assess "personal suitability" by an oral interview with an examination board as the final stage in the examination process.

The Russians have come much closer to George Kennan's proposal of a West Point for the foreign service. The Soviet aspirant for a diplomatic career spends five years or more in the specialized instruction of higher education. In addition to political and economic training and ideological training, great stress is placed on a knowledge of foreign geography and languages. Candidates tend to specialize by countries or groups of countries. The Soviet model is no longer followed in all the socialist coun-

20. George F. Kennan, "The Needs of the Foreign Service," in Joseph E. McLean, *The Public Service and University Education* (Princeton, Princeton University Press, 1949), p. 101. On the British Foreign Service see particularly Donald G. Bishop, *The Administration of British Foreign Relations, op. cit.*

tries of Eastern Europe. In Poland, for instance, a diplomatic school on the Soviet model was abolished in 1960; the Polish foreign service recruits candidates of varying university backgrounds from the different institutions of higher education across the country. Likewise Czechoslovakia abolished its diplomatic school a few years earlier than Poland. Czech foreign service officers get their training at one of the regular universities, in the party school, or at the Institute for International Relations in Moscow. Hungary, on the other hand, in 1965 was in the process of beginning a facility for the university-level training of future diplomats. The Soviet Union and the countries of Eastern Europe also follow the practice of recruiting candidates with political experience but sometimes lower educational qualifications from the party apparatus, from other ministries, or from journalism and locating them in foreign relations jobs at all levels of seniority.

All political systems under examination provide various forms of in-service training. The British assign newly appointed foreign service officers to intensive language training immediately after their appointment. Professor Donald Bishop reports that of the twenty-five or thirty appointments made each year to Branch A of the foreign service, about half are assigned to the study of European languages; the others are assigned to study "hard languages" such as Russian, Arabic, Chinese, Japanese, Persian, Turkish, Siamese, and Burmese. After initial language training in London the members of the latter group may expect to be sent to the country of their language. The Americans and the Canadians insist that candidates without competence in a foreign language on admission to the foreign service must quickly acquire that competence, the Canadians particularly stressing knowledge of French. All three services provide language training and some financial benefits for such training throughout an officer's career.

The Communist countries seem to be more rigid in relating career assignments to language competence. In several of these countries a man with limited language ability is eligible for fewer foreign postings than one who knows several languages. The tendency is to try to assign officers to departments or posts in countries whose languages they know, often for longer periods than is common among their Western counterparts. Major financial incentives are provided to the officer to learn foreign languages. In the Hungarian foreign service, for example, one may earn a 20 per cent increase in base pay by learning a "hard" foreign language such as Japanese or Chinese.

One major part of an official's in-service training comes, of course, in the form of his assignments to different jobs. It appears that the Communist-bloc countries tend to specialize their personnel geographically or functionally to a greater degree than do the United States, Britain, and Canada. There are also some indications that Russian officials may be specialized according to ideological groupings: capitalist countries, socialist countries, neutral and underdeveloped countries. The caution should be offered, however, that foreign service officers in Communist countries can, like their Western counterparts, expect to be assigned to areas for which they have little training if the exigencies of international relations so demand. This is particularly true of those countries where the pool of available personnel is limited.

Apart from some difference of viewpoint on the advantages of specialization and variations in language training, there seems to be little in the structure of educational training or the expertise of the officials of the countries under examination which would suggest sharp contrast. Each country examined is developing a career service demanding higher education or its equivalent as a condition of admission. In varying degrees all are encouraging language competence for the countries of assignment. All officers are assigned to the work of international relations and must come into daily contact with foreigners and the problem of interpreting foreign data to domestic consumers. All are engaged in work requiring classified data and confidential processing, although the accounts of defectors would suggest that Communist diplomats are subject to more rigid security requirements and internal surveillance.

The education and experience of heads of missions and senior officials in the foreign ministries may vary in some instances from the pattern just described. The United States and Canada draw a portion of this group from outside the foreign service and often from outside the government. In neither country does this constitute more than a minority of the holders of such posts, and the tendency is for the percentage to be smaller in Canada than in the United States. The aim expressed by officers of the Canadian Department of External Affairs is that eventually all recruitment should be from within the government. Needless to say, the backgrounds of outside-the-service appointees differ widely, and generalizations about them are difficult. The British policy is to draw heads of missions and top officials from the government service. The Russians and the Eastern Europeans draw senior personnel and, as noted before, personnel at all levels not only from the ranks of the national foreign ministry but also from the party apparatus, from journalism, from universities, and from other ministries. Often they will try to relate the specialized requirements of a job to the previous occupation of an individual: An information officer may be a former journalist; a foreign trade officer may be a former economics professor or Academy of Sciences researcher specializing in foreign trade. This is not always the case, however. For example, the principle of rotation of jobs peculiar to Yugoslavia may bring into various diplomatic posts individuals with little experience in international affairs whose principal previous work concerned internal Yugoslav politics or economics.

When one moves from the level of the foreign affairs official to the senior political ranks of international policy formation, the contrast between the Communist countries and the constitutional democracies becomes more striking. In general, the education of all presidium and politburo members in Communist countries reaches considerably lower levels than does the education of national cabinet members and associated top policy personnel in North American and Western European countries.

Table 5 shows something of the educational attainments, as of July 1, 1965, of the foreign affairs ministers, defense ministers, and top national leaders in the nine European Communist countries, compared with nine American-European open political systems. Probably the most striking fact is that two-thirds of the first secretaries of the Communist countries have had only a high school or, in several cases, an elementary school education. In contrast, only one of the American–Western European group of top state leaders has not completed higher education.

On the other hand, it is interesting that in both groups of countries the majority of foreign ministers have received one or more university degrees. The defense ministers of the Communist countries hold military rank, and most have had long military careers. Only one appears to have received the equiva-

TABLE 5

Education of Selected Foreign Policy Leaders [a]

	Open Systems [b]	Closed Systems [c]
Senior political leaders [d]		
More than one degree	2	0
One university degree	6	1
Some university level; no degree	0	2
Secondary or elementary school only	1	6
Foreign ministers [e]		
More than one degree	3	1
One university degree	5	4
Some university level; no degree	0	2
Secondary or elementary school only	1	2
Defense ministers [f]		
More than one degree	2	0
One university degree	4	1
Some university level; no degree	1	7
Secondary or elementary school only	2	1

[a] Data as of July 1, 1965.

[b] Open countries surveyed: Belgium, Canada, France, German Federal Republic, Great Britain, the Netherlands, Sweden, Switzerland, United States.

[c] Closed countries surveyed: Albania, Bulgaria, Czechoslovakia, German Democratic Republic, Hungary, Poland, Rumania, U.S.S.R., Yugoslavia.

[d] Hoxha (Albania); Lefèvre (Belgium); Zhivkov (Bulgaria); Pearson (Canada); Novotný (Czechoslovakia); De Gaulle (France); Ulbricht (German Democratic Republic); Erhard (German Federal Republic); Wilson (Great Britain); Kádár (Hungary); Marijnen (Netherlands); Gomulka (Poland); Ceausescu (Rumania); Erlander (Sweden); Tschudi (Switzerland); Brezhnev (U.S.S.R.); Johnson (United States); Tito (Yugoslavia).

[e] Shtylla (Albania); Spaak (Belgium); Bashev (Bulgaria); Martin (Canada); David (Czechoslovakia); Couve de Murville (France); Winzer (German Democratic Republic); Schröder (German Federal Republic); Stewart (Great Britain); Péter (Hungary); Luns (Netherlands); Rapacki (Poland); Mănescu (Rumania); Nilsson (Sweden); Wahlen (Switzerland); Gromyko (U.S.S.R.); Rusk (United States); Nikezić (Yugoslavia).

[f] Balluku (Albania); Segers (Belgium); Dzhurov (Bulgaria); Hellyer (Canada); Lomský (Czechoslovakia); Messmer (France); Hoffman (German Democratic Republic); von Hassel (German Federal Republic); Healey (Great Britain); Czinege (Hungary); deJong (Netherlands); Spychalski (Poland); Salajan (Rumania); Andersson (Sweden); Chaudet (Switzerland); Malinovsky (U.S.S.R.); McNamara (United States); Gošnjak (Yugoslavia).

lent of a university degree, although four or more have graduated from military schools. On the other hand, in the non-Communist countries only one defense minister has had a predominantly military career. The others have spent most, if not all, of their careers in civilian employment, and, as a group, their educational attainments—although not quite as impressive as those of the foreign ministers—come overwhelmingly from universities rather than military institutions.

It is dangerous to speculate about the relationship between a politician's level of formal education and his political perspectives and behavior. Obviously some people retain more from their university experience than do others, and some people can learn more than others outside the prescriptions of formal education. On the actual working competence of our group in these matters we have very little data. Likewise the absence of formal education may breed in one man modesty and in another all the confidence of ignorance.

There are only two propositions which are to be offered at this time. The first is that it seems probable that the majority of the first secretaries of the Communist countries, as a consequence of their limited education and their ideological orientation, tend to be more willing to accept uncomplicated formulas, ideological slogans, and simple solutions than are their better educated counterparts in the open societies. This proposition can be strengthened by reference to the limitation of criticism and external debate which is more characteristic of totalitarian than of open societies. The second hypothesis which is derived from the relative lack of formal education of the senior leaders of Communist countries may be stated as follows: Limited formal education and the growing scope of international problems demanding decisions force the first party secretaries to rely heavily on others for both data and analysis. It can be suggested as a corollary that such reliance may also give the staff assistants special significance because their general perspectives of the world can be transferred to their leaders to the degree that the latter depend on them.

EXTERNAL, OPPORTUNISTIC, OR POLICY PRIORITIES

The factors which determine how a person charged with making foreign policy decisions views the world, establishes priorities, undertakes to acquire and analyze information, and reacts to external and internal stimuli are undoubtedly only partly indicated in a discussion of ideology and education and training levels. Other factors which enter into the personal syndrome need to be identified.

Some analysts of international relations have attempted to

explain international phenomena with respect to a single determining factor such as geography, economics, political power,
or ideology. They stress that the most important factor affecting
the individual foreign policy decision-maker is presented to him
as "given" and possesses by its very nature imperatives which
shape foreign policy whatever the wishes of the decision-maker
may be. If one rejects this notion of a single determining factor
and looks instead for a combination of factors, it is nevertheless
difficult to escape the proposition that factors completely beyond
the control of given national decision-makers may have a profound effect on their thought and behavior. These include such
elements as the existence of friendly or unfriendly neighbors,
relative strengths of the military establishments of allies, an-
tagonists, and neutrals, geographical strengths and vulnera-
bilities, the economic assets and needs of one's own country in
relation to others, treaties and alliance patterns, the attitudes
of leaders and the "publics" of the various actors in the international system, and the limitations of one's own national capabilities in existing and potential interaction with other states or
international participants.

Along with these more or less permanent elements that define
the role of a state and its policy decisions are the day-to-day
events of diplomatic dynamics. These can force a decision-maker
to act in a mentality of crisis without recourse to his usual
sources of information and analysis. They may force on him
an order of priorities which contradicts his long-run judgments.
They may force factors of personal emotion and personality
into situations where such factors are irrelevant. In fact, as
Charles F. Hermann and others have suggested, a decision-
maker whose time is almost completely taken up with frequent
and demanding crises may find that his perception of importance and his methods of analysis become almost completely
determined by day-to-day events.[21]

The ordering of existing policy priorities can also affect the
perception of decision-makers. In open societies it is not unknown for senior political decision-makers seeking reelection
to high office to espouse foreign policy positions with an eye to
the ballot box rather than in accordance with their considered

21. See, for example, Charles F. Hermann, "Some Consequences of
Crisis which Limit the Viability of Organizations," *Administrative Science
Quarterly*, 8:1, June 1963, pp. 61–82.

judgments. In situations strongly related to internal domestic politics, therefore, it is difficult to separate motives of personal advancement and political popularity from scientific analysis. Likewise there may be a transference of the slogans, values, and methods applicable to local business or home-town affairs to the analysis of the international polity. For the political leaders of constitutional democracies it may also be useful to take attention away from internal political problems by stressing international affairs. Thus, for example, the late Prime Minister W. L. Mackenzie King of Canada on more than one occasion used Canadian conflicts with British foreign policy as a device for furthering internal national political support on his own behalf.

Such opportunistic political behavior has a different idiom in totalitarian societies, but there are similarities. The ideology of capitalist encirclement provided Stalin with a permanent bogeyman, which supplied a justification for the policies of economic and political repression which served to consolidate his personal power. From 1949 to the end of 1952 Stalin used the imagined threat of Titoism and capitalistic attack as justification for hostility and repression aimed at consolidating his East European empire and maximizing its economic deliveries to the Soviet Union. All the way down the line, junior officials and middle-level officials cited such supposed external foreign policy threats to justify unpopular actions or personal failures. If a factory did not produce up to its quota, this was not due to bad management or poor planning but to foreign spies and agents or mysterious capitalist counterrevolutionaries. Thus in open and in closed societies political leaders who have roles in both domestic and international policy formation may perceive the international policy area as one which can be manipulated to serve their domestic interests. The subject matter and the methods may be varied, depending upon whether the political system is open or closed, but the manipulation of the one sphere to consolidate position in the other seems to be a shared tactic.

These last words suggest another generalization about the way the national leader and his cabinet or an equivalent body, in their roles as top foreign policy decision-makers, perceive the world and their tasks. In both open and closed societies the top policy group has responsibility for both national and international policies and probably many hours of the day have to be devoted to national policies. A crisis in Soviet agricultural productivity is probably more important to the Soviet leaders than foreign policy conflicts in distant countries. The internal political and economic need to dispose of an enormous wheat surplus prompted a Conservative Canadian government, against its ideology and the admonitions of its American ally, to make enormous wheat deals with Communist China. Likewise, internal agricultural problems in China and the Soviet Union, associated with these countries' need for wheat, led them to improve political relations with Canada and benefit that country's capitalist economy in order to serve their own internal economic and political interests. Similarly, pressures which were of an internal economic and political nature inspired the British government to refrain from interfering in the private sale of British buses to Cuba, in spite of the disadvantageous effect of such sales on British-American relations and even on general British policy toward Cuba.

The importance assigned to external, as contrasted with internal, policy seems to be a highly variable factor which may be only slightly related to the open or closed nature of the political system. It is possible that the use of international crises to take attention away from internal problems or to strengthen the internal political position of national decision-makers is a device more common in the closed society than the open. Nevertheless one can think of a sufficient number of examples of its use in open societies so that one must view this generalization with considerable caution.

THE DECISIONAL CONTEXT

The second of the categories suggested by Snyder, et al., to be used here to group data on open and closed societies and foreign policy, is "the decisional context as a set of intervening variables." The discussion of this category begins with an examination of the organization of the decision-makers in relation to each other and their immediate bureaucracies. This will be followed by a discussion of the interaction between decision-makers and their internal national populations. Both discussions attempt to highlight variables of relevance in assessing the

international roles and decisions about international relations
for the foreign policy decision-makers identified.

ORGANIZATION OF DECISION-MAKERS RE EACH OTHER AND THEIR IMMEDIATE BUREAUCRACIES

The very bigness of governmental activity demands compart-
mentalization and specialization. Open and closed political
systems alike are faced with the necessity of dividing the functions of government and allocating them to various institutional
compartments, generally designated as ministries. Most ministries have some responsibilities in the international area, and
a few tend to be primarily concerned with this area. Three of
the latter are the foreign ministry, the defense ministry, and
the ministry responsible for foreign trade. The foreign ministry
is organized into geographical and functional divisions of varying degrees of specialization. Typically a foreign ministry faces
the problem of coordinating the information and analysis of
people in different divisions who are concerned with a given
problem and of coordinating its conclusions with the analysis
and data of other interested governmental agencies. A foreign
ministry also faces the problem of coordinating the data, analyses, and actions of foreign missions with the home office. These
are problems of organization common to all foreign ministries,
regardless of whether their political systems are open or closed.

For closed systems Professor Fainsod has suggested that in
the process of data gathering and transmission "when the views
of the leadership are well known, the words which subordinates
throw back at it tend to confirm its beliefs rather than to challenge its analyses. . . . The danger in the case of the Soviet
Union is accentuated by the rigid doctrinal stereotypes about
the outside world which acceptance of Communist ideology im-
poses." [22] He suggests that the Soviet system now partly protects
itself by establishing independent hierarchies for information
gathering, which thus make it less necessary for the top leadership to rely on any single source of data. Several former Soviet
officials in their writings have also alluded to the existence of
competing information-gathering hierarchies which report di-

22. Fainsod, *op. cit.*, p. 341.

rectly to the top.[23] This system would seem to impose a very heavy burden on the top level of the hierarchy, both in coordinating information and then in screening it.

Open political systems tend to coordinate the data-gathering and analysis process within and between departments at different levels of the hierarchy. They may thus avoid some of the bottlenecks that can occur when top decision-makers are overburdened with excessive responsibilities. True, in parliamentary and congressional systems security restrictions and the value of privileged information in interdepartmental policy bargaining do sometimes make lower level coordination less than ideal, but it is probable that these problems are far more serious in more closed polities.

One of the special characteristics of totalitarian organization is a dualism of the party and the state bureaucracy. In the Soviet Union and in the Eastern European countries there exist in the top party organization one or more sections devoted to international affairs.[24] Certain members of the Central Committee of the Communist party specialize in international affairs. And it appears that in several of the presidia or politburos of the respective central committees, there are one or more individuals

23. For examples of such sources, see Hon. Mr. Justice Robert Taschereau and Hon. Mr. Justice R. L. Kellock, *Report of the Royal Commission to Investigate the Facts Relating to and the Circumstances Surrounding the Communication by Public Officials and Other Persons in Positions of Trust of Secret and Confidential Information to the Agents of a Foreign State* (Ottawa, King's Printer, 1946), pp. 19–41. Also Aleksandr Kaznachev, *Inside a Soviet Embassy* (Philadelphia, Lippincott, 1962), pp. 79–95, 179–87.

24. In the Soviet Union there are at least three sections of the Central Committee organization devoted primarily to international affairs: (1) the International Section, (2) the Section for Liaison with Communist and Workers' Parties of Socialist Countries, and (3) the Section for Travel Abroad. In the Communist parties of Eastern Europe there is normally only one foreign or international department. This department seems to be particularly concerned with relations with foreign Communist parties and Communist and left-wing movements. Some countries' departments seem also to be concerned with assessing organized anti-Communist movements. Most of these offices seem to have a responsibility for the analysis of broad lines of general foreign policy. They undoubtedly have access to data from relevant ministries in addition to the ministry of foreign affairs. The organization for foreign policy of party and state authorities in Yugoslavia differs from other Eastern European socialist countries. Although party bodies are concerned with foreign party contacts, long-range policy, and major crisis decision-making, the state organs have greater responsibility for day-to-day policy and are subject to significant supervision by the active parliamentary committee on foreign relations.

also specializing in international affairs. In the theory of Communist organization, these party officers make the policy decisions. The respective ministries of foreign affairs simply carry out decisions made by the party. Professor Aspaturian, writing in 1958, states: "The foreign minister's role and influence in Soviet diplomacy depends almost entirely upon his party rank. When the minister is of relatively low rank in the party, he constitutes little more than a caretaker of the department." As of July 1965, Mr. Gromyko was not a member of the presidium of the Central Committee of the Soviet Communist Party. In the case of the nine Communist governments of Eastern Europe, only Foreign Minister Adam Rapacki was a politburo member. *Prima facie,* such arrangements would seem to promote important gaps in the communication of both information and analysis.

The location of actual points of power for decisions of foreign policy in a Communist regime is by no means easy. One suspects, for example, that the relationship between the ministry and the party organization varies from country to country. The fact that, as of January 1966, Mr. Rapacki had been for more than sixteen years a member or candidate member of the politburo probably meant that in Poland there had developed a higher reliance on the ministry of foreign affairs (MSZ) than in countries whose top foreign ministry officer has no party politburo rank. One might suppose that Minister Rapacki and Vice-Minister Winiewicz, for example, had a great deal to do with the formation of Polish policy toward the United States. The relatively small department of foreign affairs of the Central Committee of the Polish United Workers Party, under Mr. Czesak and Mr. Kowarz, seemed to lack the expertise and numbers needed if its role were to be very substantial in the formation of Polish foreign policy.

It may be that there are tendencies in the Soviet Union and other Communist countries which will elevate the significance of the ministry of foreign affairs, the foreign minister, and his senior colleagues in the formation of foreign policy. It is true that Professor Aspaturian's assessment of 1958 has been echoed by many seasoned diplomats in the United Nations who have offered as their private opinion the belief that Mr. Gromyko is little more than an errand boy carrying out foreign policies made by the party. Nevertheless, one must remember that in recent

TABLE 6

Politburo Memberships for Selected Foreign Policy Positions *

	On Politburo	Not on Politburo
First party secretary	9 Albania Bulgaria Czechoslovakia East Germany Hungary Poland Rumania U.S.S.R. Yugoslavia	0
Defense ministers	5 Albania Hungary Poland Yugoslavia Rumania	4 Bulgaria Czechoslovakia East Germany U.S.S.R.
Foreign ministers	1 Poland	8 Albania Bulgaria Czechoslovakia East Germany Hungary Rumania U.S.S.R. Yugoslavia
Foreign trade ministers	0	9 Albania Bulgaria Czechoslovakia East Germany Hungary Poland Rumania U.S.S.R. Yugoslavia

* Data as of July 1, 1965.

years there has been taking place in the Soviet Union both an accelerated development of social sciences related to international relations and an enhancement of the role of the professional expert in relation to the slogan-quoting party *apparatchiki*. It is doubtful if there is any senior official in Moscow with higher qualifications of experience and scholarship in Soviet-American relations than Mr. Gromyko. This special competence may well give him an important policy role, particularly on policies concerning the United States.[25]

One suspects also that there may be, now and in the future, real rivalries for policy influence among members of the party apparatus and the foreign ministry in selected subject-matter areas, especially those in which the foreign ministry has unique access to data or analytical competence.

The biographical information presented in Tables 5 and 6 on the party first secretaries, the foreign ministers, and the defense ministers has special relevance in this discussion. In all Communist countries the first secretary assumes an important role in the formation of foreign policy. And yet in most instances he is a man of very little formal education, trying to deal with a highly complicated field in which the competence of the foreign affairs specialist may appear impressive. But his foreign minister in every country but Poland and his defense minister in several countries are not on his politburo.[26] In no Communist country is the minister of foreign trade a member of the politburo.

The first party secretary can seek help from foreign affairs specialists in the party secretariat, but they may not always have at their command the knowledge and analytical skills available to the foreign ministry or other ministries. For help in policy formation he may call on the foreign ministry resources. Or he and his politburo colleagues can make foreign policy decisions on the basis of inadequate knowledge and analysis. It is worth noting that Khrushchev asserted that Stalin did this on many important occasions.[27] It is also worth remembering that in the Hitler experience, where there was also a separation between the experts of the Wilhelmstrasse and Nazi party leaders, there developed around Hitler the so-called "ring of silence"

25. Bibliographical data on Mr. Gromyko's training and experience are available in *Diplomatichesky Slovar*, Vol. 1 (1960), *op. cit.*, pp. 413–14; and H. E. Schulz and S. S. Taylor, *Who's Who in the U.S.S.R.* (Montreal, Intercontinental Book and Publishing, 1962), p. 273.

26. In the Soviet Union the top policy committee of the Central Committee is called the presidium. Several of the Eastern European countries retain the term politburo. Accordingly here the two terms are used to refer to the same organ.

27. N. S. Khrushchev, "Speech to XX Party Congress," Moscow, February 24, 1956, reprinted in the *Congressional Record*, June 4, 1956, and issued as a press release by the United States Department of State, Washington, D. C.

which allegedly kept from him major information and analysis.[28]

The problem of important gaps in the communication of data and analysis from foreign ministry to the leaders of state is not unique for totalitarian systems. It seems intensified in those systems partly because of the duality of party and state bureaucracies and partly because of the centralized authoritarian character of top leadership. There have certainly been occasions, however, when American presidents have relied more heavily on "kitchen cabinets" or special advisers than on the Department of State. In the Dulles era only selected elements of the Department of State received attention. In the days of Senator McCarthy there was undoubtedly a tendency within the Department of State to refrain from reporting or judging in such a way as to offend the wishes of certain senior officials or politicians. It is contended that on certain issues former Canadian Premier John Diefenbaker distrusted and ignored the information and advice of his Department of External Affairs.[29] Similar periods have occurred in British experience. Nevertheless, the congressional and parliamentary systems do place the secretary of state or the foreign secretary institutionally close to the president or the prime minister and make them members of the cabinet.

In open societies the role of legislatures in foreign policy formation provides sharp contrast with the experience of more closed societies. The Supreme Soviet and the comparable bodies in most other Communist countries provide little more than forums for the airing of party and state policy decisions. They do not initiate, block, or substantially amend policies presented. The Hitler experience would assign no role of significance to the Reichstag in the formation of foreign policy. On the other hand, the British and Canadian parliaments, and to a much greater

28. Paul Seabury, *op. cit.*, pp. 90–110. German Ambassador to London Dr. Herbert von Dirksen is cited as reporting that in 1938 Ribbentrop ordered that reports from abroad disagreeing with his personal views were to be ignored. British Ambassador Sir Neville Henderson is also quoted as reporting to Lord Halifax that Ribbentrop kept vital information on British reactions and policy from Hitler.

29. Peter C. Newman, *Renegade in Power: The Diefenbaker Years* (Toronto, McClelland and Stewart, 1963). "Diefenbaker, in turn, had little respect for officials of the External Affairs Department. He regarded most of them as intellectual snobs and, even worse, as Pearson partisans" (p. 252). See, generally, Chap. 19, pp. 249–74.

extent the American Congress, do have an influence in the formation of national foreign policy. It is true that usually in the parliamentary systems the legislative body is relatively docile and confines itself to asking questions, setting limits on policy, and suggesting alternatives. But as Mr. Diefenbaker discovered on the night of February 5, 1963, an outraged parliament can defeat a government on its foreign policies and put its leadership out of office.[30] Professor Robinson has cautioned against imputing to the American Congress too important a role in the initiation of foreign policy.[31] Yet by amendment of presidential bills, by the occasional rejection of treaties or legislation, and by the manipulation of the power of the purse, the American Congress can at least negatively enter the decision-making process in foreign affairs. These congressional powers place on the American higher official a need to placate legislators to a much greater extent than is required in Canada or Britain, where the burden of party politics falls almost exclusively on the shoulders of the responsible ministers and the cabinet.

There appear to be possibilities for greater continuity in office and the implementation of long-range plans under the Communist system and the parliamentary system than under the American congressional system. The assumption in the American system that policy officials of the highest and next to highest ranks will change when the President or even the Secretary of State changes inhibits personnel continuity and may make difficult certain kinds of long-run planning. The parliamentary system assumes that all officials below the rank of minister will stay on, regardless of changes in government.

One of the problems of totalitarian systems is the existence of less orderly procedures for changing top leaders. Substantial changes in the top foreign policy groups occurred in Poland and Hungary after the events of 1956. On the other hand, Professor Aspaturian points out that "down to 1949 the typical tenure of a Soviet foreign minister was ten years, and nearly thirty-five years of Soviet diplomacy have been directed by only three individuals, thus giving Soviet diplomacy a measure of

30. Canada, *House of Commons Debates,* Official Report, 107:72, 1st Session, 25th Parliament (Ottawa, Queen's Printer, February 5, 1963). For the vote of want of confidence see pages 3462–63. Part of the debate is on pp. 3437–61.

31. James A. Robinson, *Congress and Foreign Policy Making* (Homewood, Illinois, Dorsey Press, 1962).

enviable continuity." [32] Nevertheless, in the periods of adjustment following Stalin's death, three individuals successively held
the portfolio.

DECISION-MAKERS AND THEIR INTERNAL
NATIONAL POPULATIONS

One of the most obvious and striking differences between
open and closed political systems concerns the relative influence
of public opinion and interest groups. Totalitarian political systems endeavor to control all interest groups and place them
under the single policy guidance of the party. It is true that
this has not been totally successful in the Communist countries,
as recent trends in the Soviet Union indicate. The problem is
exacerbated by the development of factional groups within the
party. One of the most important groups outside the party
which resists party policy control is made up of organized religions. Professors Friedrich and Brzezinski have identified three
other such "islands of separateness": the family, the universities, and the military establishments. [33] Nevertheless, modern
totalitarian regimes make continual efforts to draw these groupings into the party political system and at the same time make
the party as monolithic as possible.

Likewise there is no encouragement of disagreement within
the populace. Patriotism consists in reacting favorably to a monolithic system of propaganda ultimately controlled by the ruling
party. External debate is confined as far as possible to narrowly
circumscribed areas of subject matter and to designated groupings of people. The system, to a very considerable extent, denies
foreign policy leadership the benefits which may be gained from
external nongovernmental criticism and the identification of
policy alternatives. It also makes more difficult the articulation
of conflicting interests in the policy process. The absence of
genuine election alternatives and the dangers for the individual
in voicing critical opinions combine to make judgments about
popular opposition and support both difficult and uncertain.

The open societies have both the disadvantages and advantages of pluralistic public opinion, competitive political parties,

32. Vernon V. Aspaturian, *op. cit.*, 1958 ed., p. 184.
33. Carl J. Friedrich and Z. K. Brzezinski, *op. cit.*, pp. 279–339.

and vigorous interest-group articulation. Trends of opinion can be identified and taken into consideration in the formation of policy. Governmental leadership judged inadequate may be replaced. When a consensus on a foreign issue or course of action has been identified, leadership can embark on policy with some assurance of national support. The top leaders in foreign policy always have available the advantages of a community of professional external critics in research institutions, universities, and the mass media.

On the other hand, those who fashion foreign policy must often lose the diplomatic advantage of surprise when many actions are announced in advance and discussed in the mass media. Popular scrutiny may make normal processes of advance and retreat in international bargaining more difficult for the diplomat from the open society than for the diplomat from the closed. Furthermore, in situations where a government may acquire maximum advantage for foreign actions—such as the giving of economic aid—the leaders of open societies may lose some of their advantages by having to spell out in detail crass justifications before legislative bodies and face the domestic popular debunking of propaganda intended for foreign consumption.

Writing in 1938, Professor Friedrich drew attention to other difficulties of constitutional democracies in foreign relations. As in the "khaki election" in Britain, following the armistice after World War I, the pressures of press and public may exemplify "the temporary outburst of reckless emotionalism in an electorate" and sanction "bad" policies.[34] Furthermore, the close connection between domestic and foreign affairs may cause purely domestic considerations and special interests to affect national foreign policy and press for inconsistent and particularistic outcomes.

A further disadvantage faced by the open system in the relationship between foreign policy leaders and the national public is in the area of internal penetration. The considerable freedom of the individual citizen makes it possible to identify alienated individuals and recruit them as spies, policy agents, propagandists, or fellow travelers for hostile foreign states. Similar penetration of closed societies is much more difficult. Nazi and

34. Carl J. Friedrich, *Foreign Policy in the Making, op. cit.*, p. 56. See generally pp. 40–61.

Communist party organizations in open societies have provided various degrees of institutional organization and even legitimacy for the penetration of open societies, whereas political party organizations sympathetic to open societies are prohibited in closed political systems.

Likewise, the competitiveness and wide coverage of the mass media in open societies provide opportunities for the foreign manipulation of public opinion on foreign policy. For example, the East Germans, well aware in 1963 and 1964 of the role of public opinion in the West German political system, successfully altered the membership of the West German cabinet by conducting propaganda campaigns against certain individuals who subsequently resigned or were released from office. The campaign to open the Berlin Wall for travel by West Berliners to East Berlin on religious holidays can also be regarded as an effort by the German Democratic Republic to develop public opinion pressures to change the foreign policy of the German Federal Republic. Here the object was probably to encourage the West German government to embark on a policy whose by-product would be a measure of de facto recognition of the East German government and Communist arrangements for the division of Berlin. Certainly other examples could be cited of foreign efforts to influence foreign policy decision-makers in open systems through internal public opinion. On the other hand, the open society runs into serious difficulties if it attempts reciprocal methods, because of state-regulated mass media and general restriction of interpersonal contact. It must be admitted that the restrictions on communication have been reduced in European Communist states since 1956 by substantial discontinuance of radio jamming, by some increase in the flow of printed materials, and by the travel of individuals in various leadership elites as well as general tourists between the competing political systems. Nevertheless the possibilities of communication are far from reciprocal.

This discussion of the relationships between foreign policy-makers and the public must include some concern for the problem of political alienation. The open political systems under discussion tend to obtain the loyalty of the great majority of their populations. On the other hand, Western observers of the Eastern European countries which have become Communist since World War II share wide agreement that substantial and politically significant percentages of the population have become alienated from the system. The Hungarian revolt adds some hard evidence in support of these impressionistic generalizations.[35] However, it is very difficult to obtain even consistent impressions on the degree of alienation in the Soviet Union itself. In fairness it should be admitted that political alienation in these countries may well be related to factors other than the open or closed nature of the political system. About the most that can be said is that the Communist systems do have a problem in making themselves popular.

DECISIONAL OUTCOMES

It remains to make explicit some generalizations about policy outcomes which may have been implicit in the previous discussion of decision-makers and the decisional context in the open and closed societies under examination.

At least seven characteristics of substantive foreign policies seem in one way or another to be influenced by the extent to which a political society is open or closed: information derivations, analysis derivation, intentional change, planned durability, time of decision, revisionist versus status quo orientation, and scope of diplomatic instruments comprehended by policies. The comments which follow are intended more as suggestions of hypotheses for further research than as conclusions with pretensions at definitiveness.

INFORMATION DERIVATION

The openness and pluralism of constitutional democratic societies may foster tendencies toward scientific objectivity in the gathering of data on which foreign policy decisions can be based. This objectivity is enhanced by institutionalized sources of criticism and external research. The closed society is hampered by ideological dogmatism and the centralization of

35. Free Europe Committee, *The Revolt in Hungary: A Documentary Chronology of Events Based Exclusively on Internal Broadcasts by Central and Provincial Radios* (New York, 1956). This collection of radio broadcasts provides some documentary basis for judgment about the nature of political alienation.

authoritarian leadership. Data may be biased both by ideology and by the fact that subordinates transmit to the top only that information which they believe will not annoy the consumer. Institutional structures and personal factors may cause the "ring of silence" problem, thus blocking the flow of essential data to senior foreign policy decision-makers. It remains a matter of conjecture whether such a ring of silence may have kept Mr. Khrushchev from acquiring vital information that might have impeded his downfall in October 1964.

Communist societies, particularly since 1956, have, however, attempted to minimize the problem of interrupted information flow and biased reporting by diminishing ideological dogmatism, fostering parallel and competitive data-gathering and reporting facilities, promoting personal on-the-spot visits to foreign countries, and developing party secretariat and administrative co-ordination machinery. These measures may mean that Soviet and Eastern European foreign policies are now based on broader data resources and more accurate data than was the case in the Stalin era. Notwithstanding these changes, it seems probable that when open societies are not going through a period like the McCarthy era they may have greater advantages in that they avoid ideologically or institutionally derived bias in gathering information on which to base foreign policies and in transmitting that information to decision-makers.

ANALYSIS DERIVATION

Many of the considerations discussed in regard to the factual data from which policy is developed are applicable to the analysis which leads to policy. An open society fosters and publicizes analytical alternatives. Different elements in government are encouraged to express diverse views. There is always a Fulbright or a Goldwater forcing the Secretary of State to defend his policy and at the same time to examine the alternatives. There is a large community of scholars and journalists constantly evaluating and criticizing. It becomes more difficult (though admittedly not impossible) for the decision-maker to espouse a single dogmatic line of analysis. It has been suggested that the open society must sometimes pay a price for this pressure against dogmatism and its drive toward pluralism in analysis. Policy results may be inconsistent, indecisive, or stalemated because recognizing the validity of many alternatives may make it much more difficult to choose a single policy or a series of consistent national policies.

The information available about the latter days of Stalin and what we know about the dogmatic irrationality of some of Hitler's analysis suggest that throughout at least part of the history of modern totalitarian closed societies analysis has been biased by ideological dogmatism and by excessive assurance on the part of senior decision-makers that their judgment had a special inspiration which must override the disagreement of others.

To some extent the great debate in the Communist world between Peking and Moscow and the smaller debates between Moscow and some of the capitals of Eastern Europe may have injected a new challenge to dogmatism of analysis into the Soviet system. It is still true that the area of permissible general debate in foreign relations appears far more highly restricted in the Soviet Union than in the Western open societies. It is also true that in the U.S.S.R. until very recently several forms of social science analysis which might be of particular relevance in reaching decisions about foreign policies were rigidly restricted, and social science still operates under important limitations. Until the latter years of Khrushchev's power quantitative methods were viewed with great suspicion. The data and analysis of one official might not be accessible to another. The fear pressures and inertia of the system sometimes have made it safer to retain old formulas and slogans than to develop new policies more applicable to changing conditions. It is suggested that the institutional arrangements of the open society create conditions more conducive to objective foreign policy analysis than exist in the totalitarian society. It is recognized that the Soviet and several Eastern European societies are making great strides in the effort to overcome their weaknesses in this respect, but the nature of their organization may place a limit on how far this process can go. There is a point beyond which it becomes dangerous for the survival of a totalitarian regime to submit its leaders and their policies to informed and sustained critical analysis without at the same time developing mechanisms for the orderly change of leadership.

INTENTIONAL CHANGE

Closed political systems seem better able to change their foreign policies radically and intentionally than do open political systems. Both the Soviet Union and Nazi Germany dramatically demonstrated this fact on August 24, 1939, through the signing of a nonaggression pact. Here both countries radically altered both their announced foreign policies and their diplomatic classifications of friends and enemies. For the Soviets it was a fundamental reversal of the popular front, collective security against Hitler, and years of propaganda citing the Nazis as the vilest enemies of the Soviet Union. For the Nazis it made nonsense of the Anti-Comintern Pact which the same Foreign Minister Ribbentrop who signed the documents of August 24 had himself fashioned only a few years before.

While the record of Soviet and Eastern European changes of foreign policy contains few examples as dramatic as the pact between Hitler and Stalin, there has been a succession of shifts of policy. The shifts of Soviet policy toward Yugoslavia indicate the capability of closed systems to make substantial changes in foreign policies.[36] A partial list of these shifts must include the denunciation of Tito on June 28, 1948; the effort at rapprochement in the speech of Khrushchev at Zemun Airport on May 26, 1955; the resumption of Soviet-Yugoslav conflict in the months immediately preceding and following the Ljubljana Congress, April 22 to 26, 1958; and the cordial words between Belgrade and Moscow during the Moscow-Peking ideological dispute. The West has also witnessed the Soviet capacity for dramatic change in the imposition of the Berlin blockade on April 1, 1948, and its withdrawal on September 30, 1949; in the Soviet missile buildup in Cuba in October 1962, and the withdrawal of Soviet missiles from Cuba following the Kennedy-Khrushchev agreement of October 28, 1962; and more generally in the sharp Soviet changes from intransigence to pleasantness and back to intransigence again which have

36. The Cominform Resolution, June 28, 1948, excerpts from the bitter charges and counter-charges, and the Khrushchev speech reversing previous Soviet attacks and calling for friendship with Yugoslavia are reprinted with comments and other documents in R. Barry Farrell, *Jugoslavia and the Soviet Union, 1948–1956* (Hamden, Conn., Archon Books, 1956). See pp. 75–106, 176–82.

characterized Soviet policies toward the United States and other
countries.

Deliberate quick shifts of extreme magnitude are far more
rare in the foreign policies of open political systems. Distinct
limits are placed on what decision-makers can do and the speed
with which they can do it. They must explain their actions and
persuade legislators, interested groups, political party supporters, and the public in general. If President Roosevelt would
have preferred to enter the war against the Nazis earlier than
December 7, 1941, he did not feel he had the mandate until
that day, with the events at Pearl Harbor. If President Wilson
would have wished the United States to be a party to the Treaty
of Versailles, the United States Senate on November 19, 1919,
and March 19, 1920, demonstrated that an American chief
executive could be blocked in his desires both of policy and of
timetable. Likewise, if Prime Minister Diefenbaker had felt he
could safely withhold from the Canadian Parliament controversial policy information on the implementation of Canadian-
American defense agreements, the House of Commons' vote of
want of confidence on February 5, 1963, demonstrated that the
legislatures even in parliamentary cabinet systems can reject
the foreign policies of a prime minister.

It is not the intention here to suggest that the closed systems,
because they may have greater freedom than open systems to
change policies quickly and to adopt radical policy alternatives,
have unlimited freedom. The decision-maker of the closed system has, to a relatively greater degree, the widened choice
which comes from greater freedom from external controls. On
the other hand, when policies which require for their success
substantial, active public participation—the most obvious being
a war—the leaders of the closed societies must be concerned
whether such proposed policies will meet with public support,
indifference, or opposition.

PLANNED DURABILITY

By "planned durability" is meant a policy characterized by
long-term perspectives and commitments whose implementation
can be expected. It is often asserted that totalitarian closed
systems have long-range blueprints and timetables for policies
of international behavior, whereas the democracies tend to re-

act to day-to-day events without long-range plans. The data would seem to suggest that there may be something to this assertion but it is a capacious exaggeration.

The relatively long periods in office of Lenin, Stalin, and Khrushchev or of Chicherin, Litvinov, Molotov, and Gromyko suggest that Soviet leaders may serve in power long enough to implement long-range policies. Against this it should be noted, however, that substantial changes may be expected at the times of transition from one leader to another and during the power struggle that precedes consolidation. Furthermore, Communist ideology, as a theory of historical development, counsels its followers to think of long-run strategy in addition to day-to-day tactics. The whole Communist system is dedicated to concepts of planning over time intervals of several years. It is probable that detailed, long-range plans are worked out in the area of foreign policy just as they are in other areas.

But this does not seem to be the whole story. The Eastern European parties and the Soviet Communist party itself have shown indications of considerable in-fighting and the rising and falling of various individuals who have been associated with different policy positions. Biographers of Stalin and Hitler suggest that a large amount of caprice may be injected at the top to distort plans for long-range policy emanating from other sources in the system.[37] There are also problems posed in the coordination of the needs, interests, and personal desires of a vast totalitarian bureaucracy. Furthermore, internal developments may destroy foreign policy plans. An ideological dispute with Communist China may necessitate revisions of plans for sharpened contests with the United States or the disciplining of Marshal Tito. Plans may be made, but they may have to be frequently changed. Internal and external factors may limit the possibilities for their implementation.

Admittedly, the open societies do less planning in foreign affairs, and many policy decisions are day-to-day responses to initiatives taken by competitors. It has been argued that the foreign policy of democracies has lacked the perception of its

37. Alan Bullock, *Hitler, A Study in Tyranny* (New York, Harper, 1953). Isaac Deutscher, *Stalin: A Political Biography* (New York, Oxford University Press, 1949). The capricious aspect is particularly stressed by N. S. Khrushchev, *Speech to XX Party Congress*, February 24, 1956, *op. cit.*

opponents in planning for needs and events which could be anticipated.[38] This could have been true in the period when the competitor was Nazi Germany; it may likewise be true when the competitors are the Soviet Union and its allies. Nevertheless, there has been substantial durability over time for various lines of policy. For example, since World War II the United States, as a matter of long-range policy, has given foreign aid not only to countries in alliance with it but to countries whose neutralism seemed preferable to Communism. Moreover, for a period of several years the United States, under both Republican and Democratic administrations, gave military and financial aid to Communist Yugoslavia. Republican and Democratic administrations gave their support to an American policy of nonrecognition of Communist China and support for Nationalist China in the United Nations. In the interwar period Republican and Democratic secretaries of state showed considerable consistency in minimizing United States involvement in Europe. Liberal and Conservative administrations in Canada during the same period sought to limit Canadian involvement in European affairs except within the framework of the British Commonwealth and the American alliance.

The institutional arrangements of the British political system seem so designed as to enhance the development of long-range policy. The fact that chiefs of foreign missions and all senior personnel below the cabinet level retain their posts, whichever political party happens to be in power, makes for great continuity. In contrast it could be argued that in the United States the changeover of senior policy personnel below the level of secretary with shifts in political leadership makes continuity of policy more accidental than planned. Continuity of policy in the United States is less than in Britain a function of long tenure of senior policy personnel in senior office. In Britain the relative permanency of senior policy officials gives them the capability of thinking in long-range terms and the possibility of carrying in their heads a knowledge of earlier decisions and precedents. The relative insulation of officials from party politics spares them from some of the political interventions caused by the intertwining of the party and bureaucracy in the Soviet

38. Franklin A. Lindsay, "Planning in Foreign Affairs: The Missing Element," *Foreign Affairs,* January, 1961.

Union, or the interventions of pressure groups and party politics which may occur in the United States.

The British system may have greater or less stability depending on the strength of the majority of the government party in the House of Commons. The very tenuous majority with which Mr. Wilson's Labor Party took office in the fall of 1964 could raise doubts on the durability of the foreign policies he might undertake. On the other hand, when—as often happens—a British government has a substantial majority in the House of Commons, the officials of the Foreign Office who advise on policy can think about foreign policies in the four- or five-year periods between elections. This gives permanent civil servants, rightly or wrongly, time to persuade the foreign secretary and other ministers of the wisdom of their positions and thus implement such elements of continuity of policy as may be agreed on by the permanent civil service senior establishment. It is also significant that in Britain the permanent foreign policy officials can feel confident that their funds will be forthcoming without the need for anyone from the official establishment to placate politicians with promises and concessions.

Concerning the open, constitutional democratic political societies the conclusion seems to be that much of the time the parliamentary cabinet system has the institutional capacity and personnel organization required for the development and implementation of foreign policies with durability over time. The American congressional-presidential system, though probably more subject to day-to-day pressures and to the disadvantages of personnel turnover, has, in fact, carried consistent foreign policies over time periods. The United States may have undeveloped potentialities in planning for future situations.

TIME OF DECISION

In a diplomatic situation the time of decision-making may, in fact, have the effect of conscious policy. A bureaucratic delay may be interpreted as a decision to stall. If a policy can be announced and its provisions implemented rapidly, this may give that policy qualities of importance and attention in a bargaining situation which will work to its advantage and the disadvantage of other state participants which cannot act so quickly.

Beyond identifying time as a decisional outcome, it is unfortunately very difficult to suggest here generalizations about
the differences in the timing of foreign policy-making in open
and closed societies. It is probably true that if a policy is regarded as urgent by a national leader it will receive such
priority that the time of decision will be shortened. Conversely,
a subject of little interest to senior decision-makers will not
receive the benefits of such priority. It could be handled quickly
as routine at a low level, or it could be pigeonholed and delayed.

On this question of the time needed for decision-making,
about all that seems to be suggested by our discussion of open
and closed societies is that in a closed society a policy which
has not been tagged as of outstanding importance may be subject to relatively slow processing. This may be due to bottlenecks
brought about by the heavy load of responsibilities placed on
senior officials because of the high degree of centralization
present. It may also be due to the necessity of coordinating
the state and party hierarchies. On the other hand, the need
to coordinate may delay processing and decision-making in open
societies. In the United States, in particular, there are frequently
several agencies involved in many subjects of foreign policy,
and the coordination that becomes necessary can cause delay.
Likewise, a policy which may stir controversy in Congress may
be delayed by consultations with political leaders or by congressional debate.

The greater centralization of the British system and its tendency to locate responsibility for policy with clarity may give
Britain an advantage over the United States in speeding the
decision-making process. It is also a tendency in open societies
to give middle and higher officials considerable discretion in
making middle- and low-level policy decisions. This may, in some
instances, give them certain time advantages in comparison
with representatives from closed political systems who may feel
it wiser to avoid choice and consult with superiors, particularly
superiors in the party apparatus.

REVISIONIST OR STATUS-QUO ORIENTATION

One of the characteristic policy outcomes generally contrasted in discussions of the foreign policies of open and closed
societies concerns the postures of status quo or revisionism.

This topic has already been examined in our discussion of ideology. There it was suggested that totalitarian ideologies, and particularly Communism and Nazism, have advocated a revision of the international status quo. It was also suggested that the aggressive revisionism of present-day Soviet Communism may have declined in recent years in comparison with the desire for radical and violent international change shown by the Chinese Communists.

It is perhaps possible that a totalitarian society which assigns the power of making the great foreign policy decisions to a very small number of men and at the same time partially insulates them from many of the mechanisms of criticism and control found in open society may, by so doing, encourage them to undertake bold high-risk policies. Such individuals may receive personal gratification in the exercise of their power by aggressive acts involving radical change or high risk. Similar tendencies in a leader of an open society may be controlled by the checks and balances of the system. It is also possible that the relatively greater education of the top leaders of the open societies may make them more aware of the implications, costs, and dangers in revisionist foreign policy. Concerning the European Communist systems some might also argue that the fact that the majority of Communist defense ministers are professional military men and the majority of our sample of open society defense ministers are civilians might have some policy implications. The military man might favor military solutions to problems, since their implementation by military action could enhance the personal prestige of the military community. Against this is the argument that military training might make a defense minister more cautious in advising his colleagues in favor of aggressive policy whose military costs and risks he might be better able to understand and appreciate.

SCOPE OF DIPLOMATIC INSTRUMENTS COMPREHENDED
BY POLICIES

The data presented heretofore indicate that the closed society may have certain advantages over the open society in being able to use the widest range of instruments of international relations in the development of a foreign policy. It can penetrate the public opinion of the open society and thereby develop pressures on the shaping of that country's foreign policy. Its intelligence and other agents have a relatively easier time in gathering information and locating themselves in key points in a system which is open rather than closed. The closed political system can bluff, advance and retreat, or spend money without having to provide a full justification to a legislature or an electorate. It can shift diplomatic positions and tactics rapidly. The military instrument can use the surprise factor in local or other wars without the restrictions on aggressive action which are sometimes imposed by open societies. Foreign aid investments need not be justified to the business community as economically sound, provided they impress the party organization as politically useful.

Though factors of control may limit the usefulness of some of the instruments of international relations which may be present to a greater degree in the foreign policies of the closed systems, open societies have shown a capacity to rally all their instruments of foreign policy in times of crisis. In the Korean War, the Berlin airlift, and the Russian missile crisis in Cuba such responses have been forthcoming.

It is arguable that in more passive policy situations the open society has greater restrictions in its utilization of the instruments of military force, internal penetration and propaganda, and some areas of foreign aid. On the other hand, from a propaganda point of view the relatively greater freedom of its political system may appear sometimes more attractive. It is embarrassed less often by high officials defecting to the other side and giving opponents useful intelligence information. The open political system whose leadership has attempted to develop a broad consensus in foreign policy may have the assurance that a foreign policy decision which requires popular support, such as one using the military instrument, will not usually be jeopardized by the threat of internal revolt.

It may be true that in the open society the pressures of the public are sometimes wrong and the leaders may be frustrated in their wisdom. But perhaps the march of events since 1938 makes Professor Friedrich's concern over the capabilities of constitutional democracy in foreign policy less decisive. Both the open and closed societies have marked advantages and disadvantages which have come into sharper focus in the years since 1938. The disadvantages do not seem so clearly assigned to one side or the other. This may indeed be an area where the common man should leave his political health to the skills of an expert physician. But there may also be advantages to having the patient judge the physician by the efficacy of his cures.

PART FOUR

The Soviet Case: Unique and Generalizable Factors

THE CASE APPROACH to the study of social phenomena has been found not only in politics. In many fields the notion has persisted that studying a single situation in depth may provide insights and data that will improve possibilities for broader generalization. It seemed appropriate to represent that approach in this symposium. Accordingly Professor Vernon V. Aspaturian, a leading specialist on Soviet politics, was asked to look at the Soviet Union as a case study in the interrelationship of national and international politics. At the same time he was asked to consider particularly the identification of unique and generalizable factors.

Professor Aspaturian's work is painstaking and discerning. He begins by examining the social structure of the U.S.S.R. and then turns to the interplay of domestic interests and foreign policy in the political process, the specific internal and external political forces shaping Soviet foreign policy. There follows an interesting treatment of internal social and political polarization on foreign policy issues, observations on who "benefits" in Soviet society from international tensions and who "benefits" from relaxation of tensions. Early in his discussion Professor Aspaturian lists several generalizable factors characteristic of the Soviet experience. He concludes by identifying factors that are unique.

In addition to serving its purpose as a case study for this symposium, Professor Aspaturian's work will be of interest to Soviet specialists for its treatment of several issues of particular importance in the literature of Soviet politics.

Internal Politics and Foreign Policy in the Soviet System[1]

VERNON V. ASPATURIAN

The Pennsylvania State University

SOCIAL STRUCTURE AND FOREIGN POLICY IN THE SOVIET SYSTEM

MARXIST THINKERS were among the earliest to analyze systematically the interconnection between internal politics and foreign policy. Marx and Lenin both characterized foreign policy as the continuation of domestic politics. According to Marxist and Soviet observers, the state as the instrument of the domi-

1. The intentions and political objectives attributed to Khrushchev in this chapter are applicable with equal force to his successors, Brezhnev, Kosygin, and Mikoyan, who were members of the Khrushchev faction. They have been pursuing essentially the same policies but with less bombast, irascibility, and personal identification, and with more sophistication, rationality, and open-mindedness to innovation and criticism. Khrushchev's colleagues apparently viewed him as the chief barrier to the successful execution of the very policies with which he had come to be identified in the public eye. In the realm of foreign policy, the decision to remove Khrushchev may have been prompted by the conviction that he had become a personal impediment in the way of a reconciliation with Peking. His sudden removal, however, also plunged the Communist world into temporary confusion and provoked widespread criticism in Eastern Europe and in Western European Communist parties, whose leaders had also identified themselves with Khrushchev's policies. His removal may have also served to mollify temporarily the factional opposition to his policies in the Soviet leadership itself, although the main factional and

212

nant ruling class articulates the interests of the ruling class outside the boundaries of the state under its control. What passes as the interest of the state, the "national" interest, is in effect the interest of the ruling class in society. In foreign policy as in domestic policy, the state is viewed as the chief instrument for defending the existing social order from external threats and for promoting the interests of its ruling class abroad.

Soviet definitions of "foreign policy," "diplomacy," and "international law" have betrayed remarkable uniformity over the years in terms of their class-oriented character. A leading Soviet authority on diplomacy defined foreign policy in 1949 as follows:

Foreign policy is a combination of the aims and interests pursued and defended by the given state and its ruling class in its relations with other states, and the methods and means used by it for the achievement and defense of these purposes and interests. The aims and interests of a state in international relations are realized by various methods and means: first of all, by peaceful official relations, maintained by a government, through its special agencies, with the corresponding agencies of their states; by economic, cultural and other contacts, maintained by state agencies, as well as by public and private institutions (economic, political, scientific, religious, etc.), which provides a state with wide opportunities for exercising economic, political and ideological influence on other states; finally by using armed forces, i.e., by war or other methods of armed coercion.[2]

Elsewhere in the same book he writes that foreign policy is "closely bound up with the character of the social and state system of the states in question, since foreign policy is a direct continuation of domestic policy, and the diplomatic machinery constitutes a part of the entire machinery of state."[3] The Stalinist edition of the *Diplomatic Dictionary* observes that

---

socio-functional and socio-institutional cleavages described in this chapter have remained substantially intact. Khrushchev's successors have actually accelerated the implementation of his tension-lessening policies, and relations with China have deteriorated even more, although the new regime unilaterally suspended its public attacks upon the Chinese for over a year. Peking's characterization of the Brezhnev-Kosygin regime as "Khrushchevism without Khrushchev" appears to be substantially accurate.

2. I. D. Levin, *Diplomaticheskii Immunitet* (Moscow, 1949), pp. 4–5. In 1962 Levin expanded the introduction to his work on *Diplomatic Immunity* into a monograph entitled *Diplomatiya, Yeye Sushchnost, Metody i Formy* (Moscow, 1962), and repeated this passage, word for word, without change on p. 17.

3. *Ibid.* For a more detailed account of Soviet conceptions of foreign policy and their relationship to the social system, cf. V. V. Aspaturian,

Foreign policy is determined in slaveowning, feudal and capitalist society by the interests of the ruling classes, but in socialist society by the interests of the entire toiling people. Diplomacy, on the other hand, whilst by no means free from the influence of the social structure . . . is all the same merely the technical means for the realization of foreign policy.[4]

Diplomacy is usually defined by Soviet authorities as subordinate to foreign policy and its chief instrument during times of peace. Just as foreign policy reflects the social interests of the ruling class in society, diplomacy represents the formal expression of the interests of the state. Thus diplomacy represents the transformation of internal social class interests into official and legal state interests in foreign policy, just as domestic law represents a similar transformation of domestic class interests secured by power into legal rights. While diplomatic relations represent, in effect, the indirect collision of interests and resolution of conflicts between internal interest groups or social classes of various states masquerading as the national interests of the country as a whole, "international law can be defined as the aggregate of rules governing relations between states in the process of their conflict and cooperation . . . expressing the will of the ruling classes of these states and defended in case of need by coercion applied by the states individually or collectively." [5]

The foreign policy of the Soviet Union, like that of other states, is shaped by the interests of the dominant social groups in society, ideologically rationalized as the will of all social classes in the country and legalized as the official interests of the state. The Soviet regime in its foreign policy also purports to articulate the interests of deprived classes, particularly the proletariat, in non-Communist countries as well, although this aspect of its foreign policy is now challenged by that of Communist China.[6] "In the Soviet Union," according to a recent

---

"Diplomacy in the Mirror of Soviet Scholarship," in J. Keep, ed., *Contemporary History in the Soviet Mirror* (London, Allen and Unwin, 1964), pp. 243–85.

4. A. Y. Vishinsky and S. A. Lozovsky, eds., *Diplomaticheskii Slovar* (Moscow, 1948 and 1950), Vol. I, p. 570.

5. F. I. Kozhevnikov, ed., *Mezhudnarodnoye Pravo* (Moscow, 1957), pp. 3–4.

6. Both Peking and Moscow have challenged each other's unilateral attempts to articulate the interests of the deprived social classes in other countries. In its letter of June 14, 1963, to the C.P.S.U. Central Committee, Peking charged: "Certain persons [i.e., Khrushchev] now go so far as to

Soviet textbook on international law, "diplomacy for the first time in the history of mankind wholly serves the interests of the working people, not only of the U.S.S.R. but also of all other countries." [7]

While the foreign policy of the state is traditionally defined as being shaped by the interests of the state, more frequently called the "national interest," this becomes an empty, sterile concept unless it is related to the ideological or social substance of what constitutes the "national interest." Ultimately the concept of state interests must have as its reference point the concrete interests of people, either as individuals, as groups, or as aggregates of groups in some ordered structure of a concentrically radiating consensus. The policies of the state, external and internal, register unevenly upon the interests of various individuals and groups in society, and represent in effect a societal distribution of power reflecting either an informal or a formal consensus pattern or a nonconsensual structure of active and passive coercion. The lowest common denominator of consensus is willingness to defend the integrity of the state and its independent existence. Sometimes it is assumed that all states qualify for this distinction, but this is manifestly not the case. States have existed, and still do, whose very existence is opposed by substantial sectors of their population. This is particularly true in cases where a single nation is divided into several

---

deny the great international significance of the anti-imperialist revolutionary struggles of the Asian, African, and Latin-American peoples and, on the pretext of breaking down the barriers of nationality, color, and geographical location, are trying their best to efface the line of demarcation between oppressed and oppressor nations and between oppressed and oppressor countries and to hold down the revolutionary struggles of the peoples in these areas. In fact, they cater to the needs of imperialism and create a new 'theory' to justify the rule of imperialism in these areas and the promotion of its policies of old and new colonialism. Actually, this 'theory' seeks . . . to maintain the rule of the 'superior nations' over the oppressed nations." *Peking Review*, June 21, 1963. Khrushchev, for his part, has publicly complained: "The Chinese splitters would like to become the leaders and mentors of the revolutionary movement in Asia, Africa, and Latin America. They are maliciously counterposing the national-liberation struggle of the peoples of these continents to the workers' movements and the countries of socialism. Even here they are striving to introduce a split, distrust and estrangement. Their reactionary idea that whites will allegedly never understand blacks and yellows, that their interests are allegedly different, serves this purpose." *Pravda*, April 16, 1964. For a discussion of a related issue, cf. *infra*, pp. 234–35.

7. Kozhenikov, *op. cit.*, pp. 281–82.

states and where the basic loyalty of the population is to the "nation" divided rather than the state of which it is a part. This may even assume the pattern of giving higher loyalty to another state because it represents the interests of the nation as a whole, in which case the interests of this state assume a transcendental significance. Historical and current illustrations of this phenomenon are so abundant that concrete recitation is unnecessary.

What is more often overlooked, however, is that even within a state consisting of a single nation in its entirety, hostility may still be directed at the separate existence of the state by sectors of the population whose primary loyalty has been transferred to another state, ideology, or class. The efforts of the Communist movement to effect a transfer of primary loyalty from state or nation to the proletarian class are well known. This indicates that a level of consensus higher than that of the state and nation may exist at the level of the social system. Social groups and classes in a particular state may experience such deprivation that they seek to rupture and disestablish the existing social order to the advantage of another state, even if the cost to their own state or nation is a heavy one. Such was the case with the Bolsheviks after the Russian Revolution, the French émigrés and the French Revolution, and the American colonists with respect to their separation from Great Britain. In such instances the interests of a social group or class assume higher priority than those of the state and nation.[8]

8. The classic illustrations of states disappearing because of a higher loyalty to "nation" than to state are, of course, the processes whereby Italy and Germany were unified in the nineteenth century. The phenomenon of "Nasserism" in the Arab world represents, in effect, a higher loyalty on the part of many Arabs to Nasser and his dream of a single Arab state than to their own independent Arab states. Bi-national and multi-national states, like Belgium, Canada, South Africa, the U.S.S.R., etc., are chronically subject to internal stresses and strains because of the higher pull of "nation" on the loyalty of many citizens than of the "state." Theoretically, the nation-state was designed to eradicate tensions originating in conflicting loyalties to nation and state by making the two congruent. But the nation-state did not solve the latent tensions generated by social class differences, and a nation-state may be swallowed up into a larger state unit, such as a federation, because substantial sectors of the population see their interests served better within such a state than as an independent "nation-state." Cf., F. Hertz, *Nationality in History and Politics* (London, Kegan Paul, 1944); R. Schlesinger, *Federalism in Central and Eastern Europe* (London, Oxford University Press, 1944); A. Cobban, *National Self-Determination* (Chicago, University of Chicago Press, 1944); R. Emerson, *From Empire*

The priority of ideological or social interests (ideo-social interests) over the interests of the state and nation is by no means an exclusive monopoly of deprived or revolutionary groups. It is not unknown for privileged or ruling groups to have also been ready to sacrifice the interests of other social groups in society, and even of the state and nation, in order to preserve or recover their former privileged status in society. This has been accomplished in the past by either merging their state into another or inviting outside powers to intervene on their behalf, in return for a guarantee that their privileged status will be preserved in one form or another.[9]

Civil wars and revolutions are thus more often the consequence of a shattered or challenged social consensus than of a disintegrating consensus at the abstract level of the state or nation.

Thus when we speak of state or national interests in foreign policy, it is necessary to examine the social structure, the interrelation of interest groups and social classes, the degree of ideo-social consensus, and the process whereby conflicts among various groups are resolved without rupturing the social consensus—and how foreign policy decisions are a product of these

to Nation (Cambridge, Harvard University Press, 1960); Karl Deutsch, Nationalism and Social Communication (New York, Wiley, 1953); Joel B. Montague, Jr., Class and Nationality (New Haven, College and University Press, 1963); and V. V. Aspaturian, The Union Republics in Soviet Diplomacy (Geneva, Librairie Droz, 1960).

9. Historical illustrations of privileged classes or groups sacrificing the interests and even the very existence of their state in order to preserve their privileged position as either subordinate local rulers or as co-opted members of the conquering ruling group can be found as far back as classical antiquity. The Alexandrine, Persian, Roman, Islamic, Ottoman and Habsburg empires were all expanded and consolidated in this manner. The acceptance of indirect rule by local aristocracies subordinate to external authority was a key factor in the establishment and preservation of the European colonial empires. Whenever a ruling group invites outside intervention to quash an internal uprising, it is often sacrificing national or state interests to its own class interests; conversely, the Bolsheviks were willing to sacrifice Russian territory at Brest-Litovsk in order to stay in power as a ruling group. According to Hertz, "in the centuries after the Middle Ages the word 'nation' was used in Germany and France for designating the higher ruling classes in opposition to Volk or peuple, which corresponded to the English word 'populace' or 'common people.' " Nationality in History and Politics, op. cit., p. 6, note 1. Cf. also, J. B. Montague, Jr., Class and Nationality (New Haven, College and University Press, 1963), pp. 44–53. Social class and nation, like state and nation are not always congruent, and under various circumstances the discrete interests of each may come into violent conflict.

processes while at the same time reacting upon them. Just as foreign policy decisions may register different consequences for various groups in society, so is the influence which various groups bring to bear upon foreign policy highly uneven.

The substantive character of the social and power structure of state and society varies considerably and so accordingly does the substantive content of the national interest. Basic alterations in the social or power structure of the state frequently generate different perceptions of national interest, although the territory, resources, and population of the state may remain largely intact. The foreign policy of Castro differs substantially from that of Batista because the nature of the social order and the threats which its dominant groups perceive are correspondingly different, not because Cuba has been transplanted geographically or because its population has been replaced or its history altered.

Generally speaking, all social groups which have a common interest in preserving a given social and political system will develop a process for resolving their conflicts into decisions in such a way as not to injure seriously the social system from which they benefit, even though deprivations in individual cases might be severe. When severe deprivations result systematically and with great frequency for certain groups or social classes, however, one can expect an alienation of these groups and classes from the system and the state which protects it and articulates its interests.

In foreign policy, as in domestic, the interests of the state reflect the socio-power structure of the community, although the precise manner in which divergent internal interests are resolved in foreign policy decisions may vary considerably. The interests of the state in foreign policy thus inevitably reflect the spectrum of domestic interest groups which are affected by foreign policy decisions and are capable of making their demands known and their influence felt in the shaping of these decisions.

Those individuals and groups whose tangible interests are either unaffected by foreign policy decisions or are incapable of making their requirements known or their influence felt remain outside the ambit of participation and are objects rather than subjects of policy. In an absolute sense, perhaps, it would be difficult to imagine a situation whereby substantial groups would be either unaffected by foreign policy decisions or incapable of even passive influence; yet it is nevertheless true that such has been the case not only in the Soviet Union but the United States as well. Under Stalin the active participation of Soviet elites and the passive influence of the nonelites were virtually nonexistent where foreign policy decisions were concerned. In the United States, relations with Latin America were largely shaped and executed to meet the requirements of the business community with investments in that area, since the great mass of Americans were largely unaffected by our relations with Latin America and hence correspondingly indifferent to policy in that region. Before World War II the American Negro community was effectively deprived of any means of exerting influence on American foreign policy decisions. With the rise of a militant Negro elite and the emergence of Africa from under colonial rule, the situation has been altered considerably and the Negro community not only can but does register an increasing impact upon American foreign policy calculations.

It is obviously impossible to quantify precisely the proportion of power which various groups and individuals can command in a given state—since this varies in time and space from one country to another and in individual countries from one time to another, and can even vary considerably in accordance with specific policies. The range is both wide and diverse, stretching from societies in which power is the exclusive monopoly of a small elite, oligarchy, or ruling class to pluralistic societies exhibiting a structural distribution of power in which virtually every group and individual has a basic minimal share in the power structure.

Even the most widely representative society, however, is graduated in its power structure in a sort of inverse relationship between the size of the group and what might be called effective power density. Thus whereas 70 per cent of a society's power may be distributed among a thousand groups, while 30 per cent is concentrated in a small number, the effective power of the latter is substantially greater than 30 per cent. A good analogy for this mode of power distribution is the modern corporation, where 10 per cent of the stock in a few hands may effectively control an organization, 90 per cent of whose stock may be widely diffused and hence relatively ineffective. Since it is impossible to be as precise in calculating the social distribution of power, inevitably some equation about the distribution of power in society is wittingly or unwittingly made on the basis of less reliable and complete data.

The foreign policy of the Soviet Union is largely formulated by decision-makers who are recruited from, and largely represent, the interests of social elites who possess a tangible share of effective political power based upon their functional skills. To the degree that these elites have interests which fortuitously correspond with those of nonelite groups in Soviet society, they also indirectly articulate the interests of the latter groups as well. But the nonelites in Soviet society exert their demands largely by indirection rather than by active participation. As in other modern totalitarian societies they may be actively involved and manipulated in the political process, but they neither directly participate in it nor exercise positive power. This is not necessarily a permanent condition, and the relationship between the nonelites and political power may change abruptly or gradually, depending upon a variety of conditions. Continued conflict among the elites may provoke certain elites to contend for the passive allegiance of the nonelites by deliberately fostering policies which coincide with the basic interests and aspirations of the nonelites. If competition becomes keen among elites for the passive support of the nonelites, dialectical quantification may take place as manipulation from above leads to *passive involvement,* which in turn may be metamorphosed into *active participation,* at first limited and indirect and then more substantial. Under such conditions, power becomes inevitably diffused and an elite power configuration may give way to an evolving system of graduated pluralistic power. Thus political conflicts originally restricted to factional groups may spread first to larger social elites representing social constituencies based upon functions, skills, and talents and finally may be extended in the process, wittingly or unwittingly, to the nonelite masses, as the elites compete with one another in searching for new increments of social power which might give them an advantage in the struggle for power. Khrushchev's consumer-oriented and tension-reducing policies, whether designed consciously or not for this purpose, provided him with a latent reserve of social constituencies which might have proved invaluable and even decisive in intraparty conflicts. Just as Khrushchev successfully mobilized a constellation of elites represented in the Central

Committee against the "antiparty group," which constituted a majority in the Presidium, it is not at all implausible that some day another leader may attempt to mobilize these numerically larger social groups (inside and outside the party) against a formal majority in the Central Committee. It is more likely, however, that skillful association or identification with the interests of these larger social constituencies may actually enable certain leaders and factions to avoid confrontations of such a nature in higher bodies.

THE INTERPLAY OF DOMESTIC INTERESTS AND FOREIGN POLICY IN THE SOVIET POLITICAL PROCESS

The state or national interests of the Soviet Union, which are reflected in its foreign policy, can be divided into four distinct components, which are wholly traditional and not unconventional in their formal abstract conception:

1. Assuring the security and safety of the state, its territory, its property, and its population, as a distinct entity.

2. Preserving or enhancing the power, prestige, and influence of the Soviet state in the international scene.

3. Preserving the social order at home and securing and promoting the social and economic well-being and prosperity of its people within the structure of priorities established by the existing order.

4. Extending the ideological values and social system of the Soviet Union to other parts of the world.

What is basically innovating and unconventional about the state interests of the Soviet Union is the substantive character of the third and fourth components, since the first two are intrinsically universal for large states in a multiple international state system. The third and fourth components are also characteristic of large states, but lack the definition and systematic explicitness that characterize Soviet behavior in international relations. This stems from the fact that the character of social groups in Soviet society, and their economic and social interests which function as inputs into the Soviet political system, represent substantially unique characteristics, as does the substantive nature of the ideological values of the system. These four components are clearly interrelated and interdependent, and frequently reinforce one another, but they are also inherently contradictory and likely to collide significantly at various points, depending upon certain internal and external variables. The contradiction between the first and fourth components has always been apparent, but it has been only in recent years that the fourth component has come into periodic collision with the second and third. Soviet leaders now perceive not only that an aggressive ideological orientation in foreign policy tends to mobilize the capitalist world against them but also that it serves to drain scarce resources required to enhance the material prosperity of the Soviet population, ideologically described as "building Communism."

While the contradiction between Soviet security interests and ideological goals in foreign policy has long been recognized by observers of the Soviet scene, a new variable in Soviet policy is the contradiction between enhancing economic prosperity at home and fulfilling international ideological obligations. In Soviet jargon, this emerges as a contradiction between the requirements of "building Communism" and the costs and risks of remaining faithful to the principle of "proletarian internationalism."

This new factor has not gone unnoticed by the Chinese. They accused Khrushchev of abandoning Soviet ideological and material obligations to international Communism and the national-liberation movement in favor of avoiding the risks of nuclear war and building an affluent society to satisfy the appetites of the new Soviet "ruling stratum"—in the guise of pursuing peaceful coexistence and "building Communism." Thus in a long editorial entitled "On Khrushchev's Phoney Communism and Its Historical Lessons for the World," the authoritative Chinese organ, *Jen Min Jih Pao*, charged on July 14, 1964:

The revisionist Khrushchev clique has usurped the leadership of the Soviet party and state and . . . a privileged bourgeois stratum has emerged in Soviet society. . . . The privileged stratum in contemporary Soviet society is composed of degenerate elements from among the leading cadres of party and government organizations, enterprises, and farms as well as bourgeois intellectuals. . . . Since Khrushchev usurped the leadership of the Soviet party and state, there has been a fundamental change in the state of the class struggle in the Soviet Union. Khrushchev has carried out a series of revisionist policies serving the interests of the bourgeoisie and rapidly swelling the forces of capitalism in the Soviet Union. . . . Under the signboard of "peaceful coexistence," Khrushchev has been colluding with U.S. imperialism, wrecking the socialist camp and the international Communist movement, opposing the revolutionary struggles of the oppressed peoples and nations, practicing greatpower chauvinism and national egoism, and betraying proletarian internationalism. All this is being done for the protection of the vested interest of a handful of people, which he places above the fundamental interests of the peoples of the Soviet Union, the socialist camp, and the whole world. . . . The members of this privileged stratum have become utterly degenerate ideologically, have completely departed from the revolutionary traditions of the Bolshevik party, and discarded the lofty ideals of the Soviet working class. They are opposed to Marxism-Leninism and socialism. They betray the revolution and forbid others to make revolution. Their sole concern is to consolidate their economic position and political rule. All their activities revolve around the private interests of their own privileged stratum.[10]

While initially the basic purpose of external security and state survival was to develop into a power center for the purpose of implementing ideological goals in foreign policy (world Communism), increasingly the primary purpose becomes in fact to protect and preserve the existing social order in the interests of the new social groups who dominate it and benefit from it.[11] To

10. *Jen Min Jih Pao,* July 14, 1964. The Chinese statement continues with its catalogue of Khrushchev's sins: "In putting up the signboard of 'building Communism,' Khrushchev's true aim is to conceal the true face of his revisionism. . . . Khrushchev has ulterior motives when he puts up the signboard of Communism. He is using it to fool the Soviet people and cover up his effort to restore capitalism. He is using it to deceive the international proletariat and the revolutionary people the world over and betray proletarian internationalism. Under this signboard, the Khrushchev clique has itself abandoned proletarian internationalism and is seeking a partnership with U.S. imperialism for the partition of the world; moreover, it wants the fraternal socialist countries to serve its own private interests and not to oppose imperialism or to support the revolutions of oppressed peoples and nations, and it wants them to accept its political, economic, and military control and be its virtual dependencies and colonies. . . . He does not regard the struggle of the working class for Communism as a struggle for the thorough emancipation of mankind as well as itself, but describes it as a struggle for 'a good dish of goulash. . . .' Khrushchev's 'Communism' takes the United States for its model. Imitation of the methods of management of U.S. capitalism and the bourgeois way of life have been raised by Khrushchev to the level of state policy. . . . Thus it can be seen that Khrushchev's 'Communism' is indeed 'goulash Communism'—the 'Communism of the American way of life.' " *Ibid.*
11. Cf. V. V. Aspaturian, "Social Structure and Political Power in the Soviet System," a paper presented to the 1963 Annual Meeting of the American Political Science Association; and R. C. Macridis and R. Ward, eds., *Modern Political Systems: Europe* (Englewood Cliffs, New Jersey, Prentice-Hall, 1963), pp. 453–72 and 492–502.

the extent that the implementation of Soviet foreign policy goals, whether ideologically motivated or otherwise, is compatible with the preservation and enhancement of the social order and serves to reward rather than deprive its beneficiaries, no incompatibility between internal and external goals is experienced. If, however, the pursuit of ideological goals in foreign policy undermines or threatens the security of the Soviet state and the social groups who dominate it (or even arrests the progress of their material prosperity), the primacy of internal interests is ideologically rationalized, and the energies and efforts devoted to external ideological goals are correspondingly diminished.

It must be realized that the relationship between internal interests and external ideological goals is a dynamic one which fluctuates in accordance with opportunities and capabilities but that in the long run the ideological goals which threaten internal interests tend to erode and to be deprived of their motivating character. The persistence of ideological goals in Soviet foreign policy, which tend to raise international tensions, reflects socio-functional interests which have been traditionally associated with the Party Apparatus and professional ideologues. The fact that the concrete policies which have resulted from the pursuit of ideological goals in foreign policy have created special vested interests for other socio-political or socio-institutional groups, like the secret police, the armed forces, and the heavy-industrial managers, should not obscure the fact that the definition, identification, and implementation of ideological goals, whether in foreign or domestic policy, has been the special function of the Party Apparatus and its attendant ideologues. The area of common interest which remains among some members of the Party Apparatus and the armed forces and heavy-industrial managers in pursuing policies which are tension producing will be discussed later in another connection. Tension-producing policies in an era of increasing technological complexity, however, not only tend automatically to enhance the power of professionalized and technologically oriented groups in the Soviet Union—to the relative detriment of the status and power of the Party Apparatus—but also tend to alienate from the Apparatus other more numerous social groups whose interests are more in consonance with tension-lessening policies. Among these groups are the consumer-goods producers and light-industrial managers, the intellectuals, artists, professionals, agricultural managers, and finally the great mass of Soviet citizenry, comprising the lower intelligentsia, workers, peasants, and others, whose priorities are always low during periods of high international tensions. Since these latter social forces are more numerous than those whose interests are served by tension-producing policies, the social function of the Party Apparatus was in danger of being rendered superfluous as it lost relatively in power and influence to the professional military and the heavy-industrial managers. At the same time its own ideological interests were being increasingly alienated from those social groups that would benefit from a relaxation of tensions.

In an endeavor to avoid this impending collision between the interests of numerically large and potentially powerful social groups in Soviet society and the international ideological commitments of the Party Apparatus, and thus simultaneously to preserve its primacy in the Soviet socio-power structure by finding larger and more numerous social constituencies to rely upon, Khrushchev's policies appeared to have been designed to provide the Apparatus with a more durable internal ideological function —the building of Communism, i.e., raising the standard of living of the Soviet people. This was reflected periodically in Khrushchev's preferences for cutting down on defense expenditures, bringing about a relaxation of tensions in the international scene, and shifting more money and resources to the production of consumer goods and services. Even more cogently, Khrushchev in August 1964 introduced pensions for collective farmers and hiked the salaries of teachers, doctors, medical personnel, service workers in communal housing and in the trade and public catering enterprises, and local government officials. Some 30 million people were the beneficiaries of these social welfare policies and wage increases, and Khrushchev specifically mentioned that one purpose of the wage increases was to enhance the social status of these groups. He also clearly revealed the relationship between tension-lessening policies and a higher standard of living for the Soviet population:

Comrade deputies: The projected wage increase is one of the most important measures envisaged by the Party to further raise the well-being of the Soviet people. It had been intended to implement the measures under discussion at the present session earlier in 1962. But then, for certain reasons of external and internal order, we were obliged to postpone their implementation temporarily. The international situation obtaining at that time forced us to take certain measures to strengthen the country's defense. In this connection it was necessary to increase the allocation of funds for these purposes, and this found full approval from the Soviet people. Our efforts aimed at achieving agreement on disarmament have not yet been crowned with success. So we must keep our powder dry so that the enemy knows that it is impossible to attack us unpunished, and that if an attack is made he will receive an answering crushing blow.[12]

He cryptically noted that "not all our people in leading positions have really understood how important it is to increase constantly the output of consumer goods," and after citing an innocuous illustration, he chastised the Gosplan, the U.S.S.R. Sovnarkhoz, and party organizations for deficiencies in this connection.[13]

Indications of such resistance to these goals can be surmised from the periodic attacks upon members of the "anti-party group," particularly Molotov, who supposedly represented constituencies external to Soviet society; cryptic references to resistance or opposton from various social groups to particular policies; and charges against the Chinese that they were either utilizing or seeking to create factional differences within the Soviet hierarchy for their own purposes.

At the Twenty-second Party Congress, for example, F. R. Kozlov's justification for the retention of the ban on factionalism in the new party statutes was an oblique admission of a continuing and chronic condition in the Soviet political process:

12. *Izvestiia*, July 14, 1964. The fact that Peking issued its statement on "Khrushchev's Phoney Communism" on the day after Khrushchev's address to the Supreme Soviet is not entirely accidental. Peking has also apparently perceived Khrushchev's alteration of the class character of the C.P.S.U. as part of his design to provide the Party Apparatus with a new internal social function. "Besides making a great fuss about a 'party of the entire people,' Khrushchev has also divided the party into an 'industrial party' and an 'agricultural party' on the pretext of 'building the party organs on the production principle.' The revisionist Khrushchev clique says that they have done so because of 'the primacy of economics over politics under socialism' and because they want to place 'the economic and production problems, which have been pushed to the forefront by the entire course of the Communist construction, at the center of the activities of the party organizations' and make them 'the cornerstone of all their work.' Khrushchev said: 'We say bluntly that the main thing in the work of the party organs is production.' . . . The real purpose of the revisionist Khrushchev clique in proposing a 'party of the entire people' was completely to alter the proletarian character of the C.P.S.U. and transform the Marxist-Leninist party into a revisionist party." *Jen Min Jih Pao*, July 14, 1964.

13. *Izvestiia*, July 14, 1964.

Under present circumstances, need the statutes contain any formal guarantees against factionalism and clique activity? Yes, . . . such guarantees are needed. To be sure, there is no social base left in Soviet society that could feed opportunistic currents in the party. But the sources of ideological waverings on the part of particular individuals or groups have not yet been entirely eliminated. Some persons may fall under the influence of bourgeois propaganda from the outside. Others, having failed to comprehend the dialectics of society's development and having turned . . . into dying embers, will have nothing to do with anything new and go on clinging to old dogmas that have been toppled by life.[14]

Although factionalism is usually associated with the antiparty group as a transitory problem and Soviet leaders had been coupling denunciations of factionalism and Molotov with charges of Chinese attempts to undermine Khrushchev's position in the Soviet party, it was hardly likely that Peking was directing its appeal to defunct members of the antiparty group. Rather it had reason to believe that the Soviet professional military and individuals in the Party Presidium and Secretariat might have shared a common interest with Peking in ousting Khrushchev from power, if for different reasons.[15] It was also plausible that the periodic denunciation of Molotov and the association of his views with those of Peking were in fact veiled warnings against those within the Soviet hierarchy who might have seen an opportunity in Peking's invitation to upset the Khrushchev faction. That these internal dissensions existed was more than implied by Suslov—who may have been a specific target of Peking's appeal—in his report to the February 1964 Plenum of the Central Committee. He confirmed the Chinese bid for factional support in the Soviet leadership and simultaneously protested much too much that Khrushchev and the Central Committee were solidly united. Suslov's statement may actually have been an esoteric signal to the Chinese that for one reason or another Peking should not rely upon him for its intrigues:

In their struggle against the C.P.S.U. and its Leninist course, the Chinese leaders are concentrating their fire primarily against Nikita Sergeyevich Khrushchev. Of course, they cannot fail to see that it is Nikita Sergeyevich himself who stands at the head of those remark-

14. *Pravda*, October 29, 1961.
15. For an interesting exposition of this point, cf. Sidney I. Ploss, "Mao's Appeal to the Soviet 'Conservatives' " (Princeton University, Center of International Studies, 1963).

able processes that arose in our party and country after the 20th Party Congress that are ensuring the Soviet people's successful progress toward Communism. This is why, for their subversive purposes, they would like to isolate Comrade Khrushchev from the Central Committee and place our Central Committee in opposition to the Party and the Soviet people. But this filthy scheme is adventurist and hopeless; it is doomed to complete and shameful failure. Our Central Committee, headed by that true Leninist, Nikita Sergeyevich Khrushchev, is united and monolithic as never before, and the Chinese leaders—and not they alone—should make up their minds to that. Comrade N. S. Khrushchev . . . is the recognized leader of our party and people. He expresses the most cherished thoughts and aspirations of the Soviet people. The Leninist line pursued by our party cannot be divorced from the Central Committee, from Nikita Sergeyevich Khrushchev.[16]

While Stalin subordinated the interests of the world Communist movement to the security and foreign policy interests of the Soviet state, the material prosperity of the Soviet population was rarely viewed by him as a significant factor in coordinating Soviet interests and those of the Communist movement. When Soviet security and foreign policy interests were not threatened, Stalin apparently—like Molotov and Mao—welcomed heightened international tensions, even at the expense of material prosperity at home, since they functioned to rationalize totalitarian controls. Hence Soviet ideological commitments abroad were rarely subordinated to the interests of raising the Soviet standard of living under Stalin.

Since Stalin's death, and particularly during the rule of Khrushchev, the balance between Soviet internal economic and cultural needs and the ideological imperatives of foreign policy had been increasingly altered in favor of the former, so that it now seems to enjoy priority in the formulation of foreign policy. Under attack from Peking for allegedly betraying the world Communist movement, Khrushchev did not directly deny the Chinese charge but in effect rationalized that the most effective way in which the Soviet Union could meet its ideological commitments to the revolutionary movement was constantly to raise the

16. *Pravda*, April 3, 1964. Suslov's report was delivered on February 4, but publication was delayed until April for obvious internal political reasons. Cf., also *Pravda*, September 22, 1963. After Khrushchev's removal it was widely rumored in Communist circles that Suslov delivered the main indictment of Khrushchev at the Central Committee Plenum which demanded Khrushchev's resignation.

standard of living of the Soviet people, which would have
presumably stimulated revolution in other countries because of
the attractiveness of Soviet society. Thus, M. A. Suslov, in his
report to the C.P.S.U. Central Committee in February 1964, re-
iterated this position in asserting that "Communist construction
is the greatest contribution to the fulfillment of the internationalist duty of the Soviet people." He then amplified as follows:

The prime role in the world revolutionary process belongs to the
socialist countries. This is demonstrated first in the fact that the
working class, the working people of these countries are . . . creating a new society . . . for the sake of which the peoples are working toward revolution. In creating the material and technical base of
socialism and Communism, the socialist countries are delivering imperialism blow after blow in the decisive sphere of social activity—the
sphere of material production. . . . All this revolutionizes the
masses, helps accustom them to the active struggle against the capitalist system and for social and national liberation. . . . It is the
internationalist duty of the Communists of the socialist countries to
build the new society well and successfully, to develop the economy,
to strengthen defense capability, to consolidate the socialist camp,
and to strive to ensure that through practical implementation of the
ideas of socialism they become increasingly attractive to all working
people. . . . Distorting the essence of the matter, the C.P.C. leadership is attempting to prove that economic competition allegedly
means that "the oppressed peoples and nations have in general no
need to wage a struggle, to rise up in revolution" . . . and that "it
remains for them only to wait quietly, to wait until the Soviet Union
overtakes the most developed capitalist country in the level of production and material well-being. . . ." Such myths are being circulated from Peking expressly to discredit the idea of economic
competition between the two systems. In fact, Marxist-Leninists see
the revolutionary importance of the victories of socialism in economic
competition precisely in that they stimulate the class struggle of the
working people and make them conscious fighters for socialism.[17]

Thus, in summary, we can isolate six characteristics of Soviet
foreign policy which can be termed generalizable and applicable
to the foreign policy behavior of all states:

1. Foreign policy is a continuation of domestic policy.

2. The interests of the state in foreign policy are a function
of the interests of internal social groups.

3. Internal policy requirements generally have primacy over
external policy requirements in the event of incompatibility.

17. *Ibid.*

4. Foreign policy, including external defense, is more a function of preserving the social order and the interests of its dominant groups than of the state or the national interests in the abstract.

5. Foreign policy, including external defense, functions more to serve tangible internal interests than intangible or abstract ideological interests abroad.

Thus we can also conclude that if the pursuit or achievement of ideological goals in foreign policy threatens or undermines the interests and security of dominant social groups, these will not be pursued even if the necessary capability is available.

In the realm of motivating factors, two unique factors in Soviet foreign policy can be isolated:

1. In the past when there has been no incompatibility between the security and/or internal power interests of social groups and the promotion or implementation of purely ideological goals in foreign policy, the latter has functioned as a significant motivating force in shaping foreign policy, and the Soviet regime has diverted relatively substantial resources and devoted considerable energies in the pursuit of ideologically determined goals in foreign policy. The fact that at some stage in the process, ideological goals were converted into instruments serving Soviet national interests should not obscure the fact that this was not always the case during the early years of the Soviet regime. Whether Soviet foreign policy will continue to be shaped by ideological considerations and whether ideological goals can still be converted to Soviet national purposes are becoming moot questions. Not only are the psychological and material drains on the Soviet system becoming increasingly burdensome and costly, but the emergence of Red China as an ideological rival threatens to render ideological goals in foreign policy dysfunctional and counterproductive for the Soviet system. This is particularly the case if the Soviet charge is true that the Chinese advocate a policy which would artificially reduce the economies of developed Communist countries to a common level. In October 1963 *Kommunist* claimed that the Chinese "asserted that the obligation of socialist countries that had moved forward in their economic development allegedly consisted in 'waiting for' the lagging ones and giving them everything that had been created by the forward-moving coun-

tries, as distinct from the lagging ones." [18] This charge was to be repeated by *Kommunist* in the following year in even blunter terms:

The Chinese interpret the question of internationalism in relations between the socialist countries in a spirit of national egoism. It was not too long ago when they were saying that the most economically developed countries must turn over to the backward countries the entire portion of their national income that exceeded the level of the backward ones. [19]

Not only does the Sino-Soviet dialogue on this point demonstrate how international ideological commitments can be subordinated to internal economic requirements by a developed and underdeveloped Communist state sharing a common ideological commitment, but it also illustrates how each can perceive its ideological obligations in such a way that their implementation automatically serves the internal interests of the state concerned. Thus while Moscow asserts that the enhancement of the Soviet standard of living furthers the promotion of world Communism, Peking controverts this view and argues that the world revolution can best be furthered if the developed Communist states postpone their affluence in favor of bolstering the economies of their deprived Communist allies. In either case it reduces itself to the crude formula: "What's good for the Soviet Union (or China) is good for the world revolution." In the past this formula was applied by Stalin almost entirely in terms of the foreign policy and security needs of the Soviet state as the bastion of the world Communist movement; only since the death of Stalin has this formula been applied to purely domestic economic considerations. To be sure, Moscow insists that raising the standard of living in the Soviet Union strengthens the most powerful Communist state and hence alters the global balance of power in favor of world revolution, psychologically if not militarily, but this proposition is both dubious and transparently self-serving. It also serves to support the Chinese charge that in the face of possible thermonuclear

18. "Marxism-Leninism Is the Base for the Unity of the Communist Movement," *Kommunist*, No. 15, October 1963, p. 15.
19. "Proletarian Internationalism Is the Banner of the Working People of All Countries and Continents," *Kommunist*, No. 7, April 1964. Citation is from the version published in *Pravda*, May 6, 1964.

war, the Soviet leaders have lost their revolutionary militancy and may be willing to settle for a status quo which will allow them to divert resources and energies from a counterproductive and dysfunctional policy of revolutionary aggressiveness to bolstering the standard of living at home and expanding and solidifying the social legitimacy of their power and authority.

The history of Soviet foreign policy thus demonstrates that the Soviet elite has been and may still be willing to divert considerable resources and energies to the pursuit of ideological objectives in foreign policy, although their achievement may result in little more than psychological satisfaction, as long as its security and vital interests are not undermined. Enthusiasm for ideological causes wanes, however, if their implementation subjects the dominant social groups in Soviet society to chronic and continuous exposure to destruction or deprivation for an indefinite period. It should be noted that Soviet behavior in this regard is not a simple counterpart to the altruistic and humanitarian efforts exercised in foreign policy by other countries, since the Soviet state has exerted itself in behalf of international ideological goals to a degree which other states would normally regard as seriously self-denying or self-depriving.

2. The second unique characteristic in the content of Soviet ideological goals in foreign policy is that the Soviet Union desires the ultimate restructuring of the social order of the outside world in its own image. This process started with the Stalinization of the Comintern and foreign Communist parties before World War II and was implemented in areas that fell under Soviet control after the war. Soviet policy was not content with the simple establishment of economic, political, or military control of client states, but rather dictated their total social transformation and restructuring of the internal social foundations of authority and power. This aspect of Soviet policy is not *historically* unique, but it cannot be generalized either. It is generally a characteristic of revolutionary great powers and thus is currently applicable to the foreign policy configurations of Communist China.

Five factors, however, have developed outside the Soviet Union that have tended to blunt the cutting edge of Soviet ideology in foreign policy and to deny the Soviet system a universalist character.

1. The growth of polycentrism and diversity within the Soviet orbit, which allowed local Communist leaders to reshape their

policies so that they were more responsive to the internal needs of their own countries than to the interests of Moscow.

2. The real possibility of new adherents to the Communist world emerging spontaneously out of initially non-Communist revolutionary movements and regimes, of which Cuba is a prototype. This allows for an even more diluted and impure type of Communism and greater deviation from the Soviet norm.

3. The implied diversity in even more radical dimensions of future Communist social orders in Western Europe and other areas, as reflected in the changing programs and strategies of the Italian and French Communist parties, to say nothing of the bizarre nature of emergent Communism in tropical Africa.

4. The appearance of intermediate-type noncapitalist, non-Communist social systems in Africa and Asia, like those in Algeria, Egypt, Ghana, Guinea, Indonesia, etc., which subscribe to a local "national" or "ethnic" socialism that Moscow wishes to attract to its ideological and political orbit.

5. Finally the most crucial factor, the emergence of Red China as a revolutionary rival to the Soviet Union within the Communist world and its objective of universalizing what Moscow calls "sinified" Communism.[20]

All these factors have impelled the Soviet leaders to adjust and accommodate to the proliferation of revolutionary movements and regimes—Communist and non-Communist—and settle for a strategy which will disestablish capitalism and

---

20. According to *Pravda*, "Our party . . . has buried the very idea of the 'hegemony' of one party or another in this movement. The Chinese leaders, however, clearly wish to revive this idea, assuming the right to decide by themselves theoretical and political questions that concern the entire movement. What else can explain the hullabaloo raised in China about the 'ideas of Mao Tse-tung' as the summit of Marxist thought for all peoples, for the entire movement? In Peking they have gone so far as to declare that the theoretical generalization of the historical tasks of the present day has become incumbent upon Mao Tse-tung alone, that our epoch itself is the 'epoch of Mao Tse-tung'. . . . Such statements not only are permeated with an adulation and glorification of the leader that is unworthy of Communists. Behind them are obvious feeble attempts to assert a 'monopoly' in Marxism-Leninism on the part of Chinese theoreticians. To counterpoise the great doctrine of Marx, Engels, and Lenin, the Chinese leadership is attempting to foist the so-called 'sinified Marxism' upon the Communist movement as its ideological banner." "Marxism-Leninism Is the International Doctrine of the Communists of All Countries," *Pravda*, May 10, 1964. Cf. also, *Pravda* for May 11 and 12, 1964, and "Against Splitters, for Unity of the Communist Movement," *Partiinaya Zhizn*, No. 11, June 1964, pp. 8–20.

imperialism without necessarily replacing them with variants of the Soviet social order.

The challenge of China and its implied threat to mobilize the underdeveloped, nonwhite areas of the world against the European and developed areas, including the Communist countries, in a kind of global war between the Northern and Southern hemispheres, has, however, caused Soviet and European Communist leaders even to doubt the wisdom and productivity of prematurely encouraging the proliferation of Communist regimes in the underdeveloped regions of the world. Such a proliferation might result not only in contributing incrementally to China's power in the Communist world, but also in radically upsetting the balance between developed and underdeveloped Communist countries and imposing serious burdens on the economies of the Soviet and Eastern European Communist states in the name of "proletarian internationalism" and "fraternal assistance." The European Communists are equipped neither temperamentally nor in terms of resources to divert their energies from internal construction in order to protect militarily or bolster economically a profusion of underdeveloped Communist states. The Sino-Soviet dispute thus reflects microcosmically the global confrontation between the European "haves" and the non-European "have-nots." This has been explicitly confirmed by Moscow and implicitly by Peking, although both have conspired to subsume such an East-West or North-South conflict in a smoke screen of jargon about whether the main feature of the current epoch is the contradiction between the working class (mainly European) and capitalism or the national liberation movement (mainly non-European) and imperialism. Thus the Soviet leaders perceive Chinese motives as follows:

The Chinese leaders represent matters as though the interests of the peoples of Asia, Africa, and Latin America were especially close and understandable to them, as though they were concerned most of all for the further development of the national-liberation struggle in order to turn them into a tool for the realization of their hegemonic plans. . . . The C.P.C. leaders have circulated their infamous myth that the C.P.S.U. "underestimates" the historical role of the national-liberation movement, that the Soviet Union, under the pretext of the struggle for peaceful coexistence, is "refusing to help" the national-liberation movement. . . . The Chinese delegates at this conference [Afro-Asian Conference in Moshi] . . . suggested to the representatives of the African and Asian countries that inasmuch as the Russians, Czechs, and Poles are white, "you can't rely on them," that they will allegedly "always be in collusion with the Americans—with whites," that the peoples of Asia and Africa have their own special interests. . . . In the light of the Chinese leaders' practical activities in recent years, the true political meaning of the slogan they have advanced—"The wind from the East is prevailing over the wind from the West"—has become especially clear. . . . This slogan . . . substitutes for the class approach a geographical and even racist one. It plainly bespeaks a belittling on their part of the role of the world socialist system, the working class and popular masses of Western Europe and America. . . . The long years of enslavement and exploitation by the imperialists . . . are nurturing among part of the population of the former colonies and semicolonies a mistrust of people of the white race. The Chinese leaders are trying to fan these feelings, in the hopes of setting the peoples of the former colonies and semicolonies against the socialist countries, against the working people in the developed capitalist countries. . . . For if one is to expose the secret scheme that stands behind the Chinese slogan, if one is to reveal the long-range goal of the C.P.C. leaders, it consists of the following: China, they reason, is the largest country of the East and embodies its interests; here are born the "winds of history" that are to prevail over the "winds of the West." Thus this slogan is nothing but an ideological and political expression of the hegemonic aspirations of the Chinese leadership.[21]

INTERNAL AND EXTERNAL FORCES SHAPING SOVIET FOREIGN POLICY

Soviet foreign policy decisions, like those of any state, are products of internal responses to both external factors and domestic political considerations operating in dynamic interrelation or as discrete variables. Increasingly, however, the distinctions between foreign policy and internal policy decisions have become blurred, and nearly all policy decisions have both internal and external effects which are continuously feeding back and forth in a reciprocal, if uneven, manner. Bearing this *basic interconnection* in mind and recognizing that foreign policy decisions may result from external or internal factors separately or in fortuitous or calculated combination, and correspondingly have internal and external effects separately or in combination,

21. Suslov's report to the February 1964 Plenum of the Central Committee, *Pravda*, April 3, 1964.

fortuitously or otherwise, expected or unexpected—we can nevertheless enumerate some of the more significant external and internal influences upon Soviet external behavior.

EXTERNAL FACTORS

It has been frequently and mistakenly assumed in the past that foreign policy is largely a patterned response to the behavior or condition of the outside world and that internal factors and effects are largely fortuitous, incidental, or supplemental. External factors which influence Soviet foreign policy can be either defensive or nondefensive in character or a combination of the two. Although nondefensive factors cannot always be discretely distinguished from defensive and security considerations, defensive factors, generally speaking, have priority in the event of conflict. Under Stalin the security interests of Soviet client or ideologically allied states generally had priority over the non-security interests of the Soviet Union. This may no longer be the case, although Soviet leaders continue to vow that all socialist states (with the possible exception of China and Albania) will be defended with the same alacrity and effort as the Soviet Union itself. Since the Cuban missile crisis, however, the credibility of this commitment has been rendered dubious and has been openly doubted by China. This in turn has elicited Soviet reactions which can be interpreted as withdrawing the protective umbrella of Soviet strategic power from China, although the Sino-Soviet military alliance has not yet been formally or publicly denounced.[22] The external factors (defensive and non-

22. In the Soviet government statement of August 21, 1963, Moscow charged the Chinese with having the audacity to criticize the Soviet Union only because Peking enjoyed the protection of Soviet nuclear power: "Can the C.P.R. leaders place their hands over their hearts and say that without the nuclear might of the U.S.S.R. . . . China could today peacefully engage in solving its internal problems of economic and state construction? No, the C.P.R. leaders would have to admit that they can permit themselves even the luxuries of their . . . rude attacks against the Soviet Union and the C.P.S.U. only because the external security of China is protected by the might of the Soviet Union and the whole socialist commonwealth." *Pravda*, August 21, 1963. *Krasnaya zvezda*, four days later, carried the implied threat of withdrawing Soviet nuclear support one step further: "China today is indebted to the power of Soviet nuclear weapons for the fact that it can calmly engage in solving its internal tasks of economic and state construction. The leaders of the Chinese People's Republic ought to recognize that they can permit themselves such luxuries . . . as their gross attacks on the Soviet Union and the C.P.S.U. only because the external

defensive) that shape Soviet foreign policy are listed below in the order of priority most probably perceived by the Soviet leadership today:

1. Threats or objective conditions that have a direct, adverse effect on the security, safety, and well-being of the Soviet state, its territory, property, and population.

2. The fulfillment of international legal obligations to other states or international organizations which are interrelated with the first factor, i.e., treaties of alliance with Communist states, whose security is intimately connected with the security of the Soviet state.

3. The fulfillment of international legal obligations to other states or international organizations, which serves to reduce the danger to Soviet security, i.e., treaties of alliance with non-Communist states, of nonaggression, neutrality, and international cooperation, such as the test ban treaty.

4. Opportunities which enhance the power and prestige of the Soviet state, not directly connected with security *per se.*

5. Opportunities in international relations which enhance the material well-being of the Soviet state and its people (defined in terms of the Soviet structure of social priorities).

---

security of China is guarded by the might of the Soviet Union and of the whole socialist commonwealth. . . . The great Chinese people have an ancient proverb: 'When you drink water, remember who dug the well.' It seems the Chinese leaders, judging by their statements, assume this wisdom can be disregarded." Colonel A. Leontyèv, "Dogmatists at the Well," *Krasnaya zvezda,* August 25, 1963.

And in June 1964, *Izvestiia* hinted that perhaps Peking may have taken itself out of the socialist camp and out from Soviet military protection: "Casting doubts on the efficacy of the Soviet-Chinese treaty of friendship, alliance, and mutual aid, C.P.R. Minister of Foreign Affairs Chen Yi alleged in December 1963 that Soviet assurances are of no value. 'Such promises are easy to make,' he said cynically, 'but they aren't worth anything. Soviet protection is worth nothing to us.' Trying to justify the C.P.R. government's flirting with reactionary regimes, Marshal Chen Yi today declares that China is a 'nonaligned' country. In political language, this means in fact that Chen Yi does not consider China a part of the world socialist camp. . . . True, the Chinese leaders assert occasionally that in a 'complex situation' the U.S.S.R. and the C.P.R. would line up together against imperialism. A legitimate question arises: When are the Chinese leaders to be believed?" "Combine National and International Interests," *Izvestiia,* June 4, 1964.

For further details on the Sino-Soviet dialogue concerning nuclear weapons and the Sino-Soviet alliance, cf. Alice L. Hsieh, "The Sino-Soviet Dialogue: 1963" (Santa Monica, RAND Corporation, 1964); and "Communist China and Nuclear Force" by the same author in R. N. Rosecrance, ed., *The Dispersion of Nuclear Weapons: Strategy and Politics* (New York, Columbia University Press, 1964).

6. Threats or objective conditions adversely affecting the security interests of Communist allies, but not necessarily of the Soviet Union, which require the fulfillment of international ideological and/or legal obligations, i.e., a treaty of alliance or informal commitment to defend a small client state only remotely connected with Soviet security interests, like Cuba or North Vietnam.[23]

7. The fulfillment of unilaterally assumed international ideological obligations to Communist parties, revolutionary movements, and "oppressed peoples" everywhere, i.e., the obligations subsumed under the rubric of "proletarian internationalism" not covered by formal legal commitments.

8. The fulfillment of international legal obligations to non-Communist states or international organizations, which have little or no connection with the direct interests of the Soviet Union or its ideological allies.

The Sino-Soviet conflict, or what we know of it to date, has raised significant questions concerning the interrelationship of Soviet interests with those of other Communist states, particularly Red China. According to the Chinese view, which is not entirely unmerited, the Soviet Union now gives higher priority to the nondefensive external and internal interests of the Soviet Union than to Chinese security interests, to say nothing of Soviet international ideological obligations to the "world revolution" in general. The test ban treaty is held up as a scandalous example of the sacrifice of Chinese security interests at the altar of the Soviet passion for affluence—since from the Chinese point of view the primary purpose of the test ban treaty was to deny nuclear weapons to China in return for a lessening of international tensions. It is difficult to assess the Chinese accusation precisely, since it is not yet sufficiently clear whether Soviet leaders have actually subordinated Chinese security interests to their passion for affluence or whether they really perceive Chinese demands for the satisfaction of Chinese national interests as jeopardizing their own security.

The issue, of course, is not this clear-cut. What the Soviet leaders may believe is that China in reality is trying to maneuver the Soviet regime into giving higher priority to Chinese non-

23. The mild Soviet reaction to the systematic U.S. bombing of North Vietnam for over a year would seem to confirm the relatively low priority of these obligations in Soviet policy, just as Peking has charged.

security interests than to its own by masquerading them under the rubric of security considerations. This interpretation is plausible because of the emphasis the Chinese leaders place on the obligations that the developed Communist countries allegedly have to their underdeveloped Communist brethren and because of the indignant manner in which they condemn the new Soviet party program designed to usher the Soviet Union into the epoch of Communist abundance.

In any event, the Soviet leaders have openly questioned the legitimacy of Chinese motives in foreign policy, as being unrelated to Chinese security interests and hence unworthy of being defended by the Soviet Union and the Communist camp as a whole:

If the leaders of China are actually following the principles of proletarian internationalism, why are they striving so hard to obtain their own atom bomb? People who stop at nothing in their desire to provide themselves with new types of destructive weapons must have some motive. What is behind this desire? From our point of view, the very idea of the need to provide themselves with nuclear weapons could occur to the leaders of a country whose security is guaranteed by the entire might of the socialist camp only if they have developed some kind of special aims or interests that the socialist camp cannot support with its military force. But such aims and interests can manifest themselves only among those who reject proletarian internationalism . . . and . . . peaceful coexistence. After all, it is impossible to combine with the peace-loving foreign policy course of the countries of the socialist system plans for nuclear weapons of one's own in order, for example, to increase one's influence in the countries of Asia, Africa, and Latin America or to create for oneself a "position of strength" in disputed international questions, or, finally, to exacerbate international tension. We say directly: We would not like to think that the C.P.R. government is guided by such motives.[24]

The Chinese, in turn, have charged that Soviet power serves exclusively the interests of the Soviet Union and that "in fighting imperialist aggression and defending its security, each socialist country has to rely in the first place on its own defense capability." [25] And even more emphatically, the Chinese Foreign Minister, Chen Yi, has declared:

Atomic bombs, missiles, and supersonic aircraft are reflections of the technical level of a nation's industry. China will have to resolve

24. *Pravda*, September 21 and 22, 1963.
25. *Jen Min Jih Pao*, August 15, 1963.

this issue within the next several years; otherwise, it will degenerate into a second-class or third-class nation.[26]

While the Soviet leaders may feel that a powerful China armed with nuclear weapons might embark on independent adventures in foreign policy which might inflame the international situation and thus force unwanted and difficult choices upon Moscow, Peking perceives in the Soviet position a desire to control the foreign policy of China and subordinate it to the interests of Russia. "Soviet protection is worth nothing to us," Chen Yi has asserted. "No outsiders can give us protection, in fact, because they always attach conditions and want to control us." [27]

INTERNAL FACTORS

All decisions, whether internal or external, frequently bring about unexpected or unanticipated consequences bearing on both internal and external affairs, which in return may modify the original action in one way or another. It is not always clear whether the effects of foreign policy decisions upon the internal situation in the Soviet Union were intended or unintended. Thus a whole series of fundamental decisions in Soviet foreign policy since Stalin's death have left their impact upon the Soviet domestic scene. This is the case with respect to foreign policy decisions concerning the rapprochement with Tito, the de-Stalinization of the satellite system, the regularization and then fracturing of relations with China, the repudiation of the doctrinal propositions concerning the "inevitability of war," "capitalist encirclement," and "peaceful coexistence," frequent resort to summit meetings and personal diplomacy, the Austrian peace treaty, the test ban treaty, etc. It is extremely difficult to determine whether these decisions were deliberately designed to bring about the internal consequences which eventuated or whether the internal changes were the incidental or unanticipated consequences of external policy decisions made for other purposes. Cause and effect are intertwined and cannot always be disentangled in any meaningful way. Undoubtedly some of the effects were intended and anticipated, and others were not;

26. As reported by KYODO, Tokyo, October 28, 1963, and cited in A. L. Hsieh, "The Sino-Soviet Nuclear Dialogue: 1963," p. 29.
27. As reported in the *Washington Post*, December 8, 1963.

some constituted a welcome fall-out, and some did not. Events and forces were often set in motion which could not be easily reversed and thus were either arrested, domesticated, permitted to run their course, or adjusted to.

There is little question but that the relaxations of Soviet society which have progressively taken place since Stalin's death are closely related to foreign policy decisions and that these relaxations in turn have influenced subsequent foreign policy decisions. But to what degree foreign policy decisions were made for the purpose of justifying these domestic relaxations and to what degree these internal changes came about as consequences remains a methodological enigma.

Internal pressures shaping Soviet foreign policy decisions, not involving security considerations, have in the past been assigned a subordinate role. Yet even during the early years of factional strife in the Soviet Union—like that between Stalin and Trotsky —Soviet leaders and personalities saw opportunities to shape their foreign policy views in a manner calculated to bolster their internal political position in the struggle for power, and these opportunities thus played a significant role in the formulation of Soviet foreign policy. Stalin's doctrines of "socialism in one country," temporary "peaceful coexistence" with capitalism, and his support of Chiang Kai-shek in China were all calculated, at least in part, on one assumption: that a foreign policy of relative retrenchment, with its promise of physical and psychological respite, and concentration on internal construction would probably find a wider response within the party and the population at large than a militantly aggressive revolutionary external policy. Hence such a policy would result in associating Stalin's political fortunes and interests with larger and more powerful social constituencies than his opposition could muster in support of its views.

Once Stalin consolidated his power, however, a political process *per se* ceased to have any existence in the Soviet system, and foreign policy calculations were subordinated almost entirely to the bolstering and reinforcing of Stalin's power at home and his grip on the Comintern and foreign Communist parties abroad. Soviet "state" interests were systematically defined in terms of Stalin's political interests, although various social and institutional groups emerged which also developed a vested interest in preserving and maintaining the Stalinist totalitarian order. After World War II a political process reemerged in which these quasi-autonomous factional, social, and institutional groups developed discretely divergent interests and imposed these on Soviet foreign policy to the degree that they were either able to influence Stalin or resort to administrative distortion in the implementation of policies with which they were charged.

After Stalin's death these differences were to erupt through the surface of totalitarian secrecy and reveal themselves in various ways, as individual Soviet leaders assumed different positions on a large number of foreign policy issues, all of which not only were to have a pronounced impact on the struggle for power among Stalin's heirs but probably were articulated in the first place to bolster the political posture of various personalities and factions. Malenkov's early bid for a relaxation of international tensions, combined with a policy of greater production of consumer goods and services and a loosening of the reins on the satellite states, was designed to widen the social basis of his political support through an appeal to those sectors of Soviet society that suffered deprivations under the Stalinist system.[28] At the same time, however, the same gesture was perceived as a threat by other groups, like the Armed Forces, the heavy-industrial managers, and members of the Party Apparatus, who saw in a policy based on the relaxation of international tensions, and greater priority to consumer goods and services, a restructuring of priorities for resources and money which would leave them relatively deprived and diminish their role, status, and power in the Soviet system. The interests of these groups during the years 1953–1955 were most vocally articulated by Khrushchev, who emerged as the personal rival of Malenkov.

Malenkov's bid for support from a wider and more numerous constellation of social constituencies appears, in retrospect, to have been premature. The light-industrial managers, the rank and file state officials, the intellectuals and professionals, the

28. Malenkov's policies were spelled out in his speech to the Supreme Soviet on August 8, 1953: "The government and the Central Committee of the Party consider it necessary to increase significantly the investments in the development of the light, food, and fishing industries and in agriculture, and to improve greatly the production of articles of popular consumption." On Malenkov's hope to reduce international tensions, cf. H. S. Dinerstein, *War and the Soviet Union* (New York, Praeger, 1959), pp. 65–90.

ordinary Soviet citizens—all of whom would be the beneficiaries of Malenkov's policies—had not yet developed either the political leverage or awareness to mobilize their latent power so as to prevail against the powerful combination of party bureaucrats, industrial managers, and the professional military, who exercised a near monopoly control over the instruments of coercion and means of production.

This powerful coalition, however, was not entirely monolithic in its outlook, and discrete but sharp divergencies of views existed among them which were temporarily submerged in the opposition to Malenkov only to reappear once Malenkov was dethroned. First, those members of the coalition with the narrowest internal constituency, like Molotov, were almost immediately isolated on questions of foreign policy, particularly as it related to relations within the Communist bloc, which at this stage was restricted essentially to bringing Yugoslavia back within the Communist confraternity and eradicating the conditions that were causing a rapid deterioration of relations with China. Thus even before Malenkov was formally removed from authority, the spokesmen for the victorious coalition journeyed to Peking and Belgrade to mend Soviet relations with those two Communist states.

After Malenkov's resignation as Premier, the anti-Malenkov coalition started coming apart and new combinations were reorganized. Khrushchev's coalition continued the policy of isolating Molotov by coming out in favor of a relaxation of tensions, but without a substantial reduction in defense expenditures or abandonment of the priority for heavy industry in economic development until after 1956. The innovations introduced by Khrushchev at the Twentieth Party Congress introduced the next stage in the political struggle and the manipulation of foreign policy for internal factional political advantage. Not only was the isolation of Molotov completed with the doctrinal emendations relating to the "inevitability of war," "capitalist encirclement," "peaceful coexistence," "peaceful transition," and negation of the Stalinist "two-camp" image, but some of the heavy-industrial managers were also threatened with isolation by the new regime's proposals to deconcentrate and decentralize the Soviet economic establishment. The denunciation of Stalin reinforced the isolation of Molotov and also was designed to tarnish Malenkov, Kaganovich, and other Soviet leaders and offi-

cials closely identified with the late dictator. Khrushchev,
however, was careful not to alienate the military, for while he
called for a relaxation of international tensions, he did not
diminish the overall military budget too drastically nor did he
decentralize the economic ministries connected with armaments
production. Marshal Zhukov was elected an alternate member of
the Party Presidium, while the denunciation of Stalin, the re-
habilitation of military victims of Stalin's purges, and the relaxation of party controls in the military widened the area of
common interest between the Khrushchev faction and the
military.

The consequences of Khrushchev's innovations at the Twentieth Party Congress were extremely complicated and mixed, for
they did not have the intended effect of simply polarizing Soviet
politics into sharp and unambiguous cleavages. Khrushchev's
emendations, however, not only served to drive his new rivals
into the arms of his old, but the wide sweep of his formulations
also either threatened members and groups within his own
coalition, or created situations which some of his allies perceived
as opportunities to preserve or advance their own political
fortunes and interests against his. Furthermore, consternation
was provoked within the Communist bloc itself, as factional
cleavages developed within satellite parties, leading to the Hungarian uprising and the emergence of a defiant Poland under
Gomulka's leadership. The denunciation of Stalin, in particular,
threatened not only Khrushchev's political rivals at home, but
some of this own allies, and various Communist leaders in
Eastern Europe and in China, all of which served to feed inputs
back into the Soviet political system which threatened Khrushchev and his faction.

The events of the Twentieth Party Congress and its aftermath
were welcomed in general by those forces which were deprived
under Stalin, such as the light-industrial managers, who saw in
the decentralization scheme a relative diminution of power and
status for the heavy-industrial managers; by the intellectuals,
artists, scientists, and other professionals, who expected de-
Stalinization at home and relaxation of international tensions
abroad to result in further liberalization of controls; and by the
rank and file Soviet citizenry, who saw in the Khrushchev
policies an implied promise for production of goods and services.
But above all, the professional military under Marshal Zhukov's

direction, felt that its interests were being amply protected by Khrushchev, and it saw in the coalition with the Khrushchev faction perhaps an opportunistic maneuver which would render it dependent upon the military, once the other groups were politically disarmed.

The net internal political effect of the Twentieth Party Congress and its aftermath was the polarization of the Soviet elites into two fragile coalitions: (1) The so-called "anti-party group" was made up of the various personalities and groups threatened by Krushchev's policies, or who saw an opportunity for more rapid enhancement of power by deserting Khrushchev. This included the so-called "Stalinist" faction, made up of those who were threatened by the denunciation of Stalin, like Molotov, Malenkov, Kaganovich and Voroshilov; the heavy-industrial managers, Pervukhin and Saburov, who viewed with distaste the economic decentralization and reorganization program, which would reduce their power and status; and the "opportunists," Bulganin and Shepilov, who deserted Khrushchev in anticipation of improving their position. (2) Within the Presidium, Khrushchev could rely on the undivided loyalty of only two full members, Mikoyan and Kirichenko, and the ambiguous support of Suslov, but among the alternate members, he was to find wider support, in particular that of Marshal Zhukov, who at a critical moment announced that the military was solidly behind Khrushchev. This caused the "anti-party group" to fracture into its separate components at various stages in the crisis, and this accounts in part for the different forms of punishment which were meted out.

The party leadership was reorganized after June 1957 with Khrushchev's supporters generously rewarded and Marshal Zhukov elevated to full membership in the Party Presidium. In the meantime, the open factional strife at the highest level of the Soviet political system unleashed political forces inside the Soviet Union and within the Soviet bloc which have since proved to be irreversible. Factionalism became rampant within Communist parties everywhere, while social groups within the Soviet Union, particularly the intellectuals, which were hitherto silent and only latent in their power, were stimulated into political awareness and assumed greater assertiveness. As the Soviet leadership divided into factions, social groups within the Soviet system were increasingly drawn within the vortex of the struggle as various factions issued direct or indirect appeals for support. As a consequence, the Communist party has been considerably expanded in numbers, and increasingly larger numbers of people, especially within the intelligentsia, are being drawn directly or indirectly into the Soviet political process. Whether by design or default, the Khrushchev faction of the Party Apparatus was increasingly shifting to broader social foundations of support, and its internal and external policies increasingly registered this tendency.

The Soviet military in the person of Marshal Zhukov, however, emerged as a potential threat, since if Zhukov's support could enable Khrushchev to prevail over a majority in the Presidium, could it not also support a minority against Khrushchev? Acting swiftly and skillfully, and relying upon personal animosities and factional cleavages within the military, Khrushchev sent Zhukov to Albania on a junket and effectively removed and separated him both from the party hierarchy and the military upon his return. No professional military man has since occupied a seat on the Presidium.

The neutralization of the Soviet military as an immediate political threat allowed for pressures to develop from within Khrushchev's new constellation of social constituencies to couple his policy of relaxing international tensions with a radical shift in emphasis from heavy industry to consumer goods and services. Such a policy would entail a reduction in investment for both heavy industry and the military, and consequently residual, but effective opposition has come from both sectors—enough to slow down the shift but not sufficient to arrest it completely, except when international developments render it unavoidable, as was the case during the period between the U-2 crisis and the test ban treaty.

As a result, a new sociopolitical balance has emerged in the Soviet political process, whereby the previous gross disparity in power among various groups has been sharply diminished, so that the Soviet system has assumed the characteristics of a limited quasi-pluralistic polity. This has brought about a greater relaxation of controls at home, a higher level of tolerance for diversity and dissent, and less fear of severe deprivation or punishment. Policies and views which have been advanced and defeated survive to be advanced once again, to be repeatedly rebuffed, or to emerge as finally victorious. Discussion and debate of an internal character (in public or in camera), preceding decisions, are becoming increasingly significant characteristics of Soviet domestic policy, although discussion and debate concerning foreign policy still remain largely behind closed doors. But even in this connection, significant differences in opinion concerning both military and foreign policy are increasingly apparent in journals, periodicals, and books. Furthermore the open polemics with Red China have been a useful surrogate for a public debate on foreign policy, particularly for outside observers.

Thus while foreign policy has always been subordinate to internal political needs, this was not always apparent during the Stalinist era. During the past decade, however, it has become increasingly obvious not only that foreign policy decisions reflect internal political processes, but that the consequences of these decisions feed back and affect the fortunes of various individuals and groups differently. Whereas under Stalin the interplay between foreign policy and internal politics was extremely narrow—the interests of Stalin and a handful of other personalities and groups being the only social inputs into the process and all other Soviet citizens being subject to the consequences—now the spectrum of individuals and groups whose interests constitute inputs into the Soviet political system is incomparably larger. In some respects Soviet foreign policy now reflects a social spectrum of interests—numerically, not substantively—similar to the initial phases of the de-aristocraticization and gradual democratization of foreign policy in Western Europe and the United States.

Increasingly many Soviet foreign policy decisions are designed principally for the impact they will have on various internal forces. Without any attempt to organize these internal purposes served by foreign policy into a structured pattern of priorities or to distinguish among them too discretely or precisely, it can be said that the following internal purposes have influenced and will continue to influence Soviet foreign policy decisions, separately or in combination with one another or with external purposes discussed earlier:

1. To provide a faction or coalition of factions in the Soviet hierarchy with an advantage in the struggle for power.

2. To justify the continuation, modification, or repudiation of existing policies, practices, institutions, and decisions.

3. To justify the perpetuation of the existing distribution of resources, rewards, and deprivations.

4. To justify the redistribution of resources, rewards, and deprivations.

5. To pacify or satisfy the demands of particular social groups.

6. To use foreign policy decisions as a diversionary maneuver to conceal, obscure, or falsify the real reasons for certain internal policies, actions, and failures.

7. To encourage the creation or alteration of a particular internal mood.

8. To justify the retention, modification, or repudiation of certain ideological propositions whose effects are substantially internal in character.

INTERNAL SOCIAL AND POLITICAL POLARIZATION ON FOREIGN POLICY ISSUES

Soviet foreign policy decisions are nearly always marked by controversy and conflict. The allegedly monolithic will and policy of the Soviet regime has been repeatedly exposed as little more than a veneer beneath which conflict rages more or less continuously. This was true even during Stalin's rule, although conflict was largely muted. Six months before Stalin's death on the eve of the Nineteenth Party Congress Stalin ominously reported that serious controversy had taken place within the Politburo over basic questions of both internal and external policy. The "doctors' plot," which unfolded in January 1953, was apparently designed to resolve these conflicts in a way characteristic of Stalin's rule—the blood purge. Khrushchev's secret speech at the Twentieth Party Congress provided the outside world with further information and insight as to how foreign policy decisions were made under Stalin. Since these matters have already been treated in greater detail, they need not detain us here.[29]

What is significant, however, is that in spite of these fierce inner conflicts the Soviet elite at the very top has demonstrated an unusual degree of ideo-social consensus, which has been

29. Cf. *supra*, pp. 240–42.

sustained over a long period of time. It is some sort of tribute to the Soviet system that after nearly half a century of cataclysmic existence, no significant coterie of prominent exiled Soviet politicians exists anywhere. The indisputable truth is that not a single Soviet official with the former status of government minister, Central Committee member, or high Union Republican or party official has defected since the forced exile of Trotsky in 1928. This is all the more remarkable since many Soviet officials stationed abroad, including heads of diplomatic missions, returned home to Stalin's abattoir and concentration camps rather than defect. Many high Soviet state and party officials have had and continue to have opportunities to flee abroad or to remain outside the country. Even during the war, no prominent Soviet official defected or went over to the opposition. The same has not been true, of course, of lower ranking officials from the secret police, armed forces, diplomatic service, and elsewhere.[30]

This indicates that members of the Soviet elite at the very top assign highest priority to the preservation of the Soviet social order, even if it results in their individual self-destruction. Even the Soviet secret police, formerly one of the principal institutional actors in the Soviet political system, was dismantled and its elite decapitated without producing more than an insignificant ripple of defection.

The Soviet elite, we can therefore assume, assigns highest priority to the security and survival of the Soviet state and its social order. Whether the Soviet elite would sacrifice the social order to assure the survival of the physical components of the Soviet state—its territory, material property, and population— is difficult to say, but the author's guess would be that it would not; that is, it would risk thermonuclear destruction rather than allow the Soviet social order to be disestablished. This high degree of ideo-social consensus is not characteristic of other Communist countries, with the possible exception of China.

Soviet foreign policy decisions are formulated within the

30. Cf., for example, Alexander Barmine, *One Who Survived* (New York, Putnam's, 1945); W. G. Krivitsky, *In Stalin's Secret Service* (New York, Harper, 1939); Alexander Orlov, *The Secret History of Stalin's Crimes* (New York, Random House, 1953); Peter Deriabin and Frank Gibney, *The Secret World* (Garden City, Doubleday, 1959); Aleksandr Kaznacheev, *Inside a Soviet Embassy* (Philadelphia, Lippincott, 1962).

party and executed through state organs.[31] Differences and conflicts over foreign policy in the party may result from several factors, individually or in combination:

1. Personality differences at the very highest levels, involving personal ambitions for power, prestige, and status.

2. Group differences at a lower level of the hierarchy, a factor which may reflect itself in factional conflicts—resulting from divergent perceptions of the impact of foreign policy decisions upon the status, role, and power of the various social elites, institutional groupings, regional combinations, national groups, and cliques and factions within these major groupings —for ascendancy within their particular grouping or institution. This factionalism may reflect itself in conflict between state and party institutions, between various state institutions, between various party organizations, between young, ambitious individuals and their older superiors, between various sectors of the economy, between local and national priorities, and between various geographical and nationality areas.

3. Differences over doctrinal interpretations, stemming largely, under existing conditions, from differing perceptions of how doctrinal positions may affect the role and status of the individual and collective actors in the system as each attempts to define and shape ideology to accord with its own interests. While doctrinal interpretations are frequently shaped to meet social interests, very often, because of the peculiar role ideology plays in the Soviet system, ideological differences may assume a separate significance which transcends conflicts of social interests.

4. Differences over strategy and tactics; that is, differences over the most effective way to achieve agreed-upon common objectives, defined in terms of the social priorities established in the process of implementing common goals. Frequently several strategies or tactical approaches may have equal chance of success, but a different set of social priorities may be involved in the process in each case. This type of conflict has become very explicit with respect to the Sino-Soviet dispute as was discussed earlier in another connection. Just as individuals, groups, institutions, etc., seek to shape ideology to satisfy or ac-

31. Cf. V. V. Aspaturian, "Soviet Foreign Policy," in R. C. Macridis, ed., *Foreign Policy in World Politics* (Englewood Cliffs, New Jersey, Prentice-Hall, 1962), pp. 152–76.

cord with their particular interests, so are strategies and tactics subject to similar distortion.

Soviet doctrine considers personality factors to be of little consequence in policy decisions, but ever since the denunciations of Stalin and the "cult of personality," it has become virtually impossible to sustain this view in word or deed. Indeed, since Stalin's death, Soviet sources have repeatedly conceded that personal ambitions and personal animosities have played an important role in Soviet political behavior. Stalin is characterized as having abused his position in order to enhance his personal power, while Beria, Malenkov, Molotov and the anti-party group, and Zhukov have been successively accused of seeking personal power or making decisions which would settle "personal scores." [32]

Even more important, Soviet sources seem to emphasize that these individuals were acting as representatives of groups and using institutional structures as vehicles of power against the Party Apparatus (always identified as "The Party"). Thus Beria was charged with using the secret police as a vehicle of power,[33] Malenkov with the state bureaucracy, Molotov with the Foreign Ministry and the Ministry of State Control, Pervukhin and Saburov with various economic agencies, Kaganovich with the Ministry of Supply, and Marshal Zhukov with the armed forces.[34]

32. Kosygin, for example, charged that the "basic motive" of the anti-party group was "personal resentment and ambition"; that they "felt they had little power." *Pravda*, July 4, 1957. S. D. Ignatiev revealed Bulganin's craving for more power and prestige by asserting: "Nikita Sergeyevich [Khrushchev] was right when he said: 'Bulganin ran after a piece of gingerbread which the antiparty group offered him. Although the gingerbread was poisonous, Bulganin, being dissatisfied with his position in the Party, nevertheless ran after it when it was promised to him.' " *Plenum Tsentralnovo Komiteta Kommunisticheskoi Partii Sovietskovo Soyuza, 15–19 Dekabria 1958 Goda, Stenograficheskii Otchet* (Moscow, 1958), p. 350.

33. The statement announcing the arrest of Beria made the following charges: "It has been established by the inquiry that Beria, using his position, forged a treacherous group of conspirators, hostile to the Soviet State, with the criminal goal of using the organs of the Ministry of Internal Affairs, both central and local, against the Communist Party and the Government of the U.S.S.R. in the interests of foreign capital, striving in its perfidious schemes to set the Ministry of Internal Affairs above the Party and Government in order to seize power and liquidate the Soviet worker-peasant system for the purpose of restoring capitalism and the domination of the bourgeoisie." *Pravda*, December 17, 1953.

34. For details concerning this aspect of the factional struggles in the Soviet hierarchy, cf., H. S. Dinerstein, *War and the Soviet Union* (New York, Praeger, 1959); Robert Conquest, *Power and Policy in the U.S.S.R.*

It might be pointed out that in all cases mentioned above the personal passion for power, and the attempt to use institutional structures successfully as power bases, failed because Khrushchev, the chief beneficiary of all these failures, was able to use the Party Apparatus skillfully, in alliance first with one group and then another, to establish the supremacy of the Party Apparatus in the system and the dominance of his faction within it.

Without going into a detailed accounting of the intricate maneuvers and intrigues involved, it can be assumed that these factional conflicts arise because a symbiotic relationship becomes established between the interests of certain individual leaders and the interests of certain elites. While these functional elites are fairly well defined, considerable lateral mobility exists at various levels among them, and personal attachments to certain institutions are likely to be transitory and opportunistic rather than permanent, insofar as the leaders are concerned.

Furthermore, the institutional and functional-interest groupings are themselves divided by personality and factional conflicts over the relative importance of various branches and sectors of the government and the economy, the allocation of budgets, and the assignments of role and mission. To the degree that foreign policy decisions affect these relationships, they give rise to internal factional strife.

The foreign policy and defense posture of the Soviet state establishes a certain configuration of priorities in the allocation of budgetary expenses and scarce resources. Various individuals and groups develop a vested interest in a particular foreign policy or defense posture because of the role and status it confers upon them. Correspondingly, other individuals and groups in Soviet society perceive themselves as deprived in status and rewards because of existing allocation of expenditures and resources; hence they might initiate proposals that could alter existing foreign policy and defense postures or support proposals submitted by other groups or individuals.

Herbert S. Dinerstein has demonstrated rather impressively how Khrushchev cleverly manipulated the fear of war to his advantage in his struggle first with Malenkov and then with the antiparty group in 1957. "Alarms of war," he writes,

---

(New York, St. Martin's Press, 1961), esp. pp. 292–328; Roger Pethybridge, *A Key to Soviet Politics* (New York, Praeger, 1962); and Aspaturian in Macridis, *op. cit.,* pp. 152–68; cf. *infra,* pp. 267–68.

may offer political advantage to the alarmist in a factional fight. To the factionary, of course, his attaining office, or continuing in it, is a matter of major ideological import. The opponent's faction, he believes, will take the country to the dogs by perverting true Bolshevism or by failing to adjust it to the changing situation. When, in the early months of 1957, Khrushchev raised a wholly contrived danger of war, he himself and those who supported him probably believed that his displacement would be accompanied by dangerous political changes. The alarm of war was raised to keep one faction in office and this suggests that a lower probability was assigned in fact to the likelihood of war.[35]

The Soviet Union, like the United States, is involved in a continuous great debate over foreign policy and national security matters centering around the issue of whether the heightening of international tensions or the relaxation of international tensions best serves the "national interests." In both countries there are important spokesmen on both sides, although in the Soviet Union those who may be interested in maintaining international tensions make their views known only behind closed doors or in the esoteric type of communication which has inspired the profession of "Kremlinology." The polemics with Peking, however, provide the outside world with some idea of how the debate behind closed doors may be taking place. Thus on June 19, 1964, *Izvestiia* published the substance of an alleged interview between a Latin-American Communist and Mao Tse-tung, in which the Chinese leader purportedly said:

Who benefits from international tension? The United States? Great Britain? The world proletariat? In this lies the problem. Personally, I like international tension. The United States will realize that the tension they themselves have created is not advantageous to them, since it can force the supporters of peace and all working people of the entire world to think, and will bring a greater number of people into the Communist Parties. . . . There is a Chinese proverb: "People dare to touch the tiger's whiskers." This is why I think that we should not fear international tension.[36]

And a year earlier, Moscow, in an "open letter" to Soviet party members, bluntly asserted:

One gets the impression that the leaders of the C.P.C. think it to their advantage to maintain and intensify international tension, especially in relations between the U.S.S.R. and the U.S.A. They obviously think that the Soviet Union should answer provocations with provocations, should fall into the traps set by the "madmen" from the

35. Dinerstein, *op. cit.*, p. 93.
36. *Izvestiia,* June 19, 1964. Cf. also *Pravda,* September 21 and 22, 1963.

imperialist camp, should accept the challenge of the imperialists to enter a competition in adventurism and aggressiveness—i.e., a competition not to ensure peace but to unleash war.[37]

On the other hand, the official Soviet position is that a relaxation of tensions is beneficial to the Soviet Union, the Communist world as a whole, and the revolutionary movement:

In a situation of rising international tension war hysteria strengthens the influence of militarist and reactionary forces; with the successes of the policy of peaceful coexistence, on the other hand, more favorable conditions arise for the masses' gains on the side of socialism, for development of the revolutionary movement.[38]

Only Molotov and the antiparty group have been specifically identified by the Soviet leadership with a policy of favoring international tensions. Nevertheless the factional conflicts in the Soviet Union—over budgets, military strategy, the likelihood of war and violence, the nature of imperialism, perceptions of American "ruling class" behavior, and the proper balance between the production of consumer goods and services and heavy industry in the Soviet economy—clearly indicate that tension-producing policies tend to favor certain groups within Soviet society and tension-lessening policies tend to favor others. Although a residual fervor of an ideological commitment to

37. *Pravda*, July 14, 1963.
38. "For the Triumph of Creative Marxism-Leninism, Against Revising Course of the World Communist Movement," *Kommunist*, No. 11, July 1963, pp. 19–20. Yury Zhukov, in an article entitled "Who Is For, Who Is Against?" linked the Chinese position with the "madmen" in the United States on the basis of the formula embodied in the title of his article. *Pravda*, July 29, 1963. Another Pravda writer, F. Burlatsky, in an article entitled "Concrete Analysis Is a Major Requirement of Leninism," rejects the Chinese view "that the revolutionary struggle of the working class in capitalist countries and the national liberation movement can develop successfully only if there is constant international tension—'cold war,' " and rhetorically asks: "What effect does an increase in international tension and a heightening of war psychosis have on internal conditions, on the political struggle of the masses? There can be only one answer to this question: a highly negative effect. . . . By using the bugbear of the 'threat of war' and inflaming nationalist prejudices and chauvinism the ruling classes in the capitalist countries have striven and are still striving to undermine the international solidarity of the proletariat and to isolate its advanced forces. An atmosphere of war hysteria makes it easier for the forces of reaction to carry out repressions against the Communists. . . . On the other hand, a slackening of tension and successes of the policy of peaceful coexistence are accompanied by an intensification of the workers' movement and a new upsurge of class struggle in the capitalist world." *Pravda*, July 25, 1963. Cf. also N. Inozemtsev, "Peaceful Coexistence and the World Revolutionary Process," *Pravda*, July 28, 1963.

specific goals and policies remains operative in the thought and behavior of Soviet leaders, there has also been an inexorable tendency for individual leaders and factional interest groups to perceive the interests of society as a whole through their own prism and to distort and adjust the national interest accordingly. Ideological distortion takes shape in similar fashion in order to impart the necessary symbolic legitimacy to policies and interests demanded by the Soviet system as part of its political ritual.

A particular interest group or social formation may often have a role or function imposed upon it by events, circumstances, policies, and the mechanism of a given social system in response to certain situations not of its own making or, in some instances, situations that objectively provided the basis for its very creation and existence. Particular interest groups may not have sought such a role, or have taken any initiative in acquiring it; they may not even have existed before the function was demanded. Yet once this role or function has been thrust upon them, they adjust to it and develop a vested interest in it as the source of their existence and status. As individual members adjust to their role, develop it, and invest their energies and careers in it, they almost automatically resist the deprivation or diminution of this function in their self-interest.

The same is true of groups which have been assigned limited or arrested roles or functions in society—except that they develop a vested interest in expanding the role, dignifying it with greater status and prestige, and demanding greater rewards. Consequently it is extremely difficult to distill out of Soviet factional positions those aspects of thought and behavior which express conflicting perceptions of self-interest on the part of various individuals, factions, and groups as opposed to authentic "objective" considerations of a broader interest, whether national or ideological—since they are so inextricably intertwined and interdependent.

All that we can assume at this point is that certain individuals, factions, and socio-institutional functional groups seem to thrive and flourish and others to be relatively deprived and arrested in their development under conditions of exacerbated international tensions, while the situation is reversed when a relaxation of international tensions takes place.

Without attempting to speculate on the motives for a particular foreign and security policy, let us examine the possible impact upon the interests of various social groups in Soviet society of a foreign policy based upon expectations of high international tensions (whether generated from without or within) as opposed to one which would be based upon the expectation of a relaxation of international tensions and *détente* (irrespective of whether generated from without or within). It should be made clear that a one-to-one relationship between cause and effect is much too simple an explanation even for hypothetical purposes, but the reconstructions below are based on actual reactions of individual Soviet spokesmen representing various groups in Soviet society, as reported in the Soviet press or attributed to them by other Communist sources, including the Chinese.

"WHO BENEFITS" IN SOVIET SOCIETY FROM INTERNATIONAL TENSIONS?

Soviet writers are fond of citing Lenin's injunction that the rewards of a particular social system should not be defined in terms of "who favors" a particular policy but rather of "who benefits" from a given policy. Thus one Soviet writer, in applying Lenin's maxim to an examination of the role of the "military-industrial complex" in American society, made the following observation:

Lenin taught us that behind every proposal and every measure are the real interests of quite definite political and social groups and that in each specific case it is necessary to elucidate whom these proposals and measures benefit. "The important thing is not *who* directly upholds a certain policy, for to defend any of his views in the conditions of the noble modern capitalist system a rich man can always 'hire' or buy or enlist any number of lawyers, writers, even members of parliament, professors, priests, and so on. We live in the business times when the bourgeoisie is not ashamed of trading in both honor and conscience. . . . No, in politics it is not so important who directly upholds certain views. The important thing is *who benefits* by these views, these proposals, these measures." [39]

A great deal has been said and written about the military-industrial complex in the United States and its alleged vested

39. I. Yermashov, "The Warfare State," *International Affairs* (Moscow), No. 7, July 1962, p. 19.

stake in maintaining and even fanning the Cold War. While individuals and groups undoubtedly exist in the United States whose interests might be adversely affected by a relaxation of international tensions and a *détente*, it is not generally recognized that a counterpart to the American military-industrial complex exists in the Soviet Union, whose interests are also favored under conditions of international tension and Cold War. We already have it on the highest Soviet authority that the social foundations exist in Communist-governed societies for individuals and groups to develop a vested interest in maintaining international tensions, since the current Soviet leadership has explicitly charged that both the antiparty group in the C.P.S.U. (which almost seized power in 1957) and the Chinese Communist leaders at the present time have a vested interest in keeping international tensions at a high pitch.

It would be absurd to maintain, as Lenin does implicitly, that because certain individuals and groups are favored by policies flowing from an exacerbation of the international environment these groups necessarily favor or deliberately promote policies designed to sustain or create international tensions, any more than it can be asserted that individuals and groups favored by a peacetime economy would deliberately favor or promote policies which would expose the country to external danger simply to avoid a rise in defense expenditures which might adversely affect their interests. It cannot be excluded, however, that motivations of this character also exist. The problem is much more complicated than conscious motivation. Aside from the phenomena of "false consciousness," false perceptions, mistaken judgment, false or incomplete information, misinterpretation, etc., which are always involved in attempting to relate social motivation to policy behavior, there is the more serious problem of genuine and unconscious distortion of the objective situation through the prism of individual or group self-interest. Perception itself is frequently a reflection of self-interest rather than objective reality, and even more frequently it is simply a distortion of objective reality to a greater or lesser degree.

What can be assumed, because of these complicated psychological dialogues between perceptions of self-interest and perception of objective reality, is that groups that are favored by a particular policy or situation have a greater inclination to perceive objective reality in terms of their self-interest. Hence groups that are objectively favored by heightened international tensions might have a greater propensity to perceive external threats and a corresponding disinclination to recognize that the nature of a threat has been altered, reduced, or eliminated, thus requiring new policies which might adversely affect them. On the other hand, groups that are objectively favored by relaxation of international tensions or a peacetime economy might be more prone to perceive a premature alteration, diminution, or elimination of an external threat and a corresponding tendency to be skeptical about external threats which arise if they would result in a radical upsurge in defense expenditures and a reallocation of resources and social rewards.

Even sophisticated Soviet writers now find it difficult to apply consistently the Leninist maxim of "who benefits" to the American political and social scene in a simplistic manner, since it would result in contravening other cherished dogmas of Soviet ideology. Thus one influential Soviet specialist on U.S. affairs, after a trip to the United States, revealed an increasing sophistication in observing and reporting on American society and politics:

The picture of political and intellectual life in the U.S.A. is extremely complex and varied and is in many ways contradictory; we saw this more than once during our trip. It is perfectly natural to find completely different ways of thinking among people occupying diametrically opposite positions in the social structure—representatives of "big business" and of the working class, say. But there are considerable differences even within the basic classes. For instance, there are great differences in position and views between the 4,000,-000 unemployed and the best-paid strata of the working class. We also encountered the following situation: In conditions where the overwhelming majority of the American working class favors a disarmament program, the segment of workers who are directly connected with arms production favors the preservation of this production in full. . . . It is common knowledge that in the conditions of capitalist reality, monopoly capital is the center of political reaction. However, the monopolistic bourgeoisie of the U.S.A. is by no means unified or homogeneous; by no means all of its representatives support the "madmen" or the "war party." . . . There are deep contradictions between the group of influential monopoly associations directly engaged in war production and all the other industrial and banking corporations, some of them very large but still deprived of access to the "pie" of government military orders. These contradictions find acute expression in the approach to many practical questions: tax cuts, the military budget, foreign economic policy and others.[40]

Factional differences over foreign policy and budgetary questions are not directly expressed in Soviet media of information and communications, since neither political factions nor the social foundations for divergent interests on such questions are supposed to exist. Only after a serious debate, which leads to an open struggle for power, has been definitively resolved are retrospective factional activities admitted, but the standard Soviet ritual is that they have been eliminated and that no social basis exists for their perpetuation or revival.[41] Some Soviet sociologists, with empirical and behavioral orientations— which is a distinctive intellectual innovation in itself—are beginning to concede that social and other differences in Soviet society influence and shape social and political attitudes. "The opinion of each person polled," according to a Soviet experimenter with public-polling techniques, "is influenced by the nature of his attitude toward life, by his moral evaluation of his personal goal and means of attaining it," which, in turn, is dependent on "how the respondent's social situation, age, and so on influenced his opinion." Thus he explained:

The poll permitted determining the degree of dependence of the judgment of different groups of youth on the nature of their activity (factory workers, collective farmers, officeworkers, engineers, professional people, servicemen, students, and school children, as well as the nonworking); education (incomplete secondary, secondary, higher); age (under 17, 18–22, 23–30); place of residence (Moscow, large cities, other cities, countryside); and sex.[42]

40. N. Inozemtsev, "The Hopes and Anxieties of Americans," *Pravda,* December 25, 1963.
41. Cf. Kozlov's explanation at the 22nd Party Congress cited above, p. 227. The statement announcing Beria's arrest, for example, asserted: "Deprived of any social support within the U.S.S.R., Beria and his accomplices based their criminal calculations on support of the conspiracy by reactionary imperialist forces from abroad." Yet, he was also accused of undertaking "criminal measures in order to stir up the remains of bourgeois-nationalist elements in the Union Republics, to sow enmity and discord among the peoples of the U.S.S.R., and, in the first place, to undermine the friendship of the peoples of the U.S.S.R. with the great Russian people," which indicates that he was looking for internal social support among the border nationalities. *Pravda,* December 17, 1953.
42. M. Kh. Igitkhanyan, "The Spiritual Image of Soviet Youth," *Voprosy Filosofii,* No. 6, June 1963, pp. 75–84.

The tyranny exercised by the international situation on Soviet budgetary allocations and the fortuitous and objective impact they have on the fortunes, status, rewards, and deprivations of various groups in Soviet society was more than implicit in Khrushchev's frequent complaints about the allocation of money and resources.

It is necessary to state frankly: When the government reviews questions of the distribution of means by branches—where to direct how much of the available resources—difficult puzzles often have to be solved. On the one hand, it would be desirable to build more enterprises that make products for satisfying man's requirements, that produce clothing, footwear, and other goods for improving people's lives. It would be desirable to invest more means in agriculture and to expand housing construction. We know that the people need this. The leaders of our party and government themselves come from the people; they know their needs and share their life. To give more good things to the people—this is the basic goal of the Communist Party of the Soviet Union. . . . On the other hand, life dictates the necessity for spending enormous funds on maintaining our military power at the required level. This reduces and cannot help but reduce the people's possibilities of obtaining direct benefits. But this must be done in order to defend the victories of the October Revolution, the victories of socialism, and to keep the imperialists from attacking our homeland, from unleashing a general war. That is why when calculating available resources we must soberly consider the needs of the peaceful economy and the requirements of defense and must so combine the one with the other that there will be no overemphasis on either.[43]

43. *Pravda*, February 28, 1963. A year later, at the February 1964 Plenum of the Central Committee, Khrushchev, in discussing the plan to expand chemical production, once again revealed in graphic, if only schematic form, how various groups protected their interests against attempts to reallocate resources to their detriment. "How is it possible to explain such an attitude toward chemistry in a country that has given the world such great figures of chemical science? . . . Only by the fact that a section of the workers of the Gosplan, by force of their departmental attachment to specific branches of production, did not appreciate the importance of chemistry in time. . . . It would seem beyond question that chemistry should be given priority, . . . that more capital investments should be devoted to the development of the chemical industry. . . . In 1958 we adopted a decision and outlined a program for the development of chemistry, but it is not being fully carried out. Why? Is it that funds have been insufficient? Nothing of the kind. We are overfulfilling the plan for metallurgy, oil extraction, and in other branches. But in chemistry . . . the tasks envisaged by the May Plenum of the Central Committee have not been accomplished. How is this to be explained? How is the process of the distribution of funds among different branches proceeding in our country? Let us take as an example the metallurgy committee. The heads of this committee are little interested in chemistry. They concern themselves pri-

The social and institutional groups in Soviet society which appear to benefit from an aggressive foreign policy and the maintenance of international tensions are (1) the armed forces, (2) the heavy-industrial managers, (3) professional party *apparatchiki* and ideologues. By no means do all individuals or subelites and cliques within these groups see eye to eye on foreign policy issues. Some individuals and subelites, for opportunistic or careerist reasons or functional adaptability, are able to adjust to a relaxation of tensions by preserving or even improving their role and status. The significant point is that the main impetus for an aggressive policy and the chief opposition to a relaxation of tensions find their social and functional foundations within these three socio-functional or socio-institutional groups, whose common perception of interests results in an informal "military-industrial-apparatus complex." Their attitudes stem almost entirely from the function and role they play in Soviet society and the rewards in terms of prestige, status, and power which are derived from these functions in time of high international tensions as opposed to a *détente*.

The professional military, on the whole, has a natural interest in a large and modern military establishment and a high priority on budget and resources; the heavy-industrial managerial groups have a vested stake in preserving the primacy of their sector of the economy; and the Party Apparatus traditionally has had a vested interest in ideological conformity and the social controls

marily with the way metal production is going to develop. . . . Huge quantities of various materials are necessary to build Communism. Hence, workers responsible for the production of steel must understand what is new and draw the necessary practical conclusions. It is this kind of understanding of which there is a shortage in some leading workers. The Gosplan is called upon to correct the narrow-mindedness of branch workers. It is duty bound to redistribute in good time material and financial resources for the benefit of new, progressive branches and to maintain reserves for this purpose. . . . By contrast, we have at times taken the position that a definite place is assigned to every sector of every branch and it is very difficult to change existing proportions. . . . Everyone then guards his own sector within the limits assigned to him. . . . And what shall we do with what is new in the economy, since it is emerging every day and demanding attention and material safeguards? The resources are already distributed among the old branches and trends. This approach impedes the development of new branches, and technical progress. . . ." *Pravda*, February 15, 1964. Cf. also Carl Linden, "Khrushchev and the Party Battle," *Problems of Communism*, September-October 1963, pp. 27–35; S. I. Ploss, *Recent Alignments in the Soviet Elite* (Princeton, Center of International Studies, 1964).

which they rationalized, thus ensuring the primacy of the
Apparatus over all other social forces in the Soviet system. All
these functional roles are served best under conditions of international tension. Consequently, these groups wittingly or unwittingly have developed a vested interest in either maintaining
international tensions or creating the illusion of insecurity and
external danger, which would produce the same effect.

To the degree that individuals or subelites within these
groups are able socially to retool their functions and adapt them
to peacetime or purely internal functions, then do they correspondingly lose interest in an aggressive or tension-preserving
policy.

THE PARTY APPARATUS

The major enigma in relating socio-functional and institutional groups in Soviet society to various internal and external
policy positions is the precise nature of the factional pattern
within the Party Apparatus. It is relatively easier to decipher
internal factional cleavages within the armed forces and heavy
industry because of the greater spectrum of technical and functional divisions which characterizes their activities. The Party
Apparatus, on the other hand, is the only major socio-institutional group in the Soviet system which performs neither a
productive nor a clear service function. While it guides and
audits both the economy and the government, and members of
the Apparatus have assumed formal administrative responsibility in both the economic and governmental establishments from
time to time, it is neither an executive nor an administrative
elite. Its sole function in Soviet society stems from its unilaterally preempted role of manipulating and articulating the
will of the party. It sets the ideological norms of the Soviet
social order, formulates both internal and external policy, and
finally audits or checks on their fulfillment by other socio-functional and institutional elites.

Traditionally the Apparatus has been associated with the internal missions of ideological conformity and political direction
and the external mission of promoting world revolution. As
pointed out earlier, these missions of the Party Apparatus were
increasingly alienating it from the numerically large and

potentially significant social constituencies, whose will it was allegedly expressing. On the other hand, the dismantling of the special instrument of coercion erected by Stalin as a counterpoise to the armed forces, the secret police, left the Apparatus increasingly dependent upon the armed forces and their allies, the heavy-industrial managers.

Khrushchev's response to the social dilemma of the Apparatus was to provide it with a more durable social function by associating its ideological mission more directly with the will of the Soviet people in the concrete rather than in the historical abstraction of a predetermined proletarian mission. This has assumed the goal of "building Communism"—that is, raising the Soviet standard of living within the ideological norms of a Communist society, which, in turn, required a relaxation of international tensions so that a radical reduction of defense expenditures could be realized.

This social retooling process has been viewed with skepticism by many old-time Apparatus careerists and has given rise to new patterns of factional conflict within the Apparatus, whose outlines are still extremely fluid and hazy. Since the expulsion of the antiparty group in 1957, there are no Stalinists, *per se,* remaining in the Apparatus. Differences, however, have arisen over the degree and extent of the de-Stalinization process and the treatment of the antiparty group. What can more properly be described as a "conservative" faction—also anonymously called "dogmatists" by their detractors—whose leaders appear to have been the late Kozlov and Suslov, seems to have played a significant role in opposing, slowing down, or arresting Khrushchev's policies and actually may have been in a position to oust him in the spring of 1963, after the Cuban missile crisis. After Kozlov suffered a heart attack in April 1963, Khrushchev's fortunes seemed to take a turn for the better.

This conservative faction represents two subfactional groups within the Party Apparatus, the professional ideologues, whose major spokesman is Suslov, and those who are more directly involved in control and audit functions, whose spokesman seemed to be Kozlov before his heart attack and subsequent death. To the degree that the interests of this faction require greater investment in military and heavy-industrial expenditures, it also serves to articulate the interests of the professional military and of heavy industry, since neither of these groups is directly represented in either the Party Presidium or the Secretariat.

The conservative faction of the Apparatus saw in Khrushchev's policies a threat to the very existence of the Apparatus itself, for if the external ideological function of the Apparatus erodes and its internal functions can be more efficiently performed by technical and administrative specialists, what is the Apparatus to do? The fact that Yugoslavia is still considered to be a "socialist state," although its Communist party has withered into a "league," must be a source of grim anxiety for this group, since it establishes the precedent of a socialist state without a separate party machine.[44]

Other differences between various factions in the Apparatus reflect themselves in divergent perceptions of the American "ruling class" and the likelihood of an American surprise attack, the level of military expenditures, the balance between heavy and light industry, on methods for increasing agricultural production, the degree of ideological conformity imposed upon the arts, sciences, and professions, and finally the degree to which Moscow can afford to alienate Peking.

The periodic and frequent rotation of personnel in the Apparatus as a whole and the constant expansion and contraction of membership in the Party Presidium and Secretariat, particularly after serious changes in the direction of policy, all attest to the factional ferment taking place within the Apparatus. Since the Chinese position on many matters seems to coincide with the views of the conservative faction of the Soviet Party Apparatus, it is likely that Peking was directing its appeal to this group to overthrow Khrushchev, while Suslov's extravagant defense of Khrushchev in response could have been interpreted as a forced profession of loyalty.[45] Peking apparently made a

44. On April 8, 1963, the May Day slogan for Yugoslavia published by *Pravda* failed to enumerate it among the countries "building socialism," although a Soviet letter to Peking on March 30, 1963, repudiated the Chinese view that Yugoslavia had "betrayed Marxism-Leninism" and emphatically affirmed that "we consider that it is a socialist country." On April 11, 1963, *Pravda* published a revised slogan for Yugoslavia, which described it as "building socialism." Cf. Carl Linden, *op. cit.*, and S. I. Ploss, *Some Political Aspects of the June 1963 CPSU Central Committee Session* (Princeton, Center of International Studies, 1963).

45. The Chinese are apparently making covert appeals to other segments of Soviet society. The noted Soviet writer Konstantin Simonov, in an article

similar esoteric overture to the Soviet military by publicly espousing a position on the validity of Clausewitz's maxim on war and politics much like that of the Soviet professional military and opposed to that adhered to by the Khrushchev faction.[46]

entitled, "A Writer's Notes: MAKE NO MISTAKE!" published in *Pravda* on May 24, 1964, broadly hinted that the Chinese apparently thought that they could make some headway among Soviet intellectuals: "The Chinese splitters . . . have no dispute, you understand, with the Soviet people, with the Soviet intelligentsia, with rank-and-file Soviet Communists, with the peoples of the socialist countries or the Communists of the world! They are arguing, you understand, only with the leadership of our party; they have nothing to argue about with us. They are possessed by a hope that, though it reeks of provocation, is still naive in its absurdity—the hope that perhaps some one of us will fall for the bait, will believe that the dispute is not between them and us, not between the Chinese leaders and the world Communist movement, but above our heads, so to speak, only with our leaders. It seems that it is this hope that has called forth the attempts to dose us with ponderous and tedious, clumsily contrived propaganda on the radio and the attempts to distribute to private addresses various documents containing ridiculous attacks on our party and its leadership. . . . I want to say: No, it won't work! It won't work in general, it won't work in particular, it won't work anywhere or with anyone. The bait with which you are trying to catch at least something in our country is rotten, and our people are not the kind who can be caught with this rotten stuff."

46. The Chinese leaders are apparently making an even more subtle appeal to elements of the Soviet military who did not see eye to eye with Khrushchev on the relationship between politics and war, military strategy and foreign policy, and on the question of whether Clausewitz's maxim that "war is a continuation of politics by violent means" is still a valid proposition during the nuclear age. Although the first edition of Sokolovskii's *Military Strategy* was attacked by various political writers on these points, the second edition reflected little change from the view expressed in the first. Cf. Leon Gouré, *Notes on the Second Edition of Marshal V. D. Sokolovskii's "Military Strategy"* (Santa Monica, RAND Corporation, 1964), and Thomas W. Wolfe, *Soviet Strategy at the Crossroads* (Santa Monica, RAND Corporation, 1964), esp. pp. 71–82. The Chinese in their polemics with Moscow have charged that Khrushchev had abandoned the Leninist twist to the Clausewitz maxim, and the Khrushchev faction confirmed this by asserting that the Clausewitz formula was now outmoded in its traditional application. One Soviet commentator, Viktor Glazunov, has gone so far as to say that the formula no longer even applies to imperialist countries and that war can no longer be considered as a rational instrument of foreign policy: "In general, the views of the Chinese leaders on nuclear arms and the nature of modern warfare can only cause extreme bewilderment. It is said that nuclear rocket arms are merely a 'current type' of weapon introducing nothing new to the nature of war. Consequently, Clausewitz's old narrow formula that war is a continuation of policy still holds true in another form. And Clausewitz is at the moment very popular in Peking. . . . Hitherto there have been victors and vanquished whereas now entire countries and peoples would disappear. For them thermonuclear war would no longer be a continuation of policy, good or bad, just or unjust. For them it would be the end of everything on earth. How, then, can one

THE SOVIET ARMED FORCES

Unlike the Party Apparatus, the Soviet military has an important and highly valued function to perform in Soviet society, which since World War II has carried the armed forces to a new pinnacle of prestige, esteem, and power. It is axiomatic in any society which is subject to civilian control and ideologically dedicated to the values and goals of peace that in time of war or external danger, the value and esteem of the military is maximized and its role and influence in society magnified, while in time of peace or reduced danger, the opposite effect is likely to take place. Soviet society is conventional in this regard since, unlike fascist or chauvinistic ideologies, war is not glorified in the Soviet Union as a value-end in itself and neither is the martial spirit. Ideologically the Soviet system is committed to the abolition of war and of all military establishments. Yet unlike the Apparatus, which has alienated many groups in Soviet society, the armed forces are a genuinely cherished and popular institution and are considered more or less indispensable. Differences do arise, however, as to the size, composition, and cost of the military establishment, and it is at this point that interest configurations assume shape, and influence the political process and the role of the military in it.

War and international tensions maximize the threat to the state and hence almost spontaneously enhance the role, status, prestige, and power of the armed forces as an institution and its individual members. It guarantees a very high priority in the allocation of money, resources, and personnel. High military officials assume greater influence in the formulation and execution of policy because of their indispensable expertise; this results in a significant spill-over into nonmilitary areas and retains a high residual political force even as war and external danger recede.

As specialists in manipulating the instruments of violence and coercion and with a high value placed upon its services, during periods of insecurity the military threatens to become a powerful entity in its own right while it dwarfs the immediate power of other elites in Soviet society. Since the Soviet military

say that nothing has changed in the nature of war since the appearance of nuclear weapons?" *Moscow International Service* (radio), July 22, 1964.

has rarely been employed as an internal repressive force, its standing and popularity with the public are enviable in the Soviet system, whereas other elites have been tarnished in one degree or another with the stigma of Stalinist repression. This makes a large military establishment even more menacing to the political authorities, who remain haunted by the possibilities of a Bonapartist coup. The recurring fear of a military coup has been dealt with by the party in a number of ways. Stalin not only subjected the military to party and secret police controls, but he also ensured compliance through periodic purges and decapitation. Since Stalin's time, the incubus of police repression has been lifted and techniques of terror no longer employed. The question of party controls and indoctrination remains a source of continuous friction with the professional military, which seeks to limit the role of the party while the Apparatus endeavors to maximize it. Khrushchev also skillfully used personal and clique rivalries and animosities within the military, whether based on professional divisions of military labor, cronyism, or simple opportunism, in order to fracture it into internal factions and keep it disunited. The professional military probably reached its maximum point of development as an autonomous political actor under Marshal Zhukov in 1956 and 1957, when Zhukov not only had administrative direction and control of the military as Minister of Defense but sat on the Party Presidium as well, where his presence was first a comfort and then a threat to Khrushchev and his faction. The fact that Zhukov had also reduced party controls in the military to the vanishing point was also a source of anxiety to the civilian authorities.

The charges leveled against Zhukov after his removal in October 1957 were essentially four in number: (1) he tried to separate the armed forces from the party; (2) he encouraged and promoted a "cult of Zhukov" in the military; (3) he tried to organize the armed forces into a personal political machine; and (4) he was planning to seize power in a Bonapartist coup. Thus the statement issued by the Central Committee contained the following charges:

The Plenary Session of the C.P.S.U. Central Committee notes that of late the former Defense Minister Comrade Zhukov has . . . pursued a policy of curtailing the work of Party organizations, political organs and military councils, of abolishing the leadership and control of the

Party, its Central Committee and Government over the Army and Navy. The Plenary Session of the Central Committee has established that the cult of Comrade Zhukov's personality was cultivated in the Soviet Army with his personal participation. . . . Comrade Zhukov . . . proved to be a politically unstable leader disposed to adventurism.[47]

All Zhukov's personal enemies and professional rivals, including his successor as Minister of Defense, Marshal Malinovsky, were mobilized to heap criticism and abuse upon the fallen warrior. Marshal Konev repeated the charge that Zhukov sought "a separation between the Army and the Navy on the one hand and the Party on the other" and further specified that he betrayed "a definite tendency to regard the Soviet Armed Forces as his own domain." [48] And two years later Malinovsky intimated that Zhukov was planning to seize power and establish a military regime:

The C.C. of the C.P.S.U. discerned in an extremely timely manner the aspiration of the former Minister of Defense, Marshal Zhukov, to sever the Army from the Party, and gave this new Bonaparte a sharp rap over the knuckles.[49]

Since the removal of Marshal Zhukov, the armed forces have not been directly represented on the Party Presidium or Secretariat, and Malinovsky's position as defense minister does not entitle him to sit on the Presidium of the Council of Ministers, the chief policy-making organ of the government. He as well as other military professionals, however, are frequently invited in for consultation and discussion.

While the professional military does not currently loom as a direct threat to the party regime as it did under Zhukov, it nevertheless still functions as a powerful political force with its own perception of its interests in Soviet society. On the whole, the professional military assumes a harder position than Khrushchev on foreign policy issues and its outlook was more in tune with the views of the conservative faction in the Apparatus. In general, the professional military has resisted troop cuts and reduced military expenditures; is skeptical of disarmament and arms control measures; is more prone to view U.S. intentions as implacably aggressive; is more concerned with the possibilities of preventive war by the United States; has con-

47. *Pravda,* November 3, 1957.
48. *Ibid.*
49. *Pravda,* February 4, 1959 (speech at the 21st Party Congress).

sistently supported a large military establishment, demanded greater defense expenditures, and more advanced military weapons; and has with equal constancy called for vigilance, preparedness, and readiness to fight any type of war from a local conflict to an all-out thermonuclear war.

The military is by no means united in its outlook. Aside from traditional service rivalries among branches and services, the military is also plagued within each service with internal divisions between "radicals" and "traditionalists"; between technically oriented officers and the conventionally trained professionals; between rocket and nuclear forces and conventional forces; between those who emphasize reliance on missiles and nuclear weapons and those who call for "balanced forces"; between those who think the initial phases of a future war will be decisive and those who anticipate a long war of attrition; between those who favor preemption and those who do not; between those who think that the military should be prepared for all kinds of wars and those who think that all wars involving the United States and the U.S.S.R. will inevitably escalate to total thermonuclear war.[50]

Superimposed upon these divisions, which are essentially professional in origin, are, of course, personal rivalries, clique and factional activities which may be independent of professional or technical considerations. Various factions, groups, services, and individuals in the military seek support from various factions and personalities in the Apparatus, so that some groups within the military were closely associated with Khrushchev, while others appear to have been in a state of continuous resistance to his foreign policy and the military policy which was derived from it.[51]

While, generally speaking, the professional military benefits

---

50. For a discussion and elaboration of divergent views between the party and the military and within the military on issues of strategy and foreign policy, see the following: V. D. Sokolovskii, ed., *Soviet Military Strategy*, analyzed and annotated by H. S. Dinerstein, L. Gouré, and T. W. Wolfe (Englewood Cliffs, New Jersey, Prentice-Hall, 1963); Leon Gouré, *Notes on the Second Edition of Marshal V. D. Sokolovskii's "Military Strategy"* (Santa Monica, RAND Corporation, 1964); Roman Kolkowicz, *Conflicts in Soviet Party-Military Relations: 1962–1963* (Santa Monica, RAND Corporation, 1963); Thomas W. Wolfe, *Soviet Strategy at the Crossroads* (Santa Monica, RAND Corporation, 1964).

51. Cf. Roman Kolkowicz, *Conflicts in Soviet Party-Military Relations: 1962–1963* (Santa Monica, RAND Corporation, 1963).

from international tensions, this is not true of some forces, particularly the technically oriented and the rocket specialists, who are viewed with a mixture of awe and contempt by the traditional ground-force officer. Khrushchev's periodic calls for troop cuts and reductions for military spending were invariably accompanied by proposals to increase spending for missile and technical development in the military. Since a *détente* and relaxation of tensions would require in any event the maintenance of a deterrent capability, these forces are not threatened, but in fact may be favored, by a relaxation of international tensions. Furthermore, of all the officers in the military, these are most likely to adjust to peacetime careers without difficulty.[52]

Since 1955, when the first major troop cuts were made in the Soviet military, the size of the military establishment and budget has varied in almost barometric fashion with the state of international tensions. As the prospects for a *détente* and relaxation of tensions went up, as after the Camp David talks, Khrushchev would call for sharp troop reductions and smaller budgetary allocations for the traditional military; as the prospects for a *détente* diminished, as illustrated by the U-2 incident, troop cuts were arrested, military expenditures were increased, and the role of the military enhanced. Thus during the period between the U-2 incident and the Cuban missile crisis, the size of the Soviet military budget and establishment was maintained at a high level; once Khrushchev successfully overcame the opposition of his conservative critics in league with the professional military in the spring of 1963, he signed the test ban treaty; and as the prospects for a *détente* became even brighter, he called for reduced defense expenditures.

Whenever international tensions are reduced and the military's budget correspondingly cut, the professional officers among the traditional services are faced with agonizing choices confronting few other comparable groups in Soviet society: the termination or suspension of a professional career in which half a lifetime or more may have been invested. Factional conflicts between arms and services and various branches of the armed forces are unleashed over the redistribution of a diminished budget. Personal conflicts ensue as difficult decisions concerning

52. Cf. Roman Kolkowicz, *The Impact of Technology on the Soviet Military: A Challenge to Traditional Military Professionalism* (Santa Monica, RAND Corporation, 1964).

the retirement of professional military officers must be made.[53]

Since the Soviet military's chief function is external defense and it plays little role in maintaining internal order, it is threatened with the deprivation of its function as the security of the state is maximized and international tensions are reduced. This means not only the demobilization of thousands of career personnel but also a diminished role and status in society for those who remain on active service. It creates serious morale and recruiting problems, since the military function suffers a depreciation of social value and esteem and suffers a corresponding reduction in social rewards. While these effects are universally applicable to military establishments everywhere, the problem is particularly acute in the Soviet system. Contrary to a widespread misapprehension, the demobilized Soviet officer is likely to suffer more than his counterpart in other countries. Unlike the retired military officer without a peacetime skill in the United States, who might, among other options, go into business for himself, this option and the entire spectrum of possibilities and opportunities offered by a free enterprise economy are closed to his Soviet counterpart.

When Khrushchev's new military policy, enunciated in January 1960, called for a troop reduction of 1,250,000 men, including 250,000 officers, Marshal Malinovsky specifically emphasized that "the demobilization of 250,000 officers will be accompanied by various difficulties." [54] Of the 70,000 officers previously demobilized, he noted that only 35 per cent were able to find civilian occupations commensurate with their previous military positions, while nearly two thirds had to assume lower skilled jobs as ordinary workers. Letters to the Soviet press and interviews with demobilized officers confirmed Malinovsky's account. One demobilized major bitterly complained:

I am 46—that's the trouble. . . . What pleasures are ahead of me? Am I to eat up my pension and wait until I die? Too soon for that. And work does not come easily for me. I need a place in life, do

53. Under budgetary pressures it is usually the officer least equipped to adjust to civilian life by training and education who is the first to be demobilized. Thus Marshal Malinovsky noted in 1960 that "Not even regimental commanders are assured of remaining in their position. If they do not have an academic education, then the cadres personnel don't even want to talk to them." As cited in R. Kolkowicz, *ibid.*, p. 20.

54. *Krasnaya zvezda*, January 20, 1960.

you understand? I need active service. . . . I am an old platoon officer; where does a company officer belong in a civilian job? [55]

Serious morale problems among officers remaining on active duty also develop as they face the prospects of demobilization—and *déclassement*. The social degradation of the demobilized officer also has the effect of insidiously undermining the status and deference shown to officers remaining on active duty by both civilians and conscriptees under their command. *Krasnaya zvezda* reports the case of an impertinent young conscriptee who scorned the advice of his commanding officer by contemptuously noting:

I don't need any teachers. I was in Grade 6 in the factory and had a former major as a metal worker apprentice working under me.[56]

Reports of mistreatment, abuse, and unsympathetic consideration of demobilized military officers by local party and government officials also appeared periodically in the Soviet press.

The clever Chinese leaders apparently perceived political capital in the dissatisfactions of the Soviet traditional military and actually made a bold public appeal to the discontented elements of the Soviet military, seeking to associate the interests of Peking with theirs against Khrushchev. The Chinese charged, no less, that Khrushchev intended to destroy the traditional branches of the military in favor of the rocket forces:

We wish to point out that the great Soviet people and Red Army have been and remain a great force safeguarding world peace. But Khrushchev's military ideas based on nuclear fetishism and nuclear blackmail are entirely wrong. Khrushchev sees only nuclear weapons. According to him, "The present level of military technique being what it is, the air force and the navy have lost their former importance. These arms are being replaced and not reduced." Of course, those units and men having combat duties on the ground are even less significant. According to him, "In our time, a country's defensive capacity is not determined by the number of men under arms, of men in uniform. . . . A country's defense potential depends in decisive measure on the firepower and means of delivery that country commands." . . . Khrushchev's whole set of military theories runs completely counter to Marxist-Leninist teachings on war and the army. To follow his wrong theories will necessarily involve disintegrating the army and disarming oneself morally.[57]

55. *Literaturnaya Gazeta,* May 24, 1960.
56. *Krasnaya zvezda,* February 3, 1961.
57. "Two Different Lines on the Question of War and Peace," *Jen Min Jih Pao,* November 18, 1963, as translated in *Peking Review,* November 27, 1963, pp. 6–16.

Even more seriously, from the standpoint of the military as an institution, the general relaxation of international tensions and the increasing prospects for a *détente* have engendered a quasi-pacifist and antimilitarist spirit and attitude among the population in general and among artists, writers, and intellectuals in particular. The impact of these tendencies on the status and image of the military was having such an effect upon the morale of the officer corps that in February 1964 the Ministry of Defense and the Chief Political Administration of the Soviet Army and Navy held a conference with writers and artists to arrest these tendencies. General Yephishev, head of the Chief Political Administration, noted that:

Certain mistaken tendencies that have appeared in recent years in individual artistic works devoted to the military-patriotic theme have been subject to serious and merited criticism. The note of pacifism that was beginning to resound in certain books, films and paintings concerned with the Great Patriotic War has been justly condemned; the mistaken and basically harmful striving by certain masters of the arts to belittle the heroic spirit of military events has been dethroned.[58]

Marshal Malinovsky chastised the writers and artists in the same vein:

In recent times mistaken tendencies in representing the last war have appeared. Motifs of pacifism and the abstract rejection of war have made themselves felt in certain works of literature and painting and in the movies. Is it correct to represent the war our people waged as merely an accumulation of horrors and deprivations, to trot out onto the stage in naturalistic detail little, confused people? We reject this one-sided approach to an important theme. . . . Of course, this does not mean that we are in favor of depicting war as one long triumphal march. . . . Neither can we ignore certain views that have appeared . . . calling for a rejection of enthusiastic words, of the heroic aspect in works about the war, and claiming, if you please, that all this used to be a feature of the period of the cult of the individual.[59]

Other speakers at the conference bemoaned the negative image of the Soviet officer which was increasingly creeping into Soviet literature and the visual arts; some speakers criticized the artists for belittling the military profession, taking a cynical attitude toward military-patriotic themes, for promoting the "so-called 'theory' of deheroization" and for writing "books

58. *Krasnaya zvezda*, February 9, 1964.
59. *Ibid.*

that cast doubt on the commander's orders." [60] All this, according to Marshal Malinovsky, was having a baneful effect on the morale of the Soviet officer and the duty and pride of soldiering:

Through the efforts of our party and the entire people both in the fire of war and in the painstaking work during peacetime, we have reared splendid command cadres. They are leading people in the country. The soldier's unquestioning obedience to his commanders acquires special importance in the army under present-day conditions. In the orders of their commander, Soviet fighting men justifiedly see the orders of the homeland, and they execute them not only because of the law but because of their internal convictions. . . . It is important to us now as never before to preserve the commander's authority, to strengthen it, and to reveal the essence of one-man command as an expression of the collective will. Therefore, for example, certain works that discredit Soviet officers and soldiers evoke a feeling of dismay.[61]

As the relaxation of tensions progresses and the expectations of war recede and pacifist trends grow, the status and prestige of the professional military in Soviet society will continue to diminish. Already the Soviet military is being confronted with the serious problem of attracting and recruiting new officers. Several students in military academies, for example, sent a letter to Marshal Budenny in which they questioned the social values of military service as a profession:

There can be no beauty where, they say, people are training to kill others. . . . They say that there have been and are bourgeois philosophers and generals who talk of the beauty of war. . . . They say that though the officer profession is necessary at present, it is uninteresting and unromantic and that any civilian profession is better than a military one.[62]

There is little question but that the Soviet professional military as a socio-institutional group views unenthusiastically its diminished stature in Soviet society and the real possibility of a mass *déclassement* of the officer elite in the event of an ex-

60. *Ibid.* In a letter to the editor of *Krasnaya zvezda,* published on January 29, 1961, twenty-five officers, including several Heroes of the Soviet Union, complained about an article which appeared in *Komsomolskaya Pravda* because the typical officer "in the sketch appears as a veritable horror, an aberration, a spiritual Quasimodo. . . . The incriminating sketch concentrates all sorts of imaginable nastiness exclusively in the person of the officer and presents this monstrosity, without concern, to the public."
61. *Krasnaya zvezda,* February 9, 1964.
62. *Krasnaya zvezda,* January 13, 1963.

tended *détente* leading to extensive disarmament measures. Yet it would be incorrect to maintain that the Soviet military is unusually aggressive or warlike or glorifies war. The Soviet military is not particularly interested in actual war, since it is aware that in a thermonuclear conflict it risks not only the lives of its members but its very existence as an institution as well. What the Soviet military seeks is social and institutional security guaranteed by the appearance of insecurity for the state. To ensure its existence as a socio-functional institution, the Soviet military seeks to couple durable security and peace with a large military establishment as the principal guarantor that the aggressors would not dare unleash war for fear of destructive retaliation. Soviet military leaders apparently place little reliance upon a possible political settlement which would lead to a *détente* based upon mutual reduction of military arms and expenditures.

The Soviet armed forces, apparently like armies everywhere, would like to be the final judge of their own requirements, and this can best be accomplished under conditions of heightened military tensions. The peculiar characteristic of the Soviet military is that it is both a social and an institutional entity, whose members are threatened with a mass *déclassement* in the event of an extended *détente*. Until the Soviet system can devise a formula which will enable the Soviet officer to transfer his relative social status to the civilian sector of society, the Soviet military will continue to view an extended relaxation of tensions with grave apprehension and perceive a *détente* as incompatible with its interests.

HEAVY INDUSTRY

Unlike the Party Apparatus and the Soviet military, the managers of the heavy-industrial sector of the economy do not constitute a socio-institutional group, but rather are a socio-functional interest group whose organizational or institutional existence is amorphous and inchoate. Since 1956–57, when the economic ministries were decentralized and deconcentrated, the heavy-industrial managerial elite has been badly crippled politically and dispersed throughout the country—and has lost what centralized control it had over the levers of industrial production. Consequently it is unable to articulate its interests or to make its influence and pressures felt as pointedly and effectively as the Apparatus and the military.

Traditionally, heavy industry has been associated with defense and international tensions, because of its obvious necessity for the production of armaments. While the primacy of heavy industry assumed virtually the status of sacred writ under Stalin and ritual obeisance continues to be paid to this theme, increasingly it has become apparent that a radical upsurge in the development of the other sectors of the economy cannot be accomplished without subverting this principle. Although Khrushchev was the chief proponent of expanded consumer goods production, he was always careful to pay continued lip service to the primacy of heavy industry. Thus when he proposed his chemicalization of industry and agriculture programs in December 1963, he emphasized the benefits for agriculture and the consumer goods industry, but in February 1964, in order to answer his critics, he emphasized that 61 per cent of chemical production was still for heavy industry.[63]

Although a productionist-consumptionist debate of sorts has been carried on in the Soviet press since 1959, the ideological rationalizations for Khrushchev's policies were provided for by Academician A. Arzumanyan in a two-part article in *Pravda* on February 24 and 25, 1964, entitled "Current Problems of the Development of Our Economy," in which he suggested not only an equal balance between light and heavy industry but an even higher rate for light industry.[64] Arzumanyan, like Khrushchev

63. "The ill-wishers of the Soviet state are also racking their brains as to how to understand the decisions of the December Plenum: Is it a retreat or is it not a retreat from the general line for the preferential development of heavy industry to which the Soviet Union had adhered unwaveringly until now? Voices can be heard now saying that under the blows of reality, because of crop failures, the Soviet Union and the Communist Party are renouncing industrialization and setting a course for the development of light industry and agriculture. We have never renounced the development of the means of production industry. . . . The chemical industry has always been a part of heavy industry. . . . Chemistry, figuratively speaking, synthesizes well the interests of the state and the people in the development of heavy industry, and the interests of Soviet people in the rapid increase of the manufacture of consumer goods. . . . The Party will continue to insure the development of heavy industry. It has never regarded it as an end in itself, however. The Communist Party forced the development of heavy industry in order to create a . . . foundation to achieve a high standard of living for the people." Khrushchev's report to the February 1964 Plenum of the Central Committee, *Pravda*, February 15, 1964.

64. Cf. A. Arzumanyan, "Urgent Problems of Developing Our Economy," *Pravda*, February 24 and 25, 1964. According to Arzumanyan: "First of

earlier, used the experience of the United States to demonstrate that under certain conditions economic growth is consistent and possible with a higher rate of production for light industry.

While the managers of heavy industry were no longer sufficiently powerful to arrest or resist Khrushchev's policies by themselves, the traditional association between heavy industry and a large military establishment, and the traditional association between the latter and national security, is so habitual that the interests of the managers were in fact being defended and promoted by the military and the conservative faction in the Apparatus. The article by Arzumanyan and the program of welfare and wage benefits introduced by Khrushchev in July 1964, however, seem to indicate that the social role and prestige of the heavy-industrial manager will suffer at the expense of his light-industry rivals as the *détente* with the West progresses. Undoubtedly many of the heavy-industrial managerial specialists can convert to light industry, and to the degree that this is possible, resistance by this group will diminish. Its future is by no means as bleak as that of the demobilized military officer or the unhorsed party *apparatchik*.

"WHO BENEFITS" FROM A RELAXATION OF INTERNATIONAL TENSIONS IN SOVIET SOCIETY?

While the socio-institutional and functional groups in Soviet society who benefit from international tensions are few in num-

---

all, the question arises of the dynamics of groups 'A' and 'B' in industry. To this day, the establishment of the proportions between them has been hindered by certain theoretical survivals that have their roots in Stalin's erroneous dogmas. . . . Stalin thought it possible to combine a rapid expansion of industrial production with a systematic lag in consumer-goods output. . . . Nevertheless, some of our economists adhere to this day to erroneous views on the question of the relations between production and consumption. Intentionally or unintentionally, they divorce the law of preferential growth of the production of the means of production from personal consumption in a socialist society and . . . the law of preferential growth of the production of the means of production is transformed into an end in itself. . . . During the past decade the Party, while comprehensively developing heavy industry, has at the same time taken an enormous stride forward in expanding group 'B', in increasing the personal consumption of the Soviet people. . . . Life today insistently advances the task of bringing the rates of growth of groups 'A' and 'B' closer together. N. S. Khrushchev was profoundly right when he asserted at the February plenary session of the C.P.S.U. Central Committee that *'there can be no counterposing of group 'A' and group 'B.'* "

ber as groups, and in absolute numbers constitute but a small fraction of the total population, they represent highly concentrated power constituencies in terms of levers of power to which they have access. The military constitutes the only organized structure of violence in the system. The Party Apparatus controls the symbols of legitimacy and functions as an organized power structure to manipulate them. The heavy-industrial managers have access to, if not control of, the basic means of production in Soviet society.

On the other hand, those social groups which tend to benefit from a relaxation of international tensions are more numerous as group entities, more diverse in terms of function and social status, and make up the overwhelming proportion of the population. While the three groups who benefit most from international tensions are relatively small in total membership, they represent power structures as well as social constituencies. The groups who would benefit from a relaxation of tensions represent the whole motley spectrum of social forces in Soviet society, from relatively powerful subgroups within the Apparatus, military and heavy industry, through the politically awakening cultural, professional, and scientific elites, to the passive and politically impotent and largely inarticulate members of the lower intelligentsia (white collar groups), the working class, and the peasantry. Thus whereas the three groups in the first category are social elites which represent a high proportion of members in the party, the second group consists of both social elites and social nonelites, whose overall distribution of party membership is very low—ranging from 100 per cent for the subelite in the Apparatus to only 5.5 per cent for the peasantry.[65]

For purposes of analytical convenience, those social groups which would seem to benefit from a relaxation of international tensions can be classified into four general categories.

THE STATE BUREAUCRACY

The state officialdom in the Soviet Union, though not always precisely distinguishable from members of the Party Apparatus,

65. For an analysis of the social composition of the C.P.S.U. and its higher organs, cf. Aspaturian, in Macridis and Ward, eds., *Modern Political Systems: Europe*, pp. 492–502, and Aspaturian, "Social Structure and Political Power in the Soviet System," *op. cit.*

the economic bureaucracy, or even the military, nevertheless appears to constitute a distinct socio-institutional grouping. While there has been considerable overlap and mutual interpenetration of the party and state bureaucracies, the two institutions are separate, and often rival, entities. The state represents in effect the structure of legality which is supposed to mirror the structure of legitimacy embodied in the party and to translate the social will of the latter into official acts of state. The party, strictly speaking, has no legal or coercive authority except through the state.

The state represents an older institution in Soviet society than does the party (strictly speaking, its Apparatus), since it constitutes a continuation of the historic Russian state and in some degree is the symbolic heir to its legacy and the deep emotional and passionate sentiments it arouses. Loyalty to the state is patriotism, while loyalty to the party is ideological rectitude. Furthermore, the state is more inclusive in its membership, while the party is selective and exclusionist: citizenship is universal, party membership restrictive. Thus although the state is identified with legality in the official dogma, it is also endowed with a residual element of the prerevolutionary repository of historic legitimacy which the Russian state embodied, and hence remains a competitor to the Apparatus *cum* party.

It was this residual symbolism of patriotism and legitimacy which Stalin relied upon during World War II to inspire the Soviet population to resist the Germans. Stalin's assumption of the position as head of the Soviet government and his appointment as generalissimo of the armed forces tended to blur the distinction between state and party, to the disadvantage of the Party Apparatus. If Khrushchev can be believed, during the war and down to Stalin's death, the party as a distinctive ruling elite was virtually on the verge of withering away, since its highest organs were no longer being used by Stalin to govern the country.

After Stalin's death, Malenkov misjudged the situation and apparently assumed that the state had eclipsed the party in power and prestige and decided to use it rather than the Party Apparatus as his socio-institutional base of power. Seeking to expand his social base of support, Malenkov decided to adopt a policy based upon increased consumer goods production at home and a relaxation of tensions abroad. This seemed to accord more with the interests of his new social constituency, the state bureaucracy, than the policies pursued by Stalin or now advocated by his rival, Khrushchev, who assumed the mantle of First Secretary of the party. The rank and file employees of the State Apparatus would be among the first to benefit from a relaxation of international tensions and a higher standard of living. Thus it was more than coincidence that among those given substantial salary increases by Khrushchev in July-August 1964 were rank and file employees of the State Apparatus. Traditionally, high administrative officials of the state have been associated with a policy of less tension abroad and a higher standard of living at home. The first three post-Stalinist chairmen of the Council of Ministers—Malenkov, Bulganin, and Khrushchev—reversed themselves and became advocates of peace and plenty once they assumed the office of premier.

As the power and prestige of the state is enhanced, the power of other institutions diminishes, most notably that of the Party Apparatus (whose functions become increasingly superfluous), but also that of the military, since the latter is legally subordinated to the state as its legalized coercive arm. Furthermore, Khrushchev, like Stalin and Malenkov before him, appeared to have shifted his main institutional base of power to the State Apparatus as well, not only because of the ineluctable advantages already mentioned but also because increasingly the glow and aura which he derived as the chief personal symbol of the Soviet Union in international affairs radiated back into the Soviet Union. Because diplomacy and foreign policy are official activities of states and not parties, a Soviet leader who chose to govern only through the Party Apparatus would be denied this new powerful increment to his internal authority.

LIGHT-INDUSTRIAL, CONSUMER GOODS AND SERVICES, AND AGRICULTURAL MANAGERS

These social constituencies represent a numerically impressive, geographically diffused, and politically weak constellation of interest groups. Generally speaking, their status, prestige, and material rewards have had low priority in the Soviet system, especially during periods of war and international tension. This stems from three principal causes: (1) During periods of external danger, their services and products are not as highly valued or needed. (2) Their geographically dispersed character diffuses their power and limits their possibilities for organized and focused articulation of their point of view. (3) Their functions give them little or no access to important institutional levers of power.

These groups become important and rise in the socio-power hierarchy to the degree that they become useful to one or more of the principal socio-power groups. But as their usefulness as social allies grows, so does their relative power position become enhanced, to the degree that they too might become more significant as political actors in their own right.

One of the oldest components of Soviet mythology from Lenin to Khrushchev has been the promise to raise the Soviet standard of living to a level second to none once the problem of external security was solved. A policy of peace and plenty obviously places a higher demand and value upon the services of these groups, resulting in commensurate increases in budgetary allocations and hence status, prestige, and power. This was concretely reflected by Khrushchev's policies. Whenever Khrushchev thought that relations with the United States had improved, he called for greater budgetary allocations for these sectors of the economy; when the international situation turned sour, they were arrested or deferred. The latest acts in this cycle were increased budgetary allocations for agriculture in late 1962 and early 1963 and a steady shift of budgetary allocations to light industry and consumer goods and services, which has been in progress since the Cuban missile debacle.

THE CULTURAL-PROFESSIONAL-SCIENTIFIC GROUPS

Except for the professional ideologists, propagandists, and hacks whose positions depend upon their servility before the Party Apparatus, these groups as a whole seem to benefit most during periods when international tensions are relaxed. International tensions are associated with ideological controls and conformity, strict rules of censorship, reduced international contacts, and greater restrictions and restraints on artistic, scientific, and professional expression and development. Relaxation of international tensions is associated with the "thaw" and the "new freedom" for Soviet intellectuals, a freedom which has been progressively expanded since Stalin's death.[66]

The Soviet artistic and intellectual community is one of the most potent forces arguing in favor of a continued relaxation of international tensions. This has found expression in quasi-pacifist and antiwar sentiments expressed in an increasing number of works, much to the dismay of the military, as noted earlier. The artistic and intellectual groups are unique in that they not only have access to media of communication and information whereby to make their views known, but they are among the few social groups in Soviet society who are legally permitted to exist as separate organized societies and associations. While these associations in the past were strictly under Party Apparatus control, increasingly they are becoming vehicles whereby the interests of their members are given voice. The Party Apparatus periodically attempts to reimpose ideological controls, but this has by no means been fully successful. Although Soviet intellectuals are likely to exercise self-restraint during periods of real danger to the state, they are unlikely to accept as supinely as before the ideological controls which the party ideologues would like to impose.

THE SOVIET "CONSUMER": THE WHITE COLLAR GROUPS, THE WORKING CLASS, AND THE PEASANTRY

These three groups, taken together, account for some 90 million of the 100 million adults in the Soviet population. The organized political power of these large social groups is virtually nil. Yet they will be among the principal beneficiaries of the policy of peace and plenty, and this has already been reflected in wage increases for white collar and service groups like doctors, medical personnel, teachers, and restaurant and catering

66. A pertinent illustration of the barometric relationship between the relaxation of international tensions and relaxations of ideological controls over the arts took place in the spring of 1963. When Khrushchev appeared to be in difficulty and was in danger of being ousted by his factional opposition because of the Cuban missile debacle, the Party Apparatus called for an ideological conference which was designed to establish more stringent ideological controls, but after Kozlov suffered a heart attack and Khrushchev's fortunes took a turn for the better, the ideological conference was delayed for a month and, when it met, turned out to be a rather tepid affair. The test ban treaty followed soon thereafter.

personnel; higher prices for agricultural commodities; relaxation of controls on collective farms; pensions for collective farmers; and higher wages for factory workers.

Since these groups are among the first to be deprived and to suffer during war or periods of international tension, they constitute a numerically impressive group whose political power, though latent and passive, might be of signal importance if allied to one of the major socio-power elites in the Soviet system.

Some Concluding Observations

One of the most conspicuously unique characteristics of the Soviet system is the virtual absence of any meaningful distinction between a public and private sector in Soviet society. Private organizations, associations, and pressure groups, as such, are nonexistent in the forms known to the non-Communist world. In the sense that the public and private sectors are virtually coterminous, the Soviet system is totalitarian, although no longer encumbered with the institutions of terror and arbitrariness which characterized the Stalinist era. This means that its political system is closed; that is, the pluralistic interplay of autonomous and spontaneously organized political organizations and associations is legally prohibited. As a consequence, several aspects of Soviet decision-making in foreign policy appear unique.

1. No internal Soviet interest groups have a vested private interest in countries abroad which might result in the distortion of foreign policy. There is, in general, none of the economic "conflict of interests" on the individual or corporate level which often complicates foreign policy-making in other countries. Private economic interests of a domestic character which might exert pressure upon decision-making also do not exist. What Soviet property exists abroad is owned by the state, and foreign trade is an absolute state monopoly. Thus the Soviet abdication of joint stock companies and other state-owned enterprises in foreign countries could be executed purely on the basis of state policy with no private interests complicating the situation.

In foreign aid and trade policies no internal pressures or lobbyists representing private economic interests can materialize to distort and shape policy. This is also true of geographical and regional pressures. There are no demands for the inclusion of certain commodities, tariff reductions or increases, etc., stemming from interest groups, private or public—although as the Soviet economy increasingly shifts to a consumer-oriented one, foreign trade and aid might become increasingly important to interest and regional groups whose internal markets have been exhausted or eliminated.

2. Soviet officials devote full time to public interests and public policy, and hence they do not divide their time and energies between public and private domains. There are no private fortunes or estates, no private businesses or professions which can drain away energies from their public responsibilities. Their status, prestige, and power in Soviet society stem solely from their public functions.[67]

3. Foreign policy debates are largely secret. While foreign policy is discussed much more widely in the Soviet Union than heretofore, there is still no criticism of a systematic character about Soviet foreign policy.[68] Soviet decision-makers still act without prior public discussion and need not render an accounting in public, although increasingly reports on foreign policy are made to the Supreme Soviet.[69] Foreign policy is too crucial a matter to debate in public, since it would alert the outside world to Soviet intentions. Thus there is no political opposition which can publicly offer an alternative program or policy. Opposition does exist, but behind the closed doors of higher party and state organs. These criticisms and alternative policies are sometimes revealed indirectly through denunciation, rejection, allusions to "bourgeois thinkers," "metal eaters," "certain comrades," "some people," "anti-Marxists," etc. In the condemnation of the

67. Cf. Zbigniew Brzezinski and Samuel P. Huntington, *Political Power: U.S.A./U.S.S.R.* (New York, Viking, 1964), for a pioneering and penetrating comparative analysis of the social background and behavior of Soviet and American political elites.

68. For a discussion of the upsurge in monographic and scholarly discussion of international and foreign policy issues and problems, cf. V. V. Aspaturian, "Diplomacy in the Mirror of Soviet Scholarship," in J. Keep, ed., *Contemporary History in the Soviet Mirror* (London, Allen and Unwin, 1964).

69. Cf. V. Vadimov, *Verkhovny Sovet SSSR i Mezhdunarodnye Otnosheniya* (Moscow, 1958); and *Sbornik Osnovnykh Aktov i Dokumentov Verkhovnovo Soveta SSSR po Vneshnepoliticheskim Voprosam 1956–1962* (Moscow, 1962).

antiparty group in July 1957, the foreign policy criticisms of
Molotov were revealed to be, in effect, an alternative policy.[70]
This revelation constituted the closest approximation to a debate
on foreign policy until the initiation of open polemics with the
Chinese.

5. The professional military in the Soviet Union is not subordinated in the ordinary sense to civilian control but rather is
integrated into the political and administrative apparatus of the
Soviet system. The military has direct, active, regular, systematic, and predictable participation and membership in party
and state organs which are nominally civilian in character.
They are co-opted at all levels and in all branches. In the party,
professional military representatives have sat on the Presidium
(Zhukov) and are regularly represented in the Central Committee, the Party Congress, and the party organs of the Union
Republics and other administrative-territorial regions.[71]

In state institutions they are found in the Presidium of the
Supreme Soviet, are regularly elected as members of both
chambers of the Supreme Soviet, serve on its committees, and
also serve on the Council of Ministers. The defense ministry is
administered almost entirely by professional soldiers, who are
at all times on active military duty as professional officers. They
also serve in Union Republican state institutions.

6. Defeated political leaders have no political base to return
to, no private business or law practice, no free opportunity to
offer services commensurate with their formerly exalted positions, no status of loyal oppositionists. Under Stalin, defeated
political leaders inevitably suffered political and physical obliv-
ion, but now only the former. The net effect is to deprive the
country completely of the services of experienced statesmen and
politicians.

This more than nullifies the unique advantage of political
leaders fully committed to public responsibilities. It should be
noted, however, that this situation is not necessarily permanent
and that the retiring of defeated opponents or the assigning of
menial positions to them may result in toleration of their dis-

70. For a discussion and description of the Molotov foreign policy "program," cf., Aspaturian in Macridis, *op. cit.*, pp. 150–52.
71. Cf. T. W. Wolfe, "Role of the Soviet Military in Decision-Making and
Soviet Politics" (Santa Monica, RAND Corporation, 1964), and his *Soviet
Strategy at the Crossroads.*

sident views, particularly if factional stalemates become a permanent feature of the Soviet political system. It is not even inconceivable that factionalism may eventually lead to the organization of competing slates and programs within the Communist party, just as they exist in other one-party systems.[72]

7. One final unique characteristic, which still requires greater exploration, is that Soviet internal politics are closely intertwined with the domestic politics of other Communist states. Factional conflicts assume an intrabloc character, with factions in the Soviet hierarchy reflected in the hierarchies of allied states and parties; the result is the formation of interparty factional alliances designed to aid kindred factions in other states in their struggle against rival factional groupings. In this way the leaders of one state may actively cultivate the allegiance and support of an opposition faction in another state and vice versa. To a certain degree the course of factional conflicts in other Communist states affects the fortunes of factions within the Soviet hierarchy.[73]

The relationship of internal politics to foreign policy in the Soviet system remains in a state of flux and has yet to find its characteristic equilibrium. The tendency, at present, appears to be that foreign policy objectives will increasingly be accommo-

72. That a multi-party Communist system is not inconceivable is attested to by the fact that the Chinese have actually called for the toleration of dissident Communist parties in other countries, including presumably the countries of the socialist camp in Europe. This has infuriated the Soviet Party, which has naturally reaffirmed its incompatibility with Marxism-Leninism: "One cannot agree with the concepts now current in the Communist movement that justify fragmentation of the ranks of the Communist movement and the creation of 'several Communist parties' in one country. The supporters of these concepts say that the international Communist movement is now allegedly undergoing a process of 'selection, crystallization, and condensation' and that there are at present in the world Communist movement four types of Communist and Workers' Parties, namely: '(1) the Marxist-Leninist party; (2) the party whose leadership is under the control of revisionists but that has a Marxist-Leninist opposition within it; (3) the party that is completely under the control of revisionists, while the Marxist-Leninists who have been expelled from the party have formed Marxist-Leninist groups; (4) the party whose leadership is under control of the revisionists and alongside which a new Communist Party has formed.' Meanwhile, certain comrades consider it possible for themselves —and call on others—to support to an equal degree liaisons with all the above groups and parties. They thereby support a kind of 'Communist multi-party system.'" "Against Splitters, for Unity of the Communist Movement," *Partiinaya Zhizn*, No. 11, June 1964, pp. 8–20.

73. Cf. article cited immediately above.

dated to internal interests rather than abstract ideological commitment, although for the moment they remain an inextricable combination of both elements in undecipherable proportions at any given time. As the social consensus within the Soviet system expands and becomes more pluralistic, the tendency will be for ideological norms to have less influence in the shaping of foreign policy. The Chinese ambition to displace the Soviet Union as the center of the world revolutionary movement and usurp the ideological initiative will have an ambivalent impact on the relationship between ideology and Soviet foreign policy. On the one hand, it may drive the conservative faction of the Apparatus to more desperate measures in reasserting the ideological preeminence of the Soviet party in the Communist movement; on the other it may serve to reinforce the conviction of the Khrushchevite faction that the internal burdens of an ideologically oriented foreign policy are too heavy to carry, and hence counterproductive in character.

PART FIVE

Some Research Challenges

W HERE do we go from here? It remains to examine the specific question of research possibilities on the relationship between domestic and foreign politics, to pose problems not just for the specialists in comparative politics and in international relations but for others as well. Of course many of the writers who have gone before in this symposium have raised interesting avenues for future research, and their suggestions must be put alongside the four papers which follow.

Professor Roland Young calls for categories of analysis broad enough to include the legal order as well as the political, which encompasses non-Western systems as well as Western. He sees the essential problems as concerned with order and change. "In meeting the challenge of change it is necessary constantly to create new patterns of order."

The paper by Professor Chadwick Alger was, unlike the others, first published elsewhere. It was, however, known well by the participants in this symposium, and Professor Alger was a participant in the conference at which the other papers were presented. Alger raises several significant issues of relevance for future research. One of the most interesting concerns the study of primitive societies to derive insights on international relations. In defending his proposal he holds that "in terms of the development of governmental institutions, and some aspects of the structure of society crucial to politics, international systems are less complex than many national systems. On the other hand, primitive societies seem not to be as simple, in terms vital to the social scientist, as has been presumed."

Professor Raoul Naroll brings to the reader the vantage point of anthropology. He calls upon the researcher to acquire an awareness of international systems other than his own and a perspective on the relative unimportance of some of the conflicts within our own system in the face of commonalities shared by all its members. As an anthropologist Naroll provides a useful evaluation of the suggestions made by political scientist Alger on the relevance of the experience of primitive tribes for international relations. Naroll concludes by calling for the utilization of rigorous scientific methods in undertaking analysis of the kinds of problems posed by this symposium, arguing both for the examination of carefully selected single cases and the undertaking of comparative statistical studies across many political systems.

The final paper in the symposium is by Professor Oliver Benson. He provides both an excellent survey of existing literature relevant to this symposium and a survey of some of the most important things he feels the several papers in the symposium have contributed. He suggests several problems which the focus on the interaction between international relations and comparative politics brings to the fore: applied *vs.* theoretical research, the use of models, the problem of unaccustomed fields, the problem of values. He brings the symposium to an end by suggesting specific research challenges it has posed, selecting for this purpose several typical hypotheses which might be tested with a view to the enlargement of our theoretical resources.

Political and Legal Systems of Order

ROLAND YOUNG
Northwestern University

T HIS SYMPOSIUM has been attempting to clarify the relationship between comparative politics and international relations, an undertaking which reflects the belief, held by many contributors to this volume, that these approaches have much in common and that the desired integration of approaches should be reflected in our research. The close relationship between the internal political structure of a nation and the nature of its foreign relations is often observable. A simple illustration is found in the story of two tribes, living on opposite sides of a river, who had traded together peacefully for many years. When nationhood inevitably arrived, the river became an international boundary, and the peaceful trade was branded as smuggling.

In attempting to establish the relationship between comparative politics and international relations we may at times be the prisoners of our own concepts; that is, we may rely on categories for gathering and analyzing our material which on the whole are unsatisfactory, or at least have proved to be less appropriate than we would wish. They do not provide a conceptual framework broad enough to fit the facts, and they may deter us in finding practical solutions. The question has been raised whether research in this area should be theoretical or practical. Whatever the answer—and I should think it would be both—the type of research is conditioned by our choice of categories, with their implicit assumptions, which in turn may affect policy proposals.

The categories under consideration here are comparative politics and international relations. We all recognize that categories of this nature are merely broad terms, used for convenience, which can be further refined; but we should also be aware that they may contain certain assumptions about the nature of the political process, that they may skew the evidence in certain directions, that they do not seem to point in the direction of solutions, and that they seem to be unduly restrictive. The emphasis on politics, narrowly construed, stresses the more manipulative aspects of the political process, and the role played by law in the resolution of conflict is included only indirectly if it is included at all. To limit our comparisons to what is normally called political may be to overlook significant aspects of cultures found in other areas of the world which do not have the Western type of political orientation and to pass over other useful methods of social control which have developed in the West. Finally, we are expected to conceptualize interaction in terms of relations between nations, a limited formulation which implies, somewhat subtly, that development in world politics should proceed in certain directions. Although I know that discussion of concepts may seem arid and tedious, I take refuge in the fact that the use of these supercategories may actually conceal the nature of the problem, and that is the sole reason the issue is labored.

What, then, is our problem? As I see it, the problem is to develop a framework of analysis which will encompass, in its various manifestations, the political and legal order as it exists in the world today and which will be useful both in future research and in policy-making as well. In achieving this purpose, we can build on our Western-derived concepts, but it is desirable that, when generalizing, we give a true picture of our material and that if we use broad categories we do not exclude important elements of cultural diversity which should be taken into account. In making this argument, I would like to consider first some of the major aspects of the Western political order, including in particular the role of law. I will then pass on to a consideration of the creation of the newer states and the impact of these developments both on the internal order and the relations between states, and I will conclude with a brief statement on the significance of these changes for our own research.

THE WESTERN SYSTEM

It is relatively commonplace to say that we have developed in the West a unique system of government; it is unique in the sense that it is largely a product of Western thought and experience, whereas other areas of the world have not been organized traditionally in the same fashion. The danger of distortion lies in applying Western ideas indiscriminately in speaking of other political systems and of their relations to each other. Our political ideas have developed over a long historical period and are the product of considerable intellectual cogitation; they are held implicitly throughout the West; and they have had a considerable impact on other parts of the world. We are all familiar with the basic formulations in which Western law and politics are expressed. There is a tendency to define the political system abstractly and to consider authority in terms of duties and powers; institutions and procedures have been especially created which are not part of the family structure; and the public is brought into the system of government through various types of representation. We have developed a convenient mental shorthand in discussing the political system which at times is abstracted in such a fashion that it seems to be independent of society itself.

We also abstract the political system so that it appears to exclude the role of law in providing a structure of order in society. We are permitted to do this because we assume that a system of law exists and that political competition takes place within the confines of law. Moreover, we have excluded law because, in the concrete operation of government, it is agreed that political influence should not be permitted to influence judicial decisions. However, these various assumptions concerning the role of law in society are not always tenable when applied to non-Western political systems.

In the Western world we assume that society is organized on the basis of law and that interrelationships between individuals,

groups, and governments occur largely within a legal framework. The individual is a part of the legally oriented society.
He can come and go within the system, and he has certain
rights and claims which he can assert in law. Maine's hypothesis
that there has been a progression from status to contract has
some validity when applied to the West, where a person possesses legal rights which enable him to make contracts and
exercise his freedom in many ways. Although a legally oriented
society is essentially Western, it should not be implied that there
are no other types of legal systems or that law, as such, is
confined to the West. However, the concept of a free person,
a legally independent person, possessing rights independent of
his family or clan, has had considerable impact on the change
which is taking place throughout the underdeveloped areas of
the world, and it is also implicit in the civil rights movement in
this country.

The basic concepts of law, and the idea that law limits and
controls the government, prevail throughout the great cultural
area of the West. Law and politics are interrelated, and if we
emphasize only the political we will produce a distorted picture
of how the Western world is organized and how conflict is
resolved. Law and politics perform somewhat different functions:
They react on one another, and for some purposes political
action may be described as the conflict which precedes the legal
resolution of social conflict. The law determines not only the
rule by which conflict is to be resolved but also the external
limits of the process to be followed. When law or authority
breaks down, political issues arise, and an attempt is made to
provide a solution through the political process in terms of law.
There is a continual interweaving of the political and legal processes, and politics and law are both essential in creating and
preserving a pattern of order.

We may, then, consider politics to be the public process of
creating new law and carrying out policy based on law. Issues
are raised for discussion and resolution in the political sphere,
but the solution, creating a new pattern of order, is stated in
terms of law. Moreover, the process itself by which the decision
is reached must be legitimate in order to make the solution
binding. Under this formulation, the law determines the basic
structure of society; it unites the political community by ties
which transcend those of kin or race or political parties; and it

provides the framework for carrying on relationships between people belonging to different societies.

It remains to be added that the Western cultural area, where society is to a large extent organized on a legal basis, is broader than the nation-state, but it is certainly not universal. The legal systems of the West, derived as they are from a common heritage, are similar to each other, and the political systems are also similar. However, it would be misleading to suggest that Western political systems have uniformly followed a constitutional pattern. We are still groping to achieve a legal order, and claims for political legitimacy have been based on factors other than law. The West has not been without dictators. It is interesting to note, though, that a legal system has been evolved in the Soviet Union, where it was once believed that the law as well as the state would wither away; however, the external controls remain totalitarian.

The Non-Western World

There are extensive areas of the world which, for the most part, are non-Western in background, which are underdeveloped economically, and which have attempted to create a modern system of government, overlapping several layers of traditional, tribal, and familial organizations. The introduction of Western political ideas, with their centralized controls and rigorous methods of enforcing compliance, has often been a heady dose. The truncated controls of traditional life may be modified and partly replaced by a political system based on conformity to a single party. The new system may be neither Western nor traditional, and the emphasis on the acquisition and use of political power may actually block attempts to create more stable patterns of legal order.

These traditional systems are often extremely complex, cumbersome, and idiosyncratic, and they have been losing ground to the relatively simplified ideas of Western politics, which are often expressed in terms of one man—one vote and which offer the lure of personal independence, where rights do not depend on custom or tradition or status. It is not easy to generalize on the underdeveloped areas, for the variety of extant political and legal systems is matched by the paucity of our knowledge of them. From the days of Aristotle to modern times, Western scholars have made facile generalizations about nonliterate peoples, and these observations, when tested, are often found to be false, misleading, inaccurate, or irrelevant. The traditional systems still perform many essential functions in society, and in particular they often exercise considerable authority over the use of land. They may provide some element of stability, even though failing to meet other tests of modernity. What is required, it seems to me, is the creation of legal and political structures which do not destroy the traditional culture and which at the same time can be related to broader systems of national and international order. This is not an impossible task; certainly in Western history new systems of order have been created out of conditions which were chaotic and despairing.

THE STATE SYSTEM

The state system of the West developed in a cultural area where many aspects of law and politics were implicitly accepted, including the legal basis of government, the language of diplomacy, the purpose of civil authority, and the basic concepts for organizing power. In its earlier years the system was not universal, and its membership was restricted to states which met certain standards, such as government stability and the willingness to live up to treaty obligations. The American Declaration of Independence can be read as an argument that the North American colonies were sufficiently responsible and mature to join the society of nations. The state system, in short, was based on certain well-known assumptions. However, one may expect modifications in the system now that it is all but universal in scope and contains states with heterodox, rather than similar, cultural orientations.

The state system has not been static, and the more highly capitalized nations have had to adjust their policies, both external and internal, to the impact of industrialization. The shrinkage in space, brought about by improved transportation and communications, has led to increased contact between people of various cultures; the power of military weapons has grown to frightening proportions; and the coverage of press, radio, television, and propaganda has also grown. It has become increasingly difficult for any country to maintain a closed system, economic or political, and remain unaffected by external ideas or world prices. However, there has also been an increase in scientific knowledge which may actually make it possible for the developed nations to be more self-sufficient, a result which in turn would have a devastating effect on the underdeveloped nations of the world. In short, then, it is not only the newer countries which have been forced to absorb change on a vast scale; the Western nations have also been compelled to modify their institutions and patterns of thought, and this challenge still persists.

THE PROBLEM RECONSIDERED

Now to return to the question raised earlier: How are we to study and comprehend these tremendous events which are taking place in all parts of the world? What major concepts are we to use in organizing our material? It seems to me that we are essentially concerned with order and change, and in meeting the challenge of change it is necessary constantly to create new patterns of order. In this vast social upheaval in which we are living, where the framework of society is being challenged on a broad front, it is necessary that we do not construct any false barriers which prevent our grappling with the central problem: viz., the establishment of effective patterns of order. In achieving this goal, it is necessary that we know something about the patterns of order found in the underdeveloped areas of the world. These are often the places where political crises occur, where dissatisfactions are acute, where conflicting ideologies meet, and where cultural conflict is profound. It is here, in these peasant economies, that the old order and the old loyalties are breaking down and techniques have not yet been developed to meet expectations and provide satisfactions.

Although the categories of international relations and comparative politics cover a wide area, it might be apposite if we directed our attention specifically to the study of legal and political systems and the part they play in creating patterns of order. We would then be able more clearly to consider Western political development in all its manifestations, to consider law as a mechanism of social control which is not confined to government but which is found in all associations; to examine the institutional expression of cultural assumptions; to relate the systems of law and politics in the underveloped areas to broader and more extensive systems of control; and to study relationships, whether concerned with individuals, groups, or nations. Moreover, our attention would be directed toward the function of law and politics in creating order, an example of which is the extended process of political and legal integration now taking place in Europe. In the area in which we are working we also require a high level of creativity in devising systems of order to control the conflict and violence which at times seem on the point of overwhelming all of us.

Comparison of Intranational and International Politics[1]

CHADWICK F. ALGER
Northwestern University

T HE STUDY of international relations has been considerably advanced in recent years by the application of findings from other areas of the social sciences.[2] These have included decision-making, game theory, conflict, bargaining, communication, negotiation, systems, geography, attitudes, and simulation. International relations scholars such as Morton Kaplan, Charles McClelland, Richard C. Snyder, and Harold Sprout have built important bridges between international relations and other disciplines. It has been fortunate that such innovators have often found men from other disciplines, such as Kenneth Boulding, Harold Guetzkow, Charles Osgood, and Anatol Rapoport, in the middle of the bridge. The volumes of the *Journal of Conflict*

1. This paper was published in the *American Political Science Review,* Vol. LVII, June 1963, pp. 406–19, and is reproduced here with permission.
2. Useful discussion may be found in Karl Deutsch, "The Place of Behavioral Sciences in Graduate Training in International Relations," *Behavioral Science,* Vol. 3 (1958), pp. 278–84; J. David Singer, "Behavioral Sciences and International Relations," *Behavioral Science,* Vol. 6 (1961), pp. 324–35; and Richard C. Snyder, "Some Recent Trends in International Relations Theory and Research," in Austin Ranney (ed.), *Essays on the Behavioral Study of Politics* (Urbana, University of Illinois Press, 1962), pp. 103–71.

Resolution offer one example of how far this remarkable effort at cross-fertilization has gone.

SOME CRUCIAL ISSUES FOR INTRANATIONAL AND INTERNATIONAL COMPARISON

It seems, however, that there has not been as much effort devoted to bringing to bear new data being collected on intranational political [3] behavior. If data on labor-management negotiation, racial conflict, and decision-making in business firms has relevancy, why not data on metropolitan politics, the politics of primitive tribes, and the politics of the new nations? [4] This seems to be a timely question for two reasons: First, political analysts have been extending dramatically the varieties of political behaviors which they are examining. Second, changes in the international system, such as the growth in the number and size of international organizations, the increase in the number of independent units, and changes in patterns of recruitment for international political roles, impel us to look for new analytic tools for handling our data. The resources from nonpolitical behaviors help, but there may be value in enriching the models of political processes in which we attempt to apply these resources.

Inadequacy of "classic" nation-state model.—What are the models that we tend to use? Fred W. Riggs concludes that we have a predilection for two "ideal" types. "At one extreme is the political *order* characteristic of the nation-state; at the other an

3. "Political" is used here as a means for referring to the concerns of most political scientists. I agree with Dahl that customary political-nonpolitical distinctions may at times assume differences that do not exist. He concludes: "I do not think we have nearly enough evidence . . . [to conclude] that the differences among particular types of polyarchies, e.g., between nation states and trade-unions, are so great that it is not likely to be useful to include them in the same class." Robert A. Dahl in *A Preface to Democratic Theory* (Chicago, University of Chicago Press, 1956), p. 74.

4. This is not to say that the literature of international politics is not potentially useful to scholars working on other kinds of political phenomena. For a stimulating application of the work of Karl Deutsch, Ernst Haas, and Morton Kaplan to metropolitan politics see Matthew Holden, "The Strategy of Metropolitan Integration: Three International Models," unpublished paper, and "The Governance of the Metropolis as a Problem in Diplomacy," a paper prepared for delivery at the Annual Meeting of the American Political Science Association, Washington, D. C., September 1962.

anarchic system of interstate relations." [5] In 1956 Secretary of State Dulles enumerated the six means whereby "order is maintained and violence is prevented" in the nation-state—characteristics which he says the interstate system lacks. Riggs calls these the "classic" formulation of the characteristics of the nation-state:

1. "Laws, written or unwritten, which reflect the moral judgment of the community."

2. "Political machinery to change these laws . . . as conditions change . . ."

3. "An executive body to administer law."

4. "Courts which settle disputes of a justiciable character in accordance with law."

5. "Superior public force which deters violence by its ability to apprehend and punish adequately any who breach or defy the law."

6. "Well-being sufficient so that the people . . . are not driven by desperation to follow ways of violence." [6]

An examination of international relations textbooks and other general treatises on international relations reveals additional distinctions between national and international politics. For example, Morgenthau probes further into the characteristics of the society than does Dulles and discusses the "social pressures that in national societies tend to keep dissenting groups within the bounds of law and peace," "expectations of justice," and "suprasectional loyalties" that result from overlapping group membership.[7] Hoffmann asserts that "the domestic order . . . regulates a great mass of individuals" whereas "the international legal order regulates a small number of subjects." [8]

5. Fred W. Riggs, "International Relations as a Prismatic System," *World Politics*, Vol. XIV, 1961, p. 144.

6. John Foster Dulles, "The Institutionalizing of Peace," address before the 50th Annual Meeting of the American Society of International Law, April 25, 1956 (Washington, D. C., Department of State, Public Services Division, Series S—No. 46, 1956), p. 3.

7. Hans Morgenthau, *Politics Among Nations* (New York, Knopf, 1960), pp. 502–7.

8. Stanley Hoffmann, *Contemporary Theory in International Relations* (Englewood Cliffs, New Jersey, Prentice-Hall, 1960), p. 206. Kaplan makes a similar point when he states that nations have "hundreds of thousands of cross-cutting social roles," but the international system has "only a small number of major actors or nation-states." Morton Kaplan, "Problems of Theory Building and Theory Confirmation in International Relations," *World Politics*, Vol. XIV, 1961, p. 14.

Kaplan concludes that "the international system is not a primary sphere of action in the same sense that national political systems are" since "internal political pressures . . . may have major consequences for international political decisions." [9] Riggs thinks that a significant difference between the international system and other political systems is that "an international system is a power structure in which the weight of external pressures approaches the vanishing point." [10] Thus he calls it a *macro-rule*.

Comparisons made by international relations scholars do, however, tend to emphasize, along with Dulles, the fact that national systems have governmental machinery that international systems do not possess [11] and also emphasize differences in the control of instruments of violence by government as well as the frequency with which it is utilized.[12] Although these distinctions are emphasized, they are often handled with restraint. For example, Van Dyke states that: "The outstanding fact is that, for some countries, civil war is a much less frequent event than international war." [13] But Van Dyke's careful statement of difference alerts us to ask the usefulness of the national-international distinction. If a generally agreed difference is frequency of use of violence, but the distinction applies to only some countries, there may be value in being more explicit about the fact that we have developed our notions about national-international differences by comparing *some* national systems with *some* international systems.

Our biased sample of political systems.—In his criticism of the "classical" description of the characteristics of nation-states, Riggs lucidly calls our attention to the fact that our "ideal" model of the national system has been developed from those we know the best—a few Western democracies.[14] We tend to

9. Kaplan, *op. cit.*, p. 16.
10. Riggs, *op. cit.*, p. 151.
11. See Kaplan, *op. cit.*, p. 14; Morton Kaplan and Nicholas Katzenbach, *The Political Foundations of International Law* (New York, Wiley, 1961), pp. 4, 7, 20, 235; Vernon Van Dyke, *International Politics* (New York, Appleton-Century-Crofts, 1957), p. 14; and Kenneth N. Waltz, *Man, War and the State* (New York, Columbia University Press, 1959), p. 11.
12. See Hoffmann, *op. cit.*, p. 206; Morgenthau, *op. cit.*, pp. 501, 505; Charles P. Schleicher, *International Relations: Conflict and Cooperation* (New York, Prentice-Hall, 1962), pp. 259–60; Van Dyke, *op. cit.*, p. 14; and Quincy Wright, *The Study of International Relations* (New York, Appleton-Century-Crofts, 1955), p. 134.
13. Van Dyke, *op. cit.*, p. 14.
14. Riggs, *op. cit.*, p. 151.

compare this model with an international model derived from the international system with which we are personally most preoccupied, i.e., the system composed of the analyst's nation and other nations with which it has the most intense conflict.[15] To a large degree this results in comparisons between the most orderly and stable national systems on the one hand and the most disorderly and unstable international systems on the other. This kind of selectivity tends to lessen our concern with national systems such as those exhibited recently in the Congo, France, and Peru on the one hand and also international systems such as the United States–Canada and Ghana-Guinea-Mali on the other.[16]

If we construct a fourfold table which includes disorderly and unstable national systems (in addition to orderly and stable ones) and orderly and stable international systems (in addition to disorderly and unstable ones), our attention is not so readily diverted from these "deviant" cases. This might also lead to a different set of distinctions between the national and international realms. Furthermore, it might also cast some doubts on the validity of our tendency to think first of "governments" and monopoly of instruments of physical force when we wish to indicate the prerequisites for order and stability. In his intensive study of ten cases of attempted political integration in the North Atlantic area, Karl Deutsch found it necessary to establish a fourfold table to describe the development of security communities, i.e., the attainment of " 'long' time, dependable expectations of 'peaceful change' among [a] population." [17] This was because he found that the development of the conditions for a security community did not necessarily coincide with the development of common governmental institutions. Thus he found security

15. See Leonard Binder, "The Middle East as a Subordinate System," *World Politics,* Vol. X, 1958, pp. 408–29 for a relevant discussion of "the inapplicability of the theory of bipolarity to Middle Eastern international politics" (p. 410).

16. Gabriel A. Almond indicates the same kind of bias in another area of political science when he reports that "the differences between Western and non-Western political systems have generally been exaggerated. This is in part due to the fact that the 'limiting case' models of the Western system, on the one hand, and of the traditional and primitive systems, on the other, have been greatly overdrawn." In Gabriel Almond and James S. Coleman, *The Politics of the Developing Areas* (Princeton, Princeton University Press, 1960), p. 17.

17. Karl Deutsch, et al., *Political Community in the North Atlantic Area* (Princeton, Princeton University Press, 1957), p. 5.

communities both with governmental institutions (amalgamated) and without such institutions (pluralistic). And he found that in some cases non-security communities had governmental institutions and in others they did not.

This suggests that the classification of political systems into national and international may have limited usefulness and raises considerable doubts about Stanley Hoffmann's strong plea for an autonomous discipline of international relations. He may be right in stating that "many of the mistakes of contemporary theoretical attempts in international relations and international law come from the systematic misapplication of the model of the integrated *Rechtsstaat*—the modern state characterized by a sense of common purpose, a rational organization of power, a bureaucracy and the rule of law—to the decentralized international milieu, either as a norm for analysis or as a goal." [18] But his criticism may apply equally to the analysis of national politics. Deutsch's findings tend to support Hoffmann's criticism of the use of the "integrated *Rechtsstaat*" model when he indicates that at times the establishment of the institutions that accompany "over-all amalgamation" and the "monopoly of violence" were "more of a burden than a help" to integration.[19] But Deutsch's study of "political communities" handles both national and international communities within the same analytic framework.

Whether or not we choose to think of international relations as a separate discipline, there are indications that the study of international politics could benefit from the utilization of resources from a wider variety of political systems, both national and international. This paper will examine some of the findings in studies of two intranational foci: "developing" nations and "primitive" political systems. Examples will be selected in order to suggest how examination of a wider range of political phenomena might offer useful stimuli for the scholar of international politics, particularly toward the end of freeing him from "classical" or *Rechtsstaat* models of political systems.

Nations as multiple actors.—Fruitful application of these examples requires taking a different perspective on the international political system than is customary in much of the literature. Look upon those persons, from whatever nation, who

18. Hoffmann, *op. cit.*, p. 3.
19. Deutsch, et al., *op. cit.*, 1957, p. 105.

carry on international relations as a society of individuals. In this society there are groups—religious, professional, ethnic, national, etc. The importance of nation groups is a matter that must be empirically verified, since it will vary in different parts of the society and change through time. For purposes of this discussion, we can precisely define the actors in the international political system as that part of international society which consists of national officials who engage in face-to-face contact with officials of other nations and members of secretariats of international organizations. We can focus on the global political system or on systems that are of lesser scope. If our perspective is global, we see a society that has population centers in such places as Paris, London, Brussels, Washington, Tokyo, and Moscow. It is also a society that is presently undergoing considerable population growth and whose population has shown remarkable growth in technological skills.

This perspective is helpful in raising questions that may not be raised when we concentrate on a system of *nations*. From the system-of-nations perspective it is quite proper for Kaplan to conclude that a distinguishing characteristic of international systems is that these systems have "only a small number of major actors or nation-states." [20] Arnold Wolfers effectively points, however, to phenomena overlooked by this perspective:

Some democratic states have exhibited such pluralistic tendencies that they offer to the world a picture of near-anarchy. They seem to speak to the world with many and conflicting voices and to act as if one hand—agency or faction—does not know what the other hand is doing. . . . [In] some . . . new states . . . integration is so poor that other states must deal with parts, rather than with a fictitious whole, if diplomacy is to be effective.[21]

When we use the international-society-of-individuals perspective, data such as this are not lost, but there may also be less dramatic characteristics of this society that are of potential significance. For example, on the basis of whatever definition of "major" we might choose, does it make any difference how many major individual actors nation "X" has in the system at one time? Does it make any difference where they are located and to what kinds of issues they are assigned? Would other

20. Kaplan, *op. cit.*, p. 14.
21. Arnold Wolfers, "The Actors in International Politics," *Theoretical Aspects of International Relations* (Notre Dame, University of Notre Dame Press, 1959), p. 102.

nations be more effective if they dealt with the United States
as one actor or would they be more effective if they related to the
United States as a number of actors? To what extent was *a*
United States revealed in the events of the U-2 affair? When
the officials of a nation who are involved in international relations are numbered in the thousands and sometimes tens of
thousands, and are in all parts of the globe, coordination of
their activity into something resembling that of a single actor
may be a goal, but it is only partially realized. The difference
between the goal and degree of achievement may be a significant
factor in international relations.

The environment of the international system.—The international-society-of-individuals perspective also raises questions
about Riggs's conclusion that the global international political
system is different from other political systems because "the
weight of external pressures approaches the vanishing point." [22]
This leads him to call this system a macro-rule. The term
"macro" is often used to describe the global international political system, but this analytic posture may inhibit our comprehension of potentially significant aspects of international
relations. It is true that the individuals in the system span the
globe and this may be important, but it does not appear analyti-
cally fruitful to subsume everything under international politics.
Therefore, the global international political system can be
viewed as one with external pressures, just as we view national
political systems as having external pressures (which come
both from within and outside the nation). This perspective gives
us a framework for applying what we know about external
pressures on national political systems to international systems.

A distinctive characteristic of external pressures in international systems is that there is greater territorial fragmentation
of these pressures than is the case in many nations. When
certain groups in the environment coalesce where there was
formerly territorial separation, the performance of international
political systems may be significantly affected. For example,
Ernst Haas reports that the development of international
interest groups has been important in the evolution toward
greater political integration of Europe.[23] He also refers to other

22. Riggs, *op. cit.*, p. 151.
23. Ernst Haas, "The Challenge of Regionalism," *International Organ-ization*, Vol. 12, 1958, p. 452.

important environmental factors when he asserts: "Governmental negotiators and high civil servants working in isolation from political pressures and democratic accountability achieve mutual responsiveness more readily than groups resting on mass support." [24]

THE "DEVELOPING" NATIONS

One of the major contributions to the study of politics in recent years is *The Politics of Developing Areas,* edited by Gabriel A. Almond and James S. Coleman. The ambitious goal of this book is "to construct a theoretical framework that makes possible, for the first time, a comparative method of analysis for political systems of all kinds." This task is undertaken through the comparative analysis of the political systems of seventy-five nations in Asia, Africa, and Latin America, areas "in which dramatic social and political changes are taking place." [25]

Common features of "developing" political systems.—Coleman concludes that three common or modal features stand out when he attempts to generalize about all seventy-five nations.[26] *First,* there is "ethnic, religious, racial, and cultural pluralism" that retards integration. Because "interests are primarily rooted in and find expression through communal groups, they are far less amenable to aggregation in a competitive and bargaining process." International societies of national and international organization officials in face-to-face contact share this characteristic. *Second,* because the "developing" nations are undergoing dramatic change, they have social, economic, and political processes of "mixed" character; i.e., they include both "modern and traditional elements." The "modern sector" tends to erode the divisiveness of ethnic, religious, racial, and cultural pluralism.

24. *Ibid.,* p. 454.
25. Almond and Coleman, *op. cit.,* p. v. The parts of *The Politics of Developing Areas* most useful to this discussion are the Introduction (by Almond, pp. 3–64) and the Conclusion (by Coleman, pp. 532–76). In these chapters the editors generalize about data provided by other contributors in the chapters that fall between on the politics of Southeast Asia, South Asia, Sub-Saharan Africa, the Near East, and Latin America. Citation of this book will hereafter be to Almond or Coleman separately, although all the contributors and others collaborated in the development of the analytic approach of these chapters.
26. Coleman, *op. cit.,* pp. 535–36.

"Only in the modern sector of these mixed societies does one find the emergence of noncommunal functionally specific interest groups." *Third,* in "developing" nations a wide gap exists between the traditional mass and the essentially modern subsociety. The modern subsociety "controls the central structures of government and essays to speak and act for the society as a whole." The "modern sector" of international societies can be seen as the permanent organizations that are being developed in both universal and regional international systems, with the national capital sites as the traditional sector.

The tendencies of the "modern sector" of international political systems to erode communal boundaries and develop norms and procedures different from those of the traditional sector are causing tension between the two. For example, the writings of Sir Harold Nicolson and Charles Thayer support the norms and procedures of traditional diplomacy and severely criticize the practices in the "modern sector." Nicolson's "suspicion" of "new methods of diplomacy such as diplomacy by conference" is such that Kertesz characterizes him as having a "19th Century frame of reference." [27] Thayer, with many years of traditional experience, asserts that the United Nations has brought "debasement of the very language of diplomacy," "has added to diplomacy the oddly incongruous innovation of the vote," quotes approvingly an Italian diplomat's assertion that lobbying at the United Nations brings "hypocrisy" and "blackmail," and asserts that "the U.N.'s parliamentary diplomacy somehow lacks the quality of reality." [28]

Senator Henry M. Jackson delivered a widely noted address before the National Press Club in early 1962 which also reveals tension between the traditional and the "modern." He asserts that the United States Mission to the United Nations should be staffed "more as other embassies," dissents from the view that the U.S. Mission has a "unique role," and objects to the role this mission is playing by asserting: "The Ambassador to the United Nations is not a second Secretary of State, but the present arrangement suggests a certain imbalance in the role assigned

27. Stephen Kertesz, "Diplomacy in the Atomic Age," *Review of Politics,* Vol. 21, 1959, pp. 151–152. See, for example, Sir Harold Nicolson, *The Evolution of Diplomatic Method* (New York, Macmillan, 1954), p. 120.
28. Charles W. Thayer, *Diplomat* (New York, Harper, 1959), p. 112.

to the U.N. delegation in the policy-making process." [29] He also objects to the press, radio, and television coverage of the United Nations, observing that "the space and time devoted to our U.N. delegation does not correctly reflect the relative importance of what is said in New York against what is said in Washington." [30] C. L. Sulzberger's explanation of the removal of General Norstad as Supreme Commander Allied Powers Europe reveals similar tension between Washington and Paris NATO Headquarters. He explains that one of the reasons for removal was Norstad's "belief in the theory that the SHAPE commander was not only an American general but wore fifteen hats as an international Allied servant—a theory discounted by contemporary Washington." [31]

M. H. Cardozo strongly argues the "modern" viewpoint in a book devoted to diplomacy in European international organizations, *Diplomats in International Cooperation*. The book's subtitle calls diplomats in these organizations "Stepchildren of the Foreign Service." Cardozo asserts: "It is hardly likely that the skills and practices of traditional bilateral diplomacy will fit the conditions of the changed international spirit and structure" to be found in the European international organizations.[32] He further underlines the conflict between the traditional and "modern" by describing the problems that arise when an international organization is established in a national capital, placing two diplomatic communities in close proximity:

Diplomats traditionally occupy a privileged position, representing their sovereigns, and they would not take lightly the establishment of a higher-ranking corps in their domain. The ingenious protocol officers in Brussels . . . have worked out various solutions to problems as they arise. For example, the permanent representatives to international organizations received diplomatic license plates, but their numbers started from the top of the list, whereas the diplomats accredited to the Belgian government got theirs from the more prestigious lower end.[33]

29. Henry M. Jackson, "Do We Rely Too Much on the U.N.?" *New York Times Magazine*, April 1, 1962, p. 110.

30. *Loc. cit.*

31. C. L. Sulzberger, *New York Times*, August 13, 1962, p. 24.

32. Michael H. Cardozo, *Diplomats in International Cooperation, Stepchildren of the Foreign Service* (Ithaca, Cornell University Press, 1962), p. xi.

33. *Ibid.*, p. 121.

Since existing international systems share to some degree the common characteristics of the politics of "developing" areas, it seems prudent to consider the relevance of the analytic scheme developed by Almond and Coleman to the analysis of international systems. Almond proposes a set of functional categories:

A. Input functions
　　1. Political socialization and recruitment
　　2. Interest articulation
　　3. Interest aggregation
　　4. Political communication
B. Output functions
　　5. Rule-making
　　6. Rule application
　　7. Rule adjudication

The functions that Almond chooses to call "output functions," also referred to by Almond as "governmental functions," are similar to characteristics of the "classic" nation-state. But the "input functions" are the major concern of the Almond and Coleman volume, because of their belief that they "would be most important in characterizing non-Western political systems and in discriminating types and stages of political development among them." [34] It is this emphasis that makes the volume a useful stimulus to the international relations scholar. We will suggest some international phenomena that might be considered in the application of the Almond categories to the study of international political systems.

Political socialization and recruitment.—Almond defines "political socialization" as the "process of induction into the political culture. Its end product is a set of attitudes—cognitions, value standards, and feelings—toward the political system, its various roles, and role incumbents." [35] Coleman draws our attention to the fact that political socialization is taking place in both the traditional and "modern" spheres. In the international system, socialization is not only taking place in the "modern sectors" but also at traditional sites. At both kinds of sites persons are being recruited from a broader spectrum of the environment

34. Almond, *op. cit.*, p. 17. Dahl makes an even stronger plea for the importance of what he terms "social variables" in an eloquent paragraph which concludes: ". . . the first and crucial variables to which political scientists must direct their attention are social and not constitutional." In Dahl, *op. cit.*, p. 83.

35. Almond, *op. cit.*, p. 28.

as new skills are being added to those of the foreign affairs generalist, such as those of physicists, information specialists, and agricultural and industrial technicians. But this is not being done without internal strain, since "the foreign offices of the world have continued to reflect the careerists' preference for the generalist in diplomacy." [36] Thus the Wriston Committee, which studied the United States Foreign Service in 1954, found this "outmoded," "nineteenth-century" philosophy still dominated the thinking of the Foreign Service. The committee concluded that "specialization has become so vital an element in the day-to-day conduct of diplomacy, no less than in complex corporate undertakings, that to allow the 'generalist' to pre-empt all but a small segment of the Foreign Service Officer category is to deny American diplomacy full flexibility and depth." [37]

Coleman notes a "progressive shift in the geographical bases of recruitment" [38] in India, Southeast Asia, and Sub-Saharan Africa. As in the "developing" nations, the geographic base of recruitment to the international system has been broadened both within some nations and, perhaps more dramatically, as a result of the independence of former colonial territories. The change in the geographic base of recruitment was forcefully brought to the attention of the observer of the resumed session of the Sixteenth General Assembly of the U.N., where the rostrum was occupied by U Thant of Burma (Acting Secretary-General), Mongi Slim of Tunisia (President), and C. V. Narasimhan of India (Under-Secretary in charge of General Assembly Affairs). Only a year before the occupants of these seats were from Sweden, Peru, and the United States. Paul-Henri Spaak suggests that the impact of extended geographic recruitment of United Nations participants has seemed profound to him:

I left the United Nations for a period of five years—from 1949 to 1954, when I was in the Belgian Opposition—and the state of the Organization I found on my return after this short interlude gave me a profound shock. . . . Never have I found myself so hedged about

36. Cardozo, *op. cit.*, p. 120.
37. *Toward a Stronger Foreign Service,* Report of the Secretary of State's Committee on Personnel (Washington, D. C., Department of State, Pub. 5458, 1954), p. 13. See the Report of the Committee on Foreign Affairs Personnel, *Personnel for the New Diplomacy* (Washington, D. C., Carnegie Endowment for International Peace, 1962), especially pp. 54–55, for a more recent commentary on the prejudice of the United States Foreign Service against "specialists."
38. Coleman, *op. cit.*, p. 547.

by prejudice, passion, and rank obstinacy. . . . Unbridled nationalism and demogogy hold the field and many young nations, which ignore the rules of democracy because they lack the faith and have not been through the struggle, seem deaf to the voice of compromise.[39]

But extended geographic recruitment at the United Nations, and at other diplomatic sites, is accompanied by the socialization of these new inhabitants. One study of the "learning experiences" of U.N. delegates suggests that socialization important to the global international system may be taking place.[40] It reports that participation in the "modern sector" extends the knowledge that participants have about specific issues and about nations other than their own. It also develops involvement in, and feelings of responsibility for, an extended portion of the global international system, and requires participants to learn new norms, procedures, and social skills. Experience at the United Nations, for example, seems to have been important in making Henry Cabot Lodge and Paul Hoffman advocates of multilateral economic development programs. These men and the Hammarskjölds, Thants, Slims, Spaaks, Hallsteins, and Monnets have played important roles in shaping the development of universal and regional organizations, but also have been themselves socialized by their experiences in these organizational settings.

Interest articulation and aggregation.—Interest articulation and aggregation are undefined by Almond and Coleman, although they offer numerous examples of phenomena which they place in these categories. They indicate that interest articulation is not synonymous with the functions of interest groups and aggregation with political parties, but their discussion of articulation and aggregation largely uses interest groups and parties as examples. Commenting on the difficulty of drawing a clear distinction between the two, they "reserve the term 'aggregation' for the more inclusive levels of the combinatory processes, reserving the term 'articulation' for the narrower expressions of interest." [41] Political systems differ in terms of whether or not there are special organizations for performing these functions

39. Paul-Henri Spaak, "The Experiment of Collective Security," in *Perspective on Peace*, 1910–1960 (New York, Praeger, 1960), pp. 84–85.
40. Chadwick F. Alger, "Participation in the United Nations as a Learning Experience," *Public Opinion Quarterly*, XXVII, No. 3 (Fall 1963), pp. 411–26.
41. Almond, *op. cit.*, p. 40.

and with respect to whether or not one individual or organization performs both, and sometimes other, functions. Almond points out that a headman of a primitive society may perform intermittently as interest articulator, aggregator, and rule-maker.

Coleman concludes that three modal characteristics are discerned in interest articulation in the "developing" nations.[42] First, "there is persistence and importance of non-associational groupings of an ascriptive or communal character." Second, there is limited development of associational interest groups. Associational interest groups are defined by Almond as "specialized structures of interest articulation—trade unions, organizations of businessmen or industrialists, ethnic associations, associations organized by religious denominations, civic groups, and the like. Their particular characteristics are explicit representation of the interests of a particular group, orderly procedures for the formulation of interests and demands, and transmission of these demands to other political structures such as political parties, legislatures, bureaucracies." [43] Third, there is a predominance of institutional interest groups (armies, religious groups, or bureaucracies). Coleman concludes that "the strength and tenacity of communal and similar groupings militates against the emergence of functionally specific groups as the foci of interest identification and expression." [44] Likewise, the absence of functionally specific (i.e., associational) interest groups serves to perpetuate the communal groups and "to invite, if not to compel, institutional groups to assume a preponderant role." [45]

International systems also tend to have the communal organization of interests that is prevalent in "developing" nations. Communal (nationalistic) identification inhibits the development of specific interest groups that cut across national boundaries. As a result "institutions," in this case national and international officials engaged in international relations, are often called upon to articulate and aggregate interests for international systems. But unlike many of the "developing" nations, these institutions are not "filled mainly by statist and nationally minded modernists," [46] i.e., persons dedicated to building strong

42. Coleman, *op. cit.*, p. 548.
43. Almond, *op. cit.*, p. 34.
44. Coleman, *op. cit.*, p. 548.
45. *Loc. cit.*
46. *Loc. cit.*

international "governments." Partially because of recruitment and socialization procedures, the traditional sector is more influential in international systems than in many of the "developing" nations.

There are, of course, different degrees of development of interest articulation and aggregation in different international systems. In Europe, trade associations and trade unions have individually combined across national boundaries to lobby in the new institutions of the European Coal and Steel Community and the European Economic Community.[47] The aggregation of interests through political parties has apparently moved more slowly, although delegations of national parliamentarians to the European Parliamentary Assembly do sit in the Assembly according to party rather than by nation. These international political groups meet frequently, whereas national contingents meet only rarely.[48] Like the interest groups, parties seem to be finding it necessary to coalesce across national boundaries in order to attempt to influence the increasingly important Community "executives." Developments in the NATO system have not gone so far, although the Chief of Staff of the Foreign Relations Committee of the United States Senate reports:

A survey of the resolutions adopted over the past four years reveals a growing sense of influence and a tendency for the [NATO Parliamentarian's] Conference to think of itself in terms of a "continuing body" capable of pushing the North Atlantic Council and member governments in certain directions.[49]

Though the universal system has not progressed as far in interest articulation and aggregation, evidence of such development is not wholly absent. The United Nations provides a permanent organized setting in which nongovernmental organizations have impetus to cooperate in their activities similar to that of the European lobbyists. But the articulation and aggregation of international interest in the universal system, when it is achieved, is largely delegated to national and international officials active in United Nations activities. Though groups have

47. Haas, *op. cit.*, pp. 451–52.
48. Eric Stein, "The European Parliamentary Assembly: Techniques of Emerging 'Political Control,' " *International Organization,* Vol. XIII (1959), p. 235.
49. Carl Marcy and Norella Hansen, "A Note on American Participation in Interparliamentary Meetings," *International Organization,* Vol. XIII, 1959, p. 438.

not developed in the United Nations that bear much resemblance to parties found in national systems, the aggregation of diverse interests around specific policies does take place. We can take the development of United Nations policy in the Congo as an example. Through the diplomatic procedures of the United Nations (General Assembly, Security Council, Secretary-General, special advisory bodies, etc.), a policy has been formulated and executed by United Nations officials. Supporters of this policy represent different interests: anticolonialism, strengthening of central "governmental" institutions, preservation of peace, and a variety of national goals. The same takes place in other problem areas such as the development of United Nations policies and programs in economic development and independence for colonial territories.

Political communication.—Coleman concludes that the underdeveloped nations are characterized by "gross discontinuities" in political communication.[50] He finds that these discontinuities tend to be of two types: cleavages between communal groups and gaps between the "modern" and traditional sectors of societies. In words that might very well have been taken from a description of international relations, he writes that "one frequently finds near-autonomous communications systems strengthened in their isolative tendencies by linguistic distinctiveness." [51] In the traditional sectors he finds communications processes that coincide "with patterns of personal relationships," [52] while in the "modern" areas he finds these patterns altered through the construction of political groups and the development of mass media. The new diplomatic sites also introduce communications patterns that are different from more traditional sites. At a site where virtually all nations in a system are represented, and where each represents itself to all instead of to one other nation, there is a tendency for new groupings to emerge. For example, in the traditional sector, diplomats from Paraguay and Chad would likely have only slight contact. In the aggregative process that takes place in the United Nations, however, they will most likely—as small, underdeveloped, land-locked, cotton-exporting nations—occasionally join together in political activity. Patterns of communication also change because

50. Coleman, *op. cit.*, p. 557.
51. *Loc. cit.*
52. *Loc. cit.*

of common membership in an organization which puts diplomats in more constant contact, under different environmental conditions. Therefore, restraints on communication at traditional sites, such as rank-differential and recognition practices, are less effective.

In addition, the documentation produced by secretariats provides a "mass medium" that is not controlled from within any of the nation units. If Almond's discussion of the importance of "an autonomous, neutral, and thoroughly penetrative system of communication" is true, this may be a very crucial role for the international organization.[53] He writes that the "availability of neutral information about the functioning of the political system tends to create an informed stratum of citizens—public policy-oriented, rather than interest-oriented in the narrow sense. . . . In addition, this attentive stratum constitutes a special political subculture in which special kinds of interest groups thrive—interest groups concerned with general policy problems rather than with special interests." [54] The members of a U.N. "presence" or an Organization of American States investigating committee are the "foreign correspondents" of the neutral "mass medium." Those active in an international organization are more informed of the content of this medium than those at traditional sites and elsewhere.

Whatever the reader's attitude toward the selection of international analogues to the Almond-Coleman variables, or his attitude toward the fruitfulness of these particular variables for political analysis, it is hoped that this discussion has helped to show that the lack of "governments" in international systems does not preclude wider application of knowledge and concepts from intranational politics to the study of international politics. Hopefully, we have also shown that "developing" international systems can be more fruitfully studied with concepts that are able to handle crucial kinds of change, and that also offer links to new knowledge being gathered in other areas of politics. So

53. For a provocative account of the independence of the Office of Public Information of the United Nations, see Leon Gordenker, "Policy-Making and Secretariat Influence in the U.N.," *American Political Science Review*, Vol. LIV, 1960, pp. 359–73. He reports: "Repeated attacks have left OPI almost unaltered, either in form or function" (p. 371). "The ability of the Secretariat to return from the General Assembly time after time with a renewed mandate to carry out its own public information program reflects real influence" (p. 373).

54. Almond, *op. cit.*, p. 48.

as not to let our argument depend on one contribution to the literature of politics, we will now attempt to show the relevance of other literature. We have selected contributions to the study of the politics of primitive societies.

PRIMITIVE SOCIETIES

The study of the politics of primitive societies has not been a matter of major concern until recent years.[55] One of the reasons is that anthropologists, to whom we are indebted for most of our knowledge of primitive societies, tended to think "that many of the institutions which are fundamental to Western society developed fairly late in the history of mankind." Since they considered "government and law" to be among these, they concluded "that primitive societies pursue no activities which deserve the name of politics." [56] Recently, however, anthropologists have provided a number of works on primitive politics.[57] These works have given much attention to societies without elaborate governmental organizations, sometimes called "stateless societies." This makes these works of particular interest to the international relations scholar.

According to Max Gluckman, the term "primitive" can be applied to societies that range from Eskimo and Bushmen to states such as Dahomey.[58] Lucy Mair uses "primitive" to refer to "peoples of simple technology." [59] MacIver uses "primitive government" for "all those systems that preside over a near-to-nature economy." [60] For our purposes the definition of "primitive" is not crucial, since the intent of this section is to examine some characteristics of politics which seem to have characteristics in common with international systems.

55. M. Fortes and E. E. Evans-Pritchard, *African Political Systems* (New York, Oxford, 1940, reprinted 1961), p. xi.
56. Lucy Mair, *Primitive Government* (Baltimore, Penguin Books, 1962), p. 9.
57. Mair, *op. cit.;* Fortes and Evans-Pritchard, *op. cit.;* Isaac Schapera, *Government and Politics in Tribal Societies* (London, Watts, 1956); John Middleton and David Tate, *Tribes Without Rulers* (London, Routledge and K. Paul, 1958).
58. Max Gluckman, "Political Institutions," in *The Institutions of Primitive Society* (Oxford, Basil Blackwell, 1954), p. 66.
59. Mair, *op. cit.* p. 9.
60. Robert MacIver, *The Web of Government* (New York, Macmillan, 1948), p. 156.

Some may question the reasonableness of an attempt to derive insights on international relations from primitive, or what have sometimes been called simple, societies. Perhaps international societies appear to be on one end of a simple-complex continuum, with primitive societies on the other. If this is indeed the case, it still may be possible to make some general statements that apply to both, such as about the lift capacity of the single-engined Piper Cub and a multi-engined jet liner. However, the assumption of both international complexity and primitive simplicity can be challenged. Certainly in terms of the development of governmental institutions, and some aspects of the structure of society crucial to politics, international systems are less complex than many national systems. On the other hand, primitive societies seem not to be as simple, in terms vital to the social scientist, as has been presumed. According to Max Gluckman:

Here the most striking conclusion of modern anthropological research is that the organization which was required to hold together a thousand people on a South Sea island was almost as complicated as that which rules a city like London. The organization was complicated even though these island societies, like many others in continental Africa and elsewhere, did not have a cultural apparatus as complex as ours.[61]

Contingency and differentiation.—In a bibliographic essay on the political anthropology literature, David Easton evaluates primitive societies in terms of the degree to which their politics are contingent and the degree of differentiation of political roles. Easton makes a provocative attack on the practice of some anthropologists in dividing primitive societies into a state-stateless dichotomy. He disputes their assertion that stateless societies are "completely devoid of organized authority." [62] He finds that "even in stateless societies there are some structures for adjusting differences among the maximal lineages," [63] and declares that "some decisions are taken, even though the scope of these decisions may be limited to the parties to the dispute and even though an informal structure may arise only as the occasion

61. Gluckman, op. cit., pp. 66–67.
62. David Easton, "Political Anthropology," in Bernard J. Siegel, ed., Biennial Review of Anthropology (Stanford, Stanford University Press, 1959), p. 235.
63. Ibid., p. 236.

dictates it." [64] Therefore, rather than arranging societies in a state-stateless dichotomy, he finds it more fruitful to locate them on a contingent-continuous political system continuum. In discussion Easton cites scope of decisions, number of decisions, degree of compliance, and whether the system is in continuous operation as criteria for differentiating more contingent systems from those less contingent. The less a system has of each of these qualities, the more contingent it is.

An application of Easton's analysis to international systems suggests that a national-international dichotomy not be set up on the basis of the presence or absence of "government." Instead Easton would ask that systems from both categories be ranked along a contingent-continuous continuum. It would seem likely that international systems would tend to be distributed toward the contingent end of the continuum. Even when organizations are established in which the entire system is represented, decisions that are made in these organizations are often limited in scope, and the degree of compliance is low. The development of organizations does, however, sometimes provide international systems with a continuously operating machinery to replace occasional *ad hoc* conferences. Nevertheless, these organizations find it necessary to use *ad hoc* machinery for handling many tasks that some nations handle through continuing mechanisms.

Easton, "in an entirely tentative and exploratory spirit," suggests the use of role differentiation in classifying political systems. By role differentiation he means (1) extent to which political roles can be distinguished from other social roles, (2) extent to which political roles can be distinguished from each other, and (3) degree to which political roles fulfill specific or multiple and diffuse functions. The literature on primitive societies stimulates him to ask whether differentiation is related to other characteristics: size of society; ethnic composition; mode of subsistence; frequency, volume, and type of demands made; nature of communications network; technical requirements for implementation of decisions; attitudes toward authority; social structure; types of personalities prevalent in society; and accessibility of physical means for usurpation, rebellion, and conquest. On the basis of analysis of data on primitive societies, Easton sees a relationship between role dif-

64. *Ibid.*, p. 237.

ferentiation and segmentation (i.e., lineage fragmentation where primitive societies are concerned). He observes that "in systems with a low degree of differentiation, there is no group of political leaders or administrative organization that views the whole political system as its constituency. There is accordingly no group of persons that has an interest in interfering with the increase or decrease of segmentation." [65]

International systems are also systems in which role differentiation is not highly developed. Segmentation resulting from national, rather than lineage, divisions is accompanied by the existence of only a small number of political leaders who see the entire system as their constituency. International systems seem to have, however, an increasing number of officials with such a view. They serve as chairmen, as presidents, and in other leadership roles in *ad hoc* and international organization conferences. The expansion of the number of international organization secretariats has increased the number of international officials "who see the entire system as their constituency." The increase in size of secretariats is permitting greater role specialization. Clusters of officials with particular specialties, including officials from a number of nations and international secretariat officials, occasionally form "interest groups" that erode segmentation. Rather dramatic erosion of segmentation is taking place in the European system, but many international systems show striking similarity to "stateless" societies in this regard.

Physical force.—One kind of role specialization in political systems is the development of specialists in the use of physical force. In some regional international systems there has been remarkable development of specialized military roles with a system perspective. In the United Nations there are commanders of international forces and military advisers to the Secretary-General in the Secretariat, though these developments in the United Nations have fallen far short of the provisions for international military forces in Chapter VII of the Charter. Since primitive systems share some of the characteristics of international systems, the experiences of primitive systems in the development of coercive institutions may offer useful insights. These experiences might throw some light on the "classic" nation-state proposition that asserts that physical force is a necessary tool

65. *Ibid.*, p. 246.

for the preservation of order. In addition, they might help us to know better the requisites for the establishment of specialists in violence in political systems.

Force has played an intriguing role in the study of politics. Following in the tradition of Hobbes and the later utilitarians, "generations of professional students of politics" [66] have considered the use of physical coercion to be a distinguishing characteristic of politics. Thus Almond considers the political system to be identifiable from other aspects of a society by virtue of its "employment, or threat of employment, of more or less legitimate physical compulsion." [67] This follows from Weber's classic definition: "The state is a human community that (successfully) claims the *monopoly of the legitimate use of physical force* in a given territory." [68] Weber also concluded: "If no social institutions existed which knew the use of violence, then the concept of 'state' would be eliminated, and a condition would emerge that could be designated as 'anarchy,' in the specific sense of this word." [69]

This definition of politics has been applied by a number of anthropologists,[70] including Malinowski,[71] Radcliffe-Brown,[72] and R. H. Lowie.[73] Schapera, however, in his study of *Government and Politics in Tribal Societies,* considers this usage "inappropriate" because "communities such as those of Bergdama and Bushmen are able to lead an orderly existence despite their lack of courts and despite the inability of their chiefs to punish offenders in other ways." [74] Schapera thus chooses to redefine "political organization" and chooses to call it "that aspect of the total organization which is concerned with the establishment and maintenance of internal cooperation and external indepen-

66. *Ibid.,* p. 218.
67. Almond, *op. cit.,* p. 7.
68. Max Weber, "Politics as a Vocation," in Gerth and Mills, *From Max Weber* (New York, Oxford, 1958), p. 78.
69. *Loc. cit.*
70. See Schapera, *op. cit.,* pp. 94–95, for a review of anthropological literature in which this definition is used.
71. Bronislaw Malinowski, *Scientific Theory of Culture* (Chapel Hill, University of North Carolina Press, 1944), p. 165.
72. In Fortes and Evans-Pritchard, *op. cit.,* p. xiv.
73. R. H. Lowie, "Some Aspects of Political Organization Among American Aborigines," *Journal of the Royal Anthropological Institute,* Vol. 78. 1948, p. 11.
74. Schapera, *op. cit.,* p. 217.

dence." [75] It is, of course, the prerogative of any scholar to define his terms as he pleases, but Schapera raises an issue of great import. He is basically interested in "order" and finds that it can be achieved, although in small communities, without physical force. Since problems of order are a major preoccupation of most international relations scholars, he offers data vital to their concerns, no matter how they define politics.

Schapera concludes that "apart from maintaining territorial boundaries and resisting external aggression the only function common to all forms of government is the organization and direction of cooperative enterprises often involving the whole community." [76] Schapera's statement can be reinterpreted to mean that he observes a pattern in the development of "mechanisms making for orderly life in any community." [77] In this pattern cooperative enterprises precede the organized exercise of coercive authority, which does not emerge until there is a "wider range of activity and complexity of governmental organization." [78] In a review of the literature of political anthropology, Easton offers a proposition similar to Schapera's: "The greater the degree of differentiation and specialization in the political structure, the greater will be the tendency to reinforce the authority of the administrative organization. Structures will emerge through which the rulers can generate support, including a greater reliance upon the monopolization of the legitimate use of force." [79]

Thus we find some evidence related to our question on the prerequisites for the establishment of monopoly of force in political systems. It appears that it may be one of the attributes of centralized governmental institutions that appears late in institutional development.[80] It also appears that cooperative enterprises are feasible before it is possible to establish organized coercive authority. The discovery of societies in which there is order without monopoly of force and other characteristics of the

75. *Ibid.*, p. 218. Almond is mistaken when he says that Schapera "does not offer an alternative definition" of "politics" (Almond, *op. cit.*, p. 5).

76. Schapera, *op. cit.* p. 217.

77. *Ibid.*, p. 218.

78. *Ibid.*, p. 220.

79. Easton, *op. cit.*, p. 245. This work includes a very useful annotated bibliography of political anthropology prepared by John D. McCaffrey.

80. This is in agreement with Deutsch's findings in his study of ten cases of attempted political integration in the North Atlantic area during the past five centuries. In Deutsch, *op. cit.*, 1957, pp. 25–26.

"classic" nation-state model demands an inquiry into what factors make order possible in these societies. Several anthropologists offer explanations that are provocative for those interested in international relations.

Overlapping memberships.—"The critical result of their analysis is to show that these societies are so organized into a series of groups and relationships, that people who are friends on one basis are enemies on another. Herein lies social cohesion, rooted in the conflicts between men's different allegiances." [81] The importance of overlapping memberships as a means whereby "society is sewn together" [82] has been of concern to sociologists such as Ross, Coser,[83] and Simmel.[84] Morgenthau also cites it as one of the factors that "make for peace within the nation." [85] But the role of overlapping memberships in *international* systems has not been a paramount interest of international relations scholars.

Max Gluckman has been particularly attentive to what he terms "cross-cutting memberships" and describes their relevance to a small society in terms readily applicable to international relations:

Thus a thousand people on an island in the South Seas, or a couple of thousand in a Plains Red Indian tribe harried by constant attack, seemed unable to hold together as a political unit unless they were involved in cross-cutting systems of alliance, so that a man's opponents in one system were his friends in another.[86]

Gluckman cites friendship, kinship, trading, and ritual ties as examples of the bases of "cross-cutting relationships." Fortes and Evans-Pritchard write about societies in which "the stabilizing factor is not a super-ordinate juridical or military organization, but is simply a sum total of intersegment relations." [87] Peristiany is of particular interest because he discriminates between territorial and nonterritorial "institutions." His considera-

81. Max Gluckman, *Custom and Conflict in Africa* (Glencoe, Free Press, 1955), p. 4.

82. Edward A. Ross, *The Principles of Sociology* (New York, Century, 1920), p. 164.

83. Lewis Coser, *The Functions of Social Conflict* (Glencoe, Free Press, 1956), pp. 75–80.

84. Georg Simmel, *Conflict and the Web of Group Affiliations* (Glencoe, Free Press, 1955), pp. 146–61.

85. Morgenthau, *op. cit.*, p. 504.

86. Gluckman, *op. cit.*, 1954, p. 74.

87. Fortes and Evans-Pritchard, *op. cit.*, p. 14.

tion of the significance of nonterritorial memberships which cut across territorial membership boundaries places the overlapping membership question in a setting quite similar to its setting in international relations. In a discussion of the Kipsigis, a tribe in the highlands of Kenya, he points out that a man is identified with a clan, a regiment, and his initiation age-mates. These affiliations extend beyond the residential unit "so that a man journeying far from home in a society which lacks a police force and a welfare organization, is assured of help and protection wherever he may be." [88]

Gluckman considers "cross-cutting memberships" to be so crucial to "political institutions" that he asserts that "all the various ties of friendship linking one small group with another have political functions and are political institutions." [89] Greater attentiveness to multiple membership phenomena might enable international relations scholars to supply useful insights to policy-makers who are now making crucial decisions about the structure of the world in which we will live in coming decades. For example, what may be the effect on future world order if British entrance into the Common Market results in rupturing ties with Commonwealth nations? It has often been debated whether regional integration is an aid or impediment to universal integration. The literature on multiple memberships suggests that regional integration may facilitate universal integration, *if* regional groups are "sewn together" by overlapping memberships. But if memberships do not overlap, they may tend simply to create a system of larger nations. From this perspective the British Commonwealth may be a valuable cross-pressure on the tendencies toward regional integration. Thomas Hovet, Jr., concludes that the Commonwealth Group in the United Nations "plays a harmonizing role because its members belong to other groups." [90]

88. John G. Peristiany, "Law," in *The Institutions of Primitive Society* (Glencoe, Free Press, 1956), p. 40.
89. Gluckman, *op. cit.*, 1954, p. 68.
90. Thomas Hovet, Jr., "Political Parties in the United Nations," paper prepared for 1962 Annual Meeting of the American Political Science Association, Washington, D. C., September 1962, p. 6.

CONCLUSION

Through the use of contributions to the study of the politics of "developing" nations and primitive societies, this paper has suggested a number of variables used in the study of these polities that might prove fruitful in the study of international politics: political socialization and recruitment, interest articulation, interest aggregation, political communication, contingency, differentiation, and overlapping memberships. These variables seem particularly relevant because of apparent similarities between some aspects of the politics of the "developing" nations and primitive societies on the one hand and international politics on the other. Material relevant to these variables is not all found in the literature on "developing" nations and primitive societies, nor exclusively in political science. These two literatures have simply been used to pinpoint seemingly crucial variables in apparently similar contexts.

Variation measured by these variables could indicate significant developments in an international system. If this change is in the appropriate direction, it may indicate developing capability to support new kinds of integrated political organizations. (On the other hand, it may be that such change could make some organizations unnecessary.) Indicators of this type of change might be increased applications of national diplomats for posts in international organizations (recruitment); increased differences between accepted norms and procedures of diplomats in national capitals and those in international organizations (socialization); increase in public statements, declarations, resolutions, etc., supported by national officials or private citizens from more than one nation (articulation and aggregation); increase in quotation of documents of international secretariats by national officials (political communication); increase in days in operation per year of international bodies and establishment of new permanent bodies (contingency); establishment of new international roles and division of old roles (differentiation); increase in overlapping membership revealed by a study of voting, resolution sponsorship, and other cooperative activity in governmental and nongovernmental international organizations.

The literature on primitive societies has been particularly

helpful in raising questions about the sequence in which certain roles can be introduced into political systems, particularly with regard to physical force. In this case the definition of politics as that agency which has "a monopoly on the legitimate use of physical force" seems to have led at times to implicit assumptions about the role of force in building social order. Those interested in building social order cannot prudently neglect to examine a broad range of means for achieving it. Such means are not necessarily circumscribed by particular definitions of politics.[91]

Finally, this effort to show international political analogues to political phenomena in "developing" nations and primitive societies suggests the potential value of greater integration of research and theory development in international politics with that in intranational politics. This should be particularly useful in providing the international scholar with a broader range of concepts for collecting and analyzing his data, as well as for providing links to other data relevant to his interests. The study of international politics has demonstrated proclivity for gross variables such as "diplomacy," which includes such processes as negotiation, communication, aggregation, and socialization. Greater differentiation would lead toward more effective data collection and analysis. Hopefully, scholars now occupied solely with intranational politics will find it fruitful to include international systems in their research designs. This may be as provocative for their investigations as the examination of "developing" nations and primitive societies is to the student of international politics.

91. For a useful discussion of definitions of politics, see Easton, *op. cit.*, pp. 213–27. Easton concludes that the "legitimate use of force" to identify politics "is an approach that research in American political science has all but abandoned, although it still has enough vitality to raise its head from time to time" (pp. 218–19).

Scientific Comparative Politics and International Relations

RAOUL NAROLL

Northwestern University

T HE QUESTION we are discussing is the question of the similarities and differences between the internal politics of national states on one hand and the international politics of the interstate system on the other.

As members of one national state, we frequently visit and communicate with members of other national states—Canada, France, Mexico, even the Soviet Union. I submit, however, that few of us have much awareness of other international *systems* than our own; that the world today is almost exclusively occupied by members of the Western European state system, which is subdivided into three major blocs: the Communist bloc, the North Atlantic bloc, and the neutralists. It is only when we carefully study comparative history that we perceive in earlier centuries the existence of multiple international state systems, each linked together, as ours is, by direct trade and diplomatic relations and governed by common concepts of morality. Each of these earlier systems was commonly referred to as "the world" by its participants, even though its members were usually dimly aware of uninvolved outsiders. Thus the ancient Mediterranean world of the successors of Alexander the Great consisted of states with important communication commitments to the Mediterranean Sea, either because they gained their livelihood largely from commerce upon it or because they were part of the Greek language intellectual community. At the same time Eurasia had two other well-developed state systems: In North India were a collection of states with religions of the Hindu-Buddhist type writing in variants of the Devanagari alphabet, and in China were another collection of states writing in Chinese ideographs and sharing a common increasingly secular body of historical and philosophical literature, which they looked to for moral guidance.

Our perception of our own system is sometimes blurred by our sensitivity to the essentially minor differences between the philosophies of the two rival blocs. From our point of view, focused as we are on the issues between those of us who are capitalist and libertarian and those who are socialist and authoritarian, it is easy to forget that we share with our Communist associates and trade-partners a common body of rules on international behavior which all obey about as well as drivers obey speed laws in California; a common philosophical and scientific literature which is read either in translation or in the original Western European languages by expert specialists who teach in the universities of our countries; and a common set of social values derived from eighteenth-century Western Europe, particularly England and France, and embodied in such slogan words as *liberty, equality, democracy,* and especially the word *people,* used to mean all the people of a state. (The Communist states are called "people's democracies," while our nation was long ago dedicated—in words now inscribed in stone on one of our most conspicuous monuments—to government "of the people, by the people, for the people.")

My impression of students of international relations today is that they overemphasize the importance of the difference between so-called "international affairs" and internal governments. Such a distinction makes better sense in discussing European-world affairs before 1918 or the affairs of other state systems, than in discussing the affairs of our own time. For since the establishment of the League of Nations in 1920 the European world has had a central governmental organization with a charter and a peace-keeping function and in this way has been as effectively governed as many true states. To be sure, we have had much internal war within our so-called international system since 1920; our system has not worked at all well. But it has worked about as well as the internal system of the Roman Empire during the years between the death of Marcus Aurelius and the accession of Diocletian.

There is, true, a vital conceptual difference between the Roman Empire of the third century and our international world today. In the Roman Empire, whereas in practice a very provincial general exercised an option to intervene on his own with his legions in the political affairs of the empire, still the notion of legitimate monopoly of force was present in theory; in our international world of today this notion is absent. The distinction, then, is between a polity with such an ideal concept, which we agree to call a *state*, and a polity without it, which we call *stateless*. The international world today *is* a single polity, embracing all human beings except some of the natives of the interior of New Guinea and Brazil, but it is not a state. Thus the difference between the theoretical nature of our international polity and the polities of its component national states is a difference like that between the polity of the segmentary Nuer or the consensual Naron Bushmen on one hand and the authoritarian Baganda on the other. If students of international relations are searching for general theory they can hardly avoid taking the advice of Alger and studying comparatively the affairs of primitive tribes.[1]

Such tribes (whom many of us anthropologists define as "peoples without cities") do lack many important characteristics of our own international polity. But if we are interested in general theory, this is an advantage rather than a disadvantage. The real issue before us today, I think, is the matter of Galton's problem, which boils down to the problem of ideographic versus nomothetic generalization, the problem of describing a particular situation on one hand and discerning general laws on the other hand.

Alger lists six characteristics of the nation-state; these were stated by John Foster Dulles as characteristics which Dulles said were absent from the international system. I submit that all six of these characteristics are indeed present in the international system—and that they are not fully effective within any nation-state, including our own—so that the difference between the

1. All references to Alger here refer to the preceding chapter in this volume.

United States and the United Nations with respect to all six of
these factors is a matter of degree rather than of kind. Let us
consider them in turn:

1. *"Laws, written or unwritten, which reflect the moral
judgment of the community."*

The Charter of the United Nations, like the Covenant of the
League of Nations, together with a number of widely-subscribed-
to treaties, forms a small body of written laws, supplemented by
important unwritten understandings. This body of international
morality includes many generally accepted, nowhere publicly
challenged laws, embracing matters like the following:

A. Warfare is an evil to be avoided; aggressors who com-
mence it are to be frustrated and punished. (Those whom we
consider to have violated this rule conspicuously, like Japan in
1931 or Germany in 1939, are careful to *claim* to conform and to
assert that they are the aggrieved parties.)

B. Accredited diplomats are throughout the international
system entitled to the same body of special privileges and immunities. Even between two countries at war with one another,
these privileges and immunities are in fact usually respected.

C. International intercourse is facilitated through an effectively operated international postal system and through generally
agreed-upon maritime traffic and harbor rules.

2. *"Political machinery to change these laws . . . as conditions change."*

Both the League of Nations and the United Nations provided
machinery to make new international law to supplement and
change old rules. The adoption of generally-subscribed-to treaties
like the International Postal Convention and the Kellogg-Briand
Pact constituted additional machinery of this sort. That such
machinery was often clumsy and inadequate and ineffective is
true; but our own United States lawmaking machinery is not always effective, as witness the bottling up of legislation by congressional committees or its blocking by Senate filibusters. In
other words, the difference in effectiveness of political machinery between our own nation and the international polity is one
of degree rather than of kind.

3. *"An executive body to administer law."*

Both the League of Nations and the United Nations had secretariats which administered and administer some laws effectively.
That they have not administered all international law effectively

has been and remains a problem. Neither the executive branch of the United States government nor that of the state of Illinois is able to administer effectively all the laws either is charged with administering. The federal laws against the importing of narcotics are notoriously flouted, and within Illinois, laws against gambling and prostitution and narcotics sales are also flouted by criminal organizations whose membership is likewise notorious. Again the difference is one of degree and not one of kind.

4. *"Courts which settle disputes of a justiciable character in accordance with law."*

Here Dulles seems to be on stronger ground. There is a generally recognized international court for the settlement of international disputes at the Hague, but this court takes cognizance only of controversies submitted to it voluntarily by the litigants. However, both the old League of Nations and the United Nations endowed their assemblies and councils with judicial functions. Such functions lacked the procedures associated with law courts in Western countries and so Dulles may not have realized that they existed, but to anthropologists the eighteenth-century notion of separation of legislative and judicial functions is not a universal truth but rather a Western policy or attitude. Thus even in the matter of courts to settle disputes, our international order has them, with jurisdiction over all international disputes which threaten to result in war; if our international courts do not function particularly well compared to our national courts, this again is a matter of degree rather than kind. Hamlet complained of the law's delay, and others have pointed out that our own law courts are not really accessible to impoverished citizens. In the 1930's the judicial processes were defied successfully by midwestern farmers who saw no justice in the enforcement of mortgage contracts. And no one ever called President Andrew Jackson to account for successfully and openly defying the United States Supreme Court in the Cherokee case. "John Marshall has made his decision," said Jackson. "Now let him enforce it."

5. *"Superior public force which deters violence by its ability to apprehend and punish adequately any who breach or defy the law."*

Both the Covenant of the League of Nations and the Charter of the United Nations called for use of contingents of national armies to enforce international decision when needed. This system was never effectively applied by the old League, but it has been used with some success in Israel and the Congo by the U.N. The Swiss state, though it has a small national police force, otherwise resembles the U.N. in that it lacks any national army distinct from the local and cantonal formations, organized like our own National Guard. In case of dispute between federal and state authorities in our country, federal authorities are supposed to be able to count on the support of the National Guard of the states concerned. Presidents Eisenhower and Kennedy found state militias responsive to their calls when such disputes arose, but President Lincoln did not.

But even in centralized states, the problem of control of the armed forces by the civilian officials responsible for law enforcement is always present. Who guards the guardians? What happens when the armed forces themselves breach or defy the law? Who has called General Francisco Franco to account for his breaches of the laws of republican Spain?

So again we find that parallel institutions exist, some more effective than others, some in which practice more closely accords with theory than others, but with no clear qualitative distinction.

6. *"Well-being sufficient so that the people . . . are not driven by desperation to follow ways of violence."*

Ways of violence are followed by people who see themselves driven by desperation in most states. Our own nation is rather more given to this than most other Western members of the European state system. We have not only our gangster syndicates but our southern mobs, our western desperadoes of the 1880's and 1890's, our labor-strife thugs of strikers and/or strikebreakers, our Appalachian mountaineer family feuders; and finally only a century has passed since we had a first-rate civil war with hundreds of thousands of killed and wounded men.

To sum up, in the world at large today we have an international polity which does not achieve its stated goals or conform to its ideal plan nearly as well as many of our state polities do, but does contain theoretical machinery which is supposed to provide for the enforcement of international law and order. Most of our states, though usually working more effectively than our international polity, also often fall short of perfection in functioning to carry out in practice their announced theoretical roles. Dulles found qualitative differences by comparing the actual operation of the international system with the theoretical operation of the state system. But in fact since 1920 the actual differences have chiefly been those of degree rather than of kind.

It seems to me more important, for the purposes of this discussion, to contrast the generally nomothetic character of the study of international relations with the generally ideographic character of the study of comparative politics, rather than to contrast the character of the national state with that of the international polity. Most recent students of comparative politics have sought to describe the political systems of prominent members of our modern Western state system. They have not in recent generations interested themselves much in the systematic search for general principles of government. In this they have departed from an earlier Western tradition. Aristotle, Montesquieu, James Madison, John Adams, and James Wilson come to mind as analysts who sought to discover fundamental propositions about the nature of political systems and who studied comparatively particular constitutions with this purpose in mind. Whatever may have been their limitations, they were political scientists. Most recent students of comparative politics have rather been political ethnographers. This is, however, an accident of recent intellectual history and has nothing to do with the fundamental nature of the comparative politics field as such. Contemporary international relations, as I have indicated, seems to me merely a special branch of comparative politics, studying a rather loose kind of confederation like the Holy Roman Empire of the eighteenth century or the old Delphic Amphictyony or the old Swiss Confederation.

To seek laws of political relationships and thus to discover a political science has not been the aim of most students of comparative politics in recent decades. It is, however, the aim of many—perhaps most—of those present here today. What ought to be the characteristics of such a discipline of comparative politics, including its subdiscipline of international relations? It ought to seek correlations between variables and, once such correlations have been discovered, to seek the underlying causal influences which produce them. To discover correlations, variables must be identified—and variables, to be identified, must vary. Consequently one must study *varied* political systems.

Furthermore, one must beware of ideographic correlations, of multiple instances of the same type which repeatedly occur through merely historical accidents of the diffusion of culture—its spread through borrowing and especially through migration. This problem can be exemplified in the correlation between the twelve-man jury system and the precedent-oriented common law system, both characteristic of English jurisprudence spread by English-speaking jurists not only to English settlements abroad but also to non-English-speaking populations administered for a time by English colonialists. For these reasons a science of comparative politics must give careful heed to the admonitions of Alger and beware of its biased sample. Not only should it give careful attention to primitive societies but also to non-Western civilized societies. Since all civilized societies today are more or less westernized, this means that students of comparative politics must, like Montesquieu, John Adams, and James Madison, give keen attention to historical materials—to the political systems of medieval Europe, of classical antiquity, of the Moslem world, of India, and especially of the pre-nineteenth-century Far East. We find rich documentation not only in China but also in Vietnam, Korea, and Japan. Japanese political history is a particularly fascinating field for the true political scientist. Here the delegation of supreme authority has been carried further perhaps than anywhere else, especially in the late Minamoto Shogunate, where an administrator actually ran the state, in the name of a regent who supposedly was acting for a shogun, who in turn derived his authority in theory from the emperor.

The methods of study must surely be varied. There is much need for the case study of a single case—studied, however, not with the aim of mere description but rather with the aim of seeking a sort of "crucial experiment" in which a case is chosen for its special nature, perhaps because it constitutes a special exception to a general rule or because certain variables happen to be present together; in short, a case chosen after much sophisticated comparative study of many other cases. There is also much need for the comparative study of a few carefully chosen cases, in which it may be that the crucial variables vary while other factors remain constant. If one wishes to test theories about the difference between the cabinet and the presidential systems of government, for example, one is better advised to compare Manitoba and North Dakota than to compare Great Britain and the United States, since with respect to all other variables Manitoba and North Dakota are very much alike while Great Britain and the United States have many other differences. Or one may wish to study a number of cases in which other factors vary widely while the crucial factors are constant, as Fred Eggam studied a number of disparate communities of the Western Pueblo Indians.

Finally, a leading role must be played by comparative statistical studies of the cross-polity survey and cross-historical survey type. For such studies, which have already begun at Northwestern and elsewhere, one needs to be sensitive to six major methodological problems to which anthropologists working on cross-cultural surveys have long given considerable attention: (1) sampling unit definition; (2) sampling bias; (3) Galton's problem (historical interdependence of cases; i.e., ideographic correlations); (4) trustworthiness of source material; (5) cross-cultural conceptualization of categories; and (6) causal analysis of correlations.

Challenges for Research in International Relations and Comparative Politics

OLIVER BENSON
University of Oklahoma

Focus on the interaction between international relations and comparative politics gives rise to many fruitful areas of co-operative research, but also suggests a number of problems. To some extent these are the same problems as have plagued researchers in both fields, but the welcome emphasis this symposium adds to coordination of the two also emphasizes the importance of seeking solutions. Only a few outstanding problems are selected for brief comment here, with mention of some research challenges suggested both by the essays in this volume and by other recent and current work.

THE PROBLEM OF APPLIED VS. THEORETICAL RESEARCH

Modern theory building and model construction in both international relations and comparative studies have frequently faced the age-old dilemma of whether or not the scholar should concern himself with practical policy. Given the widespread involvement of government in financial sponsorship of research, the question put years ago by the Lynds, "Knowledge for what?" might almost be rephrased, "What for knowledge?" Certainly the relationship between research and policy is inevitable; the question is, To what extent should it be planned? Stanley Hoffmann feels that problems of peace and world order "command all others" and that neglect of them will drive us into generalized irrelevance if not into an academic cemetery of bygone ideas.[1] Richard Snyder raises cogent questions regarding policy-oriented research, with particular reference to international relations: What is the price? What is the relationship between the theories of the scientist and those of the policy-maker? Should the policy-maker's role responsibilities and values inhibit the scientist? If the scientific approach involves trial-and-error, how can effective research be done at the policy level without serious danger of crippling effects? [2]

An encouraging aspect of recent government-sponsored research is that to an increasing extent it includes highly theoretical work as well as that which is obviously "practical" to the layman's eye. More and more frequently financial aid of the Arms Control and Disarmament Agency, the National Science Foundation, or of the armed services proper is acknowledged in support of projects which closely approach the "pure science" level.[3] If this trend continues, perhaps some of Snyder's concerns will be allayed. McClelland reports a more serious form of the problem, in the comment by Father Robert Bosc, who raised the question of incompatibility between the aim of establishing a firm and effective science of international relations and the purpose of indoctrinating college students and citizens with certain relativistic beliefs which we then represent as American moral behavior in world affairs.[4] Perhaps some resolution of this

1. Stanley H. Hoffmann, ed., *Contemporary Theory in International Relations* (Englewood Cliffs, New Jersey, Prentice-Hall, 1960), pp. 186–87.
2. R. C. Snyder, "International Relations Theory—Continued," *World Politics*, 13:2, January 1961, pp. 300–12.
3. An example is F. J. Anscombe, et al., *Application of Statistical Methodology to Arms Control and Disarmament* (Princeton, Mathematica, 1963).
4. Charles A. McClelland, *College Teaching of International Relations: Problems of Organization and Collaboration* (San Francisco, San Francisco State College, 1962), pp. 11–12; see also the more extended discussion in Robert Bosc, *La Société internationale et l'église: sociologie et morale des relations internationales* (Paris, Spes, 1961), Chap. 6, "Philosophes et moralistes devant la communauté internationale. Les différentes philosophies politiques de la Société internationale," pp. 329–56.

dilemma is found in the closer association of international relations with the comparative approach, especially in the study of comparative foreign policy, where influences from the internal society and polity are given what is hopefully the impartial treatment demanded by scientific criteria, and the place of the United States in the array simply comes out where the data locate it.[5]

A useful device for identification of some research areas which seem most relevant to the association of international relations and comparative government is McClelland's ladder-of-abstraction concept. McClelland classifies research in five stages, ranging from simple assembly of data, through low-level generalization, to a middle stage of highly generalized explanations based on conventional and socio-cultural data, then to supracultural explanations, and finally to purely formal statements of universal scope.[6] He puts most international relations research to date at the two lower stages, a point equally true of comparative politics. It is in the middle stage that he sees the greatest difficulties, but by the same token it is in this stage that the most tempting range of research challenges lie. What are the prospects for assembling the formidable masses of empirical data and low-level generalizations which have accumulated and are accumulating with bewildering speed at the earlier stages of abstraction? [7]

The Use of Models

One centralizing possibility for study of the role of policy in international relations and comparative government is that of the exploration of specific models of international interaction in terms of their usefulness for dealing with specific problems. The emphasis of such an exploration would be the "problem relevance" of the model. It is an approach which is equally applicable

5. As is well done in Rudolph J. Rummel, *Dimensions of Conflict Behavior Within and Between Nations* (Evanston, Northwestern University, 1963), later published in *General Systems Yearbook*, Vol. 8, 1963.

6. Charles A. McClelland, "Systems and History in International Relations: Some Perspectives for Empirical Research and Theory," *General Systems Yearbook*, Vol. 3, 1958, pp. 221–47.

7. For a discussion of such prospects, see Chadwick F. Alger, "Comparison of Intranational and International Politics," in this volume.

to international relations and comparative politics and to the areas of their interaction and their mutual concern. What particular problems of the international system, historic or contemporary, help to explain the patterns and implicit values of any given model? What problems is the model suited to handle? If historic, did the model actually prove useful in its setting? Did it influence the action of political practitioners? Did it result in significant research or theory? What is its value in the present study of political systems?

Such a study should suggest parameters for the fields of international relations and comparative politics by its analysis of the usefulness of the various conceptual frameworks examined—usefulness, that is, in dealing with problems of the real world either in research or in policy planning. Relevant models fall into a typology of three groups: state-centered models of primary concern to comparative government; models of the international system—chiefly studied by international relations; and policy-process models, of interest to both fields.

Several models are presented in this symposium—or are implicit in the essays—which appear especially relevant to the problems of the contemporary world. Rosenau sketches a complete set of typologies of groups, institutions, and processes involved in policy formulation and implementation, including the two key concepts of issue-areas and penetrated societies. He identifies suggested variables—idiosyncratic, role, governmental, societal, and systemic—according to their assumed (and perhaps testable) priorities under conditions of open-closed and developed-underdeveloped continuums, and calls for research to verify or modify these priorities under actual conditions, a process essential for the construction of pre-theories from which more dependable generalization may grow.

Casanova sketches a provocative model of the present international system, which most leaders of the underdeveloped nations appear, with surprising consistency, to consider the true one. This model affords a basis for research of the most specific sort, research essential to actual and pressing problems of contemporary policy. That this model differs from those most commonly employed by Western social researchers is less significant than that it is immediately useful as a fairly complete explanation of practically all major policy positions taken by the new nations in both domestic and foreign affairs. Particularly valuable is his outline of the seamless web of principles, from national unity and independence—integral independence—to development. Western policy will be inevitably irrelevant without clear awareness that to the minds of the new nations' leaders there is a necessary linkage of such goals as political, economic, military, and cultural independence; social justice; creation of investment capital by expropriation, if need be; state intervention by socialist patterns of planning, industrialization, and resource control; definition of democracy as a close relationship between state and people—not necessarily as a freely competitive polity; and the general goal of political, economic, social, and cultural development. Casanova, of course, does not present this model as his own, but insists on the importance of understanding that it is widely held and calls further for rigorous social research to test its various hypotheses.

Other essays present briefer or more fragmentary models of particular aspects of the policy process. An example is Friedrich's three-level structure of foreign policy-making: the technical level of professional diplomacy, the particular level of interest groups, and the emotional level of broad popular involvement. This typology is similar to Rosenau's idiosyncratic-systemic continuum, differing in that Friedrich postulates that research will be useful in establishing how policy moves in and out of the three levels, undergoing significant changes in the process, whereas Rosenau suggests that priorities of influence may be generalized for various types of societies and issue-areas.

Indeed, as Farrell and Aspaturian both point out, the open-closed dichotomy itself suggests a working model of limited usefulness, which permits a few tentative generalizations that might be subjected to research testing. Both authors outline a number of such hypotheses. Farrell suggests, for example, that foreign policy formulation by constitutional democracies approaches more nearly than other governmental functions the practice of closed political systems; he adds that there would appear to be greater emphasis on ideological foreign policy factors in closed societies. Aspaturian proposes that if ideological foreign policy goals can be achieved only at the expense of the interests and security of dominant social groups in closed societies, they will not be implemented even if capability exists; he suggests further that external defense serves tangible internal interests more than intangible or abstract external interests and is more a function of preserving the social order and interests of its dominant groups than of "national interests" in the abstract.

Different models of the political world tend to predominate at different times as different problems seem to be the most crucial ones. Further investigation should attempt to identify the problems most relevant to present lines of research effort in comparative government and international relations, and the models which seem most suitable to handle them. Landau has recently outlined a set of canons for use of models, which all social researchers would do well to heed.[8] These include the warnings that models from alien fields are invariably metaphorical when applied to political science; that there is danger of stripping a model of all the clarity it possessed in its original domain as we transfer it to political science; that vagueness in much political analysis often leads to a confusion of different models (the mixed-metaphor error compounded to entire systems of analysis); that care should be taken to concentrate on relationships, not on things, especially with biological models (organs of the body are certainly not to be confused with organs of the body politic); that clear and logical correspondences between entities and processes of the model and entities and processes of politics must be established; that more attention should be paid to models which have been found powerful and relevant in the past; and finally that "due process of inquiry" requires faithful adherence to the rules and language of the model's indigenous field.

In an excellent chapter on behavioral science models, Abraham Kaplan points out that although our present fascination with these constructs may indeed be a product of a technological age, fashion does not necessarily stand in the way of scientific achievement. "The dangers are not in working with models, but in working with too few, and those too much alike, and above all, in belittling any efforts to work with anything else. That Euclid alone has looked on beauty bare is a romantic fiction."[9]

8. Martin Landau, "Political Theory and Due Process of Inquiry," paper read at the American Political Science Association, Chicago, September 1964.

9. Abraham Kaplan, *The Conduct of Inquiry, Methodology for Behavioral Science* (San Francisco, Chandler, 1964), p. 293.

THE PROBLEM OF UNACCUSTOMED FIELDS

Political science generally, and comparative and interna-national studies as components of the discipline, have by now developed fair sophistication in the use of cognate disciplines—a sophistication deriving both from the traditional association with law, economics, and history, and from the newer behavioralist orientation toward sociology and psychology. There may be anticipated some profitable additions to this list.

Anthropology, for example, has been drawn on relatively little, though, as Snyder points out, there is a substantial body of research here which might be tapped. Alger suggests the reasonableness of comparisons between primitive societies and the international society, with the informed caveat that actual study has shown primitive social structures to be about as complicated as modern ones. Both international relations and comparative politics have already profited from the work of Apter, Almond, Coleman, Macridis, and others, who have used applications of Levy's structural-functional requisite analysis and the Lasswell-Kaplan concepts on allocation of values.[10] These rigorous conceptual frameworks have already produced textbooks. Even undergraduate students have found, somewhat to their astonishment, that the approach works.[11] To the extent that anthropologists may profit from this analytic rigor in their own work, we may expect future anthropology to offer us more useful data and generalization.[12] What we can offer anthropology is perhaps as important a question as what anthropology can offer us.

SMALL-GROUP STUDIES

Contemporary small-group analysis has made rapid strides, is frequently referred to in our literature, but its contributions

10. As developed in Harold D. Lasswell and Abraham Kaplan, *Power and Society, a Framework for Political Inquiry* (New Haven, Yale University Press, 1950), and Marion J. Levy, Jr., *The Structure of Society* (Princeton, Princeton University Press, 1952).

11. Cf. especially Gabriel A. Almond and James S. Coleman, eds., *The Politics of the Developing Areas* (Princeton, Princeton University Press, 1960), Robert W. Ward and Roy C. Macridis, *Modern Political Systems*, 2 vols. (Englewood Cliffs, New Jersey, Prentice-Hall, 1963), and David Apter, *The Gold Coast in Transition* (Princeton, Princeton University Press, 1955).

12. Cf. Alger, *op. cit.*

have not been absorbed into any coherent body of generalization. Examples of work pointing in this direction are, however, starting to appear. A recent symposium by Muzafer Sherif includes two relevant chapters by Klineberg and North.[13] Klineberg points out that the Cold War and the desire of the United States to face the increasing numbers of dark-skinned peoples with "clean hands" have combined to convince us finally of the necessity of coming to grips with our domestic race problems. Concomitantly this has brought an apparent increase in isolationism among southern whites, who have traditionally supported the internationalist position. North suggests attention to perception categories, growing out of his extensive research on the origins of World War I. Besides perceptions of another state's policy conditions, he includes five basic categories: perception of power (strength-weakness), frustration-satisfaction, hostility-friendship, capability, and resolution of conflict. He feels that research into this perceptual sphere may be systematically related to the more usual "objective" sphere of study. Since in his view the perceptual sphere may often or usually be the determining one, a truly formidable challenge results for international relations research, one which entails intensive utilization of the materials of comparative government as well as those of social psychology. The work of Seymour Lipset on class structure in contemporary European politics—and indeed of the entire *Daedalus* issue "A New Europe?"—supplies sensitive insights by research making extensive use of group data and opens up a number of suggestive lines of new research.[14]

Highly relevant to the Snyder-Bruck-Sapin decision-making focus is the work of Herbert McClosky and associates with public attitudes toward foreign policy, work which has led to attempts to identify personality predispositions. As McClosky puts it, existing research suggests that personality is relevant to foreign policy attitudes, so that "there is at least a *prima facie* case for taking personality variables into account. Belief, conformity, deviation, consensus, ways of perceiving and organizing experience, likes and dislikes, affection and hostility—all these enter into the formation of political and international attitudes and

13. Muzafer Sherif, ed., *Intergroup Relations and Leadership* (New York, Wiley, 1962), Chaps. 7 and 8.
14. S. M. Lipset, "The Changing Class Structure and Contemporary European Politics," *Daedalus*, Winter 1964, pp. 271–303.

all are to some extent products of psychological states. . . . By considering personality wherever it seems appropriate to do so, we may succeed in adding an entirely new dimension to our understanding of foreign policy formation." [15]

Perhaps the most ambitious series of research runs for the investigation of attitudes and actions of human actors under conditions of simulated policy-making is the Northwestern Inter-Nation simulation. The use of such experimental methods has created a pattern whereby at least certain topics—decision-making, conflict, communication—can be investigated under carefully controlled conditions and with rigorously defined rules and concepts.

The project, which began as a joint enterprise of Richard Snyder and Harold Guetzkow during their year together at the Center for Advanced Study in the Behavioral Sciences, involved twelve major experimental runs over a period of five years. Using both human subjects and formalized computations (sometimes with computers), the experiments have involved high school, undergraduate, and graduate students; professors; ex-foreign service officers; military officers; and professional scientists. The simulation is conceived both as an instrument for teaching or training and as a research method with the potential of producing verifiable theory.[16]

MATHEMATICS

It has not been long since mathematical models of politics were so rare as to be considered oddities, commonly viewed with some scorn and amusement. Though still unusual, there is already little doubt that they will have an increasing place, particularly in the area of union of international relations and comparative politics. The fine bibliographical article by Richard Fagen makes it unnecessary to dwell on this topic, but a few

---

15. Herbert McClosky, "Perspectives on Personality and Foreign Policy," *World Politics*, 13:1, October 1960, pp. 129–39.

16. Harold Guetzkow, Chadwick F. Alger, Richard A. Brody, Robert C. Noel, and Richard C. Snyder, *Simulation in International Relations: Developments for Research and Teaching* (Englewood Cliffs, New Jersey, Prentice-Hall, 1963), and Harold Guetzkow, ed., *Simulation in Social Science: Readings* (Englewood Cliffs, New Jersey, Prentice-Hall, 1962).

recent items should be listed.[17] William Riker's *The Theory of Political Coalitions* [18] adds to Morton Kaplan's use of analogic game theory for the study of international conflict; [19] Riker's model of social and political dynamics based on the *n*-person zero-sum game is equally applicable to domestic politics. As has often been pointed out, game theory has interested social scientists from the first because of its provision for human choice and its treatment of the consequences of choice in rigorous mathematical terms. Riker draws from the general theory the principle that when players are rational and have perfect information, only minimum winning coalitions will occur. He applies this concept with some success, though so early an attempt is clearly fraught with danger, to the dissolution of the victorious coalitions which won the Napoleonic wars and the two world wars. The systematic attack by Rudolph Rummel and Raymond Tanter on the problem of conflict behavior—both conflict within nations and conflict between nations—is representative of a second approach, with use of factor analysis and sophisticated statistical methods.[20] Richard Brody's work on the *n*-power problem, and with North and Holsti on the conflict spiral or escalation problem, is promising of a wide spectrum of useful production at the Stanford center. The Political Behavior Laboratory at Minnesota introduced in 1964 a workshop in comparative government, organized by William Flanigan and Edwin Fogelman, making use of data available through the Inter-University Consortium.[21]

17. Richard Fagen, "Some Contributions of Mathematical Reasoning to the Study of Politics," *American Political Science Review,* 55:4, December 1961, pp. 888–99.
18. William H. Riker, *The Theory of Political Coalitions* (New Haven, Yale University Press, 1962).
19. Morton A. Kaplan, *System and Process in International Politics* (New York, Wiley, 1957).
20. Cf. Rummel, *op. cit.,* and Raymond Tanter, "Dimensions of Conflict Within and Between Nations, 1958–60," *The Journal of Conflict Resolution* March 1966.
21. Richard A. Brody, "Some Systemic Effects of the Spread of Nuclear Weapons Technology: A Study Through Simulation of a Multi-Nuclear Future," *The Journal of Conflict Resolution,* 7:4, December 1963; Robert C. North, Richard A. Brody, and Ole R. Holsti, "Some Empirical Data on the Conflict Spiral," paper read at Peace Research Conference, Chicago, November 1963. The Flanigan-Fogelman materials exist only in worksheet form at present, "Political Science 159, Comparative Politics Lab," but their publication as a workbook is planned.

In a ground-breaking paper on mathematical theory in international relations, Alker points out the usefulness of such multivariate methods as factor analysis for condensing a large number of indices to a small number of conceptual variables, and discriminant analysis for identifying variables which best distinguish among predefined groups—the "statistics of taxonomy." He gently suggests that Hoffmann's "wrecking operation" on mathematically inclined theorists does not give fair credit to the caution with which they usually handle their data, nor to the extent to which Hoffmann's criticisms are already taken into account by the best work in the area. The very purpose of inductive statistics is the "mathematical study of risky generalization"; it is mainly concerned with rigorous demonstration of the exact degree of risk involved in conclusions drawn from given data. Alker quite properly emphasizes that presently available statistical methods offer far greater payoffs for the examination of international relations data than are likely, in the current state of the art, from the more esoteric game theory (as used by Kaplan and Riker) or differential calculus (as used by Richardson). Among current or recent topics studied by such quantitative methods are voting blocs in the General Assembly, analysis of foreign policy editorials in newspapers, analysis of European elite and mass attitudes toward foreign policy, types of European transactions, conflict data and international transactions, and the delineation of international regions by political, social, and economic data. Much of this work has centered at Yale, under the leadership of Karl Deutsch.[22]

Much of the interest of social scientists in behavioral applications of mathematics can be traced to the seminal work of John Kemeny, whose work in restructuring the role of the Dartmouth mathematics department played a key role in the entire "new mathematics" movement. Kemeny, for example, has recently developed several applications of graph theory to business and political organizations.[23] No attempt seems to have

22. Hayward R. Alker, Jr., "The Long Road to Mathematical Theories of International Politics: Problems of Statistical Nonadditivity," paper read at the American Political Science Association, Chicago, September 1964. For an application, see Alker, "Dimensions of Conflict in the General Assembly," *American Political Science Review*, 58:3, September 1964.

23. J. G. Kemeny and J. L. Snell, *Mathematical Models in the Social Sciences* (Boston, Ginn, 1962). O. Benson has included graph theory in a

been made thus far by political scientists to follow up this lead. It is encouraging, however, to note that both mathematicians and political scientists are gradually coming to the point of asking questions of one another.

COMPUTERS

Work with computers is related to mathematics but represents a different research tool with which we will need to become increasingly familiar. Particularly is this true of computer simulations of entire societies, including the international society. Pool is developing a program comparable to his Simulmatics program used in the 1960 election for the analysis of the communications network of the Soviet bloc.[24] James Coleman has programed community political conflicts in the pattern of his theoretical model.[25] Karl Deutsch, whose interest in quantification has been a seminal influence, has used computers to analyze international community characteristics, particularly in comparisons of trade flow.[26]

Sydney and Beatrice Rome, at Systems Development, have developed the Leviathan project, a simulation of large organizations intended to reproduce the key aspects of large social groups engaged in the production of goods or services: the productive process, the productive agents, the communications nets, the technological system, the governing system, and the decision-making processes, "an elaborate engine for determining

draft workbook, "Quantitative Methods in International Relations," prepared in connection with Minnesota's promising program of political behavior laboratories.

24. Ithiel de Sola Pool and Robert Abelson, "The Simulmatics Project," in Harold Guetzkow, ed., Simulation in Social Science: Readings (Englewood Cliffs, New Jersey, Prentice-Hall, 1962); see also "Simulmatics Media-Mix Technical Description" (New York, Simulmatics Corporation, 1962).

25. James S. Coleman, "Analysis of Social Structures and Simulation of Social Processes with Electronic Computers," in Harold Guetzkow, ed., Simulation in Social Science: Readings (Englewood Cliffs, N.J., Prentice-Hall, 1962).

26. Karl W. Deutsch, "Toward an Inventory of Basic Trends and Patterns in Comparative and International Politics," American Political Science Review, 54:1, March 1960, pp. 34–57. This essay was presented in preliminary draft at Northwestern's 1959 Conference on International Relations.

the consequences of theories of an intermediate level between real life and the most general theory of social process." [27]

The computer is an ever present challenge to the development of means for significant processing of the abundance of data now available in international relations and comparative studies. It cannot work, to be sure, without scientific direction. It speaks only in the voice of its programer. Political scientists apparently must learn to converse intelligently with programers. In the fields of international relations and comparative politics more scholars have learned to do so than in most other branches of the discipline, so this injunction may be superfluous here. From computer lore, however, come three recent approaches to the testing of hypotheses which deserve special note.

1. Validity of computer simulations. Abelson has approached seriously the task of validity testing by rigorous statistical inferential methods of the computerized social simulation. The basic problem is the speed of replications, which enables the computer to apply the essentials of the Monte Carlo method to the messiest set of numerical data, depending of course on the simulation's creator for a plan of analysis. The contribution of Abelson is that of applying standard patterns of statistical analysis to a macro-universe of interacting data, by a series of checkpoints throughout the manipulative process and by appropriate methods of relating the results of the checks to the original data.[28]

2. The redundancy principle. Redundancy theory seems especially appropriate to experiment design and testing in social science, and affords simple safeguards against dogmatic conclusions. This relatively new field is based on the elementary statistical concept of independent trials. A sort of guarantee against failure of an experiment is secured by its repetition. If events are unrelated, the probability that all will occur is the product of the separate probabilities that each will occur.[29] The

27. Sydney C. Rome and Beatrice K. Rome, "Computer Simulation Toward a Theory of Large Organizations," in Harold Borko, ed., *Computer Applications in the Behavioral Sciences* (Englewood Cliffs, New Jersey, Prentice-Hall, 1962).

28. Robert P. Abelson, "Some Statistical Considerations in Social Science Simulations," paper read at Massachusetts Institute of Technology Conference on Computer Simulation in the Social Sciences, Cambridge, April 1963.

29. William H. Pierce, "Redundancy in Computers," *Scientific American*, 210:2, February 1964, pp. 103–13.

principle seems relevant, for example, to Alger's concept of over-lapping memberships as constituting an improved warranty of needed action, or to Pool's use of the basic Simulmatics program for investigation of the Soviet system of communication.[30]

3. Propositional retrieval. A field which will doubtless remain in its formative stage for a number of years, because of its encyclopedic scope, is that of information retrieval of abstract propositions. Milbrath and Janda, of Northwestern, have programed TRIAL ("Technique to Retrieve Information from Abstracts of Literature"), a computer program which can search and report in textual form propositional and information statements and data from a large store of previously coded sources. True, they report that Dennis Sullivan's effort to propositionalize international relations textbooks was "not totally successful, largely because of the fuzzy conceptual level of the materials on which he worked." The system is of course not limited in value to international relations and comparative government materials, but has been used for these among other political subject areas.[31]

THE PROBLEM OF UNACCUSTOMED FIELDS: THE OLD ONES

So energetically have the "frontier" researchers exploited the concepts of new disciplines that there has been some danger of neglect of the older (or what some deem the "underdeveloped") disciplines of history and law. A small but significant number of projects suggest, however, that a sort of feedback is going on from modern or frontier methodology to the investigation of traditional subject matter with new methods.

HISTORY

Robert North's project with the data of World War I, referred to above, is one example. Charles McClelland's "transformations" concept applied to the contemporary world opens up as well the prospect of research through history in quest of similar trans-

30. Cf. Alger, *op. cit.*, and Pool, *op. cit.*
31. Lester W. Milbrath and Kenneth Janda, "Computer Applications to Abstraction, Storage, and Recovery of Propositions from Political Science Literature," paper read at the American Political Science Association, Chicago, September 1964.

formations which could support middle-level generalizations.[32] Those he has identified as especially significant now include the expansion of the European state system into a world system, the spread of nationalism to the Afro-Asian world, the democratization of controls over foreign policy, the technological revolution, the beginnings of associational patterns among the states of European background, and the need for governments of the largest states to maintain a war footing in peacetime. New research may not discover identical transformations in the past, but the list suggests a series of projects in the search for parallelisms. In a similar way Kenneth Waltz has given us incentive in his survey of the resources of classical Western political theory for searching out analytical patterns which might help in coping with the problem of war.[33]

Adda Bozeman's magistral *Politics and Culture in International History* [34] for the first time applies the techniques of contemporary international relations theory to the broad sweep of history, and supplies us with a view of the history of international systems. The ground she breaks needs to be examined in depth, but here we have another challenge to research; only by careful testing of our ideas in this rich laboratory can we hope to verify our judgments. There are so few possible case studies of complete international systems that we need to use all we have if we are to lift historical analysis above the level of investigation of the unique, the specific, and the idiosyncratic.

LAW

Myers McDougal's program to apply the Lasswell-Kaplan concept of hominocentric politics to the entire field of international law has gone far, in the three volumes already published,[35] to add the dimension of "policy science" to the formalism of most

32. See the discussion in W. R. T. Fox and Annette Baker Fox, "The Teaching of International Relations in the United States," *World Politics,* 13:3, April 1961, pp. 339–59.

33. Kenneth N. Waltz, *Man, the State, and War, a Theoretical Analysis* (New York, Columbia University Press, 1959).

34. Adda B. Bozeman, *Politics and Culture in International History* (Princeton, Princeton University Press, 1960).

35. The latest of the series is Myers S. McDougal and William T. Burke, *The Public Order of the Oceans* (New Haven, Yale University Press, 1962); this is the third in a related group of four volumes. The others are *Studies in World Public Order* (1960), *Law and Minimum World Public Order* (1961), and *Law and Public Order in Space* (forthcoming).

traditional work. In an early essay Percy Corbett contributed the idea that international law research should focus more on the individual, abandoning the classic concept that only states are its proper subjects.[36] To the extent that international law moves into this role, it assumes to some degree the character of world domestic law, applied in part by national governments but also in significant ways by a variety of multilateral institutions. At the 1959 Northwestern Conference, for example, we recall the language of Ralph Bunche, speaking to the question of whether consideration had been given to the United Nations' assuming any "executive functions" in Berlin. That such a question could be asked and discussed without the terms startling anyone bespeaks a new phase of interdependence and calls for redefinition of traditional concepts.

That legal studies are not necessarily doomed to the legalistic tradition is well shown by Richard Falk's recent essay, *Law, Morality, and War in the Contemporary World*,[37] wherein he carefully picks his way between the twin and contradictory popular perceptions of international law—cynicism and utopianism. Such new wine in such old bottles is evidence that in this timeless field too there is ample opportunity and challenge for new research.

The Problem of Values

As always, the social researcher in international relations and comparative government finds himself in a tangled web when he deals with values. Often he is inclined to seek so detached a pattern of scientific objectivity that he avoids even the consideration of values as data. When it comes to the expression of personal beliefs as to worthwhile social goals, he is even more cautious. This is particularly true in the present era of the Cold War and conflicting ideologies. Kaplan makes a useful point that is relevant here: It is not so much values we need worry about as bias in dealing with them. Bias we must indeed seek to eliminate, either personal bias, group bias, or the most

36. Percy Corbett, *The Individual and World Law* (Princeton, Center for Research on World Political Institutions, 1953).

37. Richard A. Falk, *Law, Morality, and War in the Contemporary World* (New York, Praeger, for the Princeton Center of International Studies, 1963).

diffuse form of bias represented by an entire culture.[38] Kaplan quotes Boring to this point: "What may be said of the big *Zeitgeist* may also be said of the little *Zeitgeister* of schools and of the egoist who has no following. They have their inflexible attitudes and beliefs, their loyalties that are prejudices, and their prejudices that are loyalties." Hopefully the essays in this volume have made a major stride at least toward the merging of the little *Zeitgeister* of researchers in the two fields of international relations and comparative government. Consider, for example, the following value-relevant draft hypotheses which emerge from the studies:

—That the mutant individual, behaving with random spontaneity in his social context, is the greatest potential threat to the closed system (Long).

—That ideological influence on continuity of policy is illusory; ages of greatest change are precisely those of the greatest dominance by sweeping ideological movements (Friedrich).

—That social justice is a decision-motivating goal for leaders in underdeveloped nations, deemed by them to be closely related to independence and national development (Casanova).

—That ideological goals are subordinate to dominant group interests; that the Soviet Union will divert substantial resources and energies to those ideologically determined goals in foreign policy not incompatible with the security and interests of the dominant social groups (Aspaturian).

—That the closed-system decision-maker is more likely than the open-system decision-maker to be a prisoner of dogma about foreign policy (Farrell).

—That welfare-related problems constitute suitable content for the issue-area category of human resources (Rosenau—though his presentation is, on balance, the most value free of the group).

If values can be handled objectively, it would seem that the most valuable approach to objectivity would be the simple study of what values are most widely held, particularly in the social context of existing political systems and international institutions. It is not sheer utopianism to note that two such values essentially dominate the thinking of man today: first, the bundle of goals subsumed under the general caption of welfare and, second, the goal of eliminating war, or, minimally, nuclear war. We need not avoid these value-laden goals from any mistaken sense of scientific objectivity or attachment to realism and pure power analysis. The finding that these are significant values in the

38. Abraham Kaplan, *The Conduct of Inquiry* (San Francisco, Chandler, 1964), pp. 373–77.

contemporary world can be made much in the spirit of the Roman jurisconsults who established the *ius gentium,* as a result of observation that certain principles of law were so widely held by the many cultures which Rome had conquered that they should be acknowledged even when contradictory to the law of Rome. So too we can observe—in the revolution of rising expectations, in the programs of every underdeveloped nation, in the domestic agitation over civil rights, in the President's "war on poverty"—an essentially universal concern with the whole gamut of welfare goals. At the 1959 Northwestern Conference Richard Snyder proposed a frontal attack in terms of both theory and empirical research on the problem of international welfare in his paper, "The Present Distribution of Social Values Among Nations." [39] Since the challenge to research he presented then is still relevant and applies with special aptness to the common parameters of international relations and comparative politics studies, it is in order to call attention to the three multiple-variable measures he suggested as possible techniques for handling the combination of existing kinds of data and thus for presenting a more complete picture of the "value situation" of societies. These are (1) a value-distribution matrix, which would provide a profile of a society's situation with respect to indices known to be important or instrumental to other values—capital, technical knowledge, well-being, autonomy, and the like; (2) a value-satisfaction quotient, which would represent "a calculation of the relationship between aspirations and achievement at the subjective level at a given moment in time plus the objective probability of value achievement in the future"; and (3) a world VDM and VSQ and intersocietal comparisons, based on essential value data for a sufficient sample of societies. The challenge to handle the age-old problems of man with rigorous analytical methods of this sort is one we cannot afford to decline, either for the scientific understanding of our society or for its salvation.

With respect to the second of the values identified above, that of peace, one fruitful line of research is suggested by Falk's monograph [40]—the search for "horizontal norms," by which he

39. Richard C. Snyder, "The Present Distribution of Social Values Among Nations," paper read at Northwestern University International Relations Conference, Evanston, April 1959.
40. Richard A. Falk, *op. cit.,* p. 78.

means descriptive propositions about "what nations will probably do in light of the interplay of event, interest, conscience, and rule." Insofar as the horizontal norm is based upon middle-level generalization about real societies and real decision-making entities, it takes on the character of a ground rule with some predictive reliability. Research aimed at determining such horizontal norms can fruitfully combine the efforts of the historian, the legal scholar, the social psychologist, the game-theory mathematician, and the economist as well as of scholars in the two disciplinary fields of international relations and comparative government. Falk's concept is only one of a large number of promising lines of activity which contemporary work suggests. It seems, however, especially appropriate as a meeting ground for the areas of concern in this volume.

Specific Research Challenges of the Symposium

In concluding this account of significant current work, it seems appropriate to stress in detail some examples of hypotheses put forward, tentatively or definitely, in several of the essays of this volume, as well as certain research topics to which they direct attention. No effort is made to be complete; the selection is meant only to be typical. Not all the essays are concerned with hypothesis development; those which follow might be examined, for example, with suitable attention to the scientific criteria outlined by Naroll and, if adequately tested, might fit into the broad pre-theory presented by Rosenau. It is hoped that the interest of other researchers may thus be attracted, since only by repeated testing of such generalizations may we expect theoretical advance.

Hypotheses on closed systems (Long)

—The requirement of unquestioning ritualism is characteristic of a closed system in its prescientific period, and is harder to maintain as the society moves to more sophisticated levels.

—The closed system's fear of inability to digest external influence is reflected in the international arena as a contest of incompatible systems.

—The model of a closed system is made attractive in the early stage of any group, as a result of the group's emphasis in this stage on survival and repression of internal dissent.

Hypotheses on democratic foreign policy (Friedrich)

—The impingement of party and ideology on foreign policy guarantees its discontinuity.

—Democracy is not especially suited to effective foreign policy, nor is it particularly pacific.

—An integrated foreign policy of "national interest" is characteristic of programs of aggression and imperialism.

Hypotheses on the decision process (Farrell)

—Limited formal education may make a decision-maker more likely to accept simple solutions but may enhance the role of staff assistants.

—High-risk policies may be made more likely by (1) insulation of top policy-makers from criticism, (2) low formal education, and (3) a strong role for military professionals.

—Open systems foster analytic study of alternatives and choice among them on a more rational basis than is found in closed systems.

Hypotheses on underdeveloped nations (Casanova)

—The developed world exaggerates the importance of internal factors such as race, culture, and polity in its view of the underdeveloped world.

—The underdeveloped world exaggerates the importance of external factors such as colonialism and imperialism.

—The underdeveloped world tends to reject the historic route of Western bourgeois revolution as too difficult and lengthy a path to its goals.

Hypotheses on interaction of domestic and foreign policy (Aspaturian)

—Foreign policy is a continuation of domestic policy.

—Interests in foreign policy express the interests of internal social groups.

—Internal policy requirements have primacy over external in case of incompatibility.

AREAS FOR RESEARCH

Topics urged for research attention, but not yet studied enough to supply testable generalizations, constitute a fertile field for inquiry. Farrell suggests attention to such questions as whether the closed society must necessarily be more aggressive than the open; whether there is any pattern to the time periods and problem areas as priority is given internal problems over foreign problems or vice versa; whether policy variation depends on closeness of contact between top decision-makers and staff assistants; and whether the degree of political alienation is a product of the closed nature of a system. Friedrich calls for examination of political patterns common to both foreign and domestic policy (such as negotiation, violence, and compacts); of the role of international federalism as involved in inter-dependence of foreign and domestic policy and the conduct of affairs on two or more jurisdictional levels; and of the concept that foreign affairs may be usefully considered as the external aspect of self-contained systems and at the same time the internal aspect of supranational systems. Long asks whether the inevitability of adaptation to change by a closed system makes necessary a corresponding dilution of orthodoxy. Aspaturian notes that study is needed of the extent to which foreign policy decisions are made to justify domestic decisions, and of the degree to which domestic decisions thereby result. Casanova asks for the application of Western social science research methodology to the investigation of the political theories held all but universally by decision-makers of the underdeveloped world. Rosenau suggests (among many other problems) study of the variety of ways in which his categories of issue-areas and influence institutions and forces are likely to vary by type of country.

By no means complete, if far ranging in scope, this selection of research ideas emerging from contemporary and recent work in international relations and comparative politics and from the essays of this volume should nevertheless indicate the broad dimensions of work which needs to be done. Some of the research tools described may prove eventually to be useless; some of the lines of investigation suggested may come to dead ends; some of the hypotheses put forward may be found wanting, if not groundless. Even so, this look at research going on and needed in the two fields under consideration shows international relations and comparative government to be obviously inter-twined; both are in need of advances in theory, of continued retooling in cognate and even foreign disciplines, and especially in need of one another.

Index